# Flower
## GARDENING

# Flower
## GARDENING

A practical guide to creating colorful gardens in every yard

JULIE BAWDEN-DAVIS

Reader's
Digest

The Reader's Digest Association, Inc.
New York, NY / Montreal

A READER'S DIGEST BOOK

First printing in paperback 2012

This edition published by The Reader's Digest Association by arrangement with Dolezal & Associates

**For Dolezal & Associates**

**Editor-in-Chief:** Robert J. Dolezal

**Consulting Editor:** Victoria Cebalo Irwin

**Layout Art:** Barbara K. Dolezal

**Contributing Designer:** Hespenheide Design

**Illustrations:** Hildebrand Design

**Photoshop Illustration:** Gerald A. Bates

**Photographic Management:** John M. Rickard

**Consultants:** John E. Bryan, David Bullis, Jamie Coleman

The acknowledgments that appear on page 288 are hereby made a part of this copyright page.

Concept, editorial, and design by
Dolezal & Associates
2176 Crossroads Place
Livermore, California 94550
(925) 373-3394

**For Reader's Digest**

**U.S. Project Editor:** Miranda Smith

**Canadian Project Editor:** Pamela Johnson

**Chief Canadian Consultant:** Trevor Cole

**Project Designer:** George McKeon

**Copy Editor:** Mary Connell

**Editor-in-Chief, Books & Home Entertainment:** Neil Wertheimer

**Associate Publisher, Trade Publishing:** Rosanne McManus

**President & Publisher, Trade Publishing:** Harold Clarke

LIBRARY OF CONGRESS CATALOGING-IN-PUBLICATION DATA
Bawden-Davis, Julie.
    Flower gardening : a practical guide to creating colorful
    gardens in every yard / Julie Bawden-Davis.
        p. cm.
    Includes index.
    ISBN 978-0-7621-0502-1 (hardcover)
    ISBN 978-1-60652-362-9 (paperback)
    1. Flower gardening. 2. Flowers. 3. Color in gardening. I. Title.
SB405.B35 2004
635.9--dc22

                                    2003058756

Printed in China

1  3  5  7  9  10  8  6  4  2

Address any comments about *Flower Gardening* to:

The Reader's Digest Association, Inc.
Adult Trade Publishing
44 S. Broadway
White Plains, NY 10601

For more Reader's Digest products and information, visit our website:
www.rd.com (in the United States)
www.readersdigest.ca (in Canada)

# About This Book

Do you yearn to look out the window at a landscape overflowing with lush, colorful plants? Wish to make your outdoors a paradise where you can escape from life's stresses? Dream of having beds, borders, and containers filled with flowers? If so, this book is for you.

If you're like many of us, you may wonder where you'll find the time to create a backyard refuge filled with glorious, scented flowers. The good news is you can have a fantastic garden and still have time to relax and enjoy it. Plant wisely for a flower-filled paradise developed in your spare time, minus the concerns of an aching back and groaning pocketbook. You'll find that flower gardening with a plan in mind is a rewarding experience, one that leads you to an easy success. When you match easy-care plants with the conditions of your site, gardening becomes a cinch.

Wherever you garden—a compact city lot, a windy beach slope, an expansive yard with tall shade trees, a boggy hideaway, or high-desert terrain—you'll find suggestions for plants that will thrive in your area and bring beauty to your life. We've designed combinations for every site— from the sunniest and driest to the shadiest and wettest locations. There's a garden to fit every need, from a corner nook to a formal rose garden. If you want to customize our suggested plantings, you'll find plenty of options and suggestions for plant choices throughout the book's pages. We've also included an encyclopedia section of plant listings. It has in-depth descriptions of 480 easy-to-grow annuals, perennials, bulbs, shrubs and vines, succulents and cacti, aquatic plants, and ornamental grasses for your garden. You'll find plants to fill your beds along with practical advice on planting and care. Whether your home is found in the midst of a city or within a suburban tract, you'll find solutions for your gardening questions. Flip through the following pages and learn the formula for a low-upkeep garden filled with bountiful blossoms.

# Contents

# Construction and Planting

# the beauty of flowers

THIS GARDEN SEASON—THIS YEAR—MIGHT BE THE ONE. Each spring, our heads fill with dreams of cottage gardens overflowing with flowers of every size, shape, and color; a border of glorious spring bulbs; or the cheerful bounty of annuals blooming in the first warm breezes of the season. Is this the year to make an island bed beside the front walk and a shade garden under the tree? Can the perennials placed so lovingly in the bed by the porch yield new flowers after their blooms fade, keeping color alive? At such times, we can almost see the results of our dreams in our mind's eye. There's a yearning to plant, even as the days grow longer.

Make garden plans while these dreams are fresh. Decide whether to replant an existing bed or renovate a border. Is it time to consider an informal, natural garden or plant a formal bed? Will you use your precious space for fragrant flowers or a cutting garden?

Revisit a photo album to refresh distant memories of vacations and holidays in faraway spots and landscapes filled with flowers. Thumb the pages of nursery brochures and seed catalogs for examples of the latest plants and your old favorites. Turn on a gardening show to gain insight and inspiration. Let your imagination soar while the soil lies fallow.

Imagine creating a garden to resemble a nearby prairie of wildflowers, a blooming woodland understory, or the leafy paradise of a tropical forest. Is a family celebration around the corner? Plan to make it a party in your garden. Ideas abound. Visit public gardens, historical homes, arboretums, and nurseries to spark your creativity.

In the pages that follow, you'll see examples of flower gardens that could suit your home and yard. Take note of any with appealing features and consider using them on your site. Make this spring the season you'll fill your garden and home with flowers.

# Garden Designs

Imagine a garden design that complements your home's style and your region's flair.

The glory of a formal rose garden creates an outdoor room that welcomes visitors through its gate and under its arbor.

Under the spreading limbs of a flowering plum (*Prunus* spp.), a neatly pruned boxwood (*Buxus* spp.) hedge borders a semi-circular bed filled with bright red tulips (*Tulipa* spp.). Both formal and casual elements can be found in this springtime combination design.

While it's tempting to begin your garden year by gathering tools and selecting plants, it's best to take things a bit more slowly. Reflect about your design and what you want from your garden.

Examine the architectural style of your home. You'll want a garden that works with and enhances your house rather than one that clashes or struggles to blend in.

Formal homes with a traditional appearance suit gardens with geometric patterns; neat, orderly borders; paths lined with clipped boxwood or privet hedges; and flowers in coordinating colors. Georgian, Federal, English Tudor, and mansard-roofed French dwellings all fall into this category.

If your home is contemporary, a ranch, Cape Cod, Queen Anne Victorian, Edwardian, or gothic revival with flowery trim work, an informal or natural garden design may be more appropriate.

Finally, notice the color of the house, its trim and surrounding fences, outbuildings, and other structures. You'll refer to these colors later when you select finishing materials for beds and paths or consider matching, contrasting, or complementing them when you choose flowering plants.

## Choices for Garden Design

One of the wonders of flower gardening is the nearly endless variety of combinations and many unique effects you can create. To help you understand the possible design choices, it's valuable to review each major category.

### Formal Designs

Formal gardens, often called Italianate or French designs because of their heritage dating back to medieval Europe, are symmetrical. Formal designs such as those with strong geometric patterns stem from either an Asian or Islamic tradition. Make pleasing patterns of clean, defined lines and edges to

balance plants and architectural features. Use elements such as paths or pavings in a central area to direct the eye to specimen plants or a garden element such as an archway, fountain, pergola, sculpture, sundial, or a topiary. In extreme cases, hedges, shrubs, and trees are clipped into perfectly symmetrical balls, boxes, and pyramids to complement or contrast with the flowers inside their borders or beneath their canopy.

Reserved control is the defining characteristic of the formal garden. The all-white—monochromatic—garden is an example; imagine looking out at a mass of white tulips bordered by white forget-me-nots (*Myosotis sylvatica*).

## Informal Designs

Gardens with a casual flair are popular alternatives to the straight lines, rigid forms, and geometric frameworks of formal gardens. Sinuous rows, mounded groups of plants, and winding paths characterize many informal designs.

These gardens gained popularity toward the end of the 18th century when there was a gradual shift away from the formal layout of the English parterre gardens. The goal was to soften the boundaries between the house and the garden by concentrating on the views seen outdoors from the home's windows. Casual gardens often included more potted plants.

While casual gardens became nearly synonymous with natural gardens over time, they were different [see Natural Gardens, pg. 13].

Today, choose informal and casual designs as you wish. Informal gardens are more relaxed and inviting than formal ones, and they can assume many forms. A casual garden with plantings of mixed flowers is best for most informal settings. Use large shrubs such as azalea (*Rhododendron* spp.), camellia,

The casual elegance of yellow trumpet vine (*Brugsmania* × *candida*) trained up a doorway in a fieldstone wall contrasts with the bright blue of Russian sage (*Perovskia* spp.) in this informal cottage garden.

Fuchsia (*Fuchsia* × *hybrida*), nasturtium (*Tropaeolum majus*), balsam (*Impatiens walleriana*), and broad-leaved calla lily (*Zantedeschia* spp.) combine in this contemporary design as a perfect match to a rustic stone bungalow in a shady, woodland setting.

### CHOOSING A STYLE
To help understand the choices from which you will choose your garden's design, it's valuable to learn how to distinguish the major garden designs.

daphne, and rhododendron as background plants mixed with smaller perennial flowers and annuals in the foreground. Mingle waves of black-eyed Susan (*Rudbeckia* spp.) with drifts of purple coneflower (*Echinacea purpurea*) for height, and mounds of sweet alyssum and trailing lobelia (*L. erinus*) to divide the bed.

Mounds of brilliant red flowers cascade over and mirror the arched front entry of a home. Complementary purple and gold flowers trail over a retaining wall along a walk to repeat the arch's shape.

of roofing tiles and trim paint to flower colors in the garden. Repeat circular and oval shapes found in windows or doorways with plants that mound or vines that arch over a lattice form.

Reverse plants' roles for delightful surprises. Make paths of turfgrass lawn between flower beds instead of brick or stone. Plant tiny lawns of pearl-wort (*Sagina subulata*) in raised beds set within miniature meadows of flowers. Soften the hard edges of buildings with living walls made of climbing vines such as Virginia creeper (*Parthenocissus quinquefolia*) and balconies draped with English ivy (*Hedera helix*) or trailing lantana (*L. montevidensis*). Make container groupings on your deck mirror images of the shapes found in nearby flower beds, and fill both with plants blooming in complementary colors. Pave driveways with hollow blocks able to support your vehicle's weight, but fill and plant their hollows with a carpet of creeping thyme (*Thymus serpyllum*).

A contemporary gardens is also the right place for espalier and topiary—forms borrowed from formal garden history. Make free-form pyramids, ball-pruned bushes, spiraling towers, zigzag branches, and animals peeking from behind walls. Use these elements to express whimsy in your garden.

## VERSAILLES

The formal garden of Versailles was created to impress visitors with the grandeur of the French court and eventually became a model for the Western world. In size, design, and construction materials, it embodied extravagance. Seldom-seen tropical orange and palm trees and flowering plants from warmer climates were central to its lush effect.

### Contemporary Gardens

Contemporary gardens are informal. The organizing principles of these gardens are subtle. Soft circles, ovals, triangles, and wavelike rows with fluid edges that blend together give them a modern or even abstract appearance. Some contemporary gardens use occasional geometric beds but allow the plants in them to trail into a planned yet seemingly natural chaos of informal plantings.

Stark modern structures and contemporary gardens go hand in hand. Pick paving materials and architectural patterns from your home to repeat in paths, raised beds, and gazing pools. Mate the colors

Overall, the contemporary garden is an innovative one worth your consideration. Many are simple and well-organized and include newly introduced plants. A contemporary garden can extend and blur style boundaries. While it is built around new or different ideas, it can also incorporate the past with its design elements, plant choices, or garden accessories. At its best, contemporary gardens blend traditional style with modern design principles.

choosing water-wise plantings such as ornamental grasses that sustain themselves during periods of drought.

### Combination Designs

You may have seen gardens that seem to straddle two or more of these major design categories. Multistyle gardens of this type are called combination designs. It takes experience to grow a beautiful combination garden. Of course, plenty of gardeners acquainted with the standard garden styles can synthesize them so well that they can create new designs from scratch. They can go beyond the rules of any one design category—you can throw away the rules once you become thoroughly familiar with them—and bend several categories to their will. There are two choices for such gardens: plan them with precision from the beginning, or experiment as you go; start with one of the classic styles, then transition the garden into the combination design you want a bit at a time.

Massive brick planters and steps dominate this entry with hard, square edges. Soften them with mixed plantings of erect, mounding, and trailing plants.

A rustic rail fence begs for plants to tumble through its straight horizontal lines. Here, autumn-colored flowers, mixed foliage, and tan ornamental grass create a natural look.

### Natural Gardens

Gardens that strive to replicate the patterns and forms found in nature also fall into the informal category. These organize plant groupings in rising and falling layers and levels to create variety. Tall flowering shrubs such as beautybush (*Kolkwitzia amabilis*) and forsythia rise from ground covers and ornamental grasses. Odd numbers of plants make natural-looking S-, V-, and W-shaped groups. Natural gardens include native flowering plants or those from distant locales with similar climates and light characteristics. These plants work together to create a community that feels natural.

Consider a variety of factors when planning a naturalistic design. Provide a spot for a compost pile, small bin, or tumbler to recycle the garden's fallen foliage and clippings. Use only natural alternatives to pesticides and fertilizers. Attract wildlife by planting native plants, including shrubs and small trees where birds, butterflies, and other animals can thrive. Finally, analyze water usage and try to avoid supplementing natural rainfall by

# All about Location

Gain inspiration and choose plants to fit your surroundings.
Where does your garden grow?

A winding path invites a closer look at this flower-filled meadow on a sloping site. Its space is filled with flowers of every form, from low, prostrate, and sprawling to high and mounding.

Beautiful flower gardens are blends of a gardener's taste and a geographic region's flair. Every location, from plains to deserts to forests, hosts an immense diversity of flowering plants and permits varied garden designs. While commonly used flowers are always welcome, use new blooms to make your flower garden exciting. Get to know your region and the rich array of plants it offers, from tried-and-true annuals, bulbs, perennials, and shrubs to the resilient natives and unusual heirlooms our ancestors once enjoyed.

**VANISHING GRASSLANDS**
Despite active conservation efforts, less than 1/10 of one percent of the tallgrass prairies first seen by pioneers have been preserved in their original state.

### Meadows

Meadow gardening means growing a variety of native wildflowers and grasses on open turf; it's reminiscent of carefree spaces filled with perennials and annuals, full-sun wildflowers, and native grasses. These gardens have the openness of a manicured lawn but avoid the care of turfgrasses. Match your plantings to the minimum winter temperatures of your region. Your meadow garden will have a wide variety of naturalized annuals, bulbs, perennials, and ornamental grasses that come back year after year. Choose plants that bloom in different seasons for flowers throughout the year. Once a meadow garden is established, each season blends seamlessly into the next, bringing with it new flowering beauty.

Naturalized annuals such as calendula and nasturtium mix well with perennial plants like aster (*A. ericoides*), butterfly weed (*Asclepias tuberosa*), California poppy (*Eschscholzia californica*), goldenrod (*Solidago* spp.), dwarf morning-glory (*Ipomoea tricolor*), and lupine (*Lupinus* spp.). Break up an expanse and add interest when few other plants are blooming by including a wide selection of ornamental grasses such as blue oat grass (*Helictotrichon sempervirens*), soft rush (*Juncus effusus*), and switch-grass (*Panicum virgatum*). Meadow gardens require little care; mow or shear them once a year, in the late winter. Spent blossoms fall to the ground as new blooms take center stage. Still, plan on raking leaves and litter and removing them from the garden as the season ends.

## Prairies

Close cousins to meadows, prairie gardens are home to a rich mix of grasses and wildflowers and were once common on the Great Plains. These gardens are not only beautiful, they are beneficial; the rich diversity of native plants restores natural balance to the land. Prairie gardens mix grasses and wildflowers such as asters, purple coneflowers, sunflowers (*Helianthus* spp.), and goldenrods. Choose grass species for these gardens according to your soil. Tall grasses generally grow better in moister soils than do short grasses—many of which thrive with limited water. When creating a prairie garden, you are creating a self-sustaining landscape. Expect visitors like birds and butterflies to flock to your ocean of blooms and grassy seed heads.

## Forests

A woodland garden is a restful landscape. Create a peaceful spot in a forestlike setting with plants that grow under the tree canopy. Two or three deciduous trees will shade plantings in a woodland understory.

Three plantings are essential to woodland gardens —an overstory of trees and tall vines, an understory of flowering and evergreen shrubs, and a floor or ground layer of perennials, annuals, and ground covers. The density of your canopy, which varies with the types and numbers of trees in the overstory, affects the plants on the understory and floor. An open tree with small leaves gives dappled shade, while one with large leaves and dense limbs casts heavy shadows. The amount of shade determines which plants you can grow.

Forests grow throughout North America, and you can create a woodland garden just about anywhere—if you also consider your climate.

Like meadow plantings, plan carefully for a garden in every season. Many forest wildflowers,

such as Virginia bluebells (*Mertensia pulmonarioides*), bloom in the spring and then go dormant. Grape hyacinths (*Muscari* spp.), some tulip species, lily-of-the-valley (*Convallaria majalis*), and the fragrant wood hyacinth (*Hyacinthoides* spp.) are other choices for spring; many bloom early enough for a good show under trees that leaf out late and make deep shade. Perennials with a long bloom time include the Lenten rose (*Helleborus orientalis*), which lasts from winter through spring. Solomon's-seal (*Polygonatum odoratum*) and foamflower (*Tiarella cordifolia*) bloom in mid-spring; goatsbeard (*Aruncus dioicus*) flowers in late spring; and astilbe, ginger lily (*Hedychium* spp.), and coralbells (*Heuchera sanguinea*) flower in mid-summer. For autumn blooms, try toad lily (*Tricyrtis hirta*).

Tall conifers, spaced far enough apart to allow sun to spill through their crowns, make understory plantings possible. Choose shade-loving plants for such sites.

A hedge of red ginger (*Alpinia purpurata*), lush with foliage and showy orange-red bracts surrounding its tiny white flowers, reveals the color possible in a tropical landscape.

Cactus and succulent gardens fill with flowers in spring and after monsoonal summer rains. Many desert plants bloom with waxy flowers on tall spires and spikes, such as dyckia (*D. encho-lirioides*), a bromeliad.

## Tropics

Tropical gardens fare best in humid areas with plenty of rainfall, such as parts of Florida, the Carolinas, Georgia, eastern Texas, and southern California. It's easy to grow junglelike plants with brilliant flowers and lush green foliage in the right climate. Plants that thrive in humidity include begonia, caladium, elephant's ear (*Colocasia esculenta*), ginger (*Zingiber officinale*), moonflower (*Ipomoea alba*), and passion vine (*Passiflora* spp.).

You can also grow many tropical plants in drier, cooler regions on a seasonal basis—the concept is known as tropicalismo—but the plants may need coddling or planting in movable containers. Plan to overwinter some indoors, and expect to lose a few to unexpected frost or low humidity coupled with heat.

## Desert

Xeriscaping, or creating a landscape suited to an arid environment, is the heart of the desert garden. Plants in a Xeriscape garden survive and prosper with limited water, tolerate extreme summer heat and cold winters, and thrive in poor sandy soils.

In these gardens most gardeners use drought-tolerant cacti and succulents such as salt tree (*Halimo-dendron halodendron*). You may think of them as being thorny and uninteresting, but many have breathtaking flowers that allow you to create an oasis of color and texture. Plant them in containers in cold climates to permit easy indoor storage during winter. The elaborate flowers of succulents and cacti range from pure whites to silvery grays, greens, vibrant reds, hot pinks, and vivid yellows. The shape and size of their foliage, form, and flowers are as diverse as plants found in any other environment.

Most ornamental grasses are drought-tolerant, making them an excellent choice for the desert garden. Grasses mix well with cacti and succulents. Annual and perennial flowers adapted to scant rainfall also light up the desert garden. Many require little water no matter how dry the weather. Artemisia, centaurea, daylily (*Hemerocallis* spp.), lobelia (*L. erinus*), spider flower (*Cleome hasslerana*), yarrow (*Achillea* spp.), and verbenas are all good choices.

## The Coast

Seashore gardens vary widely, depending on the climate, geology, and geography. Think of the varied conditions found in the sandy beaches of the Gulf of Mexico and the Outer Banks, the steep oceanfront bluffs of Oregon and northern California, the damp sands and rocky headlands of Washington, British Columbia and Alaska, the Mid-Atlantic coast, Maine, Nova Scotia and New Brunswick, and the diversity of the Florida coastline.

Some constants—a prevailing wind, salt spray, and sandy or rocky soil—dictate your choice of plants. Many flowering plants thrive near the coast, even when conditions seem limiting. Species adapted to these sites include native plants with succulent or leathery leaves such as ice plant (*Lampranthus* spp.) and bearberry (*Arctostaphylos uva-ursi*), and naturalized species such as cape honeysuckle (*Tecoma capensis*), a vining shrub that withstands wind and salt air. Prevent erosion with native grasses such as fountain grass (*Pennisetum alopecuroides*) and salt-tolerant shrubs, including Texas sage (*Leucophyllum frutescens*). Install a windbreak to create an environment where more flowering plants can grow.

## Mountains

In mountainous terrain, whether on high plateaus or rocky slopes, garden soil is often thin, has a high mineral content, and is so sandy that water quickly drains away. Depending on altitude and exposure, many conditions can affect flowering plants, including amount of light, range of temperature, strength of wind, and quantity of precipitation. High peaks expose plants to intense sunlight rich in foliage-burning ultraviolet rays, low nighttime temperatures, strong winds, and snow or rain. Although these conditions are less than ideal, a surprising number of plants are adapted to this environment. The aptly named Rocky Mountain columbine (*Aquilegia caerulea*) is native to the Rockies and ranges from New Mexico in the south to the Yukon and Nunavut territories of Canada in the far north. Flowering cactus such as mammillaria and alpinelike plants such as various daisies, lupines, meadow saffron, and storksbill (*Erodium* spp.) also do well in high-elevation terrain. Visit native-plant nurseries in your area for other choices.

Iris, calla lily, New Zealand flax (*Phormium tenax*), and African daisy (*Arctotis venusta*) bloom in early spring along the Pacific Ocean's coast, a region with mild winters and dry summers.

# Specialty Gardens

It's a good idea to survey the many different garden types and choose a favorite one that's right for your setting and lifestyle before you plant.

There are flower gardens for every gardener and beautiful landscapes for almost every site:

- gardens made of colorful English borders
- gardens filled with flowers to cut, arrange, and enjoy
- gardens filled with heavenly scents and fragrances
- gardens tinkling with the sound of flowing water
- gardens that conserve resources and ease the need for care
- gardens to attract and observe birds and butterflies

Look at the landscapes found on the following pages as examples to inspire you and give you ideas for your yard. Each landscape features several gardens with a common theme. You will find photographs with descriptions of unique features that help define the garden and make it special.

Look closely at how each garden differs. When you plant your yard, use these points of difference as you match your garden to your site.

As you narrow the field to the few gardens you like best, note how each garden works with its site. The conditions in your yard may be similar to those in the example garden or quite different. The amount of sunlight your site receives, for example, could vary from the gardens shown.

Always choose plants that can thrive in your yard. Many species have similar growth habits and blooms. Fill your yard with plants that perform the same function and will grow well in your conditions rather than blindly matching a plant list. Take a moment to look up each recommended plant, noting its hardiness to cold, its requirements for sun and soil, and its height, foliage type, and bloom color [see Encyclopedia of Flowers, pg. 143].

Use the information you have gathered to choose alternate plants with characteristics similar to those of the plants shown in the examples. Foxglove (*Digitalis purpurea*), for instance, is a biennial plant that grows in partial shade in nearly every climate and has tall spikes of bell-shaped flowers. It can often be planted in place of Canterbury bells (*Campanula medium*) or larkspur (*Consolida ajacis)*, two less-hardy plants that need full sun, play the same roles, and have similar flower shapes.

Treasure each new garden, even as you come to appreciate the qualities that make it unique.

Attention to fine detail can lead to different choices of posts and fences, each unique: unfinished wood (top), wrought iron (bottom), and painted wood (right).

# Cottage Gardens

## Casual floral abundance is the hallmark of an English border and the foundation of every cottage garden.

The plants in a cottage garden mingle with abandon, making a delightful mixture of annuals, biennials, perennials, and herbs. Vines roam over fences and trellises while foxglove and hollyhock (*Alcea rosea*) stand above the crowd and roses, lilacs (*Syringa vulgaris*), and gardenias share their heavenly scents. Direct descendants of England's cottage gardens, North American versions contain blossoms in myriad colors, sizes, and shapes while taking full advantage of its greater variation in climate.

Cottage gardens often fill an enclosed front yard behind a gate and flank the walkway to the front door. They give season after season of color—the more, the better. Borders overflowing with blooms are everywhere, and pathways can lead to nooks and crannies or seating areas that allow you to admire the view. Flowers abound in these gardens. Vines such as clematis, climbing roses, and wisteria may cover an arbor or climb a wall. Whimsical garden accessories such as a ceramic frog peeking from a cluster of bachelor's button (*Centaurea cyanus*), a small birdbath among the rosebushes, or heart-shaped stepping-stones surrounded by violets (*Viola odorata*) deliver the sense of discovery these gardens are meant to give.

Cottage gardens suit most geographical locales and architectural styles. You can even create one with containers in your courtyard or on a patio or deck; make the pottery a part of the garden by highlighting it. Fill a bright green pot with orange nasturtiums or a pink and lavender one with pink and white dianthus. Include native plants that attract birds and butterflies to complete the look.

By definition, cottage gardens change appearance according to the region where they grow. A southern cottage garden is likely to spotlight colorful clematis, Confederate jasmine (*Trachelospermum jasminoides*), and Virginia creeper along with showy perennials like balloon flower (*Platycodon grandiflorus*), coral-

bells, and peony (*Paeonia* spp.). A southwestern cottage garden is likely to be home to agaves, aloes, bougainvillea, marigolds (*Tagetes* spp.), and colorful ornamental peppers. Further east, you might include cranesbill (*Erodium reichardii*), feverfew (*Chrysanthemum parthenium*), iris, lungwort (*Pulmonaria* spp.), peony, and climbing rose. Regardless of the region, you'll find a wealth of plants ideal for your cottage garden.

Cozy and eclectic, cottage gardens are typically filled with a jumble of plants and many eye-catching accessories.

# Cutting Gardens
## Bring a bounty of beautiful blooms indoors.

Some people garden solely for fresh bouquets to cut and arrange. Join them—brighten your day and enjoy your blooms long after sunset with a spring bouquet of Spanish bluebells (*Hyacinthoides* spp.), daffodils (*Narcissus* spp.), grape hyacinths, and tulips on the table or windowsill.

The secret to a plentiful cutting garden is growing several reliable varieties for each season. You can have a cutting garden most months of the year in many climates, and even in the coldest regions you can usually grow flowers from April through October. Supplement your garden blooms with filler materials gathered from landscape shrubs, trees, and grasses. For example, mix summer bulbs such as dahlias, gladioli, and daylilies with fern and plantain lily (*Hosta* spp.) leaves. Cut branches in spring from forsythia or flowering plum and arrange them with daffodils and tulips. At summer's end, gather arm-loads of asters, sunflowers, and zinnias and mix them with fountain grass or branches of colorful autumn leaves. You're the floral designer—use your skills and let your imagination run wild.

Cutting gardens can be just about any size. Even a small corner or a group of containers on your patio yield a variety of blooms when you plant one or two plants of each species. Just make certain to note necessary growing conditions before planting, then give them even watering, fertilize them regularly, and protect them from unseasonable weather that might damage their blooms or foliage.

Plant a mixture of annuals, perennials, bulbs, and filler plants for the fullest, most eye-catching bouquets. Annuals may last only a season, but they are powerhouses of blooming vigor—especially when you cut them on a regular basis. If non-hybrid cultivars reseed, they'll grow true for you in following seasons. Reliable annual choices include calendulas, cosmos, many of the daisies, larkspurs, sunflowers (especially dwarf varieties), satin flowers (*Clarkia amoena*), spider flowers, stocks (*Matthiola* spp.), and sweet peas. Perennials with stunning cut flowers include avens (*Geum* spp.), carnations (*Dianthus caryophyllus*), chrysanthemums, delphiniums, foxgloves, patrinias, phlox, and roses. Just about any bulb is an excellent cut flower: plant alstroemerias, daffodils, dahlias, gladioli, irises, and tulips. Also plant a peony as a shrub to cut for its flowers. The best-known filler plant is baby's-breath (*Gypsophila paniculata*), but bishop's weed (*Ammi majus*), dill (*Anethum graveolens*), and Queen Anne's lace (*Daucus carota*) are also excellent choices that provide delicate, airy fillers.

Create easy access to flowers in a cutting garden by surrounding their beds with paths.

# Flower Arranging

Arranging cut flowers picked from your flower beds brings the garden's beauty indoors. Grow blooms to use in floral displays in a cutting garden or in an out-of-the-way location such as behind your landscape shrubs.

Water your plants the night before you harvest flowers. The next morning, take a deep container filled with cold water into the garden. Cut annual and perennial flower stems at points close to where they emerge from the foliage; cut flowering shrubs such as roses above a leaf's junction with its main branch. Plunge each cut stem into the water immediately after cutting.

When harvesting is complete, recut each stem under running water. This two-step process eliminates any air gaps that could block water flow into the flowers, prolonging freshness.

Use floral freshener additives in the water of your arrangement to prevent bacteria and fungi from growing and causing premature decay.

**1** Remove any spent blooms and strip away greenery. Wash optional decorations such as crab apples (shown), lemons, limes, and pears. Fill the vase with the apples, which provide support.

**2** Place greenery as a foundation in the vase. It will hold the flowers in place, anchoring and supporting flower stems inserted in the arrangement's bottom tier.

**3** Place filler flowers first, such as Monte Casino (*Aster pringlei* 'Monte Casino'). Fillers provide accent color and shape the arrangement. They occupy gaps between the major flowers.

**4** Insert garden zinnas angled to the vase for balance and form. For overall color coordination, use flowers with similar hues and intensity and choose textures similar to the filler flowers.

**5** Add highlights and complement the other flowers with yellow freesia. Its contrasting color, texture, and midsized flowers are key features of a highlight choice. Freesia is also a good fragrance flower. Use it to add scent to the bouquet.

**6** Fill voids between the zinnias and freesias with flowers of Peruvian lily (*Alstroemeria* spp.), a flower with contrasting shape and color. When the arrangement is full and symmetrical, mist it with water to help keep it fresh until its flowers draw water from the vase.

# Floral Fragrances

Breezes will waft the scent of fragrant flowers into your home and tantalize your senses.

Smell is our most evocative sense, researchers claim. Aromas can alter moods, reduce stress, and promote a calm feeling. They are memory triggers for important events and treasured relationships. The scent of daphne, gardenia, pink jasmine (*Jasminum polyanthum*), or lilac gives as much pleasure as the sight of their blooms.

Fragrance is a personal thing. It's important to follow your nose to have the best results in your garden; a heavenly scent to one person may be overpowering for another. Visit public and private gardens as well as garden centers and nurseries. Sniff the plants you see. Find out what scents appeal to you before you introduce them into your garden. Remember that some flowers are fragrant

Angel's-trumpet is especially fragrant in the evening.

at a particular time of day. Night jessamine (*Cestrum nocturnum*), for example, perfumes the night, while others such as honeysuckle (*Lonicera* spp.) become aromatic in the daytime, when it is warm outdoors.

Once you've chosen all your plants, site them carefully. Grow scented plants where you'll notice their fragrance and plant them in raised beds to lift them near your nose. For example, scented geraniums —apple (*Pelargonium odoratissimum*), lime (*P. nervosum*), peppermint (*P. tomentosum*), and rose (*P. graveolens*)—work well along a pathway where you'll brush against them. You can also make an inviting welcome for visitors with a walk bordered by clethra or heliotrope (*Heliotropium arborescens* and *Valeriana officinalis*). Set potted candytuft (*Iberis* spp.), nemesia, and sweet alyssum on an outdoor table. If you spend summer nights outdoors, make sure to include several of the fragrant night bloomers such as angel's-trumpet, citrus, night jessamine, star jasmine (*Trachelospermum jasminoides*) and moonflower in beds near sitting areas and paths.

Grow enough fragrant flowers in your garden so you can dry their blooms, petals, and buds to use when making sachets, potpourri, rosewater, and other floral notions that require the pure, strong scent of fresh-from-the-garden flowers.

## Herbs

Enjoy the aromatic power of herbs, from pungent rosemary to spicy chocolate mint and from licorice-y tarragon to calming lavender. Tuck scented herbs into bouquets for a special fragrance treat in your home. But remember that herbs are more than just perfume for your garden; they also flavor food and are vital to many medicines.

# Creating Sachets

Make fragrant pouches of dried flower petals, citrus peel, and essential oils to add touches of luxury to your bathrooms, bedrooms, and clothes closets.

For the best fragrance, withhold water from your garden for a day or two before you harvest the flowers. Pick scented, large-petaled blooms such as roses in the morning after dew evaporates and before heat causes wilting or evaporates oils. Also gather a few fragrant herbs, including lavender (*Lavandula* spp.) and rosemary (*Rosmarinus* spp.)

Choose blossoms that have opened fully within the last day, with swollen anthers and ovaries at their centers. They are mature, ready for pollinating, and have the strongest fragrance.

Floral-fiber fixative (which helps hold the scent), dried citrus peel, essential oils, and sheer mesh bags are available from hobby stores.

Use sachets in dresser drawers used to store linens and clothing, in open bowls over basins and tubs, and in other places where their scent of fresh flowers will be appreciated.

> **CAUTION**
> Essential oils can cause skin and eye irritation in sensitive individuals. For external use only. Keep out of reach of children. Wear protective clothing, and protect furniture surfaces.

**1** Gently strip the flower petals from each blossom. Loosely spread them on a lingerie-drying rack or hardware cloth frame. Dry them in a dark, warm, dry location for 5–7 days.

**2** Thoroughly mix equal parts of dried petals, herbs, and dried citrus peel. To each quart of petal mix, add 10 drops of an essential oil and 3 tbsp. (45 cc) of floral-fiber fixative. Cover and let stand for 1–2 hours.

**3** Partly fill sheer mesh bags with petal mix and tie them closed with decorative ribbon or fill open containers with loose petal mix. Store finished sachets in sealed plastic storage bags or airtight containers to retain their scent.

# Water Gardens
## The melody of water brings peace to your garden.

Whether fanciful or traditional, fountains add the dimension of sound to your garden.

### Gardens to Soothe the Spirit

Other than the flowers themselves, water is the most alluring garden element. Its look and sound calm and relax everyone. Plan a water feature to make your garden a refuge from everyday stresses and concerns.

Thanks to technology, water can gush, rush, trickle, splash, pour, cascade, or drip in your garden. Install anything from a simple container fountain on a deck or patio to a pond that blends with a stream in a woodland garden. A bog garden is often a good solution for an area where water naturally tends to stand, and a wall fountain splashing into an adobe pool creates a refreshing haven in a desert Southwest garden. You can extend water gardens from an existing stream if you have one on your site, but most are entirely man-made and use pumps to recirculate the water through the water feature.

## Aquatic Plants

Water gardening offers a whole new world of plant and garden design possibilities. Plan a water garden for a location that is bright but cool. Most flowering water plants require at least five hours of sunlight a day but may fail in areas that receive hot sun in midafternoon. Sites with morning and evening sun are best. For ponds in shady areas, choose foliage plants rather than those that flower.

Make the pond at least 18 inches (45 cm) deep and cover 60 to 70 percent of its surface with plants. This will keep the water cool and cut down on sunlight, helping to prevent the overgrowth of algae. Select a mix of water plants. Oxygenating and floating plants are the best competitors for algae. Their coverage of the pond keeps algae from blooming by blocking its access to sunlight and nutrients. While bog and marginal plants also shade the water, they are usually ornamental plantings.

Algae blooms are common in new ponds. If they are left to grow unchecked, algae will choke out other plants and release toxins when they die and decay. Use algae-control methods such as floating containers filled with barley hay or periodic skimming before applying an algicide safe for your plants and fish.

Give your water garden a fresh start by always cleaning it at the beginning of each season, and prevent it from becoming overgrown by trimming back plants as they grow.

Formal gardens traditionally included reflecting pools and fountains, but today's gardeners usually opt for a more naturalistic approach. Their water features are extensions of the garden itself—designed to be small ecosystems that local wildlife can call home—and are the center of its design.

### Installing a Water Feature

Make a water garden of your own by either installing a fountain or by preparing a site, digging a hole, and placing a preformed waterproof liner in it [See Water Garden and Fountain Utilities, pg. 97].

Fountains are available as kits that are ready for installation. Finish the feature by landscaping around it with paving, loose stones, and plants.

Location is important. Make your water feature the focal point of your yard or the destination at the end of a path. Another option is to place a pond under trees; plan ahead to remove falling leaves or needles, seed pods, and other debris that will fall into the pond from overhead. Skimmers will remove such debris.

Also consider wind when installing a water garden or fountain. It can blow spray from a fountain off-course, damage aquatic plants, and lead to excessive water loss in a recirculating fountain or pond. If your water feature will be in a breezy location, make a wind-break of plants or erect fences to protect it.

Consider the potential for gardening with aquatic plants [see Aquatic Plants, opposite pg.]. To grow lotuses (*Nelumbo lutea*) or water lilies (*Nymphaea* spp.), choose an open spot with four to six hours of sunlight a day. In woodland sites, choose shade-loving

Pond shorelines are a good choice for moisture-craving flowering plants.

aquatic plants for the pond. Some species of fish such as ornamental goldfish and carp tolerate both warm sites in full sun and the cooler conditions of a shady site. Match both the fish you select and your plants to the conditions of your site.

## Koi

Having a koi pond is much like having a giant outdoor aquarium. Koi need lots of room, so these ponds tend to be large—at least 1,000 gallons (3,785 l) of water with a three-foot (90 cm) depth. This translates to a pond with an area of 50 square feet (4.8 m²), or about six feet by eight feet (1.8 m × 2.4 m).

Koi were bred in Japan during the 17th century from wild carp. They will grow a foot (30 cm) in their first two years and add an inch (25 mm) a year until they reach two to three feet (60 to 90 cm). Contrary to popular belief, koi don't grow to the size of the pond. In a tight space they will grow slowly, but they will soon outgrow a pond that is too small for them.

Koi live 20 to 50 years in ideal conditions. Because they require constantly moving water, install an appropriately sized filtration system and a fountain to keep the pond water aerated. Select rapid-growing aquatic plants, too, because koi eat most water plants. Protect your koi from fish-eating birds such as heron by placing netting over their pond.

# Flowering Xeriscapes

## Conserve precious water and still have abundant flowers.

Ice plant and other drought-tolerant plants suit a rock garden.

Choose drought-tolerant, exotic plants such as Montebretia (*Crocosmia* hyb.), torch lily (*Kniphofia* spp.), and watsonia for your Xeriscape garden's beds.

Xeriscape gardening, or gardening for water conservation, was developed in Denver, Colorado in 1981. The word Xeriscape comes from the Greek word *xeros*, meaning dry. Xeriscape landscapes, also known as dry gardens, require minimal irrigation. They are common in arid regions where summer rainfall is scarce, but you can create one anywhere, providing you follow several basic principles:

- Grow plants that are well adapted to the area and group those with similar needs.
- Limit turf and replace it with more drought-tolerant native grasses.
- Use mulch to retain moisture and reduce weed growth.
- Water plants only when necessary, irrigating slowly and deeply to encourage deep root growth.
- Perform a soil test and add the required fertilizers and the amendments needed to provide all essential nutrients and improve drainage, moisture penetration, and water-holding capacity.

Hardscape features such as brick, gravel, pebbles, statuary, and stepping-stones, as well as larger structures, including arbors, seating areas, and trellises, are also common elements of these dry gardens.

Xeriscape gardens are different from those filled with plants that grow only with abundant moisture. The flowers are brighter and more intense, gray and silver foliage is more common than green, and the leaves often are leathery or succulent. Rather than towering vines, you'll also see more ground covers such as brilliant, pink-flowered ice plant. Ornamental grasses are staples. Most of the plants in Xeriscape gardens are native. For example, in the Great Plains, they usually contain a mixture of grasses and wildflowers native to the region.

Plant carefully for Xeriscape gardens that provide colorful flowers year-round, choosing drought-tolerant plants suited to your area. Besides flowering succulents and cacti—of which there are many—select from the wide variety of ornamental grasses and the huge realm of drought-resistant native and naturalized plants. You'll find as many flowering Xeriscape plants as you need. For example, the *Echinopsis* species of cactus includes many blooming varieties. Succulent plants are equally abundant; they include aloe, crassula, echeveria, euphorbia, and kalanchoe, all of which bloom. Add plants chosen from the numerous drought-tolerant annual and perennial species such as certain bellflowers (*Campanula* spp.), blanket flower (*Gaillardia* spp.), bougainvillea, California poppy, calliopsis (*Coreopsis* spp.), cornflower (*Centaurea* spp.), purple coneflower, cosmos, perennial flax (*Linum perenne*), geranium, lupine, penstemon, pinks (*Dianthus* spp.), various poppies (*Papaver* spp.), spider flower, sunflower, thrift (*Armeria maritima*), and red valerian (*Centranthus ruber*).

All drought-tolerant plants require regular watering until they are established. Plant in the autumn and during spring when the temperatures are cooler and abundant rain aids your efforts.

Mexican bush sage (*Salvia luucantha*), agave, and succulent ground covers are low-water plants suited for arid gardens.

## Using Fieldstone and Boulders

Balanced gardens contain more than flowering plants. Bulk and presence offset greenery and blooms, making rocks and boulders a natural addition to Xeriscape and other gardens. In fact, many drought-tolerant plants are native to rocky areas and can be found sheltered beneath boulders where the soil is shaded, retains moisture, and remains generally cooler than the surrounding area.

Once you begin a search for the perfect stones and boulders for your landscape, you'll notice the subtle detail and personality of each piece. Take time to measure and mentally picture the larger ones in your garden. How will they look when the sun hits them? Will they be

effective at shading your plants or protecting them from wind? Will their colors blend in or contrast with your flowers?

Transporting large boulders requires considerable effort. Most man-made prefabricated boulders are lighter than their natural counterparts; even so, their size makes them awkward and cumbersome to move. Real boulders are very heavy and require special equipment such as forklifts, cranes, and backhoes to transport and install. Personal safety is a prime consideration when installing large stones or real boulders. Plan to enlist the aid of one or more assistants and obtain the necessary equipment to help you do the job safely.

# Welcoming Winged Creatures
Provide habitats in your garden for birds, hummingbirds, and butterflies.

Typical of visitors to a wildlife garden are a common house finch (top), a pair of Anna's hummingbirds (lower left), and a monarch butterfly (lower right).

Even a small garden corner has enough space for plants and features that attract birds. Install different kinds of birdhouses and feeders, and plant a variety of nectar- and seed-producing flowering plants.

Habitats for wildlife in North America shrink with every new housing or commercial development. While there are practical limits to your ability to help large animals, your garden does give birds, butterflies, insects, and smaller animals places where they can feed, rest, find shelter, and produce young.

Birds and plants have a symbiotic relationship. Birds pollinate blooms, protect plants from insect pests, and scatter their seed even as they consume the plant's fruits, buds, flowers, and nectar.

Plant annual flowers such as sunflower and many daisies with seed heads, and birds will flock to them.

Hummingbirds are tiny, colorful, and unique. Time seems to stand still when you see a humming-

bird. With its tiny wings pumping up and down at peak speeds of up to 200 beats per second, it zips between flowers, drinks their nectar, and quickly moves on. It's easy to attract hummingbirds. Plant a variety of tubular flowers, concentrating on red or deep orange blossoms.

Many other species of wild birds feed on seed that flowers produce. Especially important for many birds are seed-bearing stems of ornamental grasses and annual flowers that remain standing throughout the winter. Flowers can also attract desirable insects such as ladybird beetles. Many of these beneficial insects prey upon pest insect species or make a dinner for the birds.

Butterflies are probably the most admired insects. Attract them by designing a garden that provides a full season of nectar-producing flowers mixed with their host plants. Host plants—milkweed, for example, is a common host to all of the monarch, queen, and viceroy butterfly species—provide feed for the caterpillars. Remember to avoid squashing them or their chrysalises when you prune and perform clean-up chores in your garden; both must survive to produce new generations of adult butterflies.

Butterflies feed on flower nectar; their larvae—or caterpillars—usually eat foliage.

# Flowers for Intimate Spaces

Containers are the right choices for decorating patios, decks, courtyards, and balconies.

Given the wide range of container products available today, you can garden almost everywhere. Experiment by clustering a group of small potted plants such as marigolds or violets on a patio table or plant sweet peas in a larger pot beside it. Spill trailing lobelia, million bells (*Calibrachoa* spp.), and ivy geraniums (*Pelargonium peltatum*) from a window box. Flank an entry with pots of fragrant gardenias. Encircle a small courtyard's tree with overflowing pots of impatiens and hang containers with trailing fuchsias, lungwort, or dwarf periwinkle (*Vinca* spp.) from its limbs. Free your imagination and let it be your guide.

Nearly any vessel makes a good plant container. Choose a pot with at least one protected drainage hole, or bore extra holes using an electric drill, making them at least one half inch (12 mm) in diameter.

Always learn a plant's requirements—including its mature size—before potting it. Plan to transplant it to progressively larger pots as it grows. A good rule of thumb is to choose a container as large as the plant's foliage is wide.

The best-looking mixed groups usually combine both large and small plants, along with upright, tall, and trailing species.

Potted plants require more frequent watering and fertilizing than in-ground plants. Without food, plants in confined areas may flower only sparsely or fail to bloom entirely. Plants that experience drought are unlikely to reflower until they grow new feeder roots. Water yours whenever their soil dries—containers that need watering seem lightweight for their size—and fertilize blooming plants every two to four weeks with liquid fertilizer.

OPPOSITE:
Hanging baskets and planters dress up a wall with color at eye level. They expand the planting space available for gardens in a courtyard, deck, or patio.

BELOW:
Make your entry more inviting with flowers in containers. Change the pots and plants as the season progresses.

# Entertaining in the Garden

Gardens are for enjoyment, celebrations, gatherings, and informal fun.

Create a beautiful outdoors and you'll want to share it with friends and family. There's a certain magic that comes with entertaining in the garden. As you plan your garden, think about events that you might hold outdoors and how much space they'll need. For instance, you may want to enjoy an intimate brunch in a courtyard surrounded by roses and filled with the music of a fountain, or hold a wine-and-cheese tasting next to a coorful flower bed.

Consider privacy, too. Add intimacy by covering walls and fences with latticework for climbing vines. This floral background will add dimension and depth to the setting. Delineate garden areas from the space for your guests by marking them with rows or groups of planters and containers.

Amuse your young guests with old-time garden favorites such as croquet or horseshoes, or teach them a trendy retro game of bocce ball.

## Planning a Garden Party

1. Refresh bloomed-out beds about six to eight weeks prior to a party with six-packs of annuals.
2. Deadhead spent flowers and prune repeat bloomers to encourage new blossoms.
3. Fertilize using diluted 1–5–5 liquid every seven to ten days until a week before the party.
4. Add containers and hanging flowers one to two days before the party for extra touches of color.
5. Inspect the garden for safety and remove any items that could trip, snag, or injure your guests.
6. The day of the party, set each table with cutting shears and a small vase. Award prizes for the best centerpieces your guests create.
7. Provide sunblock, shade, and water in daytime; in evening, provide mosquito protection, lighting, and infrared heaters.

Make the garden part of your party decor. Gather flowers from your cutting garden and make a stunning centerpiece, put potted herbs on the table to accompany the meal, and use your sunflowers for a theme that extends to napkins and tablecloths with sunflower motifs.

While indoor entertaining can tend to the formal, backyard entertaining lends itself to greater flexibility. Take table coverings, for instance: use blankets, rugs, towels, and brightly colored sheets to accent tables, chairs, and benches. Play off the bloom colors in a nearby floral border. Match your landscape shrubs with a centerpiece brimming with flowers of similar colors and textures. Turn pots over and use them as occasional tables. Use the edge of planters as a tabletop. Fill a child's wagon with a bunch of cutting flowers just before guests arrive or load it up with soft drinks and bottles of water. Accessorize as you would indoors: use throw pillows, lanterns, candles, wall plaques— anything to make your yard look casual, homey, and inviting.

It's easy to decorate for a social event in your garden and make your guests feel special at the same time. Start with some behind-the-scenes planning and spruce up your garden [see Planning a Garden Party, opposite pg.].

Make fun, charming, and garden-themed elements to decorate for your party. Here are some great, yet simple, ideas you can use as a starting point.

**1** Fill a plant tote with clay pots for napkins and plastic flatware. Use a watering can as the vase for a bouquet of flowers surrounded by miniatures holding votive candles. Make sugared pansies from the flowers in your garden to decorate a cake. Set the cake tray on a stable, wide-based clay pot.

**2** Keep guests comfortable on warm summer days with lots of cold drinks. Loading a colorful wagon, garden cart, or wheelbarrow with buckets of ice and cold soft drinks is a good alternative to unsightly ice chests. Pull it into the shade; moving your drink service for refilling is easy. Refresh it with new ice every couple of hours to keep the drinks icy cold.

# contemporary
# and classic

GREAT FLOWER GARDENS ARE STRUCTURED ACCORDING TO SOLID DESIGN PRINCIPLES. Begin the design process by clarifying your vision for the garden; your initial design decisions will affect its overall look and feel for years to come. Define the primary purposes of your outdoor space and how you plan to use it. Do you want a formal or a relaxed area for entertaining and dining? Do you want to beautify your home's front yard and improve its appeal? Do you wish to attract birds, butterflies, and hummingbirds? Is a cutting garden your heart's desire?

It's easier to develop a garden that is as beautiful as it is functional when you are clear about its intended use and purpose. Think of landscape design as being similar to creating one or more outdoor rooms, each with its own use. Once you know what the rooms are, you can decide how they should relate to each other and how to position them in your yard.

Begin with the entry to your home, its front yard. It's the first thing a visitor will see. Many suburban homes, for example, have small lawns and concrete paths between the front door and the street. Choose between an island—a flower bed placed in the lawn and surrounded by turf—and traditional borders that line the front of the house and extend down the walk.

Should they be geometric and formal, or sinuous and casual? Will you surround your home with carefree flowers or emphasize its dignity with a row of tree roses that parallel the path to your door?

Gather ideas for your outdoor rooms by comparing your landscape to the examples shown in the following pages. Take a few moments to explore options before proceeding to your garden center. For most people, a simple freshening with annual and perennial flowers or creation of a new feature completes the change they desire. For others, evaluating purposes and uses will suggest redos that improve and dramatically alter the appearance and appeal of their homes. Let function guide your design.

# Garden Where You Are

Make a garden that relates to your home by complementing its architecture and matching regional styles.

The best gardens reflect their surroundings and look as if they belong to the region and its climate. You may already understand your area well enough to create a garden that fits seamlessly into it. Even so, take the time to discover all you can about its ecology. Research native plants and find out how they interact with or feed local wildlife.

Effective gardens also mirror a home's architecture. For example, if you live in the Pacific Southwest and your house is Spanish revival or Mediterranean-style with a low-pitched roof, clay roof tiles, stucco siding, and arched doorways, you will find a broad palette of plants to complement it. Train a fuchsia, a bougainvillea, a Lady Bank's rose (*Rosa banksiae*), or a wisteria vine over an arched entryway. Contrast the home's blue trim and rust-colored tile with red geraniums spilling from large earthenware containers in a courtyard. Plant a bed of lavender and salvia to attract hummingbirds and butterflies.

Formal gardens are appropriate for a Georgian-style home with its stately symmetry. Also use this approach with French and Italianate and other formal dwellings such as those seen in Washington, D.C., Montreal, and Toronto. In the mid-Atlantic and southeastern United States, where Federal homes are common, offset clipped hedging with soft pink camellia or myrtle (*Myrtus communis*). A boxwood-lined path at the back of your house might lead to a formal rose garden. Build uniform garden beds and fill them with bulbs such as tulips in monochromatic —single color—schemes.

An informal, cottage-style garden is needed for a Queen Anne's Victorian with its towers, turrets, a wraparound porch, gingerbread moldings, and other frills. For those set in the mid-Atlantic, central, or western states, grow cornflower (*Mirabilis jalapa*), four-o'clock, dahlia, delphinium, foxglove, holly-

> **SOUTHERN GARDENS**
>
> In the 1700s, when wealthy European settlers made the southern parts of North America their home, they established plantations with accompanying gardens that were a blend of Old and New World styles. Today, southern gardens mix styles derived from formal 17th- and 18th-century European gardens with a more relaxed and natural approach that the climate of the American South dictates.

Grow flowers in all your available space, from the mow strip between your sidewalk and the street to flower-filled containers and planters.

hock, nemesia, pansy (*Viola* × *wittrockiana*), speedwell (*Veronica* spp.), viola, and violet.

If your home is a Craftsman bungalow with a low-pitched roof, wide eaves with exposed beams, and square porch columns, an informal garden design works well. In the midwestern United States or prairie provinces of Canada, focus on a multiseason, highly diverse garden. Generally, bungalows are painted with two or three colors. Choose flowers that play off the dominant color and accent your garden with foliage or blooms that complement its trim. Enjoy fragrant daphne, lilac, and stock in spring, Shasta daisies (*Chrysanthemum maximum*) and coneflower in summer, and chrysanthemums and nerine in late summer and early autumn. Plant verbena and sage (*Salvia* spp.) for color accents from late spring through early autumn. Transition into winter with shrubs such as fire thorn (*Pyracantha* × hyb.) that develop berries that persist after frosts begin, and bulbs with hardy foliage such as cyclamen, ornamental cabbage, and kale.

To complement a Cape Cod–style home in New England or the Maritime provinces with its steep shingle roof, side gables, large central chimney, and dormers, plan a formal garden. Clean, geometric forms and stone walls, paths, gates, and trellises combine well with plants suited to northeastern coastal weather. Plant coralbell, johnny-jump-up (*Viola tricolor*), bearded iris, and peony. Use azaleas and rhododendrons, which usually appear stately, or tree roses —standards—for larger plants with presence.

In the Pacific Northwest, a ranch-style home with a low-pitched gable roof, deep-set eaves, and rambling layout looks best

surrounded by a woodland garden. Plant a combination of plantain lilies, using cultivars with solid green and variegated foliage. Mix the planting with white astilbes, goatsbeards, ginger lilies, and meadow rues (*Thalictrum* spp.), plus your favorite broad-leaved ferns and other foliage plants.

Fill vertical space with blooms. The blue flowers of passion vine (*Passiflora edulis*) contrast well with rustic yellow walls.

## Flowers with Nature in Mind

One key to creating a lush flower garden is to choose plants that appear and behave as if they were native to your region. Choose plants suited to the conditions in your yard so they can thrive with minimum care. Plant native flowers rather than introduced species and hybridized plants; natives are long-lasting and will increase in number by self-seeding or spreading. Some are invasive when first planted, but will soon intermingle to strike a balance with their companions. Before long, your garden will be filled with plants marked by mutually beneficial relationships with each other and with local wildlife. You'll sit back and enjoy the floral show as it unfolds, season after season.

# Gardens Are Outdoor Rooms

Divide your yard according to the use you plan for each area, creating floral ceilings, walls, and floors of great beauty.

Add flowers where they are least expected by growing them in containers and creating artful groups of bright color. Placed along a swimming pool's edge, they can be a practical reminder that its water is too shallow for diving.

The concept of decorating your outdoors with flowers and accompanying greenery is hardly new—gardeners have been doing it for generations. The idea may have come from observing the wild, where plants naturally layer themselves, share the same space, and work together to create glades, grottoes, and meadows. You can orchestrate a similar process and replicate natural plant communities in your yard and landscape as you choose plants for each of the situations found in your site.

## Planting in Beds and Borders

Place large plants such as shrubs and vines toward the back of your flower borders to create a graceful, tiered effect. Create height in the center of an island bed with taller plants used as a background. Place midsized annuals, perennials, bulbs, and shrubs in front of or surrounding them, and finish planting in descending order with the smallest annuals, perennials, and ground covers.

### Start with Ceilings and Walls

Our homes' walls and ceilings give us an enclosed, safe feeling. Similarly, gardens with a canopy seem more inviting and intimate than landscapes open to the sky.

Choose carefully and train large garden plants—your trees and shrubs—as they grow to give needed shade as well as privacy. When properly chosen and placed, trees are always valuable; flowering shrubs such as lilac, crape myrtle (*Lagerstroemia indica*), and sumac (*Rhus* spp.) can enclose a garden. With the right supports, flowering vines can also serve as excellent ceilings. Cover

an arbor, patio cover, or shade structure with trumpet vine (*Campsis radicans*), bougainvillea, jasmine, mandevilla, passion vine, or wisteria.

Vines also substitute for garden walls. Train a honeysuckle, morning glory, or mandevilla up a wall, trellis, or fence. Use dense shrubs such as glossy abelia (*Abelia* × *grandiflora*), photinia, and weigela to block your view of a neighbor's yard. Where yards run together, use lilac and azalea or evergreen hedges for transitional "walls" between them rather than building fences.

## Decorations and Wall Coverings

Think of small- to medium-sized perennials and annuals as accessories and wallcoverings for your out-door rooms. Bugloss (*Anchusa* spp.), lily-of-the-valley, small shrub roses, and snapdragons (*Antirrhinum majus*) are good choices. Add annuals such as floss-flower (*Ageratum houstonianum*), globe candytuft (*Iberis umbellata*), nasturtium, and wishbone flower (*Torenia fournieri*).

## Hang the Chandelier

Hanging containers create drama in the backyard, much as chandeliers do in a dining room. Suspend hanging baskets from house eaves, arbors, patio covers,

and trees. Use bright trailing plants such as bacopa (*Sutera cordata*), begonia, fuchsia, ivy geranium, lobelia, nasturtium, and verbena cultivars. Grow staghorn ferns (*Platycerium bifurcatum*) on tree trunks. Install hangers and hang plants on walls.

## Install Carpeting

Low-growing plants and ground covers are a finishing touch for the garden. Most ground covers have low, dense growth. Some species can stand in for lawn, while others such as creeping thyme and baby's-tears (*Soleirolia soleirolii*) work well between stepping-stones. Many flowers make a brilliant carpet. Try Dalmatian bellflowers (*Campanula portenschlagiana*). They create a bright purple display each spring and remain in bloom throughout summer. On sunny hillsides, use succulent ice plant with brilliant pink, purple, white, or yellow flowers or gold-blossomed Aaron's beard (*Hypericum calycinum*). Other good ground covers, depending on the species, include ornamental bindweed (*Convolvulus mauritanicus*), garden chamomile (*Chamaemelum nobile*), erodium, forget-me-not (*Myosotis scorpioides*), one of the various true gerani-ums, strawberry geranium (*Saxifraga stolonifera*), hebe, periwinkle, verbena, viola, and yarrow. In a shade or water garden, grow mat-forming true moss (*Hypnum* spp.) or one of its usual stand-ins, Irish and Scot's moss, baby's-tears, or dichondra (*Dichondra micrantha*). Experiment with small patches of ground covers in your yard until you find a species or a cultivar that you like and that will thrive in your climate, together with the soil and light conditions found in your particular site.

OPPOSITE:
Add beauty beneath a patio roof with hanging baskets of flowers.

BELOW:
Hang pots filled with flowers from the branches of trees and place others on their limbs. Plant a carpet of ground cover succulents as a floral alternative that replaces water-hungry turfgrass lawns.

# Beauty in Motion

## Mix flowers and ornamental grasses to add subtle textures, graceful arching, and seductive movement.

You probably long for the "perfect" plant: easy-to-grow; beautiful yet hardy; adaptable to a wide range of soil, temperature, and moisture conditions; relatively free of diseases and pests; requiring little if any care; suited to just about any garden location; available in a variety of sizes, shapes, and colors; and fast growing. Sound impossible? Grasses can be your dream come true.

Long a staple of European gardens, ornamental grasses add a fresh dimension to the landscape and are enjoying a surge in popularity. They are often planted alone, but many designers believe they are more striking when combined with flowers, especially Xeriscape species.

The foliage and flowers of these plants are varied; long, narrow leaves range in texture from soft and flowing to short and spiky. Stem colors include blues,

Vary the heights of your bed with low flowers in the front, tall grasses in the back.

Mix your planting of flowering shrubs and ornamental grasses, taking advantage of the beauty both add to the garden. These graceful plumes of purple fountain grass arch among spikes of Russian sage.

purples, reds, and yellows, as well as a variety of greens. Maturing leaves fade to soft blond, lime green, and red orange, making them a prized addition to fresh and dried flower arrangements as well as a persistent note of winter color. Ornamental grass species grow from three inches (75 mm) tall, as in the case of mondo grass (*Ophiopogon japonicus*), to 15 feet (4.6 m) high for pampas grass (*Cortaderia selloana*). Best of all, they make a soft rustling sound in the slightest wind.

Ornamental grasses are extremely adaptable. They look as much at home in a small balcony garden in urban New York, Dallas, or Ottawa as they do spilling over the length of a suburban garden in Pennsylvania or Manitoba. They grow well in just about any soil and will thrive in containers.

There are ornamental grasses for every situation, just as there are flowers for every garden. Grow Japanese sweet flag grass (*Acorus gramineus*) in a boggy area or by a water garden with moisture-tolerant plants such as Chinese globeflower (*Trollius chinensis*), heliotrope, and lobelia.

On the midwestern plains, big bluestem grass (*Andropogon gerardii*) combines well with lupine and Joe-Pye weed (*Eupatorium purpureum*). It is also a good choice for the tall-

grass prairies. In a woodland setting, ornamental grasses such as hakonechloa, northern sea oats (*Chasmanthium latifolium*), and tall purple moor grass (*Molinia caerulea*) grow well beside shade-tolerant perennials such as coralbells, forget-me-not, lenten rose, lily-of-the-valley, creeping phlox (*P. stolonifera*), and Solomon's-seal.

While gardeners who love ornamental grasses say that they are all excellent, there are a few that stand out. Stipa (*S. gigantea*) is a clump-forming grass with large, airy inflorescences that add light and motion to the garden. Blue fescue (*Festuca glauca*) has fine leaves that turn blue to silver white and make a good background for brightly colored flowers. The aquatic fiber-optics grass (*Scirpus cernus*) has variegated stalks with black markings that give it the illusion of being beaded. Tufted hair grass (*Deschampsia caespitosa*) has graceful, bunching clumps of arching foliage covered with flowing, cloud-like flower heads.

## ORNAMENTAL GRASS BASICS

Plant ornamental grasses as far apart as they will grow tall; place narrow, short species close together and tall or mounding grasses farther apart. They will thrive in just about any soil but prefer good drainage. Avoid overwatering.

Any discussion of ornamental grasses would be incomplete if it failed to mention the boldest grass of all: bamboo. Usually thought of as tropical plants, which many are, northern species such as yellow groove bamboo (*Phyllostachys aureosulcata*) and *Fargesia murielae* are hardy to −20°F (−29°C). Many bamboos are very aggressive and should be planted in containers or surrounded with root guards to block their spread.

Do research and seek advice from your garden center's staff before choosing grasses. Pay attention to growth habit—some grasses grow in bunches that slowly increase their width, others extend long underground runners (stolons) over large areas, and many reseed themselves with the wind.

Consider height, too. Do you want one large specimen to take center stage among a group of flowering plants or a group of ornamental grasses that gracefully blend into a sea of blooms?

Pay special attention to the mature size of grasses when making your selection. A grass in a one-gallon (3.8-l) pot may outgrow its bed in one season. Others have spreading roots and quickly become too wide for narrow borders.

# Attracting Birds and Butterflies

## Bring winged visitors to your garden to see their colorful plumage and enjoy their activity.

White-crowned sparrows and lesser goldfinches will make repeat visits to flowers in search of seed and small insects, reducing the amount of care the flowers need to keep them pest-free and beautiful.

One of the most delightful aspects of having a garden full of flowers is its attraction for many lovely birds and insects that come calling. Encourage these visitors by considering their needs and providing them with a welcoming habitat.

### Birds

Many colorful and interesting birds may visit your garden. Create a nurturing oasis in your backyard by providing their four basic requirements:

**Food.** Grow flowering plants that produce nectar, seeds, or fruits. Birds love beautyberries (*Callicarpa bodinieri*), purple coneflowers, cornflowers, cosmos, globe thistles (*Echinops* spp.), honeysuckles, poppies, snowberries (*Symphoricarpos* spp.), sunflowers, trumpet vines, viburnums, and many ornamental grasses. Tempt them to your yard by installing bird feeders to dispense seed, suet, fruit, or nectar [See Making a Bird Feeder, pg. 44].

**Water.** Birds need a good, clean source of water for drinking and bathing.

**Nesting sites.** Give birds reasons to stay in your yard by providing spots where they can build nests and raise their young. Trees and large shrubs are ideal, but to increase the number of cavity-dwelling birds you see, build and place birdhouses in your garden [see Making a Birdhouse, pg. 42].

**Shelter.** Safeguard your winged visitors from the elements and keep them protected from predators. Shrubs and trees shelter birds, and the foliage keeps them warm. Give extra protection with roosting boxes to help them retain heat in cold weather.

## About Birdhouses

Most commercial birdhouses are simply decorative. Functional birdhouses are unpainted wood or lightly coated with latex stains and sealed with organic shellac. Each bird species requires certain interior dimensions and entrance holes of specific sizes and distances from the floor; consult the staff at your nearby birding center for construction tips on houses meant for specific bird species. Also ask them for the measurements you'll need for recommended heights above the ground and distances apart.

## Hummingbirds

Hummingbirds will visit your garden when you give them an adequate supply of their favorite nectar-producing flowers: red, tubular, and pendulous. Most bees and birds can't reach into the deep centers of these flowers for nectar, so hummingbirds have the high-energy nectar all to themselves.

A wide variety of flowers attract hummingbirds, including begonia, bleeding-heart (*Dicentra* spp.), cardinal flower (*Lobelia cardinalis*), columbine (*Aquilegia* spp.), coralbells, dahlia, delphinium, foxglove, fuchsia, honeysuckle, penstemon, petunia, trumpet vine, and verbena.

## Butterflies

Butterflies will grace your garden if you include nectar plants for adults and host plants for their larvae. Nectar and pollen plants include aster, black-eyed Susan vine (*Thunbergia* spp.), butterfly bush (*Buddleia*

spp.), purple coneflower, coreopsis, cosmos, fuchsia, heliotrope, honeysuckle, impatiens, marigold, butterfly weed, penstemon, phlox, yarrow, and zinnia.

Plants to feed caterpillars—host plants—include dills, various grasses, hibiscus, hollyhocks, lupines, mallows (*Malva* spp.), milkweeds, monkey flowers (*Mimulus aurantiacus*), nasturtiums, Italian parsley (*Petroselinum crispum*), passion vines, penstemons, mustards (*Brassica juncea*), radishes (*Raphanus sativus*), roses, snapdragons, speedwells, spiraeas, viburnums, and violets.

Sacrifice host plants to caterpillars even though the results can often be untidy. Plants can look ragged as they are consumed by the hungry larvae. Whenever possible, place host plants in out-of-sight locations hidden behind your other landscape plantings. Potted plants are useful for this purpose because you can move them around.

Include a few flat rocks in your butterfly garden design. Rocks attract butterflies because they absorb and radiate heat. Heat is important to butterflies because they can't fly until their body temperature has reached 85°–100°F (29°–38°C), depending on the species. On cool mornings, you will see them basking on your flat rocks in a sunny spot until they are warm enough to fly.

Keep the visitors to your garden safe—adopt strict organic gardening practices to control pests diseases and or fertilize.

OPPOSITE:
Anna's hummingbirds are frequent visitors to the Pacific coast; in the East, look for their ruby-throated cousins.

BELOW:
Adult question mark butterflies may visit butterfly weed, but to lay their eggs they prefer nettles. The colorful larva shown is that of a monarch, a milkweed butterfly.

# Making a Birdhouse

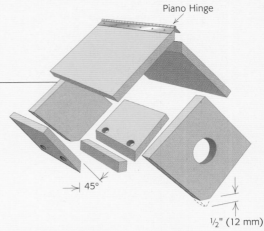

Piano Hinge

This easy-to-build birdhouse suits small, cavity-dwelling birds such as chickadees, nuthatches, tree or violet-green swallows, titmice, and wrens, including Bewick's, house, and winter; even downy woodpeckers may move in to build a nest.

Use a wood such as alder, ash, birch, or poplar. You'll need the materials listed below and an electric drill, a hole saw, a screwdriver, a hammer, and a nail set. Allow four to five hours for building and finishing the birdhouse.

Hang the finished birdhouse in trees or from eaves at least 12' (3.7 m) above the ground, or install it on a trellis as a garden decoration [see Birdhouses on a Trellis, opposite pg.].

**1** Measure, mark, and cut all pieces. Measure ½" (12 mm) in from the bottom corner of both end walls, cut off the corners, and discard the waste.

45°

½" (12 mm)

**2** Use an electric drill with a 1¼" (32 mm) hole saw to bore an entry hole centered in the front wall. With a ½" (12 mm) bit, drill two vent holes in the bottom edge of each side, equally spaced from the center and 1" (25 mm) above the bottom edge.

**3** Join the roof panels with a piano hinge along the peak. Join the end walls to the sides and base strut with the strut between and flush with the sides. Fasten the components of the wall assembly with finish nails.

**4** Lap the roof equally over the wall assembly and fasten one side only with finish nails. The hinge allows the other panel to open for cleaning.

**5** Using an electric drill with a ⅛" (3 mm) bit, drill two holes equidistant from the ends of the fixed roof panel. Attach screw eyes and a wire bridle to hang the birdhouse. If desired, use latex paint or stain only on the exterior of the birdhouse.

MATERIALS
End Walls (2) ¾" × 6⅛" × 6⅛" (19 × 156 × 156 mm)
Sides (2) ¾" × 5½" × 9" (19 × 140 × 229 mm)
Roof Panels (2) ¾" × 7¼" × 12" (19 × 184 × 305 mm)*
Brass Piano Hinge (1) ½" × 12" ( 6 × 305 mm)
Base Strut (1) ¾" × 1¼" × 9" (19 × 32 × 229 mm)†
Galvanized Finish Nails (36) 6d
Galvanized Screw Eyes (2) ¾" ( 19 mm)
Braided Copper Wire (1) No. 18 × 14" (No. 18 × 35 cm)

*Bevel one 12" (305 mm) side of each roof panel 45°
† Bevel both ¾" (19 mm) edges of the base strut 45°

# Birdhouses on a Trellis

Lattice panels to support climbing vines also make great supports for birdhouses [see Making a Birdhouse, opposite page]. Setting the posts at 45° angles adds shear (wind) strength to the trellis and mimics the birdhouses' diamond forms.

Use redwood, cedar, or cypress for the posts; framed lattice panels are available at most building centers. You will need the materials listed below and a table saw, a paintbrush, an electric drill, a screwdriver, a shovel, and a garden hose. Allow two four-hour sessions for construction and finishing.

**1** Measure, mark, and cut the posts to equal lengths. Use a table saw set at 45° to rip and bevel one corner along the side of each post. Paint the bottom 18" (45 cm) of the posts with penetrating wood preservative.

**2** Align the wide lattice panel with its top end 4" (10 cm) below the end of two posts and flush to the beveled sides. Square the assembly and fasten the panel to the posts with deck screws.

**3** Dig footing holes 16" (41 cm) deep. Set the post assembly in the footings, fill around them with posthole concrete, and add water as directed on the concrete package. Measure 2' (60 cm) out at 90° to each post face, dig a footing hole in each location, place a post in each hole, square, and set in concrete. Allow concrete to cure for two days before proceeding.

**4** Use deck screws to mount each narrow lattice panel between the assembly and the outer posts. Use an electric drill with a 1/8" (3 mm) bit to bore holes in the top of the outer posts, and attach finials to their tops. Open the tops of the birdhouses and fasten them on top of the center posts with deck screws. Finish with paint or stain, as desired.

## MATERIALS

Posts (4) 4 × 4 × 10' (8.9 × 8.9 × 305 cm)
Wide Lattice Panel (1) 4' × 8' (1.2 × 2.4 m)
Narrow Lattice Panels (2) 2' × 8' (60 × 244 cm)
Decorative Finials (2)
Clear Wood Preservative (1) qt. (0.95 l)
Deck Screws (36) No. 6 × 1⅝" (No. 6 × 41 mm)
Posthole Concrete (2 Bags) 70 lb. (32 kg)

# Making a Bird Feeder

This feeder features clear acrylic windows on both sides that show the seed and draw birds to the feeding platform area at its base. Fresh seed falls from above to refill the tray as the birds eat.

Use a wood such as alder, ash, birch, or poplar. You'll need the materials listed below and a table saw, a screwdriver, an electric drill, a hammer, and a nail set. Obtain cut acrylic from hobby or plastics retailers. Allow three to four hours for building and finishing.

Hang the finished birdhouse in a tree, from an eave 4'–5' (1.2–1.5 m) above the ground, or mount it on a log planter [see Log Planter with Bird Feeder, opposite pg.].

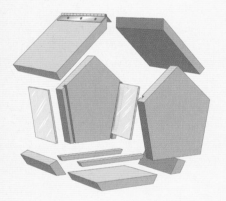

**1** Measure, mark, and cut all pieces. Bevel base, seed rails, and roof panels. With a table saw and 3/16" (5 mm) dado blade, cut a kerf 1/2" (12 mm) on both of the 47/8" (12.4 cm) edges of the end panels.

**2** Join the roof panels with a piano hinge along the peak. Fasten the short seed rails to the tray base with finish nails. Fasten the end panels to the tray base with wood screws. Fasten the long seed rails with finish nails to the tray base inside of the end panels and flush with the short seed rails.

**3** Remove the protective paper from the plastic panels and slide them into the kerf slots until they rest on the long seed rails.

**4** Fasten one roof panel to the end panels with finish nails. The other side opens for filling the feeder. To hang the feeder, add screw eyes under the eaves and a wire bridle. To mount on a post, use two deck screws through the base.

MATERIALS
Tray Base (1) 3/4" × 71/2" × 41/2" (19 × 190 × 114 mm)*
Short Seed Rails (2) 3/4" × 11/2" × 41/2" (19 × 38 × 114 mm)†
Long Seed Rails (2) 1/2" × 1/2" × 71/4" (12 × 12 × 184 mm)*
Roof Panels (1) 3/4" × 7" × 7" (19 × 178 × 178 mm)‡
End Panels (2) 3/4" × 5" × 47/8" × 41/2" (19 × 127 × 124 × 114 mm)
Acrylic Plastic Panels (2) 1/8" × 5" × 41/2" (3 × 127 × 114 mm)
Brass Piano Hinge (1) 1/2" × 7" (12 × 178 mm)
Galvanized Finish Nails (36) 6d
Wood Screws (6) No. 6 × 15/8" (No. 6 × 41 mm)
Galvanized Screw Eyes (2) 3/4" ( 19 mm)
Braided Copper Wire (1) No. 18 × 18" (No. 18 × 46 cm)
Deck Screws (2) No. 6 × 15/8" (No. 6 × 41 mm)

* Bevel both ends 25°
† Bevel one long side 25°
‡ Bevel one side 45°

# Log Planter with Bird Feeder

A rustic log planter with plants and a bird feeder is a good choice for a shady spot in your shrubs. [see Making Bird Feeders, opposite pg.].

Use a log of alder, birch, or willow. You'll need the materials listed below and a bow saw, a measuring tape, a mallet, wood chisels, an electric drill, a hole saw, and a screwdriver. Allow four hours to craft and assemble.

Set the finished planter under shrubs in your bird garden in a good viewing spot. Ground-foraging birds will gather on it to feed.

**1** Rotate the log into its most stable position. Use a bow saw to make parallel cuts centered on the log, 9″ (23 cm) apart, and as deep as required to make them 4½″ (11.4 cm) wide. Make additional cuts between them at 1″ (25 mm) intervals.

**2** Use a mallet and wood chisel to remove all of the wood between the cuts and make a flat surface 4½″ × 9″ (11.4 × 23 cm).

**3** Use an electric drill fitted with a 4″ (10 cm) hole saw to cut into the log at a point centered 4″ (10 cm) from each end. Remove wood with the chisel until the hole is 3″ (75 mm) deep and fits a 4″ (10 cm) plastic pot. Repeat, making a second pot hole at the log's other end.

**4** With a ½″ (12 mm) bit, drill a drain hole in the center of each pot hole.

**5** Fasten the bird feeder to the log with deck screws. Plant the two containers with trailing flowers such as bacopa. Set them in the pot holes.

**MATERIALS**
Log (1) 8″ × 26″ (20 × 66 cm)
Plastic Pots (2) 4″ (10 cm)
Deck Screws (2) No. 6 × 2″ (No. 6 × 50 mm)

# Vegetables in a Flower Garden

Marigolds, pumpkins, and the colorful red stalks of Swiss chard mark the calendar's turn to autumn.

When space is limited, try mixing flowering plants and vegetables. Cottage gardens often do this with flair. You're likely to see in them combinations such as lettuce and Swiss chard in front of a planting of delphinium and foxgloves or cherry tomatoes with a surrounding circle of cosmos and zinnias.

Use these concepts in your own garden. Let a pumpkin peek out of a patch of geraniums and asters. Use artichokes, with their distinctive thistlelike heads, as the focal point of a garden bed. Surround them with various annuals like baby-blue-eyes (*Nemophila menziesii*), everlasting (*Helipterum roseum*), and pincushion flower (*Scabiosa atropurpurea*). Orange, dark purple, red, and yellow peppers can add beauty; plant them as focal points in a bed with pastel blooms —cosmos, flossflower, and tree mallow (*Lavatera*

spp.), or match the peppers' vibrant colors with vivid yellow chrysanthemums, bronze blanket flowers, and bright red geraniums.

Herb plants mix well in flower beds, particularly because you can take advantage of the blooms of some mints, sages, and thymes. Various thyme species such as creeping and woolly thyme (*Thymus pseudo-lanuginosus*) also make aromatic ground covers that stand up to heavy foot traffic.

## Edible Flowers

The lure of edible flowers is easy to explain. Perhaps it's their ability to light up the garden, or maybe it's how they decorate a plate. It could even be the unusual flavors they lend to food. Whatever the draw, edible flowers provide the perfect way to combine edible and ornamental gardening. Some flowers have objectionable flavors and should be avoided; others are poisonous. Many, however, including nasturtium, pansy, rose, and violet, are tasty and safe. Check that the flowers are edible and use only strict organic-gardening practices when growing them to eat.

## Ornamental Vegetables

Ornamental cabbage and kale is an easy way to keep color in your garden long after leaves have fallen. Their leaves come in a variety of colors such as cream, purple, red, rose, and white. Though too pretty to eat, they're edible.

# Formal Flourishes

Include knotted and geometric border hedges to frame your garden and make it a work of art.

Knot gardens and parterres are natural additions to a formal garden. These forms stem from the gardens of 16th- and 17th-century Europe.

## Knot Gardens and Parterres

In knot gardens, hedges of low-growing evergreens are planted in intertwined patterns, like threads in a tapestry. Parterres have sheared hedges planted in patterns of geometric shapes, usually bisected by paths. Parterres were the vogue in England during the reign of Dutch-born King William III and his English wife, Queen Mary. They were also included in the French garden of Versailles. Conceived for viewing from raised terraces or other high vantage points, parterres are best admired from a distance where their complete design can be seen and appreciated. Aerial views reveal their intricate design, detail, and symmetry. In some cases, parterres are fashioned into symbols or emblems; the flower-filled triangular beds of Williamsburg's Custis-Maupin garden, for instance, date back to colonial times and resemble a British flag.

### Planning the Garden

**Location.** If you want such a garden, begin by choosing its location. In large yards, use a parterre along a path leading to a particular location such as a pond, seating area, statue, or other focal point. In a small-space garden, include a parterre in an enclosed front yard or line walkways leading to the front entry of the house with shrub parterres. Plant masses of colorful flowers inside the parterres' borders.

**Pattern.** Once you have picked your location, decide on a pattern. You might want to sketch out potential plans. Try making a garden path flanked by repeated geometric shapes. In some instances, squares look particularly attractive, while in others, diamonds, rectangles, or triangles work best. Mirror the pattern on both sides of the path, taking into account your shrubs' eventual size.

**Plants.** A number of hedging plants, including boxwood and arborvitae (*Thuja occidentalis* or *Platycladus orientalis*), work well in parterres and knot gardens. Add life to these patterned-hedge beds by filling their centers with massed plantings of flowers in solid or geometric color patterns. Popular choices include bedding plants such as marigold, petunia, pansy, and zinnia, spring bulb plantings of daffodil, common hyacinth (*Hyacinthus orientalis*), and tulip, and summer bulbs such as freesia, lily, and gladiolus. Fill spaces between hedges and your flowers with flossflower, nemesia, and sage.

Use the interior of a knot garden to plant colorful annuals, such as nasturtium.

# Flowers of Every Color, Shape, and Texture

Catch admiring eyes with plants that have different habits, contrasting colors, striking flower forms, and variegated foliage.

Make a gated walk and entrance inviting with an unexpected display of contrasts and bright colors.

When it comes to selecting flowers, most gardeners think first of color. It's a dramatic decorating element, and fortunately flowers come in an array of shades that can be combined for different effects. While bold colors shout for individual attention, pastels blend, creating a background. In addition, lighting changes the effect of color. White flowers that appear pale in midday, for example, seem to shimmer in twilight. Similarly, flowers in shady locations appear to have a deeper, richer hue than those planted in bright sun. Some of these flowers have an iridescent sheen and are nearly fluorescent.

Most flowers are a single color, but some are bi-, tri-, or even multicolored. Others have intricate patterns that look painted on. A red tulip may be streaked with yellow stripes. A bright red amaryllis (*Hippeastrum* × hyb.) might have a white interior, while a mahogany-red painted tongue (*Salpiglossis* spp.) may bear thin, dark purple etchings and golden veins within its throat.

Like color, flower and foliage texture also varies widely. Petals can be tissue-paper thin, such as those of bougainvillea, dianthus, and poppies, or thick and waxy, as is found in amaryllis, daylily, and various orchids and succulents. Leaves may be crinkled, hirsute, veined, or folded. Some flowers are smooth to the touch and repel water; others feel rough and tend to trap and absorb excess moisture.

Flower shape is another element to consider. Choose from plants with single, open blossoms or those bearing multiple blooms, including:

1. Large, bold flowers such as clematis, hibiscus, morning glory, and sunflower
2. Ruffled flowers such as dahlia, iris, marigold, and matilija poppy (*Romneya coulteri*)
3. Upright plants including gladiolus, hollyhock, lupine, statice (*Limonium* spp.), and tulip
4. Pendulous flowers such as abutilon, angel's-trumpet, fuchsia, and lily-of-the-valley

Use all of these elements —color and pattern, texture and shape—to achieve the effect you want in your garden. As you experiment, you'll discover new combinations that appeal to you.

## VISITING NEIGHBORS

In gardens on small lots, it's often possible —and sometimes a necessity—to work a neighbor's flowering vegetation into your garden design. When a nearby shrub or vining plant reaches onto your property, enjoy the "free" flowers and integrate them into your landscape.

# Pint-Sized and Pretty

## Miniature and genetic dwarf species are right for small-space gardens.

Thanks to the work of hybridizers, you can enjoy many traditional plant favorites in miniature form. Whether you require small plants for a tight space or just want to enjoy a miniature garden for its own sake, you can find a wide array of true dwarf species or diminutive cultivars.

Astilbe, bellflower, blanket flower, globe candytuft, columbine, cyclamen, daffodil, dianthus, foxglove, geranium, hollyhock, iris, rose, thrift, veronica, viola, and yarrow are popular flowers with dwarf cultivars. Bred especially to fit small-space gardens, such miniature plants are smaller than is typical for their species and tend to grow more slowly. They require minimal care.

Combine dwarfs with full-sized plants in garden beds or create mini-landscapes in areas that are too small for large plants.

**JUST MY SIZE**
New dwarf and miniature flowers make gardening possible in any space.

Use miniature displays for focal points or hide them as a surprise to visitors.

Miniature flower gardens are a good choice for those who garden indoors or have limited mobility. Plant miniatures in tabletop containers or specialized tables, making care easier. You can find tabletop planting systems from direct merchants or create your own. Choose tables that are sturdy and include adequate provision for drainage. Although miniature plants require less root room than full-sized ones, provide eight to twelve inches (20 to 30 cm) for soil. Other dimensions of miniature flower planting tables can be as large as your space permits.

Container choice for mini-gardens is almost unlimited. Anything from a large window box to a small dish is appropriate for some plants. Select containers that

Miniature roses in the bed, dwarf fuchsias on an occasional table, and a container filled with Swedish ivy (*Plectranthus verticillatus*) to sit on a pot shelf complete this mini-garden tucked into a nook behind a fence and gate.

have several large holes to provide good drainage or drill holes yourself through masking tape with an electric drill and a half-inch (12 mm) wood, masonry, or metal bit.

### Mini-Landscapes

Give your mini-garden an added spark by selecting plants with a theme in mind, and add a few miniature accessories from a hobby store or dollhouse retailer that coordinate with its theme.

Many seeds of miniature plants and dwarf cultivars are available at garden centers.

Match each container's style to its flower when you plant in pots.

**Southwestern Mini-Garden.** For a south-western garden, for instance, choose miniature succulents and cacti. Good options include dwarf aloe, golden barrel cactus (*Echinocactus grusonii*), hen-and-chickens (*Sempervivum tectorum*), dwarf prickly pear (*Opuntia microdasys*), and Jelly Beans (*Sedum pachyphyllum* 'Jelly Beans'). Accessorize with tumbleweeds made of thin wire and straw, a tiny cowboy hat, scaled windmill, and miniature saddle.

**Cottage Mini-Garden.** A scaled cottage garden is another possibility. Pave pathways with finely crushed rock or small polished pebbles. Include cottage-style favorites such as candytuft, carnation, dianthus, foxglove, hollyhock, pansy, and phlox. Accessorize by adding a miniature gazing globe made from a holiday ornament, scale benches, a swing, colorful stepping-stones made of flat marbles, or tiny birdhouses and birdbaths. Line the perimeter of your mini-garden with a white picket fence made from narrow slats and fasten it with fine wire. Finish your garden with a miniature arbor, pergola, or trellis, complete with a live vine or rose in miniature.

**Formal Mini-Garden.**
For a formal mini-garden, use small hedging plants such as dwarf boxwood (*Buxus sempervirens* 'Nana Variegata', 'Rosmariniflorus', or 'Suffruticosa', and *B. microphylla* 'File Leaf', 'Kingsville Dwarf', 'Koreana', 'Justin Bowers', 'Morris Midget', or 'Tide Hill') and keep them sheared to an appropriate size. Add a few flowering shrublike plants such as bog rosemary (*Andromeda polifolia* 'Grandiflora Compacta'), dwarf daphne (*D.* 'Pygmaea Alba'), heath (*Erica carnea*), miniature rhododendrons (*R. micranthum* 'Montchanin Racemosum', 'Ramapo', 'Purple Gem', and 'Ramolet'), and vinca cultivars. Fill in between the hedges and shrubs with single-color plantings of dwarf flowering plants. For these, consider white erodiums with white miniature roses or combine purple Dalmatian bellflowers and dark-blue violas (*V. cornuta* 'Blue Perfection'). For accessories, select from a variety of miniature statuary, birdbaths, and small fountains.

**Natural Mini-Garden.** Fashion a natural mini-garden with sweeping drifts of dwarf flowers and ornamental grasses. Good flower choices include miniature carpet bugleweed (*Ajuga* 'Chocolate Chip'), alliums, aster (*A. ericoides*), baby's breath, meadow rue (*Thalictrum kiusianum*), dwarf thrift (*Armeria* 'Nifty Thrifty'), dwarf flowering thyme (*Thymus* 'Elfin'), and yarrow (*Achillea ageratum* 'Moonwalker' and *A. ptarmica* 'Ballerina'). Appropriate ornamental grasses include dwarf blue-eyed grass (*Sisyrinchium angustifolium*), miniature fountain grass (*Pennisetum alopecuroides* 'Little Bunny'), dwarf lilyturf (*Liriope platyphylla* and *L. spicata*), and sedge (*Carex* spp.). Include a miniature fountain with the sound of running water. Rustic miniature birdhouses and bird feeders provide the finishing touch.

Whatever miniature garden you choose, selecting a site, planting, and care will be the same:

- First, look for a location with adequate light exposure; most plants grow best when they receive full sun for six to eight hours a day. Plant miniatures in high-quality potting soil amended with organic fertilizers such as worm castings, alfalfa meal, bat or bird guano, or cottonseed meal. Properly amended soil will release nutrients to the plants over an extended period of time, allowing for slow, steady, and strong growth.

- Space the plants correctly, leaving enough room for each one's eventual height and width. Also allow space to include garden accessories. Grade the soil to form hills and valleys and mark areas for pathways.

- After about six weeks, begin fertilizing your garden every four to six weeks with a balanced, organic, liquid fertilizer. It feeds the plants slowly and evenly, and prevents the root or leaf burns common when using concentrated granular or powdered fertilizers, particularly those with a high nitrogen percentage.

- Once your garden begins to grow, you will need to prune and pinch buds, depending on your selection. Some will grow more readily than others and will require frequent trimming; others may need it only occasionally. You will find that some plants are better than others in tight spaces. If a plant grows too vigorously, remove it and replace it with a slower grower.

Plant sweet alyssum (*Lobularia maritima*), beard-tongue, miniature hollyhock (*Sidalcea* spp.), and dwarf speed-well to make a cottage mini-garden in a tiny bed.

Whether you are growing a miniature garden as a hobby or beautifying a small-space landscape, follow these four easy steps.

# Striking Specimens

Make a single plant, shrub, or tree the focus of your garden design.

Every spring, this cottage is draped with the dangling, grapelike clusters of wisteria vine. Plant a specimen plant to create a distinctive feature for your home.

Large structural plants and specimens that bloom often serve as a landscape's focal point. Entire gardens are sometimes built around a plant with a formidable presence: a giant wisteria that covers an entire wall of the home, a bougainvillea draping a gazebo, or a clematis covering a porch swing. Certain shrubs also naturally cry out for attention, especially when in bloom. Choose a bright red azalea hedge or plant a forsythia against a wall for a dazzling seasonal display. A giant hydrangea with mounding clusters of blue flowers is a superb focal point set against the front of the house, as is a pink-flowered camellia.

Take your time when choosing specimen plants; these focal points will likely be a part of your landscape for years to come. If your garden is small, one feature plant is probably enough. For an average-sized lot, select one focal point for the front and another

for the rear of the house. In a larger landscape, you may want specimens in several sections of the yard. When you plant, take each plant's eventual size into account, and give it room to ensure it will fit your space in the years to come. Also think about how you will prune and shape your specimens when they reach their full height and spread. Consider using the advice of a licensed arborist to safely remove any excess, out-of-reach growth and maintain your specimen trees. If you garden in a small space, on the other hand, opt for less expansive plants such as various jasmines, tulip trees (*Magnolia* × *soulangiana*), yellow-woods (*Cladrastis kentukea*), or climbing roses.

Select your plants when they are in bloom, even if it means waiting a season to plant them in your yard. Examine the flower of each candidate specimen plant and choose the cultivar that matches the shape, style, and color of surrounding items in the landscape. An orange hibiscus may be stunning against a backdrop of greenery, but it may lose its impact when set against a beige home or wall.

Focal points should mirror the overall style, feel, and color of the surrounding garden. Consider a white lilac next to the front door for a light green home with dark green trim. A crape myrtle with pink to red and purple flowers looks good with a yellow house. Focus visitors' eyes on the center of your backyard with a bright pink mandevilla draping a statue. Use a giant purple lotus (*Nelumbo* spp.) or an Amazon water lily (*Victoria amazonica*) in a water garden. The right specimen plants put the finishing touch on a well-designed landscape.

# Winter Color

Chase away somber skies with color in your garden that lasts throughout the season.

Even in regions with long, cold winters, you can enjoy winter color in your garden. Berries, seed heads, and bark are all good color sources during the months when flowers are in short supply.

Many trees and shrubs hold on to their berries and fruit well into the winter months—until they are picked clean by birds. A leaf-bare tree such as flowering crab apple (*Malus* 'Red Jade') or hawthorn (*Crataegus* spp.) loaded with bright red berries or a holly (*Ilex* spp.) draped with clusters of white or red fruit can be a dramatic presence in your winter garden.

When deciduous trees drop their leaves, their interesting structural forms and spectacular bark colors and textures can add desirable winter drama. The Japanese stewartia (*Stewartia pseudocamellia*), for example, has brown bark that peels, exposing a yellow trunk. On many other small trees and shrubs such as willow (*Salix* spp.) striking bark patterns appear only in cold weather. In summer the bark is likely to be subdued or hidden by foliage.

Dried seed heads, fruit, and nuts also light up the outdoors in winter. Seed heads have an added appeal: they may rattle in the wind. Leave the hips on roses after autumn's last bloom and let your ornamental grasses and native plants go to seed for added color. In warmer climates, pepper tree (*Schinus molle*) is festooned with bunches of bright red peppercorns in autumn and winter. Plant blackberry lily (*Belamcanda chinensis*) and Chinese fire thorn (*Pyracantha crenatoserrata*) for similar effects in cooler climates.

Plan bulb and shrub plantings with the first days of spring and the last days of autumn in mind. There will still be snow on the ground when glory-of-the-snow (*Chionodoxa* spp.), hyacinth, and wintersweet (*Chimonanthus praecox*) burst into bloom, and cyclamen will last until the heavy frosts of winter.

Keep track of plants that look attractive during the winter months and emphasize them in your winter landscape the following year.

The bark of redtwig dogwood (*Cornus stolonifera*) has bright color in spring when its sap first begins to flow. In winter its branches are a pleasing contrast to white snow and will enhance any yard.

Clusters of berries cloak cranberry bush (*Viburnum trilobum*). These nodding red berries often persist into winter and will extend the season until birds eat them.

# An Oasis of Vivid Blooms

## Even a desert home can be a showplace if you plant flowering cacti and succulents.

Flower gardeners sometimes forget about cacti and succulents, but their blooms can be even more breathtaking than flowers of many annual and perennial plants or shrubs.

**Surprising Flowers.** Various species of succulents and cacti flower in colors that range from brown, lavender, pink, and deep purple to orange, red, white, and yellow. Some are muted, while others are hot and vivid. Flower shapes and styles are diverse, too. Some plants, such as aloes and echeverias, bear blooms along erect stems shooting high above foliage, while many others such as epiphyllum have large, round, and somewhat pendulous blooms. Sempervivums' delicate star-shaped flowers in hues of maroon and green with silver-white highlights are so small they command a close look, as do the funnel-like blooms of the chin cacti (*Gymnocalycium saglione*). These have variegated petals and contrasting interiors of cream, green, white, yellow, and even a deep purple that appears black. These are just some of the surprises you will find.

Ball-shaped and ribbed, *Notocactus magnificus* has terminal, yellow flowers that appear in late spring.

**Hardy in Cold Climates.** Contrary to popular thought, succulents and cacti aren't confined to deserts and desertlike terrain. They also grow in many non-desert regions—from the humid jungles of the Amazon, where the colorful Christmas cactus (*Schlumbergera bridgesii*) grows, to snow-capped mountains where many species of mammillaria thrive in rock crevices. A number of cacti and many succulents native to North America or imported from South Africa and South America grow near the ocean and tolerate alkaline soil and salt well. Trailing ice plant (*Lampranthus spectabilis*), for example, lights up coastal hillsides near the Pacific Ocean with brilliant flowers in many colors, including an intense purple-pink, deep red, and bright orange and yellow. Its smaller relative, *Delosperma cooperi*, is also called ice plant. It is a ground-hugging miniature just one to three inches (25 to 75 mm) tall that blankets large areas in neon-bright pinks, purples, and yellows. It's a favorite for everything from small rock gardens to entire hillsides.

**Many Forms and Habits.** Flowering cacti and succulents vary in form and size. There are giant aloes and tiny lithops, which break out of their pebblelike disguise in late spring with flowers. Use a treelike apple cactus (*Cereus peruvianus*) as a

Several cacti share the common name old-man cactus. The one shown here blooms in May. It is *Borzicactus sericatus*.

specimen to create a focal point. It reaches ten feet (3 m) tall and has white flowers that are fragrant at night. The old-man cactus (*Cephalocereus senilis*) makes another good focal point. Its night-blooming flowers are rose-colored, and it is covered in stiff grayish and yellow spines. To fill a hillside, plant succulent airplane plant (*Crassula falcata*) to stand above an ice plant carpet. Decorate a small space with succulents in hanging baskets. Try baby sun rose (*Aptenia cordifolia*), which has trailing stems two feet (60 cm) long covered in purple-red flowers in spring and summer. For edible fruit, plant hedgehog cactus (*Echinocereus* spp.) and prickly pear.

Adam's needle (*Yucca filamentosa*) is a popular plant found throughout the entire desert Southwest of the United States.

**General Care.** Ensure that your cacti and succulents flower well by following some general growing guidelines. Most of these plants do best in sites with full sun and good drainage. Protect them from the cold, and water them only sparingly. Succulents require more water than their spine-bearing cousins, and tropical cacti like epiphyllums and Christmas cactus need partial shade in an overall bright location plus additional moisture. Feed cacti and succulents regularly during their growth cycle, which generally runs from spring into autumn. Use a balanced organic food such as liquid fish emulsion, 5–5–5, that also contains trace minerals. These minerals are essential for flowering and are often deficient in soils in the areas where cacti grow. You should fertilize lightly every four to six weeks to get consistent blooms.

When succulents and cacti are neglected, they revert to dormancy, begin to look unattractive, and flower poorly or not at all. But give them appropriate light levels, water, warmth, and nutrients, and they will put on a magnificent floral display—right on schedule.

**Cold-Climate Cacti.** Gardeners in the coldest climates can grow cacti in containers indoors during winter. As spring arrives and danger of frost passes, move the plants outdoors for the day to harden them and return them indoors at night. After a week or two, the cacti will adjust to the outdoors and be able to tolerate its temperature variations.

Plant cacti, pots and all, in a sheltered spot protected from precipitation. Fertilize them regularly and give them water whenever their soil dries completely. Avoid overwatering or allowing cacti and succulents to stand in soggy soil.

When autumn begins, dig up the container and move it indoors. Following this method, even gardeners located in arctic Fairbanks or Whitehorse can have summer landscapes filled with cacti and succulents. The surprise of seeing a large cactus in full bloom will reward all your effort.

Trailing ice plant has a sprawling and creeping habit that makes it ideal for rock gardens, yet is hardy in cold-winter climates to USDA hardiness zone 4.

# Unique and Spectacular Color

## Plant eye-catching hues that contrast or coordinate to add visual spice.

The quest for pleasing color is at the heart of every flower gardener's efforts. Successful plantings usually follow well-established rules that are easy to learn and apply in your flower beds.

Four fundamental concepts govern color schemes for planting flowers:

- Contrast. Use the primary colors and white to make bright and dominant flower displays.
- Coordinates. Pair primary colors with their complementary opposites and with colors adjacent to them on the color wheel to create pleasing combinations.
  - Monochromatic Color. Combine mass plantings of a single hue to create large units, shapes and geometric patterns.
  - Approach and Recession. Pair light or warm tones with their opposite dark or cool colors to enhance dimension—light and warm colors feel nearer than they are, while dark and cool colors recede.

Explore possible options by experimenting with an artist's color wheel, which you can find at most arts and crafts stores. Use colored pencils to try out different pairings on paper and refer to them when you visit a garden store to choose your plants.

### Special Color Effects

For unique flower displays, choose plants that have blooms of unusual colors and take advantage of opportunities presented by your site. Plant shady locations with coordinated pastels. Bright primary colors and deep tones tend to fade away in low light, while the pastel tones of shade-loving plants such as impatiens seem to glow in dim light.

For full-sun locations, experiment with bright, fluorescent colors. The hot pinks, yellows, oranges, and reds of flowers from canna to bougainvillea and daylily to hybrid tuberous begonia (*Begonia* × *tuber-hybrida*) remain glorious in the bright, midday sun. Softer tints, hues, and pastels usually look faded and muted in these conditions.

In small gardens, create the illusion of additional space by planting short plants with yellow, orange, and red blossoms in the foreground and using taller plants with blue and violet flowers at the back of your beds to create a layered effect.

Mingle low-growing, drought-tolerant ground cover plants, such as English daisies (*Bellis perennis*), with their white petals and yellow centers, beneath a primary-color display of golden tulips to provide lasting color when the bulbs fade.

Try different combinations in small container groups, made according to the directions on the opposite page.

Place cheerful groups of containers on a porch, along a pathway, or on a deck or patio. The key to making successful container groups is to choose a few pots of a single primary color, then mate them with pots of beige, white, black, or tan. Red, yellow, and blue are the primaries. They'll stand out from the neutral-colored pots in your group.

Next, choose plants for your containers. Start with a primary that complements your pots. For example, select primary yellow chrysanthemums to fill a pot of primary blue. Choose an orange cultivar for the other pots because orange is one of the two adjacent colors to yellow (the other is green). In both cases, the chrysanthemums are tall—ideal for backgrounds in a mixed container planting.

For the front of the pot, pick shorter violet pansies—yellow's complement— and blue pansies—the complement of orange—both good with blue pots.

You'll need nine yellow chrysanthemums, four orange chrysanthemums, four violet pansies, and six blue pansies along with three large pots, two smaller pots, a trowel, moist potting soil, a watering can, and garden gloves. Allow two hours to follow these steps:

**1** Plant three yellow chrysanthemum plants in a spacious container partially filled with potting soil. Set them in an arc along the back edge of the pot. Fill the reserved space in the foreground with two blue pansies. Fill in around the plants with potting soil and tamp it firm. Repeat with two other large containers.

**2** In two smaller pots, plant two orange chrysanthemums to the rear and two violet pansies in the front. The complementary color to the blue pansies in the larger pots is orange, while yellow is the complement of deep violet.

**3** Place the three larger containers in a semi-circle and nest the two smaller containers between them. Planted containers are heavy. Fill them in place, use a hand lift truck, or dolly, to move them, or ask a friend for help.

# Accessorizing Your Landscape

Decorate your outdoor garden rooms with statuary, fountains, and accessories.

Inviting gardens, like attractive home interiors, often use accessories to direct the eye to their most beautiful features. Landscape accessories add a decorative touch, perhaps a bit of whimsy, or an element of anticipation. The right items produce a particular ambience. If they are colorful, they will add interest throughout every season of the year. Many items—hammocks, obelisks, potting benches, and thermometers—have double duty as functional parts of the garden, aid in its care, or are there to help you enjoy the time you spend outdoors. Other elements such as gazing globes and statuary simply add beauty and quiet elegance to the landscape.

Make a focal point for your garden by surrounding a sundial on a short column with rings of low, medium, and high plants such as dahlias, geraniums, and sages.

**Add Antiques and Accessories.** Personalize your garden with antiques and artifacts such as plows, wagons, and wheelbarrows or old bathtubs, hand pumps, sinks, and windmills. Create your own accessories using kits to make arbors, birdhouses, furniture, oblisks, stepping-stones, and trellises.

**Use Container Plants.** Containers are important accessories—as important as the plants they hold. Match every pot to its plants so that they complement one another. Containers come in many materials: ceramic, fired clay, terra cotta, metal, or plastic, to name just a few. Before choosing containers, consider how they will look in your garden and the space they will occupy. Do they blend with its style? Does the container's color match the colors found in the plant's foliage or flowers?

**Consider Theme.** Consider your landscape's theme and design style before you choose the accessories for your garden. A formal garden calls for arbors, fountains, gazebos, trellises, latticework, and statuary. Choose those objects that complement the textures found in the garden's paving materials such as bricks, cobblestones, pavers, quarrystone, or tiles.

An Asian-themed garden, for instance, calls for objects with an Eastern flair. Use lanterns, stones and boulders, bamboo birdhouses, Raku pottery and crane, temple-dog, and turtle statuary in a Japanese

Combine function with utility. Choose a statue planter for the edge of a walk.

Whimsy is another popular element when you accessorize. Express your personality with fanciful sculptures.

garden. An arched arbor that frames a view of the garden is reminiscent of the moon gates found in traditional Chinese gardens and should be made of black-lacquered wood. Place crane statues along the edges of garden ponds.

For a tropical look, install a waterfall, hammock, and bamboo screening. For a country cottage garden, add a windmill and decorative plaques.

**Be Practical.** Think about your use of your garden. Do you want seating? If so, will it be in the sun or shade? You will want a small table and a couple of chairs if the garden is a romantic retreat for two, but for entertaining a group, you'll need a larger table, more chairs, and maybe a bench or two. Is the area just for relaxing and taking in the view? Your best choice might be decorator objects to surround a floral point of interest or a quiet seating area at the end of a path.

Accessories can also be focal points in their own right. It's important to draw the eye to a feature in the yard. Nearly anything serves the purpose of attracting attention. Excellent points of interest in the right settings are a garden bench, a potting shed, a gazebo, a greenhouse, or even an outdoor fireplace with stone seats and cushions.

> "There is more pleasure in making a garden than in contemplating a paradise."
>
> ANNE SCOTT-JAMES

Get a sense of each accessory item's size and scale. Measure it and use a rope or hose to outline its shape on the ground at the site where you're considering placing it. Walk around the shape, imagining how the accessory will look from various angles. Will it seem too big? Not large enough? Can you see it well from each vantage point? Will it block your views of the plants, garden features, and accessories? Is it something you'd like to look at on a daily basis? How will it appear when viewed from indoors? Finally, is it placed in a location where it is safe from rocking or toppling?

Besides being functional and attractive, accessories are constant and timeless. A garden is always changing and growing. Plants may come and go, while accessories treasured by their owners may remain in a garden for generations. They also need very little care and are a fun way to share your sense of style and individuality with others.

Incorporate surprises in your garden like these amusing, larger-than-life utensils.

# flower garden plans

Now that you've seen the possibilities for a flower garden, you can begin to choose the perfect places for the colorful blooms that will soon grace your landscape. Start with your site, noting its location, orientation, sun exposure, features, and soil. Next, review your options for different garden styles and designs and select one that suits your home and region. Also choose between a formal and an informal style. If you plan a casual garden, think about including features such as native or Xeriscape plants to help adapt your garden to your climate. Follow the planting maps included here or use them as guides for planning your own original beds.

In this chapter you'll find the details of how to plan specific types of flower beds and borders. You'll learn about heirloom and heritage flowers, including old-garden roses and other long-time favorites that have been around for a century or more. For a long-lasting display you can keep, you'll discover how to grow flowers to dry and be given information on how to prepare and preserve them.

Most of the chapter is devoted to maps and plant selections you can follow to plant a great flower garden of your own. Each plan comes with a map, a helpful and complete description of the planting, options for customizing it, and suggestions for installing it on your site. Following these maps makes visualizing beautiful flower gardens easier than ever before, and planting them a snap.

If you live in a newly constructed home and have to start your landscape from scratch, you will find information on the steps to take for planting in this special situation. And you'll find ideas for creating an entire room in your garden, complete with walls and a ceiling of flowers.

# Creating Flower Gardens

For the most successful flower gardens, think in terms of plant communities that fit your climate, exposure, soil, and site.

Before shopping for plants, it's important that you understand your climate and your garden's exposure because these factors should influence your choices.

**Plant Hardiness Zone.** Take time to familiarize yourself with the climate conditions of your area. Determine the USDA Plant Hardiness Zone for your region and garden. (See endsheets.) This map tells you the average first and last expected frost dates for your area as well as the 15-year average of the lowest temperatures it has experienced. While the information used to draw the map is current, there are other factors that influence the growing conditions in your yard. In addition to the general climate in your area, also consider the variation caused by the particular conditions—microclimates—in your garden.

Bear's-breech (*Acanthus mollis*) is a versatile, shade-tolerant plant that also grows well in sun and in moist or nearly dry soils. It has showy flower spikes that appear in late spring or summer.

**Microclimates.** Depending on how your home and garden are situated and their proximity to nearby structures or large trees, the soil temperature in your garden beds might vary by as much as 10°F (6°C) from one spot to the next. Microclimates, greatly influence how plants grow.

Heat emanating from your house and other structures makes some areas located near them warmer than those in your yard's center. Elevated areas tend to be colder than protected low spots all year round since they radiate heat and are exposed to cooling winds. Such spots experience frosts both earlier and later than other nearby areas, and they are often much colder in winter. Cold air flows downhill and is also caught in valleys. Microclimates are caused by wind exposure, too, and some plants are more tolerant of wind than others. Trees offer some protection from both cold and wind, but remember that a deciduous tree offers little protection from wind and cold during winter.

**Plants and Exposure.** When you evaluate light exposure in your garden, remember that the sun casts longer shadows in winter than in summer; take this factor into account when planting full-sun flowers in the early spring. At the same time, note trees and deciduous shrubs that will soon leaf out and create shady areas under them. You might have to plant in sequences or fill with annuals as blooms fade and the seasons change.

Note how your house is situated and oriented. Follow these general recommendations when you choose plants:

- Gardens Facing North. These gardens are the coolest areas of most yards and generally receive bright, indirect light or partial shade. Select flowers for cooler temperatures. Azalea, heartleaf bergenia (*B. cordifolia*), bleeding heart, Virginia bluebells, camellia, fuchsia, forget-me-not, impatiens, pansies, and violas are suitable choices.
- Gardens Facing South. Unless shaded by large trees, these gardens will receive lots of sunlight and heat. Here you can grow a wide variety of flowering plants that thrive in sun. Among them are angel's-trumpet, bougainvillea, trailing lantana, lupine, marigold, painted tongue, various poppies, sage, sunflower, sweet pea, wisteria, and zinnia.

The heat and moisture of evaporating water from a swimming pool create a microclimate near it that will sustain warmth-loving, tender plants from impatiens to ferns.

- Gardens Facing East. These gardens are often shaded in afternoon but have morning sun. Plant flowers that tolerate four to five hours of sun daily such as columbine, cupflower (*Nierembergia caerulea*), hydrangea, jasmine, lilies, poor man's orchid (*Schizanthus pinnatus*), and toadflax (*Linaria maroccana*).
- Gardens Facing West. These gardens have shade in the morning and heat and sun in the afternoon. Plant flowers for combination conditions, including bachelor's button, coneflower, honeysuckle, California poppy, pot marigold, statice, thrift, and thyme.

Other gardens, of course, have different orientations. They might face southeast or northwest, each of which has different qualities. You can grow the widest range of flowers in yards with areas of full or filtered sun, but many flowers also thrive in shaded spots. (Think of a mid-Atlantic woodland garden. You can grow shade gardens filled with Virginia bluebells and azaleas in its conditions. Other gardeners might have landscapes filled with dazzling blooms of desert rose and bougainvillea that grow in the unrelenting glare of a Southwest desert sun.)

**Understanding Your Site.** Thorough knowledge of your site is essential to successful flower gardening. Do you have a boggy area? Look for plants that thrive in consistently wet conditions such as heliotrope, lobelia, monkey flower, and vinca. Dry sites with very little water require a different category of plants, including cleome, coreopsis, speedwell, many ornamental grasses, and a host of succulents and cacti. You can also find plants for alpine meadows and coastal shorelines. Whatever your site, you're likely to find a wide variety of microclimates within your property that will allow you to grow many different flowering plants.

Protect plants edging streets that receive sprays of deicing salt in winter by installing a stone, brick, or concrete strip and filling behind it to raise the plants above the street.

# Planting Heirloom and Heritage Flowers

## Add charm and delicious scents to your landscape and home by finding and planting old flower favorites from yesteryear.

In the 1950s, when hybridizers began introducing long-blooming and disease-resistant versions of old flower favorites, many of the flowers that had been around for centuries went out of favor. Hybridizing is expedient in many ways, but it has also resulted in the loss of many delightful flowers with effusive blooms and fantastic scents. Fortunately, in the last 10 to 15 years, gardeners have begun to rediscover many heritage flower favorites and others such as old-garden roses.

**Heirloom Plants.** Now called heirloom plants, such flowers were saved from extinction by a few dedicated plant collectors and reappeared in the 1990s. A renewed interest in the cottage garden developed about the same time.

Even experts don't agree on the definition of heirloom flowers. Some say heirlooms must have become rooted in American soil between 1600 and 1950, while others adhere to a looser classification. Whatever your choice of definition, plant an heirloom to cultivate a piece of history you can pass on to your children and grandchildren.

Find heritage flower seed at your garden center or nursery, as well as in the catalogs that arrive each spring.

Antiques, including sweet William (*Dianthus barbatus*) and black-eyed Susan, with profuse, colorful, repeating blooms, fit perfectly into these gardens. The names of others such as kiss-me-over-the-garden-gate (*Polygonum orientale*) and the delightfully named

Canterbury-bells are cottage garden favorites available in many heirloom cultivars.

bouncing bet (*Saponaria officinalis*) are playful and reminiscent of other times and places. Gardeners soon rediscovered the staying power and magnificent colors and aromas of these antique flowers. Flowers such as larkspur, love-lies-bleeding (*Amaranthus caudatus*), and love-in-a-puff (*Cardiospermum halicacabum*) have withstood the test of time. They're easy-to-grow, vigorous bloomers that reseed themselves year after year.

Growers who specialize in heirloom flowers now provide many old-fashioned favorites our grandparents once grew. You can also find new, improved hybrids of these plants. Grow them to have a literally memorable yard.

# Old Garden Roses

Bring a touch of old-fashioned elegance to your landscape with these special heritage flowers.

Roses have always been garden favorites. Species of the genus *Rosa* have been identified everywhere in the Northern Hemisphere, and fossils more than 30 million years old can be linked to modern roses.

New roses are being developed every day, but growing old garden roses is a popular hobby. Their flowers tend to be more fragrant than many new cultivars. Step back in time and enjoy the same delicate blooms and aromas as royalty did so long ago with *R. damascena* (before 1700), 'Madame Hardy' (1832), and 'Tuscany Superb' (circa 1848). Old garden roses encompass ten major groups, including these favorites:

- Chinas, everblooming and first found in Asia, arrived in Europe in the late 18th century and are ancestors of modern, repeat-blooming roses. Examples include 'Old Blush' and *R. × odorata* 'Mutabilis'.
- Gallicas, low-growing with large, fragrant flowers, are considered the oldest roses cultivated in the West. They include 'Fleurzauber', 'Cardinal de Richelieu', and 'Belle de Crécy'.
- Damasks are the most fragrant of the old garden roses, with a classic, deep-musk scent. One damask is 'Quatre Saisons'.
- Noisettes are crosses between China roses and

> ### THE ROMANCE OF ROSES
>
> Roses held many romantic meanings for Victorians. A gentleman gave a woman a single red rose to proclaim his love for her. She would, in turn, respond in one of several ways. A yellow rose would let him know she thought he was fickle, while a white rose indicated that she felt too young for love. A single rose leaf meant that she didn't care for him, and a red rose signified that she returned his love.

autumn damasks, as are Bourbon roses. One very popular climbing noisette is 'Aimée Vibert', also known as 'Bouquet de la Mariée'. A Bourbon rose is 'Bourbon Queen'.

Still other old rose classifications are moss roses such as 'Blanche Moreau'; centifolias (known generally as cabbage roses for their globelike flowers), including 'Cristata' and 'Muscosa'; and species roses such as *R. alba*, with their many offspring such as 'Belle Amour' and 'Alba Semiplena'.

Strictly speaking, old garden roses date from before 1867, when the first hybrid tea rose, 'La France', was developed. But roses such as 'Madame Pierre Oger' (1878) are also considered old roses because their parent stock ('La Reine Victoria') was a true old-garden rose dating to before 1867.

'Souvenir de la Malmaison' and 'Madame Pierre Oger'

# Heritage and Old-Garden Flowers

## Revive a bit of history by growing heirloom flowers that your ancestors planted and enjoyed.

Thanks to the efforts of gardeners who have passed on seeds and created many seed banks, you can enjoy old favorites that were nearly forgotten. Seed companies have followed the trend and now offer seed packets such as Grandma's Bouquet—a seed collection of all the flowers that one manufacturer's grandmother grew. Many mail-order nurseries also sell these flowers as small plants.

Modern hybrids, while beautiful, often lack fragrance. Heritage flowers are usually exceptionally fragrant and durable—the reason that many are still around. Most heirlooms are also easy to grow. They will readily reseed in

An arch of English ivy is an obvious choice for a home named Ivy Cottage. Use geraniums and primroses in pots to add a period touch.

your garden, and you can easily save seed for the next year's crop. These flowers and their seeds are virtual magnets for birds, butterflies, and other wildlife. Bees often fly straight to the heirlooms, leaving hybrids and hybrid cultivars alone.

Heirlooms thrive in every corner of the yard, from beds and borders to containers and hanging baskets. You may already have a few of them in your garden. Try such old favorites as Canterbury-bells, four-o'clock, foxglove, hollyhock, Joseph's coat (*Amaranthus tricolor*), larkspur, love-lies-bleeding, love-in-a-mist (*Nigella damascena*), love-in-a-puff, morning glory, musk mallow (*Malva moschata*), poppy spiderwort (*Tradescantia virginiana*), flowering tobacco (*Nicotiana* spp.), and twinspur (*Diascia barberae*).

Reserve a bed for heirloom flowers with fragrance. Choose a spot near a path or plant them in a raised bed adjacent to a deck, patio, or seating area. Grow 'Grandpa Otts' morning glory up a lattice. This flower, first introduced in the 1930s, has deep blue blooms with vivid, ruby, star-shaped centers. Other heirloom favorites are 'Carmine King' California poppy (1906), with silky, deep red blooms; 'Stella' sunflower (circa 1850), with tall, branched stems, gold petals and dark-brown centers; Crimean War poppy (*Papaver somniferum* 'Victoria Cross' (1890), with fringed red petals and centers that bear a broad white cross; and golden pink 'Miss Willmott' sweet pea (1901). Plant these in your garden and enjoy scents worth remembering.

### FOR LOVE OF ROSES

Empress Josephine, wife of Napoleon I of France, so loved roses that she tried to grow every rose in existence in the gardens of the Chateau Malmaison, outside of Paris. When she died in 1814, more than 250 rose varieties grew in her garden.

## Reviving "Lost" Flowers

Take weekend excursions that satisfy your passion for plants and help you beautify your garden. Hunt down and save lost flower species. In landscapes around abandoned farmhouses, mountain cabins, and cemeteries, you can often find plants that may now exist only in that place. If your local laws permit, take a cutting or gather seed to save flowers that might otherwise have been lost. (Check laws on plant collection by calling the nearest Cooperative Extension, the local county Agricultural Commissioner, or the provincial Ministry of Agriculture.)

# Drying Flowers

Preserve the beauty of your garden by drying cut flowers at their prime. Dried flowers can last for months or years, but be sure to display them in an area with limited sun- or fluorescent light—the uv rays of either will hasten color fading.

For drying flowers, pick blue, orange, and pink blossoms that hold their color. Harvest them in late morning after dew evaporates and before heat causes wilt.

If the flowers' natural aromas fade as they dry, renew them with essential oils [see Creating Sachets, pg. 23.].

Three common methods of drying are shown at right and below. You will need the materials described. Silica gel, a desiccant, is also available from hobby retailers. Choose a method and follow these instructions.

## Air-Dry Method

Air-dry most flowers. Stiff-stemmed flowers such as Chinese lantern, baby's breath, and globe thistle dry best upright. Succulent-stemmed flowers such as flossflower, heather, hydrangea, ornamental onion, and yarrow are best if dried right-side up with their stems in shallow water. Fasten bunches of six to eight flower stalks together, and hang them upside down in a warm, dry spot with good air circulation. In three to four weeks, most flowers will be completely dry.

## Desiccant Method

Dry flowers with a desiccant such as silica gel. Pour a layer of dry gel, 1"–2" (25–50 mm) deep, into a tight-sealing container. Dry flat-faced flowers face down, round-faced flowers face up, one species per container. Cut their stems ½" (12 mm) long, bed them in gel, separate their petals, and pour gel between them until the flowers are covered. Seal the container and place it in a dark closet. Dry the flowers for 2-3 weeks. Pour the gel from the container, then lift the flowers and dust away any clinging gel. Dry the gel periodically to renew it by following its package directions.

## Microwave Method

Dry flowers in a microwave oven and silica gel, one at a time, in an open cardboard box. Bed a single flower in the gel as you would for traditional desiccant drying [see Desiccant Method, right]. Place the box on a plate in the microwave. Set the microwave to high temperature, and run it for 30 seconds. Allow the flower to cool, remove it, and test it for dryness. Repeat cycles as necessary until you obtain a satisfactory result, then use the same process to dry successive blooms of the same type of flowers.

# Sites and Soils

Help your flower garden thrive
by understanding garden soils.

Soil is more than merely a place to put plants. It's a complex substance that contains rock particles, minerals, organic and inorganic compounds, air, water, and, of course, huge numbers of soil-living plants, animals, and microorganisms, including beneficial bacteria and fungi. These organisms accomplish a number of critical tasks. For example, many digest organic materials and convert them into nutrient forms that plants can absorb through their roots. High-quality soil contains plenty of organic matter, which gives it a rich, dark color. It is also crumbly and easy to work rather than hard-packed.

## Soil Composition and Type

**Clay.** Clay soil is composed of very fine particles with little airspace between them. Clay absorbs water slowly and tends to hold it. Such soil becomes sticky when it's wet and will dry as hard as brick.

Sloping sites can mean that uphill plants have less moisture than those lower on the grade. Choose plants that grow well in either condition, such as black-eyed Susan.

**Silt.** Silt is not as fine as clay. It is found in river bottoms and around areas where rivers have flooded the surrounding countryside. It is high in nutrients and holds some moisture.

**Sand.** Sandy soil has much larger particles than clay or silt. It doesn't hold moisture, so frequent watering is a necessity.

**Loam.** The ideal soil is loam, a mixture of all three types and abundant organic matter. It drains well but doesn't dry out too fast, holds onto nutrients, and contains air for healthy root growth. No matter what soil type you have, you can make it a rich, healthy soil in which plants can thrive by adding organic amendments such as compost. When you add organic material to soils rich in clay, the small particles are separated, creating spaces for air and water. It also bulks up sandy soils, helping them to hold onto moisture and nutrients.

**Acidity and Alkalinity.** Soil pH—its degree of acidity or alkalinity—is another important consideration. Soil pH is measured on a scale that runs from 0 to 14. Each plant species grows best within a certain pH range. The best soils for landscape plants range from 6.5 (acidic) to 7.0 (neutral). Most soils measure between 4.0 and 8.0.

The pH is vital to plant health. If it is too low, or acid—or too high and alkaline—plants cannot take up adequate amounts of some nutrients. For example, phosphorus, which is necessary for photosynthesis and healthy root and flower growth, often forms insoluble compounds when the pH is lower than 5.0 or higher than 7.0. Plants such as azaleas, gardenias, hydrangeas, and rhododendrons grow best in somewhat acidic soil, while others, such as sweet alyssum, baby's breath, cosmos, peony, and sweet pea, prefer somewhat alkaline conditions.

Landscape trees, such as birch (*Betula* spp.) develop surface roots in flower beds that are surface watered. Here, a tree has been set apart from the flowers to stop its roots from growing into them.

**Soil Testing.** The only accurate way to know your soil's pH is to test it. Send a sample to a soil-testing laboratory or test it yourself. Whatever method you use, take representative samples of the area you are testing. Gather three or four soil samples from various areas of your garden, at six inches (15 cm) deep, keeping them separate. Avoid using tools made of aluminum or storing soil samples in metal containers that might contaminate the sample.

If testing yourself, use a pH test kit or an electronic pH meter; both are available at garden centers and nurseries. A kit is sufficient if you have a small yard and don't plan on testing often. Many soil test kits also measure major nutrients. A pH meter can be used indefinitely, but it will need occasional calibration at a nursery or garden center.

If your sample is dry, mix it with distilled water for the most accurate results. Add the kit's reagent and dip a test strip or insert the meter's probe into the sample. Match the color of the solution or strip to the color chart that came with the kit for a pH estimate, or read the measurement on the meter.

Soil pH changes over the year, in response to soil temperature changes. Fertilizers can alter soil pH, as do minerals in tap water or through the leaching effect of precipitation removing salts from the soil. Acid rain, for instance, can lower the pH of garden

soil an entire point. It also varies across your yard, and spots by concrete are more alkaline. Once you measure your soil pH, alter it by adding soil (agricultural) sulfur to lower the pH and make the soil more acidic, or garden limestone to elevate the pH and make it more alkaline. Retesting is a good idea.

Prevent erosion of the soil on paths. Apply mulch in a deep layer and place stair timbers parallel to the slope to slow runoff.

# Plans for Flower Beds and Borders

Beautify your yard with these quick and easy landscape makeovers.

As you plan your flower garden, give yourself leeway to make changes later as it grows and develops. Once you master tried-and-true methods, you can expand on them and add your own gardening flair.

The following section includes a variety of garden plans that are sure to spice up your yard. Consider following the Corner Flower Bed Plan for a sunny nook in your yard [see Corner Flower Bed Plan, opposite pg.]. For the rose garden of your dreams, follow the Formal Rose Garden Plan and enjoy beautiful blooms for many months of the year [see Formal Rose Garden Plan, pg. 72]. Would you like to have a wall of flowers to fill a bed between your lawn and the street? Follow the Layered Bed Plan for great results [see Layered Bed Plan, pg. 74]. Is an English border—or cottage garden—what you're after? Start with the basics by planting the flowers suggested and add a few of your own [see English Border Plan, pg. 76]. Want a formal garden? Try the Formal Mixed Bed Plan [see Formal Mixed Bed Plan, pg. 78]. Or would you like to attract birds and hummingbirds to

your yard [see Bird Garden Plan, pg. 80]? Your greatest challenge is likely to be making a choice from the long list of many possible candidates.

As the many illustrations, plans, pictures, and ideas in this section show, you can think beyond traditional boundaries. Mix several garden styles for an eclectic imprint or follow the planting and design suggestions more closely and create a garden true to a particular style. Mix and match colors in combinations that please you. Stick to one or two colors or let the garden explode with a wild mix of hues.

In laying out your beds you may find that you have to transplant trees and shrubs. Fortunately, many species are resilient. When the move is done properly, most will survive. But some trees, such as flowering plum and many evergreens, pose a challenge when you transplant because they are tap-rooted or struggle when they are disturbed. In such cases, you'll need a backup plan. If the transplant is struggling in the seasons after the move, plant another of the same species beside it or hold a young plant in a container. Think ahead, arm yourself with good information and options, and you can create the garden of your dreams, one floral step at a time.

## Color Surprises

The wide array of flower colors is astounding and gives you enormous latitude in planning a color scheme. Light up a corner border by mixing and matching unlikely color combinations, such as purple and orange. Create a stately, elegant feel with a monochromatic grouping next to a statue, surrounded by deep red 'Mister Lincoln' rose bushes. Plant an electric blue hanging container with bright yellow nasturtiums. Cluster bunches of deep orange marigolds in a whitewashed wooden wheelbarrow and place it next to a russet-red door. Color options in your flower garden are virtually endless.

# Corner Flower Bed Plan

Corners are ideal spots for colorful beds of annual bedding plants. Try them where your driveway meets the street, at the junction of fences and walls, and on the corners of decks and patios.

This corner planting plan calls for using low-growing lobelia in the foreground (other choices are sweet alyssums, forget-me-nots, and violets). Midsized petunias fill the center of the planting (options include marigolds, pansies, and narrow-leaved zinnias) with a background of tall, colorful salvia. Choose similar plants available locally.

In larger beds, exaggerate the steps in height by choosing cultivars that are taller; in tiny beds, select dwarf and miniature plants.

**A  Edging Lobelia**
*Lobelia erinus*
'Riviera Sky Blue' and
   'Cascade Pink'

**B  Petunia**
*Petunia × hybrida*
'Midnight Madness' and
   'Ultra Pink'

**C1  Scarlet Salvia**
*Salvia coccinea*
'Red Hot Sally'

**C2  Jamé Salvia**
*Salvia × jamensis*
'Moonlight'

**C3  Blue Salvia**
*Salvia × superba*
'Blue Queen'

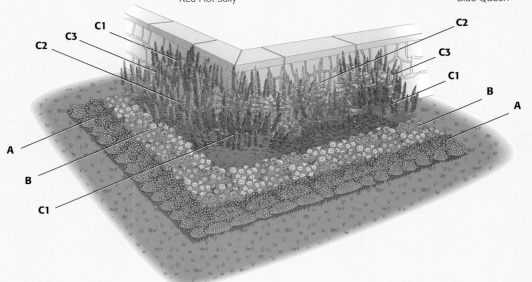

# Formal Rose Garden Plan

### A Word about Roses

Among the most treasured of flowering shrubs, roses need a good start to do well. Begin by choosing roses that are a good fit for your climate. In cold-winter regions, choose species roses such as *R. rugosa* and roses bred to be resistant to cold temperatures. In moist, warm climates, select those that will shrug off fungal diseases. In arid regions, seek out cultivars that thrive while basking in sun. After they become established, water them deeply and infrequently.

Rosemary plays a useful role in this formal rose garden. Aromatic herbs attract many beneficial predator insects such as ladybird beetles and reduce the number of aphids on the roses.

Four outer rectangular beds surround two inner square beds and a central circular bed in this formal rose garden. The garden shown was built in raised masonry beds [see Raised-Bed Masonry, pg. 90]. It would look just as nice in fieldstone planters [see Fieldstone Planter, pg. 92] or in prepared in-ground beds set between paths—a must for cold-winter climates. Whatever the style, make the entry gate grand.

The garden features some of the all-time most popular roses, including multiple prizewinners and a selection of hybrid tea, floribunda, and shrub roses. The four corner beds each hold three different cultivars; the three smaller beds spotlight single species, giving you a variety of bloom habits to enjoy. Or, you can substitute others.

Remember that roses are deep-rooted shrubs. Prepare the soil in the beds at least 32" (80 cm) deep. In cold-winter climates, protect your roses in autumn from frost heaving. Mound soil and add a layer of mulch to a depth of eight to nine inches (20–23 cm) above the crown. Rake up any debris.

**A 'Queen Elizabeth'**
Grandiflora

**B 'Peace'**
Hybrid Tea

**C 'Secret'**
Hybrid Tea

**D 'Brandy'**
Hybrid Tea

**E 'Double Delight'**
Hybrid Tea

**F 'Tropicana'**
Hybrid Tea

**G 'Scentimental'**
Floribunda

**H 'Mr. Lincoln'**
Hybrid Tea

**I 'Olympiad'**
Hybrid Tea

**J 'Touch of Class'**
Hybrid Tea

**K 'Angel Face'**
Floribunda

**L 'Bonica'**
Modern Shrub

**M 'Dortmund'**
Modern Shrub

**N 'Knock Out'**
Modern Shrub

**O 'Gemini'**
Hybrid Tea

**P 'Crimson Bouquet'**
Grandiflora

**Q Rosemary**
*Rosmarinus officinalis*

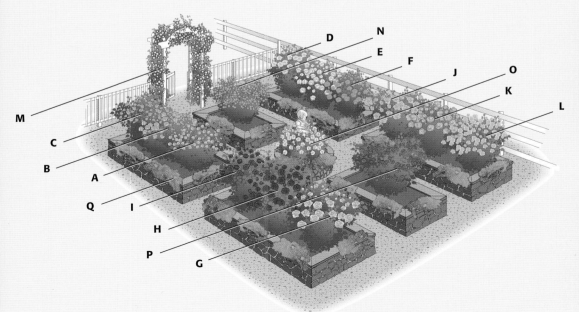

# Layered Bed Plan

Both bedding begonia and yarrow are tough plants able to withstand sun and temperatures that can reach 105°F (41°C) or higher. Blue salvia is a heat-tolerant annual flower.

As their name implies, different species of plants in varying heights make layered beds visually interesting and provide foreground cover for the foliage and stems of tall species. Layered beds appear luxurious and nearly all you see in them are flowers. They are built in tiers with short plants along their front edges, midsized plants in their middle areas, and the tallest flowers in their center or rear.

The layered bed shown here uses a low border of edging lobelia to define its edge, an inner frame of bronze-leaved bedding begonia to separate blocks of midsized yarrow and diminutive 'Blue Queen' dwarf blue salvia, and finishes in the rear with French lavender intermixed with taller 'Blue Hill' blue salvia.

Measure and mark the layout of the entire bed before planting. Next, set individual perennial French lavender plants in the rear, allowing 12" (30 cm) of free space around them, and plant blocks of 'Blue Hill' salvia between them. Plant the yarrow and 'Blue Queen' salvia blocks, dividing them with rows of bedding begonia. Finish the bed with the edging lobelia border.

## Layered Bed Plants

This design uses a selection of common bedding plants available in most areas. You can match the cultivars exactly or substitute other varieties with similar color and height characteristics.

All of the plants are tender perennials that will winter over in zones 8–11; in cooler climates, use them as annuals.

Salvia, lobelia, and begonia prefer moist conditions, while yarrow does best in drier soil. For best results, mound the yarrow's soil 4" (10 cm) high.

**A  Edging Lobelia**
*Lobelia erinus*
'Crystal Palace'

**B  Bedding Begonia**
*Begonia × semperflorens-cultorum* hyb.
'Bronze-leaf Rose'

**C  Yarrow**
*Achillea × hybrida*
'Summer Pastels'

**D  French Lavender**
*Lavandula dentata*
'French Gray'

**E1  Blue Salvia**
*Salvia × superba*
'Blue Hill'

**E2  Blue Salvia**
*Salvia × superba*
'Blue Queen'

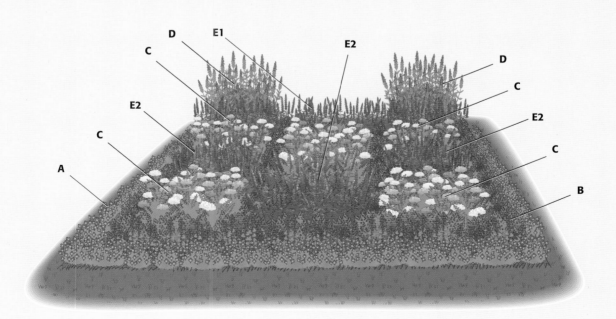

# English Border Plan

An English border's charm is a perfect accent for the rough cobblestones of this cottage. The hallmarks of this attractive border are varied heights, color, and textures.

Plant in sequence for a classic English border. Place tall flowering shrubs in the rear of the bed, progress to medium-height plants in the middle, and plant short-statured flowers in the foreground. Plant groups of three or five plants in sinuous lines, alternating with tall and short species, then repeat the pattern. Plant triangular groupings at the front and fill the space between groups with contrasting colors and varied foliage.

English-border plantings were traditionally composed of plants found in the British Isles. Today, the same carefree abandon that so appealed to Georgian and Victorian gardeners can be yours by using plants that bear lush, fragrant flowers, regardless of your climate and garden. Border plantings work best with Tudor, Cape Cod, Queen Anne Victorian, and other frame homes. Sun exposure is important for planting the border shown here; choose an area that receives some sun in the morning or evening but remains exposed to open shade during the heat of the day. If your site is more sunny, substitute plants with similar forms and greater heat tolerance.

## English Border Plants

Use the plant listings in the back of this book to obtain information about each plant shown, including options for its culture needs, flower colors, special cultivars, and soil requirements. Note the bed diagram on the opposite page and its key that identifies each flowering plant. Next, visit your local nursery; each plant shown is commonly available in many different cultivars with different appearances and habits. After making your selection, read the plant tag carefully for spacing requirements and obtain the number of plants you will need for your garden. Also note soil requirements, adding necessary fertilizer and amendments to increase acidity or alkalinity as the species requires.

**A Summer Phlox**
*Phlox paniculata*
'Snow White'

**B Purple Coneflower**
*Echinacea purpurea*
'Royal Majesty'

**C Marguerite**
*Chrysanthemum frutescens*
'Versailles'

**D1 Petunia**
*Petunia × hybrida*
'Mauve Beauty'

**D2 Petunia**
*Petunia × hybrida*
'July Fourth'; 'Apple'

**E1 Snapdragon**
*Antirrhinum majus*
'Dragon Burgundy'

**E2 Snapdragon**
*Antirrhinum majus*
'Dayglo White'

**F French Lavender**
*Lavandula × heterophylla*
'Seacrest Ville'

**G Foxglove**
*Digitalis purpurea*
'Leopard Purple'

**H Tickseed**
*Coreopsis* spp.
'Flying Saucer'

**I Flowering Flax**
*Linum grandiflorum*
'Scarlet Passion'

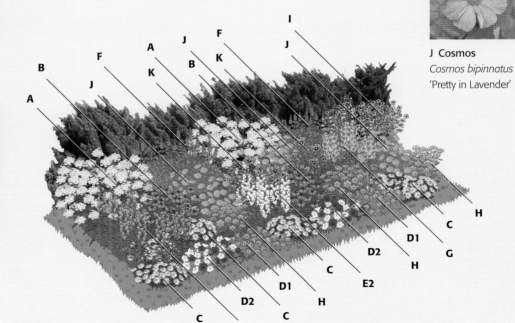

**J Cosmos**
*Cosmos bipinnatus*
'Pretty in Lavender'

**K Iceland Poppy**
*Papaver nudicaule*
'Arctic Glow'

# Formal Mixed Bed Plan

## Formal Mixed Bed Plants

All of the annuals selected for this bed grow equally well in fertile, well-drained soil and full-sun conditions. Flossflower cultivars include blue, pink, purple, violet, and white flowers. Cosmos colors are pink, red, and violet; plant *C. sulphureus* to have gold or yellow flowers. Marigolds are available in several shades of yellow, gold, and white.

Use other species of short-statured plants to vary the bed's appearance. Dwarf periwinkle, for example, is a good substitution for flossflower.

Scale the size of the island bed to fit your yard. It can be adjusted to a narrow rectangle, or made a perfect square. Similar designs work with circular and oval beds.

Neat and orderly are the watchwords for planning and planting a formal island bed. Most formal beds use plants of equal heights. This design introduces a splash of unexpected contrasting color above the low plane with five groups of taller cosmos. They are planted symmetrically around the central, four-pointed star of marigolds.

Measure carefully when you mark the bed. The arcs that define the four sides of the marigold planting are portions of circles passing through the outer bed's corners. To make them, begin by driving stakes at each bed corner. Attach to the stakes strings the same length as the bed—for a 6' × 8' (1.8 × 2.4 m) bed, the radius is 8' (2.4 m)—and stretch them taut to find the points on each side of the bed where their ends just touch. This is the center point of the two large circles that define the long-sided arcs. Repeat with strings the length of the short sides—or 6' (1.8 m)—to find the centers of the short-sided arc's circles. Drive stakes at each circle's center point, attach the string to them, and use the taut string to swing across the bed, marking the arcs that divide the plantings. Also mark the center point of the bed and a spot on each arm of the marigold plantings for a tall cosmos group.

Vary the color scheme of the bed by choosing different cultivars of the species shown. Beds with different color combinations are also possible.

**A Flossflower**
*Ageratum houstonianum*
'Pink Powder-puffs'

**B Marigold**
*Tagetes erecta*
'Inca Gold'

**C Cosmos**
*Cosmos bipinnatus*
'Imperial Pink', 'Sea Shells', and
'Sensation' mix

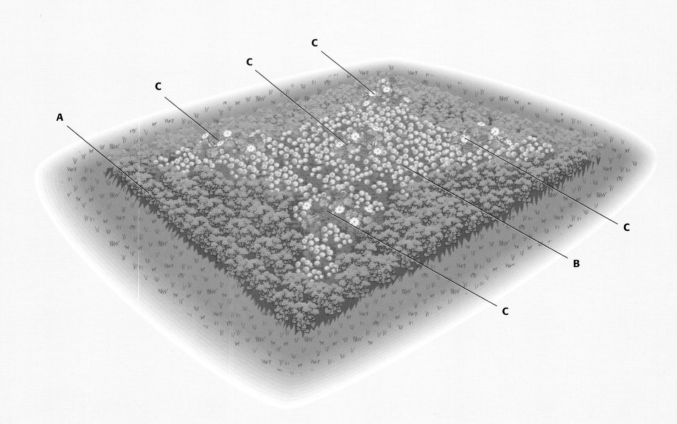

# Bird Garden Plan

### Bird-Attracting Plants

Plants attract birds and hummingbirds with their aromas, bright colors, nectar, pollen, and seed. Plant combinations of annual and perennial flowers. Leave flower heads on the plants after their petals drop; they will form seed and attract many birds.

Wholly organic culture and care methods are essential ingredients for a successful bird garden. The birds will glean many insects on the plants.

Bright and colorful birds will flock to this garden built especially for them. It's filled with seed-bearing flowers and pluming grasses as well as nectar-producing flowers for hummingbirds. Besides its birdbath—water is a powerful attractant for birds—it also has two birdhouses atop a colorful trellis [see Birdhouses on a Trellis, pg. 43]. There's always something for the birds to eat and drink, from spring until autumn.

The garden is designed for a narrow space next to a driveway or fence. From fence to front, it is 6' (1.8 m) deep at its widest point and narrows in a gentle curve to 3' (90 cm) wide at its tip. The bed is 12' (3.7 m) long. For longer beds, repeat the plantings at 12' (3.7 m) intervals.

Build the birdhouses and arbor first. Set two level, concrete stepping-stones for a plant support column and the birdbath. Plant tall background flowers and bushy shrubs: use single-stem and branching cultivars of annual sunflower, pea shrub, and shrub lantana. Next, plant the fountain grass and a morning glory vine to grow up the arbor. Then set in the mid-ground plants: use cosmos, lupine, gloriosa daisy, and black-eyed Susan. Finally, plant the foreground with mixed zinnias and set a pot of petunias on the column. Install a bird feeder on the arbor.

When first planted, the garden may seem sparse. It will take four to six weeks to grow in completely and, by midsummer, it will be crowded with blooms.

**A Petunia**
*Petunia × hybrida*
'Petunia Wave'

**B1 Zinnia**
*Zinnia elegans*
'Dreamland'

**B2 Zinnia**
*Zinnia elegans*
'State Fair'

**C1 Sunflower**
*Helianthus annuus*
'Starburst Auora'

**C2 Sunflower**
*Helianthus annuus*
'Pan'

**D1 Gloriosa Daisy**
*Rudbeckia hirta*
'Autumn Colors'

**D2 Black-eyed Susan**
*Rudbeckia hirta*
'Rustic Colors'

**E Morning Glory**
*Ipomoea tricolor*
'Heavenly Blue'

**F Cosmos**
*Cosmos bipinnatus*
'Sonata Carmine'

**G Shrub Lantana**
*Lantana camara* hyb.
'Gold Rush'

**H Dwarf Pea Shrub**
*Caragana pygmaea*

**I Fountain Grass**
*Pennisetum alopecuroides*
'Cassian'

**J Lupine**
*Lupinus* hyb.
'Russell Hybrid' Mix

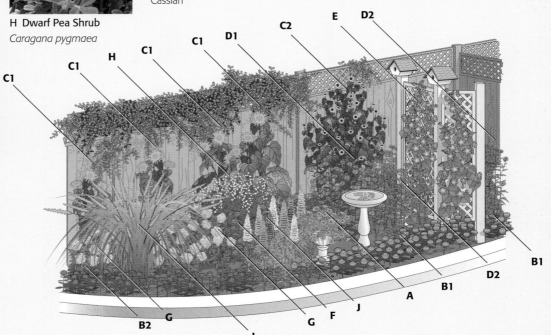

# Uncharted Territory

Create a flower paradise on a new homesite by combining possibilities with foresight.

A work in progress: the soil has been prepared for seeding the lawn, the large shrubs have been planted, and other landscape plants are being set in their final locations. In a few days, the yard and garden of this home will be complete.

Unlike an established home surrounded by a host of established plants and structural items, newly constructed suburban and urban tract houses have little if any vegetation around them. This creates specific challenges.

While the blank slate of a landscape may seem overwhelming at first, it also provides many opportunities. Start by taking a good look at your site and deciding what elements you want in your garden. Then divide the project into stages, planning and setting priorities before you ever lift a shovel. Proceed with a plan in mind, but expect to make changes along the way as realities present themselves.

Take a walk across the street and look at the front of your house with an artist's eye. Think about how you want to surround your new home with flowers. Do you desire thick, lush vegetation or is a sparser, cleaner landscape your style? Does a formal garden appeal to you? Then consider a parterre walkway leading up to the front porch. Would you prefer instead a billowy, natural border of wildflowers and other natives?

## Less Lawn and More Flowers?

Lawns require a remarkable amount of water to thrive. In addition, studies have found that maintaining turfgrass lawns causes significant groundwater pollution in the United States and Canada. Flower beds are much more colorful than lawns, use fewer natural resources, require less upkeep, and attract and feed many species of birds.

**Scope and Symmetry.** Think in terms of scale and balance. Generally, when it comes to shrubs and trees, you'll want to frame the house by placing items of equal bulk at each edge of the property. A large shrub or tree on one side may make your home look unbalanced unless you compensate by adding a tall vine or other plant on the other side. Once you've examined the front yard, do the same for the back.

**Color and Fragrance.** Next, think color. What sort of hues would blend well with your house? Though you may like lavender flowers, you might consider other options if you have a dark brown home. Pay careful attention to the house's trim and such accessories as mailboxes or pillars that could be enhanced by vining plants such as honeysuckle or star jasmine. Put fragrant plantings near your dining area or kitchen so you can enjoy their heady aromas from your open windows.

**Purpose.** Stand at the door or a window and look out at the landscape. What will you see? Think about how you will use your yard. Do you yearn for a flower bed thick with plants or a space bordered by edgings and beds? Consider adding play areas and open spaces for sports activities if you have children. For entertaining, surround a built-in barbecue with beds of flowers. Break up areas of the yard with patios and paths of stone, concrete, or brick. Take notes or make sketches.

**Implementing Your Dream.** Now that you have your general plan, decide which areas to tackle first. Some housing developments require that you landscape your front yard within a certain time from purchase, so this may be the area where you begin.

Regardless of where you start, your first task will be to develop healthy soil. The topsoil is usually removed from new homesites during construction, leaving only lifeless, rocky subsoil. It has little organic material or beneficial soil bacteria and is unsuitable for planting. Remove 6 to 18 inches (15 to 45 cm) of the subsoil and replace it with new topsoil.

Bare-root roses and other shrubs benefit from overnight soaking in water prior to planting.

Depending on the size of your yard, you may also need large amounts of topsoil. Conserve your budget by creating some in-ground beds and rock gardens planted with Xeriscape flowers that are naturally accustomed to marginal soil. Many drought-tolerant plants are native to rocky and sandy areas. Plant resilient species such as butterfly weed, white gaura, golden marguerite (*Anthemis tinctoria*), and red valerian in one bed, and fill another with topsoil to grow plants that are more delicate. Ornamental grasses tolerate unimproved new-home soil conditions better than turfgrass, so substitute them for lawns or beds of flowering plants until you can improve the soil. Still, always remember that drought-tolerant plants require good drainage even though they may grow well in nutrient-poor soils, so take this need into account and amend the soil for drainage before planting if needed.

# Vining Plants and Flower Supports

Fill the walls and overhead ceilings of your garden with flowering plants that climb, arch, vine, ramble, and trail.

Vines and other rambling and climbing plants lend height and depth to a landscape that few other plants can duplicate. How magnificent to see a wisteria draping from an arbor, its pendulous, lilac-colored blossoms perfuming the garden each spring. Passionflower looks especially exotic twining up an ornate obelisk in the center of the yard, and jasmine makes a heady statement as it crawls along a fence.

'Climbing Sally Holmes' is a profuse-blooming rose that will fill trellises and arbors in spring with pink buds that open to single-petaled, cream-white flowers and gold-to-rust centers.

**Vining Plants.** As a group, vines encompass several categories of plants. Their shared similarity is that they climb—with tendrils, growing attachments called holdfasts, or by winding stems around vertical supports. If you plan to enjoy rambling flowering vines, you will have to give them a place to grow—before you plant. It's difficult to install structural supports after a vining plant has begun to grow. Also, vines grow stronger and require less pruning when they are planted and trained properly from the outset. Attach trellises to garages, fences, and walls, giving the vines a point of attachment, or install horizontal training wires such as those used for grapevines.

Among the most beautiful of vines, clematis produces abundant blossoms.

Although they lend so much to the landscape, vines are underrepresented or sometimes left out entirely from North American gardens. In other parts of the world such as Europe, South America, and Asia, vines twine up pillars and hang from balconies. They envelop fences and blanket the sides of buildings, giving their surrounding landscapes a softer, long-occupied feeling.

Look at your garden with vines in mind. Bare walls and fences look more festive when covered with a living tapestry. Patio covers are transformed by flowering ramblers, and vines make pillars and posts more attractive. Fill arches and trellises with color or train climbers up supports attached to, but free of, your walls. Grow small vines up your mailbox.

Plant vines in containers. Let vines drape and trail from a pot or give it a support to climb.

**Supports.** If you lack permanent structures on which to attach vines, you can build new features in your garden. Add an arbor or a gazebo. Choose wooden and fieldstone structures for informal, natural settings, wrought iron and brick for more formal decor. Take into account the eventual size— and sometimes considerable weight—of the vining plant you wish to grow. While wisteria may start out small, it soon becomes large; a slow-growing alternative is the climbing hydrangea (*H. anomala* subsp. *petiolaris*). You can change your garden's appearance on a regular basis by planting climbing annuals such as black-eyed Susan vine, cypress vine (*Ipomoea quamoclit*), moonflower, and morning glory.

Add an obelisk or trellis and train the vine to cover it. Or insert three plant supports, tepee-style, and tie them at the top; let vines grow up the tepee. If the vine is very dense, roll wire hardware cloth into a narrow cylinder and place it within the inner rim of a pot. The vine will soon grow through the wire and obscure it, or plan to fill it with sphagnum moss. For small vines that require minimal support, such as a black-eyed Susan vine that grows just eight feet (2.4 m) tall, weave a group of their flexible branches into a supporting column for an unusual visual effect. Whatever type of support you choose, keep the scale of the trellis proportional to the plant and pot.

You will need to train and tie your vines as they grow. Vines climb in several ways. Like passion vine, they may send out twining tendrils that clasp onto available parallel supports such as trellises. Other vines, such as climbing hydrangea, have aerial roots or adhesive pads that attach to walls and fences. Climbing roses cling with thorns and use woody stems to stay upright, and sweet peas twine both petioles and tendrils around thin supports. Tie the stems of sprawling ramblers, including love-in-a-puff, with stretchy plastic garden tape, available from most garden centers and nurseries.

ABOVE:
An arbor is the perfect match for a walk that passes through a gate since it marks the dividing line between areas of the garden.

OPPOSITE:
Plant supports and stakes are available in many forms, with or without ornaments and decorations.

# construction
## and planting

BEFORE YOU FILL YOUR YARD WITH FLOWERS, IT'S IMPORTANT TO LAY A SOLID FOUNDATION FOR your garden. Well-planned flower beds will let you enjoy your garden for many years, even if you replace the plantings in them as your tastes change. Quality is important, too. Well-built planters will withstand the rigors of weather and remain attractive for a long time. There is also the matter of choosing the right plant for each situation and deciding how it will work with and complement your landscape. Finally, there's a correct way to plant each flower, from seed to transplant, from bulb to shrub.

This chapter will lead you through building eye-catching permanent planters and beds as well as installing irrigation systems and lighting. You will learn about soil preparation and drainage and see how to plant seeds, nursery containers, and bulbs. You'll also find out how to create different effects with techniques such as vertical layering, massed flowers of a single species, and succession plantings. Look here for the how-to's of container gardening, from preparing pots through planting flowers and installing drip irrigation systems especially suited to their needs. Discover how hanging planters can extend your garden vertically up a wall, fence, or tree. Several advanced techniques are covered as well: forcing bulbs for year-round color, caring for flowering bonsai and dwarf plants, using flowering topiary, and growing flowers in structural planters and terraced gardens.

87

# Preplanting Building and Installation

Construct permanent homes for your flowers with surface beds and raised structural planters that complement your plantings.

As you plan your beds, consider two basic options: ground-level beds and raised beds. Both have their place in your flower garden.

Ground-level or surface beds serve a variety of uses. They can line a garden path, border your home, or even fill an entire yard. You can surround them with a defining strip of concrete, stone, or brick to mark their shape and permit easy care when you mow or leave them less well defined. Beds that line a fence, wall, or house are called borders; when they are free-standing, in the middle of a lawn for instance, they're called islands. Island beds filled with flowers are landscape features that are sure to draw favorable comments and attention. Plan for a curving, ground-level bed as the border of your backyard to give it a flowing, natural look or, to have a more formal effect, install symmetrical garden beds on both sides of a sidewalk leading up to your front entry or use them to line a driveway or fence.

Your other choice is raised beds. Their advantages are twofold. First, they give you greater control over the soil they contain. Fill them with a high-quality mix perfectly suited to your chosen plants rather than your native soil;

Useful building tools for garden projects include a carpenter's level and a string level. Specialized tools such as those used for concrete work are available at rental yards. It's often more economical to rent them for a single use. Find materials and supplies at your local hardware retailer.

raised beds are a good idea for gardens with soils that are rocky, clayey, or too acidic or alkaline. They warm more quickly in the spring than surface beds and allow you to plant sooner. Raised beds are also easier to maintain. Because of their height above the ground, you'll be able to avoid bending and kneeling as you do your gardening. Design raised beds in just about any shape: rectangles, squares, hexagons, even circles. Construct your beds of wood or brick, rock or stone, depending on the look you want. Landscape timbers are another option for raised bed materials. They are durable for most landscape plantings, with a life in the soil of five to eight years. Generally, brick and stone beds last longer than wooden ones.

You'll find the complete details on how to build masonry and fieldstone raised beds on the pages that follow [see Structural Planters, opposite pg.].

To build in-ground beds, follow these steps:

1. Mark the outer edge of the planter using stakes and string or lay a garden hose to define its outer edge.
2. Use a turf-cutting tool—a flat blade with a sharp, straight edge—to divide, cut, and lift sections of lawn from the bed. Cut the turf in narrow strips and roll them up with the grass inside.
3. Fit porous non-woven landscape fabric around the edges of the bed to block grass from growing into it. Lap it up to the soil's surface.
4. Install a mowing strip border of brick, stone, or concrete, six to eight inches (15 to 20 cm) wide and flush with the soil's surface.
5. Loosen the soil for at least its top 16 inches (40 cm), add any needed amendments, and fill with soil until the bed is level or higher than the lawn.

# Structural Planters

## Raised beds made of durable materials are attractive, practical, and long-lasting features of your landscape.

Masonry planters add appeal to landscapes and are ideal planting locations for flowers of all types.

Structural planters are attractive yet functional garden elements. Build planters at the ends of a bench or at the corners or center of a deck or patio. Place an island planter in the middle of your yard where it can be viewed from a variety of vantage points. Use raised planters in the middle of a courtyard to highlight a spring-blooming lilac or a group of hybrid tea roses. Put a planter on either side of your front door to welcome visitors with several ornamental grasses mixed with native wildflowers.

Besides structural planters, raised beds are also useful in the overall design of your garden. Use them to divide the garden into sections. Flank your drive-way or build a raised bed to divide a patio from a vegetable garden or lawn. Raise and define the planting bed, bringing its flowers to eye level. This enhances the foreground and brings it into view to make the space beyond an attractive vista. From indoors, it is much easier to see and enjoy a raised bed than one at ground level.

Select from many different choices of shape for your structural planters. Give extra thought to planters located in the open, since they stand alone and their shape is more pronounced. For a formal garden, use defined, geometric shapes. Circles, ovals, rectangles, and squares comprise typical regular shapes. If you want a more natural, informal feeling, mound the soil to create free-flowing beds. You can make beds that are kidney- and paisley-shaped or vary their shape to flow in sinuous lines. On sloping lots, build them as terraces. On a lot with hills, fill the space between two of the rises with a raised planter that merges into the top of the mounds. Raised beds can play many roles in your home landscape.

When you design a raised bed, make it at least one foot (30 cm) high. Heights of 18 to 20 inches (45 to 50 cm)—seating height—are best for easiest care. Keep terraces less than three feet (90 cm) tall.

Plant an attractive trailing species such as geranium to color-fully trail down a wall.

# Raised-Bed Masonry

Build a structural planter constructed of mortared blocks and face it with natural stone, an artificial stone facing, or brick. The result will transform your yard from ho-hum to wow.

The amount of effort required and the budget you'll need varies with the size of the planter. Build a small planter in a couple of weekends—concrete and mortar requires time to gain strength after it hardens, so allow several days between steps for it to cure—or a larger one over the course of a month. Enlist the aid of an assistant or two to help with heavy lifting. If this is your first attempt at masonry construction try a small bed to hone your skills before tackling a larger structural planter.

You'll need the following tools: a 50' (15 m) tape measure, work gloves, a sledgehammer, a shovel, a wheelbarrow, a tamping tool, a carpenter's spirit level, concrete floats and steel finishing tools, a garden hose, a mason's string level, a trowel, and a grout-finishing tool.

You'll also need these materials: 4" (10 cm) perforated PVC pipe for drainage, 4" (10 cm) solid PVC pipe for utility chases through which you'll run irrigation pipe and electrical cables, porous landscape fabric, pea gravel, concrete, cinder blocks, mortar, galvanized metal brick ties, facing materials and capstones, a rubber mallet, grout, and fill soil. Consult the staff of your local hardware retailer or building center to estimate the amount of materials your bed will require and arrange for supplies to be delivered to your site.

For the raised bed shown, allow a day to lay out the bed, excavate, and prepare the trench, and about three hours to pour, level, and finish the concrete footings.

**1** Mark the outside perimeter of the island bed using stakes and survey tape. Trench a footing 12" (30 cm) wide and deep along the interior of the perimeter. Place irrigation and utility chases of PVC pipe, 4" (10 cm) in diameter, crossing beneath the trench, along with perforated 4" (10 cm) PVC drain pipes wrapped in landscape fabric at 3' (90 cm) intervals along the lowest side. You will use these pipes later. Fill the trench with a base layer of pea gravel, 4" (10 cm) deep, and compact it with a tamping tool.

On the second weekend, it will take a day to erect the block walls plus four to six hours to face the bed with stone, grouting as you go. Allow an additional three to four hours to prepare the bed for filling and topping it off with soil.

Review the entire building project before you start, then follow these steps.

**2** Fill the trench with concrete to a level 2″ (50 mm) below the surrounding soil surface. Use a carpenter's spirit level and concrete finishing tools to roughly flatten and level the surface. Occasionally mist the concrete with water as it sets and hardens. Allow it to cure for at least ten days.

**3** Set cinder blocks in mortar at the highest corner, tapping each block to set it firmly. Fill the hollows with mortar. Build the corner up to the final height of the bed, as a reference point. With a mason's string level, set and level each adjacent corner to the courses of this reference corner. Repeat for the final corner, leveling it to the adjacent and reference corners.

**4** Set a row of blocks along each side in mortar, leveling them horizontally to the string and vertically using a carpenter's spirit level. For beds to be faced with brick or synthetic stone, set galvanized metal brick ties in the mortar every 12″ (30 cm) along the bed, protruding ½″ (6 mm) out from the block. Tap each block to set it. Fill the hollows with mortar. Repeat for succeeding courses.

**5** Cover the bed with stone, facing, or brick. Start at the base below soil level and work up a corner. Spread mortar on the block face with a trowel, "butter" the facing stone with mortar, and press it into place. Tap it into place until set. For random patterns, fit stones to fill the space. For laid brick, keep each course square with a mason's string level. Grout the spaces with a grouting tool. Clean the facing with a sponge as you work.

**6** Cap the bed's wall with flat concrete blocks, molded bricks, or capstones set on a mortar base. Allow the mortar to set for at least ten days before proceeding.

**7** Backfill around each drainpipe with pea gravel and line the bed with landscape fabric to help prevent the drains from clogging. Run irrigation pipes and low-voltage lighting wire through chases for later connection to control valves and fixtures, then fill the bed above its rim with amended soil. Allow the soil to settle for several weeks until it is 2″ (50 mm) lower than the capstones, adding soil to fill any low spots.

# Fieldstone Planter

Build a dry-stacked planter of unmortared fieldstone to make an attractive casual bed. This bed is much easier to build than a masonry planter made of blocks and mortar. Tailor the size of your planter to your site, abilities, and budget and enlist the aid of a helper for the heavy lifting.

Remember that every raised planter should have good drainage to prevent it from accumulating water. Install drain-pipes when you build it, and wrap them in porous landscape fabric to stop roots and soil from clogging them.

You'll need the following simple tools: a shovel and wheelbarrow. For materials, obtain spray marker paint or flour, 4" (10 cm) perforated PVC pipe to use for drainage, 4" (10 cm) solid PVC pipe for utility chases through which you will run irrigation pipe and electrical cables, porous landscape fabric, pea gravel, soil, and large, medium, and small fieldstone boulders, rocks, and cobbles. Remember that rock is heavy for its size and always should be handled with caution to prevent personal injury.

Consult the staff of your local building center or hardware retailer for aid in estimating the amount of materials your bed will require and arranging for supplies to be delivered to your site.

For the raised bed shown, allow a day to lay out the bed, excavate, and erect the fieldstone walls, filling and topping it off with soil as you go.

Review the entire building project before you start, then follow these steps.

**1** Mark the bed's outline using marking paint or flour. Excavate the bed, from 8" (20 cm) beyond its outside perimeter to its center, making it 12" (30 cm) deep.

**2** Place irrigation and utility chases of 4" (10 cm) PVC pipe in trenches that extend into the bed from outside its perimeter. Run irrigation pipes and low-voltage lighting wire through the chases for later connection to control valves and transformers.

**3** Lay landscape fabric across the excavation, overlapping its margins 6"–8" (15–20 cm) beyond the perimeter of the bed.

**4** Pull back the landscape fabric and excavate a corner to accept a large cornerstone. Make the excavation about 12" (30 cm) deeper than the surrounding soil. Replace the landscape fabric and place the cornerstone. Set several smaller stones next to it in each direction along the bed's sides. Repeat for each corner.

**5** Add a layer of pea gravel 4" (10 cm) deep over the landscape fabric and along the perimeter of the bed. Tamp the layer firm. Fill the spaces between cornerstones with a base course of midsized rocks.

**7** Dry-stack a top course of smaller cobbles even with the bed's crown to cap it. Butt the top course flush against the sides of the cornerstones and 3"–4" (75–100 mm) lower than their tops.

**8** When the final courses are finished and the bed is full of soil, allow the soil to settle for several weeks before planting, adding additional soil as required to fill any low spots.

**6** Dry stack each succeeding course of fieldstone on the base course. Step each course 1"–2" (25–50 mm) inward toward the bed's center, filling the bed as you go with amended soil to the top of each course to support the stones.

# Installing Garden Systems

## Ease the chore of manual watering with an automated system, and add beauty after nightfall with low-voltage lighting.

Match drip systems to the plants. Set automatic timers to meter the schedule and duration of flow. Control the total water released by selecting emitters rated by the amount of water they release per hour.

Increase your enjoyment of your garden with two beneficial systems: drip irrigation and low-voltage lighting. With an automated drip system, you can water your plants exactly the right amount at the same time every day—even if you're away from your garden for days at a time. Well-placed lighting of your flowers, paths, and steps creates a welcoming feeling and makes for safer access after dark. Plan and install both systems, plus those for any water feature—bubbler, fountain, or pond— before you plant. You

will find it much easier than working around your flowers later on.

If there's a single system that every garden should have, it's automated watering. Gone forever is the time-consuming effort of dragging hoses to new spots in your flower beds and filling watering cans over and over. Equip your system with a rain sensor and it will turn itself off automatically when it rains. Add a drain fitting at the lowest point, and you can leave the system in the ground all winter, even if you live in the coldest climate.

For small-space gardens, a battery-powered timer valve attached to a garden faucet will do the job. For larger gardens, a multiple-circuit system with the capacity to water different areas is best. Attach the system to an exterior or interior faucet with a simple threaded T-fitting. Run easy-to-install PVC pipe and control cable into your garden, and place an automated irrigation controller near a handy faucet. Add a few irrigation control valves—select those equipped with built-in backflow preventers to stop irrigation water from siphoning back into your household water supply—connect the control wires, and your system is in business [see Adding Drip Irrigation, opposite pg.].

Both spray-stake and bubbler-emitter irrigation systems are installed in much the same way as drip, but use different output fittings. Consult the staff of your local hardware retailer or garden center for help in planning and installing your irrigation system.

Low-voltage lighting in your garden is, if anything, even easier to install than an irrigation system [see Adding Low-Voltage Lighting, pg. 96]. From a transformer plugged into an exterior A.C. outlet, run thick direct-burial cable to the site of each lamp. Attach it to the power with simple piercing connectors that grasp and puncture the cable. A bit of tidying up, and you'll have a complete system of low-voltage lights to illuminate your yard.

# Adding Drip Irrigation

# Adding Drip Irrigation

There are many methods of irrigation, including drip irrigation, hand watering, overhead sprinklers, and soaker hoses. Choose a drip system to water flowering plants. First, it can be automated, to free more time for other tasks or to enjoy your garden. Second, drip delivers the water only where you want it, cutting down on weeds. Last, drip irrigation applied to the soil virtually eliminates fungal diseases such as mildew.

Drip systems are quite simple. Place small fixtures, called emitters, at the base of each plant and attach them to thin, flexible tubing. In turn, attach this tubing to larger-diameter tubing or a drip-line coupler. Choose ½" (12 mm) drip hose. Add a filter to keep the emitters from clogging, a pressure regulator, and a back-flow prevention valve. Consult the staff at your local hardware retailer or garden center for advice and design help when you plan and install irrigation systems, then follow these simple steps.

**1** Turn off water at the main and open the hose bib to relieve water pressure. When the flow stops, use two opposed pipe wrenches to remove the hose bib. Attach a T-fitting to the supply pipe with a threaded nipple coated with plumber's putty. Fit one or more irrigation valves to the T-fitting with PVC nipples, 90° ELLS. Use Teflon® thread tape to seal the joints. Replace the hose bib to the T-fitting.

**2** Connect the control cable's common ground and a hot lead to the irrigation control valve using waterproof wire nuts. For multiple irrigation valves, pigtail the common ground to all valves with a separate hot lead for each valve. Run direct-burial–rated control cable to the irrigation controller site.

**3** Install batteries and connect the irrigation controller to an electrical outlet. Wire the common ground and each hot lead to the watering circuit terminals. Turn on the water and test that each control valve operates. Set the watering time and duration on the controller, following the manufacturer's directions.

**4** Run PVC pipe from the control valve to each flower bed on the circuit, connecting pipes with PVC primer and solvent. Use Teflon® thread tape and three street-ELLS to make an adjustable swing joint for each riser. Fit a drip outlet onto each riser.

**5** Water large areas in the bed with perforated drip tubing laid in S-shaped runs across the bed, 6" (15 cm) apart and up to 12' (3.7 m) long.

**6** To water large shrubs, run drip tubing to each plant and attach one or more emitters, 4"–8" (10–20 cm) from its roots. A single line can serve up to six plants.

# Adding Low-Voltage Lighting

With low-voltage outdoor lighting you can create nearly any illusion you want, from intimate to festive. Spotlight flowering shrubs or add submersible lights to highlight a pond, and for safety after dark, light pathways, stairs, and stepping-stones. Choose from a wide array of fixtures to complement any type of garden.

Low-voltage lights are generally just four to eighteen watts D.C. and require a transformer for operation. One major advantage of this type of lighting is that shock hazard is virtually eliminated. The wattage and amperage is low enough to use these lights anywhere outdoors, including underwater in garden ponds or fountains.

You'll need the following tools: a shovel and an electric screwdriver with flat-head and Phillips bits.

You will also need these materials: 12-volt D.C. direct-burial cable, waterproof wire nuts, surveyor's tape, lighting fixtures with piercing connectors, fixture mounting stakes, and a low-voltage transformer and its mounting hardware.

Consult the staff of your hardware or building center for help choosing and installing lighting.

Allow a half day to install a simple low-voltage lighting system, following the steps shown here.

**1** Dig trenches 12"–16" (30-40 cm) deep. Make wiring runs less than 50' (15.3 m) long; use T-splices with waterproof wire nuts rather than looping back. Plan your lighting run carefully. Choose a low-voltage transformer with capacity to supply the combined wattage of all of the lighting fixtures you'll install, plus 25 percent additional capacity. If your layout requires it, use more than one transformer and circuit.

**2** Partially fill each trench, leaving the cable exposed at each light fixture. Lay surveyor's tape in the trench 1"–2" (25–50 mm) above the cable to alert those who may excavate the area in the future.

**3** Fasten low-voltage lighting fixtures to the main cable with piercing connectors that contact each wire conductor in the cable when its two pieces close around it. Splice end-of-run fixtures using waterproof wire nuts. Test the lights and fill in the trenches.

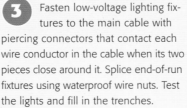

**4** Install the lighting transformer in a protected place adjacent to an electrical outlet. Follow package directions for mounting and connecting the unit to an electrical outlet and the cable, as well as for operating the unit.

# Water Garden and Fountain Utilities

## Allow for a water supply and an electrical connection when you plan to install a fountain or garden pond.

When you consider a water feature for your garden, the systems you need are as important as their design. First, you'll need a power source run from an outlet to the location of the water garden. It will operate the pump. Lay Underground Feeder (UF) direct-burial cable. It is fully armored and labeled for easy identification should it later be unearthed. Protect the cable or insulated wires by encasing it in rigid metal conduit or PVC pipe rated for use as electrical conduit. Bury metal-encased cable at least six inches (15 cm) deep, keeping in mind that it will corrode over time. Bury PVC conduit at least 18 inches (45 cm) deep. Attach the cable to an existing circuit, but protect it with a ground fault circuit interrupter (GFCI) that trips in case of shock hazard. Use existing plumbing for the water supply, but install a backflow-prevention valve to prevent siphoning and contamination.

Use only pumps made specifically for garden pools and choose one with ample capacity. Circulate the entire volume of the fountain or pond once every hour for koi ponds and once every two hours for those with small fish. In other words, for a 600-gallon (2,280-l) pond, choose a 600-GPH (2,271-LPH) pump for koi or 300 GPH (1,140 LPH) for goldfish. Calculate the pond's volume by multiplying its length times its width times its depth, and then multiply the volume by 7.5 to determine the number of gallons (by 28.5 to determine the liters) in the pond. When water is raised for a fountain, it takes more power and lowers the per-hour load capacity. To find a pump's gallon-per-hour rating, look at the head, or discharge fitting. The rating should be listed there.

Submersible pumps are the most popular choices for small water features. They are quiet and mount below the water surface. Choose one with a stainless steel shaft, sealed plastic housings, and a strainer to prevent clogging. Some big ponds use external pumps. These require protective housings and are louder than submersible pumps.

Whichever pump you need, check its wattage and make sure your circuit will accommodate it. Pumps use from as little as 5 watts to 750 watts or more. Also look at its inlet size, indicated by the interior diameter, or ID. The more powerful the pump, the bigger its ID.

Before you install a water feature, check with your municipal building department about codes and requirements. These vary from area to area.

It's easy to create a lively water feature for your garden with just a fountainhead, a catch basin, a sturdy base, and some PVC pipe or conduit, fittings, and solvent.

# Soil and Drainage

Start with good soil, the foundation
of your garden.

Bog and aquatic plants grow well in marshy areas, filling
them with flowers.

Good soil is the essence of a healthy garden. Soil
that is full of nutrients and drains properly gives
plants the best possible growing medium. Start with
high-quality soil and replenish it as your plants use
its resources.

**Soil Types.** Basically, there are three kinds of soil.
Clay is heavy and requires both organic and mineral
amendments to loosen it. Because it is so dense, it is
the slowest to warm in spring and cool down in the
autumn. It can be very fertile, however.

Silt has bigger particles than clay, but it's still very
fine. When wet, it feels silky. It is fertile, absorbs water
more quickly than clay, and drains a bit faster. Both
clay and silt soils can form hard crusts.

Sandy soil feels gritty. It is composed of large
mineral particles and has a great deal of space for air
and water. Sand drains well yet loses water-soluble
nutrients equally quickly. Plants grown in sandy soil
must be fed and watered frequently.

Attach surface drains
to runs of perforated
PVC pipe that connect
to the street's storm
drain, gutters, or
open areas of turf.
Drains collect water,
diverting it from your
home's foundation
and preventing the
erosion of soil in
your garden.

The ideal soil is loam, with roughly equal parts
of clay, silt, and sand and abundant decayed organic
material. It holds nutrients, water, and air but also
drains well. Loam is uncommon, but over time you
can create a soil with most of its characteristics by
adding compost, rotted manure, and missing minerals.

**Soil Nutrients.** Nutrients are a very important
component of soil. There are four groups: macronutrients, secondary nutrients, micronutrients, and
trace minerals. All four are important to your flowers.

Macronutrients are found in the soil in fairly
large quantities. They are listed on fertilizer bags as
three numbers separated by dashes.
This is known as the NPK ratio. N
stands for nitrogen, which is used
in the synthesis of proteins, chlorophyll, and enzymes, all necessary for
plants to live and produce. Without
nitrogen, plants yellow. It is the most
likely of all macronutrients to be in
short supply. P stands for phosphorus,
which promotes flowering, fruiting,
and strong root growth. Phosphorus-
deficient plants have stunted flowers
and fruits and weak growth. K stands
for potassium. It regulates the synthesis of proteins and starches that make
plants strong. It also helps increase
resistance to heat, cold, and disease.
Symptoms of potassium deficiency
are reduced flowering, spotted or

curled older leaves, and weak stems and roots. All three macronutrients are essential.

Secondary nutrients are important, too, but they are less likely to be deficient. These are calcium (Ca), which plays roles in both cell formation and growth; magnesium (Mg), which adds molecules that form part of chlorophyll's chemical structure; and sulfur (S), which acts with nitrogen in the manufacture of protoplasm for plant cells.

Plants need micronutrients and trace minerals in very small quantities. These include zinc (Zn), manganese (Mn), boron (B), iron (Fe), copper (Cu), molybdenum (Mo), and chlorine (Cl).

**Fertilizers.** Apply fertilizers to supplement the nutrients that are already present in the soil. Choose fertilizers according to plant needs. Single nutrient fertilizers such as ammonium sulfate (21–0–0) contain only active ingredients, in this case nitrogen. Complete fertilizers contain all three macronutrients and may contain secondary or trace nutrients as well. Special-purpose fertilizers are generally meant for use on particular types of plants or for special purposes. Use high-nitrogen fertilizer, for instance, on foliage plants and a fertilizer high in phosphorus to help promote flowering and fruiting. Fertilizers that have an ammonium form of nitrogen tend to produce an acidic soil reaction, while those that contain nitrates produce an alkaline reaction.

Natural, or organic, fertilizers have become the plant food of choice for a number of reasons. They are made up of cow manure or bat or seabird guano; materials made from dead organisms, such as fish emulsion; and naturally occurring mineral deposits. Meals—dried and ground seaweed, alfalfa, blood, cottonseed, fish, and soybean—are also common fertilizers. All organic fertilizers contain lower levels of immediately available nutrients than man-made fertilizers do. The lower percentages prevent root and leaf burn and also limit nutrient run-off into the groundwater or nearby bodies of water. Rather than dissolving in water as chemical fertilizers do, the complex molecules in organic formulations must be broken down by microorganisms in the soil to release their nutrients. This action builds soil fertility and promotes bioactivity.

**Drainage.** Proper drainage is as important to soil health as is soil fertility. Before planting, test your drainage, or percolation. Dig a hole two feet (60 cm) deep and fill it with water. If the water drains within five minutes, you have sandy, fast-draining soil. If the water stands for more than an hour, you have heavy soil and poor drainage. If it drains in 15 to 20 minutes, you have a good mix of silt, sand, and clay, and the soil is likely to support healthy plants.

When drainage is too fast, in the case of sandy soil, you will need to bulk it up. When drainage is too slow, in the case of clay soil, you will need to create more airspace. In both cases, the answer is to add organic material to the soil. Good organic additions include compost, manure, earthworm castings, mushroom compost, or coir dust—a by-product of coconut fiber often used as a substitute for peat moss.

Channel the runoff from seasonal desert downpours by making a channel or building a dry creek bed filled with rocks. Plant its borders with deep-rooted or succulent ground covers and low shrubs.

# Planting Flowers

Match your planting technique to the flowers you plant, whether they are nursery transplants, seeds, or bulbs.

Finally, it's time to plant. Before you set roots in soil, however, gather the necessary supplies. At the very least, you will need a hand trowel. Depending on what you are planting, you'll also want fertilizer, soil amendments such as compost, and mulch to control weeds and help retain moisture in the soil [see Mulches and Mulching, pg. 125]. Make sure there is a nearby water source or fill a watering can and keep it close. You will want stakes or trellises and stretchy plastic garden tape to attach vines or tall flowers to their supports. Protect your hands with garden gloves. Use an indelible pencil or pen and plant markers to label your plantings for easy reference. Record the name of the plant, the date of its planting, and any other pertinent information such as the starter fertilizer that you added.

Ease your plant's transition to native soil by scoring the side of the rootball to break up encircling roots and help it grow into the soil.

**Vertical Layering.** While it's possible to randomly plant flowers in a planting bed, you'll get a more pleasing display if you use vertical layering. To layer, place tall, large plants at the back of the bed. As you move toward the front, use increasingly shorter and smaller plants. You could include shrubs and flowering vines like glossy abelia and pink jasmine in the rear of the bed, followed by lower-growing perennials like white gaura (*G. lindheimeri*), white iris, and white evening primrose (*Oenothera* spp.). In front of this, plant a variety of smaller annuals such as wishbone flower, love-in-a-mist, and lavender nemesia (*N. strumosa*). Finish off with a ground cover such as ornamental strawberries (*Duchesnea indica*) at the front of the bed.

**Spacing.** Proper spacing is critical to plant health and successful flowering. Flowers planted too closely will compete for water and food and have fewer blooms or, with less air circulation, be susceptible to pests and diseases. Planted too far apart, the bed will seem sparse and unfinished. Find spacing requirements on nursery tags or determine how far apart to plant by noting their size at maturity and allowing that much space. Remember that mature size depends on the plant. Is it a vine that needs support as it climbs or is it a rambler that will arch or spill over the edge of a raised bed? Are its leaves large and will they take up a great deal of room, or does it have compact foliage? If in doubt, ask the staff at your nursery or garden center for advice. The encyclopedia of flowers at the back of this book notes the size and spacing of many flowering plants.

**Plant Size and Variation.** Plants vary in size depending on your particular climate, their growing conditions, and culture.

Climate is the first important consideration. A plant that is well-suited to your climate is likely to reach the mature size noted or grow even larger under ideal conditions. Plants growing far from their native habitats will usually be smaller than is typical for their species. This is especially true with shrubs and vines. Choose plants that are well-adapted to your region's climate and temperature.

Growing conditions and the care you give your plants are secondary factors that also contribute to their well-being. If conditions are ideal for a particular plant—for instance, if you put an azalea in a spot with bright shade and rich, acidic soil—it will perform well. Plant an identical azalea in alkaline soil and too much light, and it will remain small. Care and maintenance also affect how plants grow. Keep your plants well fed, weeded, pinched, and pruned to produce vigorous growth and flowers.

Garden centers offer plants ready to transplant into your garden in a variety of sizes. Popular sizes are 4-, 6-, 8-, and 12-packs; 4" (10-cm) and 6" (15-cm) pots; 1-, 2-, and 5-gallon (4.4-, 8.8-, and 22-l) containers, and boxed shrubs or trees. Shrubs and trees are also offered during the spring, as bare-root stock and year-round balled-and-burlapped. Note that some flower species tolerate transplanting only with difficulty; for these, plant seed directly into the garden soil [see Planting Seed, pg. 103].

Regardless of size, all nursery starts are transplanted the same way. You will need a shovel or spade, a rake, a hand fork, a trowel, and a hose or watering can. You will also want 2–5–5 organic fertilizer (sometimes labeled as starter fertilizer) to add nutrients to the bed.

Allow an hour to prepare the bed, and four to five minutes per plant, then follow these steps.

**1** Work the soil in the bed at least 16" (40 cm) deep. Incorporate an organic fertilizer containing abundant phosphorus and potassium but limited nitrogen, such as 2–5–5. Allow the soil to settle for at least two days before proceeding.

**2** Space plants as recommended for the species. Measure the distance between the centers of each plant and mark each point as a center for a planting hole. Dig the planting holes as deep as the rootballs of the nursery starts.

**3** Press in the sides of the growing container. Invert it as you support the plant's stem between your spread fingers. Tap the bottom of the container to slide the rootball into your open hand.

**4** Set the rootball into the planting hole. Firm the soil around it and press down with your palms to bed it into the soil. Water the plant immediately after you place it in the soil. Repeat the process for each remaining plant.

# Selecting Vigorous Flowers and Seeds

Choose fresh seed and healthy plants to make sure your flower garden will be off to a good start.

Healthy plants give you the best, most long-lived displays. Start with high-quality seed and robust plants to have beautiful, abundant blooms.

**Seed.** Ensure success if you opt to grow plants from seed by carefully selecting your stock. Choose seed packets displayed indoors or in the shade. (Seed left in bright sunlight will have lower germination rates.) Check the date of seed packets to be sure they are fresh. The older the seed, the lower the germination rate.

**Plants.** When you choose plants, look for these features:

- Green, vibrant foliage. Yellow, dull leaves may indicate a nutrient-deficient or rootbound plant. Avoid plants with damage due to handling or insects.
- Flower buds. Presence of buds means you'll soon see flowers. Examine buds for uniformity, full size, and health. Avoid plants already in full bloom and those with overly small or malformed buds.
- Signs of vigor. Dense plants with strong stems are best, with new growth that is firm, thriving, and of normal size and shape. Avoid spindly, weak-stemmed plants.
- Abundant firm roots. White or tan-colored roots free of soft spots mean a healthy plant. Avoid plants with brown or black, soft roots and droopy, wilted leaves. (The roots of some plants have brown outer casings. Inside the casings, the roots are white or tan.)

Seeds come in all sizes, from starch-filled, large sunflower to the tiny seeds of coreopsis. Plant each according to its package directions. As a general rule, large seeds should be planted after soil temperatures have already warmed.

Examine each plant's roots. Squeeze the sides of its pot, support the plant with your palm, turn it over, and tap the pot to slide it out. Choose plants with established root systems. Pass by any with roots wrapped tightly around the ball of soil. And use a magnifying glass to look for sticky residues on leaves that are telltale signs of near-microscopic insects such as spider mites.

## IN SEARCH OF FLOWERS

David Douglas, one of the greatest plant hunters of all time, belonged to the Horticultural Society of London, now the Royal Horticultural Society. From 1824 to 1827, he collected seed in western North America. Besides many coniferous trees, he discovered a number of popular flowers, including the California poppy. His journeys could be grist for a wilderness adventure movie. On several occasions, he survived attacks by Native American tribes—all so growers in Europe could enjoy new, colorful flowers.

Obtain your plants soon after they arrive in the nursery or garden center. You will have the best selection, and the plants will be fresh from the growers.

Buds ready to open

Compact, dense habit

Dark green foliage

Stem and foliage free of damage

White, firm roots

# Planting Seed

Plants such as love-lies-bleeding (*Amaranthus caudatus*) or satin flower struggle when transplanted. For this reason, you will seldom see them in your garden center's plant selection. Other cultivars and hybrids are available only as seed.

Plant seed in garden soil after the soil warms. A soil temperature of 50°F (10°C) or higher will work for most garden flowers with small seed, but wait until it reaches 60°F (16°C) or more for large, starchy seed. (Soil temperatures lag behind air temperatures by a week or more in spring.)

Prepare the bed as you would for nursery transplants [see Transplanting Nursery Containers, pg. 101]. You'll need a shovel, rake, hand fork, trowel, and hose or watering can. You'll also want 2–5–5 organic fertilizer to add starter nutrients to your soil.

Allow an hour for preparing the bed and 15 minutes for planting each area, following these steps.

**1** Fertilize and amend a bed of loose garden soil. Rake and smooth the soil's surface. For small seed, tap seed from the seed package onto the soil. For large seed, pour the seed from the seed package. Space the seed at about half the distance recommended for the species.

**2** Note the recommended planting depth indicated on the seed pack. Sift a layer of organic compost over the seed to cover them. Firm the soil by pressing it down with your open palms.

**3** Use a watering can with a diffusing rose to gently moisten the planting. Erect string around the planting to identify it. Label it with the flower species. Keep the bed evenly moist until the seed germinate and sprouts emerge. Thin them to their recommended spacing when they grow two true leaves [see Pinching and Thinning Flowers, pg. 131].

# Growing Bulbous Plants

## Add spring, summer, and autumn bulbs for a glorious display.

Store bulbs in the temperature range recommended for the bulb species, packing them loosely in dry, damp, or moist peat moss or sawdust.

Plants that sleep underground and suddenly spring forth in flower have a special beauty. Bulbs, corms, rhizomes, and tubers come in a variety of colors and unusual forms. Bulbs are also plants for all places. Sunny or shady, wet or dry—just about any spot will prove suitable for some kind of flowering bulb. Bulbs bloom in all seasons, from spring crocus that peek out in late winter, daffodils that grace the spring garden with their pert blooms, gladioli that display their flaglike flowers and foliage in the middle of summer, and sternbergia (*S. lutea*) that light up the autumn. With careful selection, you can have bulbs blooming throughout your landscape for much of the gardening season, from spring until autumn. [see Flower Successions, pg. 110].

Probably your most important task is to plant the correct bulbs for your area. Before you start, determine which bulbs grow so well in your area that they naturalize. These species will multiply all on their own. Other bulbs need more care. Some, for example, require winter chilling, and others may mildew if exposed to summer rain.

Select healthy, high-quality bulbs. Always obtain your bulbs from an established nursery, garden center, or a reliable direct source. Over the long run it's more economical to budget a little more up front for bulbs that will produce beautiful blooms in their first season and readily naturalize. Examine each bulb carefully to be sure it is firm and free of blemishes, cuts, or spots, any of which could be entry points for fungal diseases or bacterial rot. Choose bulbs that feel heavy for their size rather than those that are lightweight, shriveled, or dried up. As they grow, bulbs store energy in the form of starch, making their next season's blooms possible. Generally, the bigger the bulb, the bigger the bloom. Most bulbs adapt to various soil types, but many grow best in well-drained soil. Plant bulbs as soon as possible after you obtain them to prevent their drying out. Lilies are especially prone to drying. If you must store them, do so by packing them them loosely in damp sawdust.

## Bulb planting depths

Planting bulbs, corms, rhizomes, and tubers at the correct depth ensures that the sprouting flower stalks will reach the surface and remain healthy. Most bulbs are planted at a depth equal to three times their diameter, although some rhizomes, such as iris, are planted shallowly with parts of their structure exposed. Bulbs are planted months before they peek through the soil surface. Lift them in areas that have rain during their dormant period. Label bulbs before storing.

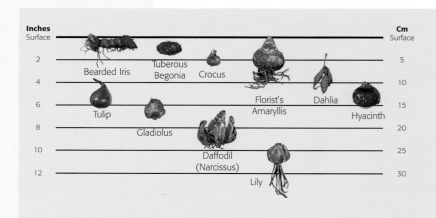

# Planting Bulbous Plants

Planting bulbs, corms, rhizomes, and tubers at the correct depth ensures that the sprouting flower stalks will reach the surface and remain healthy.

Plant true bulbs, corms, and tubers using the method demonstrated at right. Most bulbs are planted at a depth equal to three times their diameter.

Plant rhizomes following the steps shown below. Note that some rhizomes such as iris are planted shallowly with parts of their structure exposed.

Allow an hour to prepare the bed for planting, plus a minute or two for each individual bulb planted. It's faster and easier to excavate the entire planting area to the recommended depth when you plant large numbers of bulbs. Next, fertilize, set the bulbs, and cover them with soil.

Bulbs are planted months before they peek through the soil's surface and are often lifted after their foliage dies back or, for tender species, before winter. Label lifted bulbs to prevent confusion months later when you replant them.

## Planting Bulbs, Corms, and Tubers

**1** Note the planting depth for the bulb species found on its package label. Discard any dehydrated bulbs, along with those with cuts and nicks.

**2** Use a dibber or bulb planting tool to excavate a hole 2" (50 mm) deeper than the recommended depth for the species. Add 10–10–5 fertilizer to the hole and cover it with 2" (50 mm) of soil. Always bury the fertilizer to avoid direct contact between it and the bulb.

**3** Orient each bulb so that its top is up. For tubers or bulbs lacking discernible tops, plant them on their sides. Place the bulb in the hole and cover it with soil. Water the bed thoroughly after planting.

## Planting Rhizomes

**1** Note the depth recommended on the package directions for planting the species and excavate a trench to that depth; some are planted at the soil surface. Discard any that have become dehydrated.

**2** Lay the rhizomes in the furrow and cover or bank soil against them to close the furrow. For those rhizomes lacking a clear top or bottom, set them in the trench on their sides.

**3** Water thoroughly immediately after planting. In the following weeks, keep them evenly moist until their flowers fade, then limit watering and wait for their foliage to die to the ground.

# Flowers in Beds and Borders

Use your planting skills to grow flowers in spectacular plantings, filled with interesting groups and coordinated colors.

Fill the space between early-spring bulbs such as tulip or daffodil with a late-spring bloomer such as grape hyacinth.

Plants with unusual foliage color such as Joseph's coat anchor a bed and can provide texture as well as color.

When it comes to bed and border flower displays, styles run the gamut from very formal to relaxed and casual. Creating patterns of plantings is an art that takes some practice. Using a variety of organizing principles such as drifts, groups, and massed plantings, you can learn to create a flower display that looks organized and spontaneous at the same time.

**Borders and Beds.** Borders are typically long, rectangular flower beds, often in front of a stone wall, beside a driveway or path, or alongside a house.

The traditional English border discards all rigid boundaries yet retains structure and form. Natural- and undulating-style borders are even more free-flowing. Island beds are usually irregular shapes with few straight lines, though some are circles, ovals, or squares. Islands look best and make for easier care when they are approximately six feet (1.8 m) wide and less than twelve feet (3.7 m) long.

**Arranging Plants.** Your taste and the style of flower bed you are trying to create will influence your choice of plants.

When selecting plants for a mixed-group border, remember that the best-looking plantings are built around a theme such as color, texture, form, or size. For instance, tall flowers with similar growth habits and colors, like larkspur and lupine, are excellent garden companions.

Massed plantings of flowers all of the same color such as tulips and ranunculus make a stunning bed. Plant an island of red roses in the center of a lawn.

Drifts—sinuous rows and arcs of flowers—are another versatile design. Arrange groupings of five or more plants of the same type. Take into consideration color, texture, and size. A drift of purple, yellow, and white foxglove offsets one of purple, yellow, and white snapdragons, and complements a drift of white and yellow mums.

# Casual and Formal Beds

Casual beds have sinuous lines, varied heights, and irregular borders, and the plants within them blend in V's or arcs. Formal beds are divided into regular geometric patterns, and their plants are set in straight lines or regular shapes. Either design is easy to install in your garden.

Choose flowers with similar bloom periods, have varying heights and widths, and whose hues are coordinates on an artist's color wheel—either paired primary colors and their complements or trios of adjacent pastels. The complementary and adjacent colors generally work best in casual beds, while contrasting colors are the right choice for formal beds.

You will need a measuring tape, a spray can of marking paint or flour, a trowel, and a hose or watering can, plus the plants you've selected.

Allow two to three hours to plant either a casual bed, shown at right, or a formal bed, described below.

## Casual Shape

**1** Mark out a kidney-shaped casual bed, and fill its interior with U-, V-, S-, and W-shaped drifts of plants. Draw alternating V-shaped wedges in the bed with flour or marker paint. Choose a tall species such as 'Sonnet Mix' snapdragons of crimson, pink, and yellow to make two arcs dividing the bed roughly into thirds.

**2** Plant each wedge with alternate colors to complete the bed. Here, 'Midnight Madness', 'Ultra Burgundy', and 'Ultra White' petunias, respectively in blue, purple, and white, are used to fill the V's of the casual design.

## Formal Shape

**1** Formal beds rely on divided geometric shapes. Mark out a circular bed 6' (1.8 m) in diameter. Mark two of its diagonals at right angles, and set a smaller circle inside it, 2' (60 cm) in diameter.

**2** Plant contrasting or complementary colors in opposite quadrants of the outside circle, such as 'Cooler Grape' and 'Pacifica Apricot' vincas. Plant a taller flower in the center. Here, the tall center was planted using 'Peter Pan Plum' zinnia.

# Single-Species Mass Plantings

Make floral patterns and quilts of color with a mass planting using dozens of flowers all from the same species such as viola. Use varied color in a field of uniform texture and height to create geometric forms that please your eye.

A mass planting is easy to grow. Prepare the bed the same way as for planting nursery starts [see Transplanting Nursery Containers, pg. 101]. You will need a pair of gloves, a spoon, flour, and a hand trowel, plus your plants.

Allow an hour to prepare the soil, a minute or two to mark each planting location, and another minute or two to plant each flower. Follow the steps shown for a striking, mass-flower display.

**1** Choose the species you will plant and refer to the care tag to obtain the needed spacing. Measure, then use flour to mark each planting spot within the bed. Spacing plants properly is key to having a healthy bed with lots of flowers in it.

**2** Set out your plants, working from back to front of a border, or middle to outside of a bed. Plant rear and center areas while they are still easy to access. Plant a reserve area near the back of the bed with a few extra plants set at closer-than-recommended spacings. Water and keep the bed evenly moist until new growth appears.

**3** Water regularly according to the needs of the species planted. Allow the bed to grow in, fertilizing every few weeks when you water. If some plants fail, transplant healthy ones to replace them from the reserve area. When the entire bed is full and thriving, thin any remaining extras in the reserve area.

# Mixed-Species Groups

The most common alternative to beds of a single flower species calls for mixing species when planting. Use plants with different heights, foliage textures, flower shapes, and colors to create beds and borders that delight the eye. Choose plants that have similar needs for light, moisture, soil texture, and fertility.

Again, prepare the bed as for planting nursery starts [see Transplanting Nursery Containers, pg. 101]. You'll need a pair of gloves, flour, and a hand trowel, plus your plants.

Allow about an hour to prepare the soil, plus two to three minutes to plant each flower, following these steps.

**1** Use flour to divide the bed into irregular V-shaped sections, with the wide end of the V toward the outside and the tips near the center of the bed. Allow a corridor 6″ (15 cm) wide between each V. The bed should have an odd number of V's.

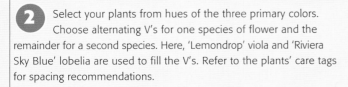

**2** Select your plants from hues of the three primary colors. Choose alternating V's for one species of flower and the remainder for a second species. Here, 'Lemondrop' viola and 'Riviera Sky Blue' lobelia are used to fill the V's. Refer to the plants' care tags for spacing recommendations.

**3** Complete the bed by planting a taller species in the median corridor between the V's. Here, 'Red Hot Sally' salvia divides the bed. To have more diversity in a larger bed, subdivide the areas and plant several different species in each.

# Flower Successions

Plant flowers that bloom from spring to autumn to keep your beds brimming with flowers in different seasons.

First up in spring are the bearded iris. In mild-winter climates, to zone 7, they can be planted in autumn and will bloom the following season. In colder areas, plant them during spring and keep them in the ground over the winter; they'll bloom in the spring of their second year.

If you plan your garden with the seasons in mind, you can have a garden and landscape bursting with blooms throughout the year. Rather than planting a bed with one spring flower that will have its days of glory and then peter out and leave the bed barren, fill each bed with a wide variety of flowering plants that will carry you through each season. Annuals naturally have their bloom times, but even perennials and shrubs have their peak periods. Veronica, for instance, looks its best in spring, while begonias only begin to perk up in late spring and early summer. Even within a flower species you'll find that some cultivars bloom earlier than others. Clematis is one good example.

The exact time of bloom for each species of flower varies by climate, light conditions, and region. Those in the Midwest and Northeast, for example, may have heat that lasts late into the summer and is followed by first frosts. Such conditions limit autumn plantings of annuals such as sweet pea because their growth is retarded by the heat and they fail to set flowers before frost kills them. Consult the staff of your garden center or nursery for advice on hardiness and planting for blooms at specific times.

## Spring Flower Display

Many flowers bloom in the bright sunshine and fair days of spring. Some flowers such as crocus and *Iris reticulata* peek out even as winter still lurks, while others begin to bloom just as summer heats up. Spring bloomers are particularly abundant and include many other spring bulbs and all of the following:

Astilbe (*Astilbe* spp.)
Avens (*Geum* spp.)
Bleeding-heart (*Dicentra* spp.)
Carpet bugleweed (*Ajuga reptans*)
Globe candytuft (*Iberis umbellata*)
Columbine (*Aquilegia* spp.)
Coralbell (*Heuchera sanguinea*)
Cornflower (*Centaurea cyanus*)
Crocus (*Crocus* spp.)
Daffodils (*Narcissus* spp.)
Daphne (*Daphne* spp.)
Firethorn (*Pyracantha* spp.)
Fringecups (*Tellima grandiflora*)
White gaura (*Gaura lindheimeri*)
Honeysuckle (*Lonicera* spp.)
Wood hyacinth (*Hyacinthoides* spp.)
Lenten rose (*Helleborus orientalis*)
Love-in-a-mist (*Nigella damascena*)
Lupine (*Lupinus* spp.)
Mountain laurel (*Kalmia latifolia*)
Pinks (*Dianthus* spp.)
Pot marigold (*Calendula officinalis*)
Photinia (*Photinia* spp.)
Poppy (*Papaver* spp.)
Primrose (*Primula* spp.)
Satin flower (*Clarkia amoena*)
Swan River daisy (*Brachyscome iberidifolia*)
Ornamental strawberry (*Duchesnea indica*)
Tulip (*Tulipa* spp.)
Windflower (*Anemone* spp.)
Wintersweet (*Chimonanthus praecox*)

## Summer Flower Display

When spring fades and the flowers of more delicate plants finish, those that bask in the sun's glory begin to bloom in full force. Among the many species of summer-blooming flowers are the following:

Glossy abelia (*Abelia × grandiflora*)
Globe amaranth (*Gomphrena globosa*)
Angel's-trumpet (*Brugmansia × candida*)
China aster (*Callistephus chinensis*)
Astilbe (*Astilbe* spp.)
Avens (*Geum* spp.)
Annual baby's-breath (*Gypsophila elegans*)
Balsam (*Impatiens walleriana*)
Beautyberry (*Callicarpa bodinieri*)
Bleeding-heart (*Dicentra* spp.)
Bugloss (*Anchusa* spp.)
Calliopsis (*Coreopsis tinctoria*)
Globe candytuft (*Iberis umbellata*)
Carpet bugleweed (*Ajuga reptans*)
Cornflower (*Centaurea cyanus*)
Swan River daisy (*Brachyscome iberidifolia*)
Daylily (*Hemerocallis* spp.)
White gaura (*Gaura lindheimeri*)
Gladiolus (*Gladiolus* spp.)
Goatsbeard (*Aruncus dioicus*)
Heliotrope (*Heliotropium arborescens*)
Hollyhock (*Alcea rosea*)
Hydrangea (*Hydrangea* spp.)
Joe-Pye weed (*Eupatorium purpureum*)
Lavender (*Lavandula* spp.)
Marigold (*Tagetes* spp.)
Pot marigold (*Calendula officinalis*)
Milkweed (*Asclepias tuberosa*)
Million bells (*Calibrachoa* spp.)
Morning glory (*Ipomoea* spp.)
Moss rose (*Portulaca grandiflora*)
Myrtle (*Vinca* spp.)
Photinia (*Photinia* spp.)
Snapdragon (*Antirrhinum majus*)
Speedwell (*Veronica* spp.)
Spider flower (*Cleome hasslerana*)
Globe thistle (*Echinops* spp.)
Tickseed (*Coreopsis* spp.)
Trumpet vine (*Campsis radicans*)
Verbena (*Verbena* spp.)

Yarrow (*Achillea* spp.)
Zinnia (*Zinnia* spp.)

## Autumn Flower Display

Certain flowers light up the garden in the cool, shorter days of autumn. These include:

Glossy abelia (*Abelia × grandiflora*)
Daphne (*Daphne* spp.)
Globe amaranth (*Gomphrena globosa*)
Japanese anemone (*Anemone* spp.)
Angel's-trumpet (*Brugmansia × candida*)
Aster (*Aster* spp.)
Bugloss (*Anchusa* spp.)
Calliopsis (*Coreopsis tinctoria*)
Chrysanthemum (*Chrysanthemum* spp.)
White gaura (*Gaura lindheimeri*)
Hydrangea (*Hydrangea* spp.)
Marigold (*Tagetes* spp.)
Mexican bush sage (*Salvia leucantha*)
Nerine (*Nerine* spp.)
Sweet pea (*Lathyrus odoratus*)
Sweet pepperbush (*Clethra alnifolia*)
Globe thistle (*Echinops* spp.)
Winter daffodil (*Sternbergia lutea*)
Zinnia (*Zinnia* spp.)

By midsummer, spikes of gladioli provide a new round of color. Of the bearded iris, only its foliage remains. Hidden between both are the straplike leaves of nerine.

In autumn, star-shaped nerine bursts onto the scene with colorful clusters on wiry stalks.

# Planning for Flower Successions

Good planning and plant selection is the key to having flowers bloom throughout the garden season.

A glorious spring bulb display is the starting point for seasons of flowers. Choose each plant according to its bloom cycle to keep beds colorful from spring to autumn.

You can have new blooms popping up just as old flowers are fading away if you think in terms of phases of bloom—not just the seasons.

There are six to eight blooming periods during the year, depending on where you live, and you'll find plants that fit into each one. You can have nearly continuous flowers when you choose plants that

bloom at the various stages of the year: late winter to early spring, early to mid-spring, mid- to late spring, early to mid-summer, and so forth. Of course, some flowers you choose will bloom simultaneously. Spread their color around by placing these plants in various areas of the yard. Others—many roses, for instance—are repeat bloomers with flushes of new flowers every four to six weeks.

**Variety.** Have a succession of blooms by planting a wide variety of flowers. Many shrubs and vines offer long periods of color. Use them to fill in blanks in left by perennials and bulbs that have finished their bloom. They will create a permanent display; your garden's surroundings change during the season but the seasonal color will return every year. Also use annuals as fillers to perk up beds that are between color. You can count on them for future seasons of easy blooms if they are good reseeders.

## Color in Winter

Plants such as the aptly named fragrant wintersweet have winter flowers. If you want to add winter color to your garden, preview plants by taking a trip to local public gardens and nurseries while they're in bloom. Once you have chosen and planted them, provide shelter from extreme temperatures, wind, rain, and snow.

### TULIPS

No one knows for sure where the tulip originated. Tulips are found in the wild in North Africa, southern Italy, southern France, Turkey, China, Japan, and Korea. Somehow, the bulb managed to make its way under the ground across mountain ranges and barren deserts.

**Make Records.** Keeping good notes goes a long way in helping to plan future gardens. Record where you bought plants and seed and where you planted them. Each month, note what is flowering, including what is just beginning to flower, what is in full bloom, and what is beginning to fade. This record will help you identify areas where you need more flowers. Also keep track of such things as pest or disease problems or unusual weather.

Bulbs are one good choice for building flower successions. They bloom reliably during distinct seasons. Varied species can be layered at different depths. Best of all, you plant them at the same time.

Another good succession option is annual flowers. Like many bulbs, they can all be planted at once for bloom in different seasons. Plant annuals with perennials and flowering shrubs for a colorful bed from spring to autumn.

You'll need garden gloves, a shovel, rake, surveyor's tape, and a bulb planter, or, for annual and perennial flowers, a hand trowel. You will also need these materials: your plants and an organic starter fertilizer such as 2–5–5.

Prepare the bed as you would for transplants of nursery starts [See Transplanting Nursery Containers, pg. 101]. Work the soil at least 16" (40 cm) deep to loosen it and amend it to correct any drainage or pH deficiencies [see Soil and Drainage, pg. 98].

Check with the staff of your garden center or nursery for the ideal planting times for the plants you select.

Allow two to three hours for the project. Follow these steps to install a bulb garden with successive blooms in three different seasons.

**1** Plant the entire bed in the prior season with a spring-blooming species, such as bearded iris. Here, irises were planted the previous spring. The bed also holds lavender and speedwell, two plants with long blooming seasons, to provide color between the bulbs' blooming seasons. When the soil warms in spring, mark new ovals with two colors of surveyor's tape, overlapping the areas' margins.

**2** Plant the areas marked by one color of tape with a midseason blooming species such as gladiolus. These summer-blooming corms will send up their greenery while the iris is blooming in spring, then will flower after the iris fade.

**3** Plant the remaining areas with one of the late-season blooming species such as nerine or autumn crocus. Like gladiolus, they will send up stalks in spring, but their leaves will die back well before they bloom in early autumn. Their dying leaves will be masked by the iris and gladiolus foliage. Wiry flower stalks will appear with large clusters of graceful, pink, star-shaped flowers.

# Flowers for Container Gardens

Grow flowers in unique containers with character to light up corners of your patio, courtyard, or deck.

Dress up entry paths with containers of bright flowers.

Many flowering plants, including most annuals, many perennials, and a surprising number of shrubs, vines, and even small flowering trees, grow well in containers. Spring or summer bulbs do very well in pots, as do ornamental grasses. And in many climates, cacti and succulents often thrive in pots.

**Advantages.** Gardening in containers may seem limited in scope, but it actually gives you a lot of leeway. One benefit is the control you have over the soil mix. True, garden soil can be amended, but you can completely change the soil in a container to meet the needs of each particular plant. If you're growing succulents, provide them with a sandy loam.

Grooming a gardenia? Give it a rich, acidic mix that will ensure a profusion of blooms.

Containers are also portable. Move plants to shadier locations if conditions become too hot and sunny in the summer months. Likewise, relocate tender container plants to a protected environment when temperatures dip in winter, and adjust the amount of light your plants receive by moving their pots into and out of the sun or shade.

Antique toys remain fun filled and precious when they have been converted to planters. Remember to give them new holes that will allow the soil to drain after watering.

**Styles.** Pots are available in myriad shapes, sizes, and materials. You'll find everything from lightweight concrete to glazed ceramic, plastic, wood, fiberglass, terra cotta, and metal. Use containers to coordinate colors. Select pots that complement your home's style and exterior colors. Use just about any container that has adequate room for the plant roots and good drainage—or widen the existing holes or add new ones with a drill.

## Drip for Containers

Add drip irrigation to your containers to avoid watering by hand. It is easy to install a drip irrigation system [see Adding Drip Irrigation, pg. 95]. All you will need is a battery-operated timer valve attached to your hose bib faucet, drip tubing, and drip emitter fixtures, which are available with a range of dispersal patterns. Emitters drip, bubble, or spray water at various rates.

Use fast emitters to release water to large container plants and slow ones for smaller plants. Hide the flexible tubing by running it along a fence, wall, patio, or underneath a deck.

Simple treatment will prepare nearly any container for planting. First, check its drain holes. Two or more should be located on the outside base of the pot rather than underneath. Enlarge or install more drain holes as needed. Next, sterilize porous containers by soaking them in a solution of household bleach and water. Wash them with detergent and allow them to dry. These steps prevent fungal spores and bacteria from infecting your plants and are essential for any containers you reuse. Finally, waterproof porous containers. This blocks water with mineral salts from leaching through them and accumulating on their outsides.

Allow two to three hours to prepare your containers by following these steps.

> **WARNING**
> Household bleach causes skin and eye irritation and bleaches fabrics. Protect your hands and clothes by wearing gloves and a smock or apron.

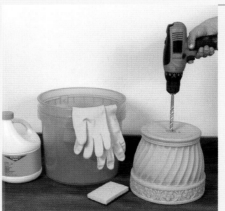

**1** Inspect drain holes. If they are less than ½" (12 mm) wide or you wish to improve a pot's drainage, use an electric drill with a masonry bit to enlarge existing drain holes and drill new ones. Bore through masking tape to prevent shards and cracking on ceramic and terra-cotta containers.

**2** Sterilize containers made of porous wood, terra cotta, or ceramic by immersing them for an hour in a bucket filled with 2 gal. (7.6 l) of water and 2 oz. (60 ml) of household bleach.

**3** Rinse all containers thoroughly in clean water, wash with detergent, then rinse again until they are clean. Allow them to dry completely.

**4** Apply non-toxic latex waterproofing compound with a paintbrush to waterproof the inside surfaces of porous containers. Pour out any excess compound, and allow the containers to dry completely before using them for plants.

# Planting a Container

Potting container plants is a simple task once your containers are ready to plant [see Preparing Containers for Planting, pg. 115].

Ensure your plants have good drainage by taking measures to keep their drains from clogging. Traditionally, drain holes were blocked with pebbles or broken pottery shards. Today, many gardeners prefer the nylon mesh netting used to keep gutters clear of debris. The mesh, covered with porous landscape fabric that contains the rootball, makes an airspace between the soil and the drain hole. When you irrigate, the water runs freely from the pot without carrying away any of the soil.

Tools you'll need include a pair of garden shears and a hand trowel. It's easiest to work on a raised surface such as a potting table. For materials, gather nylon mesh, porous landscape fabric, potting soil, and your plants.

Allow 30 minutes to pot a plant. Follow these easy steps.

**1** Protect the container's drain holes with nylon mesh. Line the bottom and sides of the container with porous landscape fabric to keep soil or roots from blocking drains.

**2** Partially fill the container with potting soil mixed with organic compost, tamping it firm. Use enough soil to position the top of the plant's rootball so that it sits 1" (25 mm) below the container's rim.

**3** Press on the sides of the nursery container, invert the plant carefully over your open hand while supporting it. Tap the bottom of the container until the plant slides out into your hand. Cut through or unwind any entwined roots. For plants in peat pots, tear down the sides of the peat pot below the soil surface in the pot.

**4** Center the plant in the container or set it relative to other plants in the container. Fill around the plant with soil, pressing it firm. Water the plant thoroughly. Keep it evenly moist until its new foliage emerges, then water the plant using the recommendation for the specific species.

Forcing is a technique you can use to have fresh bulbs in bloom throughout every season of the year, even in winter. Virtually all bulb plants have periods of dormancy followed by new growth and bloom. Keep your spring bulbs dormant by storing them at 40°–45°F (4°–7°C) for up to eight months. They'll reward you with beautiful blooms when you remove them from storage for planting.

You will need a paper bag, nylon mesh, porous landscape fabric, potting soil, and your bulbs.

Allow about 30 minutes to plant a container, two to three weeks for sprouts to form, and one to two weeks for the bulbs to bloom. Follow these steps.

**1** Bulbs suitable for forcing are available in autumn at garden centers and nurseries. Keep bulbs dormant by storing them loosely in a breathable paper bag placed in the vegetable keeper of a household refrigerator for at least 6–8 weeks prior to planting. Store bulbs away from ripe fruit, including apples and bananas. Remove them as needed after that.

**2** Protect the drain holes from clogging with plastic mesh covered by porous landscape fabric to promote evenly moist soil with good drainage.

**3** Fill 3"–4" (75–100 mm) of the container with potting soil. Crowd the bulbs upright into the container with their flat sides—if any—facing outward. Press them gently downward into the soil to hold them in place. If bulbs lack clear tops and bottoms, lay them on their sides.

**4** Fill the space around the bulbs with additional soil. Raise the container on pot feet. Water thoroughly to settle the soil, adding more soil as necessary. Install optional decorator accents. Place the container in a dark, cool spot and keep moist until sprouts form, then bring it into a warm, full-sun location. In 7–14 days, the bulbs will bloom.

# Planters for Hangers and Walls

## Add flowering color to fill the vertical spaces in your garden.

Hanging plants make a big impact even though they are small compared to other landscaping elements in your garden. Hanging plants add flair to your yard and triple or even quadruple your gardening space. They soften the appearance of a wall, block an unwanted view, filter harsh sunlight, provide privacy, and add vertical dimension to the garden. You invite the eye upward and create interest and contrast by hanging plants that cascade from above and trail down walls.

**Options.** You will find several types of hanging planters. Wire baskets can be lined with moss and planted. Some plastic and wooden containers have holes or hooks in the rim and a hanger, while other containers can easily be adapted for hanging. Log-cabin baskets suit trailing fuchsias and geraniums. Hang containers flush-mounted on a wall, set them in the crotches of a tree, or attach them to posts.

**Installing.** Hanging baskets are especially heavy after watering. Anchor stable hooks for them into a sturdy support such as the beam of a covered porch or an overhanging roof, or to the frame of a deck, wall, or door. Thick, sturdy tree limbs also work well to hang containers. Protect trees from chafing damage with a flat bridle made of rubber, use quality fasteners, and attach the hanger to them with a sturdy chain or heavy cord. Also choose the location carefully. Avoid areas where the container would be easily bumped. Hang planters above areas safe from splatters each time you water them. Match each container to your desired space to fit the location and please the eye. As a basket fills with plants, it will also grow in weight.

**Plants.** The best bets for hanging plants are those with trailing and drooping foliage. Good choices include alyssum, bacopa, fuchsia, ivy geranium, wax-flower (*Hoya* spp.), johnny-jump-up, lobelia, million bells, nasturtium, orange clock vine (*Thunbergia gregorii*), verbena, and viola.

**Care.** Hanging baskets need special care, including regular watering, fertilizing, and pruning. Baskets that are open on all sides—especially those made with potting soil inside a coconut fiber or sphagnum moss shell—dry out quickly. You may need to check them often and water daily in hot weather.

Promote thick, rich growth by feeding hanging containers every two weeks with a balanced, organic fertilizer such as 10–10–10.

Prune as often as needed. Prevent leggy plants by pinching back foliage to stimulate new, fuller growth. Trim off unhealthy leaves; they rob the plant of energy and detract from its beauty. Prune stems or branches just above a leaf or leaf node to get new growth and flowers starting at that point.

Make the walls and ceilings of your landscape more beautiful with hanging baskets or an arrangement of containers mounted to a wall.

# Planting Hanging Baskets

Use special techniques to plant hanging baskets made of wire frames lined with sphagnum moss. Such baskets will hold moisture better if they are partially lined with plastic rather than moss. Plants that seem to grow through the sides of these baskets actually grow through slits in the waterproof liner material.

Hang the finished basket from the eaves of your home, beneath an arbor or lattice frame, or from the branches of a tree.

You will need a wire frame with its hanging hardware, a dust mask, a pair of rubber gloves, and scissors.

For materials, gather dry sphagnum moss, potting soil, and your plants.

Allow an hour to plant each hanging basket. Follow these easy steps:

**1** Dampen sphagnum moss and use it to line a wire hanging frame. Press it firmly into the spaces between the wires, filling them completely.

**2** Line the partly filled frame with sheet plastic as a moisture barrier. Cut it to shape, position it, and punch drain holes in its center. Hide its edges under the moss.

**3** Cut slits in the plastic at each planting location to insert plant roots through the hanging basket's sides. Thread the roots through the plastic and the sphagnum moss to the basket's open interior.

**4** Fill the frame's center with potting soil. Firm it around the roots by pressing it down with your open palms.

**5** Open planting holes in the soil with your fingers. Place trailing plants at the rim and taller ones in the center. Water thoroughly after planting and keep evenly moist until new growth appears, then water when the soil becomes dry.

# Flowering Bonsai

## Create a garden in miniature with its roots in Asia.

A contorted flowering bonsai can grow outdoors for most months, then be moved indoors at the peak of its bloom.

Bonsai plants—carefully trained dwarfed trees or shrubs in small containers—are idealized mimicries of natural scenes. Growing bonsai combines the skills of both the artist and the horticulturist.

Although bonsai is usually linked with Japan and the term is Japanese, historians believe that the craft originated in China and that the Japanese adopted the art form in the 8th century A.D. Over the centuries, bonsai has been enjoyed by millions of gardeners.

**Plants.** Many bonsai are trees and shrubs; some flower. Flowering bonsai plants include a number of rhododendrons and azaleas such as *R. indicum, Camellia sasanqua*, crab apple (*Malus cerasifera*), flowering cherry (*Prunus serrulata*), *Gardenia augusta* 'Radicans' Japanese flowering apricot (*Prunus mume*), *Pyracantha angustifolia*, tree of a thousand stars (*Serissa foetida*), and wisteria.

**Planting and Care.** Prune back all the extra limbs on your bonsai plant at planting time. Plant as for a nursery transplant [see Transplanting Nursery Containers, pg. 101].

Allow the bonsai to grow until winter, when you will prune the plant for the first time. Bend and shape its branches into a pleasing form while they are pliable —usually the following spring or summer for deciduous plants and autumn or winter for evergreens— and twist wires around them to bind them into place. When the branches' shape has set in a year or two, you can remove their training wire.

Proper watering, fertilizing, and light conditions are important. Use rainwater, distilled water, or reverse -osmosis water—water filtered and forced through porous membranes to remove most of its minerals. Water when the soil surface dries.

Fertilize during waterings with a liquid plant food diluted to one-quarter the manufacturer's suggested strength every four to six weeks.

Grow bonsai in sites with six hours or more of bright, indirect light, such as a north-facing window.

Prune both top growth and roots regularly. Root pruning keeps the plant small and molds it to your desired shape. Gently invert the pot while supporting the plant with your open palm on the soil surface, then use a hose to wash away one to two inches (25 to 50 mm) of soil from the roots. Cut away any entwined or encircling roots that grew inside the old pot. Repot the plant in a slightly larger container using fresh potting soil.

## Flowering Topiary

You can make topiaries—decorative shapes fashioned out of plants—with flowering vines. Choose geometric shapes, hearts, or a menagerie of available animal shapes such as giraffes, bears, and swans. Grow vines such as black-eyed Susan vine, clematis, pink jasmine, morning glory, and blue potato bush (*Solanum rantonnetii*) on wire or woven-wood forms. Shape and train the tendrils as they grow, weaving them into and around the form, pinching foliage, and removing wayward shoots until they form flower buds. Water and fertilize them regularly.

# Structural Planters and Terraced Gardens

Treat large landscape containers as you would their smaller cousins—pots and planters.

Structural planters and terraced gardens both provide an excellent home for flowers. Because they hold a great deal of soil, almost any kind of flowering plant grows well in them. And both are elevated, which gives you the opportunity to create impact with trailing plants. If you have a yard with a hillside, consider a terraced garden. You can control erosion and find extra planting room by building a series of wide, steplike planting beds.

In many ways, structural planters are similar to regular containers but are better because the amount of space they have for root growth is limited only by their size.

**Plants.** Depending on the size of your planter and its location, you can grow a wide variety of plants.

For structural planters that measure at least two by two feet (60 by 60 cm), choose from a variety of shrubs to use as background material. Daphne, genista, lilac, and roses all do well. In front of the shrubs, add annuals or perennial flowers, selecting from alstroemeria, aster, baby's breath, flax, ground morning glory (*Convolvulus sabatius*), lavender, marigold, and phlox. At the front edge of the planter, plant a pendulous or trailing flower such as sweet alyssum, bacopa, ivy geranium, love-in-a-puff, love-lies-bleeding, or lobelia.

For terraces, create repeated and layered plantings. In the top bed, for example, plant a sea of yellow marigolds; in the next, a bed full of draping purple verbena or lantana; repeat the pattern to the bottom of the hill. For a layered planting from terrace to terrace, plant large flowering plants such as small specimen trees and shrubs in the topmost terrace. Plant successively smaller plants as you descend, working your way down the hillside. Choose small flowering shrubs for the second terrace, tall perennials for the third, and short annuals and trailing vines for the fourth.

**Care.** Like small containers, terraced gardens and structural planters overheat and dry out more quickly than flat gardens. Careful nutrition is also critical. Keep plants blooming with frequent feedings and by keeping the soil evenly moist.

Plant exuberant groups of mounding and trailing flowers on a retaining wall next to a driveway for a riot of color.

Treat low raised beds along the edge of your yard as a traditional flower border. Their height makes them easy to view, and also simplifies planting and routine care.

# caring for flowers

LIKE MANY THINGS OF BEAUTY, FLOWERS REQUIRE REGULAR CARE TO REMAIN IN TOP FORM. Once you plant them, you'll need to look after them. Learn to recognize when they need watering and provide the amount they require to stay in top form. Apply mulch to keep their soil moist, to insulate them from sudden temperature changes, and block weed seeds from sprouting. Cultivate and fertilize throughout cycles of active growth and provide tall plants with support for their stalks and blooms. Besides these basic care steps, you'll also thin and pinch to direct their growth and control pests and diseases.

Make frequent maintenance a priority. Spend a few minutes a day weeding and checking plants for pests; it's more effective than a marathon session every few weeks. If you perform each of these tasks regularly, your flowers will thrive. Pinch spent blooms frequently, for instance, and they will reward you with a plethora of blooms over many months. If you feed plants with high-quality organic fertilizer, they will remain healthy and fit, able to withstand occasional onslaughts by insect pests or infections caused by fungal diseases. Spread a thick layer of easily decomposed mulch in the spring after you cultivate and fertilize your flower beds' soil. You will have a lush supply of blooms all spring, throughout the summer, and into the autumn.

Think of garden maintenance as a series of steps to a beautiful garden and as part of enjoying its beauty. Caring for your flowers will give you many delightful hours in your garden. Lifting and dividing bulbs in spring after their flowers fade, an act that may sometimes seem tedious, more than repays any expenditures of time and energy with a glorious display of blooms the following spring.

Note that garden care is a constant. If you plan to be away for more than a few days, ask someone to tend to your flowers while you're gone.

123

# Early Care

## The most important days for your flowers are those that follow shortly after you plant them in the garden.

Care during the first week or two after planting will likely determine the success of your garden. During this period, a plant establishes its roots and begins true growth beyond the stored nutrients of its seed or, for transplants, its potting soil. A missed watering at this time permanently stunt or even cause a delicate plant to give up entirely.

Use temporary row covers to keep frost from harming young, tender plants. Place them so their sides and top are free of foliage and allow for good air circulation.

**Inspect Frequently.** Be sure to check new transplants daily for signs of stress—telltale symptoms include wilt, yellowing, and dying buds. Also look for signs of pests and diseases. Slugs, snails, and caterpillars eat obvious holes in the leaves, and aphids and leaf miners infest the surface and underside of leaves. Also inspect for blooms of fungal spores such as powdery mildew and rust or the browning of shoots near their contact with the soil, a first symptom of some fungal diseases.

Even after flowering plants are established, keep a close eye on them until they begin growing vigorously. Check them daily and note if new leaves are developing and if blooms are forming. If plants grow slowly or lack blooms, you may have to move them to a different location with more or less moisture, or adjust your watering schedule.

**Water Regularly.** Water your flowers immediately after planting them, and keep the soil evenly moist until the roots have a chance to establish themselves, at least seven to ten days . You'll know they're established when you see new growth from leaves and flower buds. From that time on, you can provide regular waterings as recommended for the species of flower. For most flowering plants, it's best to hold off watering again until the soil surface dries and you have checked the subsurface soil for moisture.

**Protect from Heat and Cold.** Protect young transplants from excessive sun exposure, especially in hot climates during the summer months, and shelter them from unseasonable cold or frost (see Unseasonable Weather, below left). Harden off new seedlings—slowly adapt them to outdoor weather conditions—if they have been grown in warm, indoor locations and are transplanted while temperatures outside are still cool. Expose your plants to the elements for a few hours every day but move them back indoors at nightfall, gradually increasing their time outdoors until they are fully accustomed to the conditions of their new home and its fluctuations in temperature. They'll make the transition to your garden with a minimum of shock.

## Unseasonable Weather

Flowers often suffer when Mother Nature is fickle. In areas such as continental Canada, the intermountain West, the Midwest, and the Northeast, for example, mild spring weather often brings out flowers. But every few years, a freak snowstorm buries the new blooms. Take steps during early spring to ensure that your flowers make it into the warm months. Use row covers or freezer cloth—specially designed and lightweight, translucent, breathable landscape fabrics—to protect tender sprouts from the elements. Support covers on stakes or metal hoops to keep them elevated over the plants.

# Mulches and Mulching

Beneficial, practical, and beautifying, mulches finish your garden, help flowers grow, and even prevent weeds.

Few gardening tasks are as simple and beneficial as mulching. Mulches such as shredded bark chips, salt hay, and peat moss also prevent water runoff, keep soil moist longer, discourage weeds, prevent erosion, protect fallen fruit from bruising, and keep your garden looking tidy.

**Benefits.** Spread organic or inorganic material over the soil around plants to temper the effects of temperature fluctuations. Quick and extreme changes in temperature stress plants, but mulch acts as an insulator by preventing the soil from heating and cooling as quickly as the outside air. If the mulch you use is organic, it will improve the soil and release nutrients as it breaks down. Mulching saves lots of water. According to many experts, you can reduce watering by as much as 60 percent if you mulch. Mulch can even increase the disease resistance of plants. Recent research demonstrated that the microorganisms in an organic mulch produce enzymes and other chemicals that stimulate plants to develop resistance to some plant diseases.

Some plants such as columbine, lily, and lily-of-the valley need a combination of full sun with shaded, cool soil around their roots—conditions that mulch promotes—in order to bloom and retain their flowers. Other acid-loving plants perform best when mulched with conifer needles with high pH; as the needles decompose, they continuously acidify the soil in the bed.

**Mulch Application.** Water the area well before you mulch to lock in moisture and cut down on future irrigation. Apply mulch one to three inches (25 to 75 mm) thick; err on

the deeper end for best weed control, and remove existing weeds before mulching. Keep mulch four to five inches (10 to 12 cm) from the base of plants; excessive moisture around a plant's crown can encourage pests or foster diseases.

**Mulch Options.** You can use an organic mulch—shredded or chipped bark, cedar chips, cocoa hulls, salt hay, compost, composted lawn clippings and leaves, leaf mold, sphagnum or peat moss, marsh plants, peanut hulls, and pine needles—or an inorganic one such as carpeting, black plastic (polyethylene), clear plastic, and crushed stone or gravel. Choose a mulch material that won't decompose quickly. Avoid fresh items such as grass clippings and leaves, which can mat and prevent air from reaching plant roots. Mulches that are high in carbon and low in nitrogen such as straw, sawdust, and bark absorb nitrogen from the soil as they begin to decompose. If you use any of these items for a mulch, watch for the symptoms of nitrogen deficiency in your plants—poor, stunted growth and yellow new growth—and use high-nitrogen fertilizer if you see them.

Complete your garden masterpiece by adding mulch, which insulates the soil and absorbs or holds both rain and irrigation water.

Apply a generous amount of mulch around your plants; always remove existing weeds before mulching.

# Watering Flowers

## Recognize the symptoms of over- and underwatering and adjust your irrigation to your plants' needs.

Proper watering is important to the health of your flower garden. Incorrect watering can cause wilting, collapse, even drowning. Some plants tolerate a bit of neglect in their watering, but others react quickly and overwhelmingly to interruptions in irrigation.

Shower your plants with water in the morning to allow them to dry as the day grows warmer.

**Over- and Underwatering.** Signs of over- and underwatering are often similar. Either can lead to leaf droop and drop, yellowing, and stunted growth overall. Underwatering causes the leaf cell structure to collapse, while too much water can cause fungal infection of the roots, or root rot. When root rot sets in, the plant is unable to take up water and its leaves wilt. The symptoms are remarkably similar to those seen in underwatered plants.

**When to Water.** Water your garden properly. Soil conditions vary from day to day and season to season. Set the amount and frequency of application according to the condition of the soil instead of following a routine schedule or judging the degree of wetness as you water. The soil's surface can look wet even when the soil underneath is still dry. The secret is to provide water when your plants need it, rather than according to your own timetable. Test the moisture level by inserting your finger or digging with a trowel about two to six inches (50 to 150 mm) into the soil near a plant's base. Water only when this subsurface soil has dried or is beginning to dry. For new plantings, the depth of this layer of dry surface soil should be less than one-half inch (12 mm); for established annual flowers, less than two to four inches (50 to 100 mm); for flowering shrubs, less than four to six inches (10 to 15 cm). You can also test the soil with a moisture meter with a metal probe that you insert into the soil. It will tell you if the soil beneath the surface is damp, dry, or wet. Exercise caution; moisture meters are sometimes unreliable in alkaline soils that are high in salts.

Water according to your particular soil type as well. If your soil is clayey and resists water penetration, water it slowly and deeply. Apply a small amount of water, wait for it to be absorbed, then water again. Drip systems are the best choice for heavy clay soils. Sandy soils are common in many areas. If your soil is sandy, irrigate frequently, because water will wash through it quickly.

# Proper Watering Methods

Most landscape plants require watering every few days. Hand watering a large flower garden requires effort and time. Consider automatic watering systems for such landscapes. Choose the right equipment to water smaller gardens by hand. Essentials include flexible radial-rubber hoses or coil hoses—both are free of troublesome kinking—equipped with a watering wand with a diffusing nozzle for easy reach, a watering can with a large rose on its spout to break the stream of water into gentle sprinkles, and a soaker hose.

## Hanging Containers

Water hanging containers with a watering wand. Apply liquid until it runs freely from the container, wait for it to stop draining, then repeat.

## In-ground

Water flowering plants by hand with a watering can with a diffusing rose on its spout or a hose fitted with a watering wand or diffusing spray nozzle. Apply liquid directly to the soil beneath the plants' outer edges of foliage, away from plant centers. Keep their trunks or stems, leaves, and flowers dry.

## Automatic

Water permanent plantings with soaker hose or drip irrigation. Both dispense water slowly at the base of each plant, conserving water and withholding it from weeds that can sprout and grow in nearby areas.

# Fertilizing Flowers

## Flowering plants need nutrition throughout every stage of active growth.

Flowering plants need food to start and continue blooming. Fertilizers provide healthy plants with nutrients that keep them healthy and vigorous. Many gardeners now opt for organic fertilizers. They cite two main reasons:

1. Organics have lower amounts of nutrients overall, release them over a more gradual time period, and are unlikely to burn plant roots compared with chemical fertilizers which can burn if applied incorrectly.

2. They feed the soil, which is important to the longevity and success of your garden.

**When to Fertilize.** Fertilize throughout the life of your flowering plants. First, apply a base fertilizer to the planting bed or pot before you plant. Next, fertilize regularly after your plants are established. Last, top-dress established flowers and shrubs with organic mulches that release their nutrients slowly over time at the beginning of the growing season and again midway through flowering [see Mulches and Mulching, pg. 125].

**How to Apply Fertilizer.** Rake any mulch away from your plants, exposing bare soil. Cultivate the soil's surface to loosen it and uproot sprouting weeds. Scatter granular pellets or spray liquid fertilizer around the base of the plant [see Using Granular and Liquid Fertilizers, opposite pg.]. Choose and apply the right fertilizer. If you want your hydrangea to bloom in blue, for instance, feed it a fertilizer containing sequestered iron.

Always read completely and follow exactly the manufacturer's package instructions when applying fertilizers and disposing of empty containers. Reserve a watering can or a fertilizer injector device, available at most garden centers, for fertilizing.

In general, nitrogen (N) is the nutrient that is needed in the largest amounts. It is water soluble and leaches quickly from the soil. Most nitrogen-deficient plants grow slowly or become stunted, are usually pale green or yellow, have stems that become spindly, and foliage that drops. Fertilizers such as bloodmeal and fish emulsion are rich in nitrogen. Phosphorus (P) and potassium (K) bind chemically with minerals in the soil and tend to stay in place, though potassium also may be deficient in regions with heavy precipitation and acidic soils.

Feed container plants monthly or use a time-release fertilizer. For quick results, try a foliar fertilizer. Spray it directly on the stems and leaves. Its nutrients are absorbed through the foliage.

Choose a synthetic fertilizer by its content analysis rather than the name. For example, 5–5–5 is the same, whether it's called a rose food or a flower fertilizer.

# Using Granular and Liquid Fertilizers

Either solid or liquid fertilizers will deliver the nutrients your plants need to grow strong and healthy. Both are available as organics such as bloodmeal and liquid fish emulsion or man-made synthetics formulated from petroleum by-products. Organic fertilizers have many secondary nutrients and trace elements; synthetic formulations have the nutrients listed on their labels.

Always apply fertilizer on cool, calm mornings. Choose a fertilizer and follow the steps shown for that type.

Always water immediately after you apply fertilizer to dilute the fertilizer and carry it into the soil. Lightly spray your plants' foliage to wash any fertilizer dust or liquid droplets that may have been applied to them into the soil .

## Liquid Fertilizers

**1** Read and follow exactly the manufacturer's label directions when applying fertilizers. If the fertilizer is concentrated and requires dilution, carefully measure the proper amounts of fertilizer and water, mixing only the amount required.

**2** Apply the fertilizer solution. Treat the entire surface under the plant from near the stem to an imaginary line drawn to the soil under the perimeter of its outermost foliage. Avoid wetting foliage, stem, or trunk.

**3** Water every plant to further dilute the fertilizer. Watering carries it into the soil where its nutrients are absorbed by the roots. Foliage burn is unlikely with properly applied liquid organic fertilizers.

## Granular Fertilizers

**1** Read and follow exactly the manufacturer's label directions when you apply fertilizers. Apply granular fertilizer in a circle extending from 4"–6" (10–15 cm) out from the plant's stem or trunk to an imaginary line drawn to the soil under the perimeter of its outermost foliage.

**2** Using a hand fork or a cultivating tool, work the fertilizer into the soil. Return the existing mulch around the plant or apply new mulch. Leave bare soil in a circle 4" (10 cm) in diameter around each plant's stalk or trunk.

**3** Water thoroughly immediately after applying granular fertilizer to dilute the concentrated fertilizer and carry it into the soil for ready absorption by the plant and to avoid foliage burn.

# Staking and Supporting Flowers

## Trellis Supports

Use stretchy plastic plant tape available at garden centers to loosely tie tendrils, vines, and stems to a trellis or arbor. Work from the base of the plant and up its stems or canes to build support for the top-most ties. Tie the tape snugly to the support, then loop it around and retie it around the stem. Make successive ties in the same piece of tape for multiple canes rather than bunching several together. If a branch or stem has grown thick and woody, it may resist bending close to the support frame. Cinch it progressively tighter over a period of 5–10 days until it is in the right place; a single move can break it in half or where a crotch joins the trunk or main stem.

Tie freely climbing vines such as morning glories and sweet peas to strings stretched vertically down the trellis or arbor. Their tendrils will wrap around the strings and follow them upward.

## Staking

Install wire stakes or hoops for weak-stemmed plants with heavy flower heads. Set a stake next to each as it is planted, six to eight inches (15 to 20 cm) deep in the soil and at least six inches (15 cm) from the plant's center or main stem. Allow the plant to grow freely until it begins to branch, raise flower stalks, or produce heavy buds that cause it to bend or arch. Tie the plant loosely to the stake at its uppermost point and at 12-inch (30-cm) intervals.

Some stakes have built-in holders at the top, shaped like the letter G. As your plants grow past these holders, slip their stems through the narrow opening and rotate the stake to cradle the stems in the direction of their lean. Other staking systems have one, two, or three symmetrical parts that can fit together to create a stable, circular fence for very tall, wide, and heavy flowers such as dahlias.

## Thinning

Thin plants to the appropriate spacing when your sprouting seedlings have developed at least two true leaves. Many flowers grow best when their seed is planted where they will grow because they transplant poorly. Scatter seed at a density twice that of the seed package label's recommended spacing to compensate for seed lost due to poor germination, damping off, or slugs and snails.

When the seedlings begin to develop roots, they also grow their first true leaves just above the seed leaves that appeared when they sprouted. When you see these true leaves, it's time to thin. Grasp each sprout to be removed by its growth point near the soil surface. Pinch it between your thumb and forefinger and lift up to remove the plant and its roots. Use some of the sprouts to transplant to bare areas; discard the remainder in your compost pile.

## Deadheading

Pinch all spent flower heads to promote new buds and blooms. Most annuals, some perennials, and remontant shrubs such as hybrid tea roses that set progressive groups of flowers in successive flushes can stop blooming when their pollinated blooms set seed. Pinching removes these faded heads and sends a signal to the plant, prompting new growth and fresh buds to replace the flower that has been removed. In a short time, a new flower will bloom. Pinching and deadheading will extend the bloom period of most plants.

Thumbnails are the best tools for deadheading flowers; only use sharp bypass pruning shears on woody shrubs. Grasp the flower at the junction of its stem with a main branch rather than right below the bud. Pinch it between your thumbnail and index finger; discard it in your compost pile.

# Shrub Pruning

## Prune, thin, and shape for best blooms.

Do annual pruning to shape the growth of plants. Prune woody shrubs that flower on second-season wood such as camellia and many climbing roses when their blossoms fade. Prune those that flower on new wood in spring.

Prune shrubs to remove any damaged and diseased branches and to redirect growth. You can also thin a shrub to shape it into an effective screen, or in the case of the flower garden, to enhance the quality and quantity of the blooms.

**Types of Pruning.** Basically, there are two types of pruning: annual and in season. Prune annually to restore size and shape after a shrub flowers. Prune spring- and early-summer–flowering shrubs soon after their flowers fade. Late-summer and autumn bloomers flower on the new growth and should be pruned in spring. Prune seasonally to direct growth and remove diseased wood. Avoid pruning off flower buds when performing seasonal pruning and note that some plants require special handling to ensure a good bloom.

**Fit Pruning to Need.** Learn your shrub's needs before pruning. In general, there are two types of shrubs. Some flower only on new wood grown that season, while others bloom only on old wood left from the previous year. Climbing roses, for instance, are mostly pruned after blooming; the new growth of the season bears flowers the following year. Even so, there is some variation. Some clematis cultivars, for instance, flower on old wood while others flower on new growth.

**Thin.** Thin shrubs during annual pruning so that light and air can penetrate the interior of the plant. Remove branches that are dead, rubbing against other branches, crossing through the plant's center, or look out of place. Avoid cutting a plant against its natural growth pattern. Keep pruning shears and saws clean. Refrain from using pruning paint; it can seal in fungal spores and foster disease.

**In-Season Pruning.** Throughout the season, look for and remove suckers growing from the rootstock under the variety graft, which can sap the vigor of the desirable cultivar. Also remove any broken or diseased branches as soon as they are noticed.

Always prune following damage to your shrubs. Broken limbs or crushed foliage are susceptible to disease. New growth will quickly fill any sparse area created by removing damaged elements.

Keep track of the pruning you do, noting when it was completed and the next date to prune.

Most shrubs, some perennial flowers, and bunching grasses are pruned using two distinct techniques:

**Annual Pruning:** Shrubs are pruned once each year to take out dead limbs, remove limbs with poor development, open the shrubs' interiors to light, and prepare for new cycles of growth. Prune annually in early spring those flowering shrubs that bloom on new wood; prune after bloom for those that flower on old wood [see Shrub Pruning, opposite pg.]. For ornamental grasses, shear annually down to the growth buds near the base of the bunch. Follow the steps at right for annual pruning of shrubs.

**In-Season Pruning:** For a continuous show of large flowers, shape your plants and control their growth throughout the garden season by pinching extra buds before they bloom, deadheading flower heads after they fade and trimming away the bloomed-out stalks to start new ones growing. To prune in season, follow the technique shown below.

## Annual Pruning

**1** Prune shrubs with vigorous seasonal growth such as roses and butterfly bush in autumn as they become dormant. Prune shrubs less severely in cold-winter climates or wait until the spring thaws; prune them more extensively in mild-winter climates.

**2** Remove all canes or limbs that cross the center of the plant and cut away secondary branches at their junction with the main stem. Remove all spindly canes. Prune away any diseased or dead wood. Leave four or five large canes or limbs.

**3** Strip away any clinging foliage and remove it from the garden bed to eliminate pest eggs and disease spores. Rake or blow and remove fallen leaves and foliage litter from beneath the shrub.

## In-Season Pruning

**Pinching:** Pinch back extra buds for larger, showier flowers. Pinch new foliage sprouts to redirect growth, cause branching, and make plants denser and bushier.

**Deadheading:** Deadhead any spent blossoms to stop seed production and force additional flower buds to develop.

**Trimming:** Cut back flower stems to the main branch after blooms fade; On roses, cut bloomed-out stems back to the junction of the first 5-leaflet group below the flower.

# Propagating Flowers

Grow copies of your favorite flowers
to use as gifts or to expand your garden.

After a few years of gardening, you'll probably have flowers that you especially enjoy. Perhaps you'll be enchanted by their scent, a special blend of colors, or simply the long-lasting nature of their blooms. Whatever your pleasure, you can share your best plants with friends and grow new stock for your own garden. Propagating—starting new plants from old ones—is easy. Propagating is also an excellent way to preserve a plant that may be on the decline. But note that some plants are patented, so it is illegal to propagate them commercially without a license from their hybridizer. Check your plants' tags for this information.

Use these techniques to create fresh plants from hard-to-find old favorites, increase your flower garden collection inexpensively, and regenerate plants nearing the ends of their lives.

Use hot beds—soil over green manure—or a greenhouse to start bulbs in early spring.

### TERRARIUMS

Terrariums date back to 1829 when, as a child, Nathanial Ward discovered that many plants thrived in a miniature greenhouse environment. These original terrariums, known as Wardian cases, became popular during the Victorian era. They were also used to propagate new plants and transport them by sea over long distances.

revert to those of a grand-parent. They can also inherit a weakness rather than more desirable traits from their parent plants. Choose plants that will breed true, including species rather than hybrid roses, alyssums, or poppies, when you collect seed from the flowers in your garden [see Collecting Seed to Share, pg. 137].

**Preferred Methods.** Avoid cross-pollination issues by propagating asexually. Take softwood or hardwood cuttings, divide, or layer. Plants produced from these methods are true copies of their parents.

You may have to make several tries before you succeed with cuttings. Softwood cuttings of geraniums and begonias usually root readily, but those of some shrubs are less certain. Take softwood cuttings in spring, and take hardwood cuttings in autumn.

With practice, you'll succeed most of the time. Dividing roots and layering—bending a branch to the soil and pinning it there until roots form—are easily mastered skills [see Dividing and Layering Perennials, pg. 136].

Divide and repot container plants whenever they have grown too crowded, bloom sparsely, or begin to show other signs of loss of vigor.

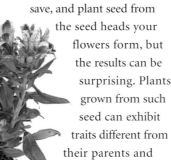

**Save Seed.** You can collect, save, and plant seed from the seed heads your flowers form, but the results can be surprising. Plants grown from such seed can exhibit traits different from their parents and

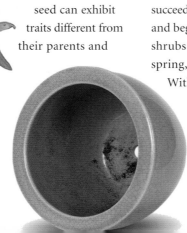

# Lifting and Dividing Bulbs

## Increasing the number of bulbs in your garden is easy; they do most of the work themselves.

Lift and divide bulbs to give your seasonal favorites necessary care as you propagate them in quantity for new plantings.

Most bulbs require a rest period with little or no water before the next season's bloom. Given too much water during this period, they can rot. If you live in a region that experiences regular rainfall in the summer, lift bulbs such as tulips and hyacinths and store them until it's time to replant them in autumn. Gardeners in cold-winter areas should dig and store tender bulbs such as dahlias and begonias before the first hard frost.

**Lifting.** Bulbs are ready to lift after they flower and their foliage dies back. Mark the location of your plantings during bloom so you can find them easily later. Remove bulbs from the ground with a spading fork and discard any bulbs you damage; open wounds might spread disease to other bulbs. Shake the soil from the bulbs and let them dry for a few days on a wire rack in a dry, warm, well-ventilated spot. Dust the bulbs with fungicide to prevent mold and store them in dry garden peat moss or cleaned, washed-and-dried sand. The best spot is one with humidity of 25 percent or less and temperatures of 45° to 50°F (7° to 10°C), such as in an unheated, attached garage during winter or a cool basement.

**Dividing.** Large bulb clumps naturally decline in vigor, especially at their centers. Divide bulbs after lifting and during dormancy to counter this and increase your stock—generally in autumn for spring bloomers and winter or early spring for summer bloomers. Use the method appropriate for each bulb type in your garden:

- True bulbs such as lilies, muscari, and narcissus produce offsets. Carefully separate the offsets from the mother bulb.
- Corms such as crocus, freesia, and watsonia produce new corms and cormels (very small corms). Divide healthy new corms from the old corms and discard the tiny cormels.
- Cut rhizomes such as iris and zantedeschia into pieces with growth points.
- Cut tubers such as begonia and cyclamen into sections with one or more growth points, or "eyes."
- Cut apart tuberous roots such as dahlia into divisions with roots, part of a stem base, and one or more growth buds.

Most bulbs produce offsets. Carefully dig the entire clump. Break off the offsets from the large bulbs, discarding those that are very small and therefore requiring several seasons to grow before bloom.

Good ventilation during storage is vital for most tunicate bulbs—those with thin, onionskin-like sheaths. Loosely pack the bulbs in a porous container set in dry peat moss or sawdust. For non-tunicate bulbs, corms, rhizomes, and tubers, dampen the peat moss or sawdust before packing and renew its moisture from time to time when it dries. Examine and discard any bulbs that have signs of decay.

Favorite plants that have grown in your landscape for a number of seasons may become crowded and bear few flowers. Give them new life with root division or layering. Dividing expands your plantings by separating the new plants from old roots. Layering grows copies of plants with trailing or vining habits by helping them produce roots.

Remember that some cultivars are patented. Their commercial propagation is illegal, though you can still reproduce them for your own personal use. Dividing and layering are two handy techniques that allow you to create additional copies of the many flowers you love.

For division, you'll need garden gloves, a sharp knife, and garden forks. Layering requires a budding knife, gloves, trowel, a U-shaped garden staple, rooting hormone, and pruning shears. For both, an elbow-high work surface such as a potting bench is an essential aid. Allow an hour to follow these steps.

## Dividing Perennials

**Rhizomes:** Divide rhizomes 6–8 weeks after flowers fade. Carefully dig them. Discard diseased, withered, or infested roots and plants. Use a sharp knife to cut each root into V-shaped sections with two growth points, cutting the foliage back to about 6″ (15 cm). Replant the rhizomes at the same depth and thoroughly water. Avoid fertilizing until new foliage forms.

**Fibrous-rooted:** Divide fibrous-rooted perennials when their centers lose vigor. Dig up the clump. Shake off clinging soil. Discard any diseased parts and the woody, old central plants. Pull the plants apart into sections, each with roots, one or more crowns, and foliage. Replant at the same depth in loosened soil. Apply a liquid fertilizer mixed at half strength.

**Large Plants:** Divide spring-blooming plants in autumn, autumn bloomers in spring. Carefully dig up the clump. Shake off clinging soil. Discard diseased parts. Force the crowns, roots, and foliage apart with two spading or hand forks set between them. Replant at the same depth in loosened soil. Apply a liquid fertilizer mixed at half strength.

## Layering Perennials

**1** Select a trailing stem with foliage rather than flowers at its tip. Bend it to the soil surface. At the point of contact, dig a hole 2″ (50 mm) deep in the soil. Nick the stem with a sharp budding knife at its junction with a leaf, or leaf axil, and dust the cut with rooting hormone.

**2** Anchor the stem in the hole with a U-shaped metal stake. Use soil to fill in the hole, covering the nicked stem. Water thoroughly and keep the buried stem evenly moist for 1–2 weeks.

**3** Carefully excavate the nicked stem to confirm that roots have grown. Use hand pruners to cut the stem between the new roots and the parent plant. Allow the new plant to grow for another 2–3 weeks, then transplant it to a new location.

Gather seed heads from your flowers to create uniquely personal gifts for your gardening friends. Harvest the seed of species known to retain their desired characteristics each generation.

To collect seed that will breed true, gather it from plants of a single species grown in isolation—a single stand of one color of California poppy, for instance—rather than from seed taken from plants of two different colors grown near each other or a mixed planting of flowers that have cross-pollinated.

Some old-fashioned flower favorites have seed with very tough seed coats, or outer shells. In the wild, tough seed coats protect the seed from being destroyed as it passes through birds' or other animals' intestinal systems. Seed from plants such as brooms (*Cytisus* spp.), lupines, and wisterias germinate poorly when planted directly in the soil. Treat the seed just before planting by rolling it between two sheets of sandpaper to nick its outer seed coat or by soaking it overnight in water to soften its coat.

For memorable gifts, combine dried or pressed flowers from your garden with personalized packets of seed.

**1** Allow flowers to set seed, wither, and dry. When they are ripe, carefully cut off the seed heads or pods. Put them in a covered, ventilated box set in a warm, dry location until they are completely dry.

**2** Crumble the seed heads in your fingers into a winnowing sieve placed over a sheet of paper—this helps you see and collect small seeds. Shake the sieve in a circular motion to separate the seeds from the chaff. Gather the seeds.

**3** Pack the collected seeds into paper envelopes. Label each envelope, then seal it in an airtight plastic bag. Store packaged seed in your refrigerator's vegetable keeper for at least 3 months, until you are ready to plant it.

# Flower Pest and Disease Control

Examine your flowers often and use organic controls to quell any infestations or infections that would mar their beauty.

Conditions that stunt or kill flowering plants and their controls: (1) use sulfur dust to control leaf spot on a hibiscus blossom that affects both foliage and flowers; (2) eliminate thrip damage to marigold leaves by washing the foliage; (3) pick or spray large beetles eating tender buds of a rose with *Bacillus thuringiensis* (BT); and (4) uproot and burn dodder before it sets seed, or solarize the bed by covering it in clear plastic during hot weather to kill the foliage and seed of this rootless parasitic plant that sucks sap from flowering plants.

Pests or diseases can become established and spread in your flower garden before you notice them. Stop garden pests and most diseases before they start by routinely inspecting your flowers. If you detect new pests and disease, you will have the best results by controlling them early on.

Examine flowers and buds for discoloration, chewed petals, or disfiguring fungal spores. Check leaf tops and undersides for stunting, yellowing, speckling, or bruised and eaten foliage. Look for powdery mildew, boring, or girdling on stems and branches. Turn mulch with a rake to see if it harbors large numbers of insects, larvae, or pill bugs. Be especially watchful in periods of cool, moist, or humid weather when fungal disease spreads quickly.

Deal with pests and diseases using safe organic methods. Generally, these are gentler and safer for the plants, you, and the environment. Once you know your foe—the specific pest or disease damaging your plants—choose the control method that is precisely right for it, starting with the least toxic approaches: hand picking, washing with water, and stripping off affected foliage. Follow by releasing beneficial predator insects such as ladybird beetles, preying mantises, and green lacewings. In most cases, using one of these methods will control the problem. If it persists or spreads despite your efforts, apply insecticidal soap, horticultural oils, or botanical insecticides such as neem oil or pyrethrin directly to the pest or affected foliage. Again, select a control that lists your plants' specific problem on its label and precisely follow all package directions. Apply soaps, oils, and pesticides only to affected foliage and plant material, and avoid broadcast spraying. Keep in mind that many of the insects you see in the garden are actually beneficial. Entomologists estimate that more than 95 percent of all insects are either beneficial or harmless. It may be surprising, but the more of these bugs you have, the healthier your garden will be.

# Flower Pests and Organic Cures

| Symptom | Cause | Remedies |
| --- | --- | --- |
| Curled, twisted, sticky leaves; stunted or deformed blooms; loss of vigor. | Aphids; look for clusters of $\frac{1}{16}''$ (1.6 mm) black, green, yellow, or gray round insects. | Spray with a stream of water; spray with solution of 2–3 Tbsp. (30–44 ml) dishwashing liquid per gallon (4 l) of water; spray with insecticidal soap. |
| White trails on or inside leaves; papery yellow or brown blotches on foliage. | Leaf miners; look for small, pale larvae and $\frac{1}{8}''$ (3.2 mm) tiny green or black flying insects. | Remove infested leaves. Move plant to sheltered outdoor spot and spray foliage with neem oil extract solution. |
| Stunted plants; white cottony clusters in leaf axils. | Mealybugs; look in the junctions between leaves and stems or at the base of leaf clusters for white or gray waxy bugs, $\frac{1}{8}''$ (3 mm) long. | Dab or spray with rubbing alcohol diluted 3:1; spray with insecticidal soap; spray with horticultural oil. |
| Stunted, discolored, spotted plants with deformed roots, sometimes bearing swollen galls; loss of vigor. | Nematodes; microscopic wormlike creatures that live in the soil and feed on plant roots. | Repot into sterile potting soil after rinsing roots in neem oil extract solution and pruning away swollen root nodules; may require several repottings at monthly intervals. In garden, release competitive beneficial nematodes or solarize soil. |
| Leaves speckle, wrinkle, turn yellow, drop; minute white webs on undersides and the plant's foliage junctions. | Spider mites; shake foliage and blossoms over white paper and look for moving red or yellow, spiderlike specks. Thrive in hot, dry conditions. | Spray repeatedly with water to rinse off dustlike pests; spray with insecticidal soap. |
| Stunted, yellow plants lacking vigor; leaves may drop. | Scales; look for $\frac{1}{20}''$ (1.2 mm) flylike insects accompanying soft or hard $\frac{1}{50}''$ (0.5 mm) mounded bumps on stems and leaves. | Remove infested foliage. Swab scales with soapy water or diluted denatured alcohol solution; rinse well after solution dries. Apply horticultural oil. Spray with pyrethrin, rotenone. |
| Brown-, silver-, or white-speckled leaves; may be gummy or deformed. Blooms are deformed and fail to open. | Thrips; shake foliage and blossoms over white paper, and look for moving winged specks. Thrive in hot, dry conditions. | Remove and destroy infested foliage. Spray with stream of water; spray with insecticidal soap. |
| Yellow leaves and stunted, sticky plants. When foliage is shaken, a cloud of white insects may fly up. | Whiteflies; shake foliage and look for $\frac{1}{20}''$ (1.2 mm) mothlike flying insects. Inspect leaf undersides for scalelike gray or yellow eggs. | Catch with sticky traps. Spray with soap solution. Spray infested foliage with insecticidal soap. Move plant to sheltered outdoor spot and spray foliage with horticultural oil or neem oil extract solution. Spray with pyrethrin. |
| Chewed leaves and blossoms; silvery mucus trails. | Slugs and snails; look after dark on foliage for shelled and unshelled mollusks. | Remove mulch used as hiding places. Hand pick after dark; dust with diatomaceous earth; use nontoxic baits containing iron phosphate; use bait gel. |
| Trampled garden with plants eaten to ground; numerous cloven-hoof prints. | Deer; look in mornings and evenings for large mammals eating garden plants, trees, and shrubs. | Apply repellents containing coyote and cat urine by spraying on foliage; repeat every 4–5 days or more frequently if it rains. Cage plants in wire-cloth barriers. Build two parallel 4′–5′ (1.2–1.5 m) fences around the garden, 4′ (1.2 m) apart. |
| Round or oblong raised mounds of soil pushed up in turf or garden beds lead to extensive networks of tunnels and dens deep beneath the soil's surface. | Pocket gophers; watch for new mounds being raised, plants being pulled down by their roots; or animals pulling plants into burrows. | Flood active tunnels with water to drive gophers from nests. Excavate the main tunnel between burrows; set traps facing each way into the tunnels, stake them in place, then cover. |
| Plants are uprooted. Cones of raised soil are pushed up in turf, connected by near-surface tunnels. | Moles; carnivorous animals cause damage by digging in garden beds while hunting insects and earthworms. | Flood active tunnels with water to drown moles. Place surface traps at fresh mounds. Excavate main tunnels and set two scissors traps, one facing into each tunnel. Stake them in place, then cover with soil. |

# Flower Diseases and Organic Cures

| Symptom | Cause | Remedies |
| --- | --- | --- |
| Oozing rotting spots of brown, pink, purple, or yellow appear on foliage, flowers, fruits, or stems. Spots merge and darken over time, girdling stems. | Anthracnose; fungal disease. Soil-borne spores and infected seed cause most infections. Spreads during garden care and watering when spores wash or blow onto leaves. | Remove fallen leaves and litter from garden soil. Space plants and divide plantings for good air circulation. Rotate plantings annually. Prune off infected branches or uproot and remove infected plants from garden; avoid composting them. |
| Trees and shrubs gradually or suddenly die. Shoestring-like white mycelium threads permeate soil, and mushrooms grow around the base of the plant. | Armillaria root rot; fungal disease. Fungal mat and rhizomorphs grow through soil and infect new plants. Air-borne spores start new fungal colonies in moist soil. | Prune and remove infected foliage and roots; avoid composting. Dig up and remove dead plants and the surrounding soil layer, 12–18″ (30–45 cm) deep; fill hole with compost and treat with beneficial soil nematodes. |
| Moist, rotting spots appear on foliage of fleshy plants and spread to become stinking, slimy patches. Plants collapse. | Bacterial soft rot; bacterial disease. Soil-borne bacteria live on fallen leaves. Insects and watering carry them to plants. Open wounds or sap-eating and rasping insects allow entry and infection. | Space plants and divide plantings for good air circulation. Control pests that may carry or facilitate bacterial disease. Water soil only; avoid wetting foliage. |
| Nightshade-family (Solanum spp.) plants wilt in afternoon heat, recovering by morning. Foliage and branches die, followed by shriveling of entire plant. | Bacterial wilt; bacterial disease. Insects carry soil-dwelling bacteria to plants, infect them as they eat stems and foliage. Stems become slimy inside and filled with bacterial threads. | Plant resistant cultivars. Rotate plantings annually. Water soil only; avoid wetting foliage. Control beetles and their larvae. |
| Old flowers become blighted; disease spreads progressively to flower stems, branches, and foliage, which become covered with many oozing spots. | Botrytis blight; fungal disease. Soil-borne spores are blown and washed onto foliage. Also spread by infected tools. Enters plant through wounds. Spreads rapidly in cool, humid weather. | Space plants and divide plantings for good air circulation. Deadhead spent flowers. Remove infected foliage from garden; avoid composting it. |
| Brown stains and softened tissue near base of stem or crown of plant; leaves may yellow or drop. | Crown or stem rot; fungal disease. Look for decaying stems. Usually associated with keeping soil overly moist. | Rarely curable; remove infected foliage, dipping pruning shears in denatured rubbing alcohol solution between cuts. Reduce watering. Repot to soil-free, well-drained mix. Root cuttings of healthy growth. |
| Young sprouts and seedlings develop brown patches at their base, topple, and fall over. | Damping off; fungal disease. Caused by many cool- and moist-soil fungi. | Plant resistant cultivars after soil warms above 60°F (16°C). Use sterile potting soil placed in clean containers. Avoid overwatering sprouts in cool temperatures. Apply bacterial treatments containing Streptomyces griseoviridis bacteria. |
| Fully mature leaves develop small yellow spots; underleaf surfaces grow dustlike gray, white, or purple mold. Spots darken and merge, foliage dies. | Downy mildew; fungal disease. Caused by many cool- and moist-soil spores that overwinter in fallen leaves. Watering and insects carry spores to plants. Worst in humid conditions. | Space resistant cultivars and divide plantings for good air circulation. Rotate plantings annually. Remove leaf debris from garden in autumn; avoid composting it. Apply garden sulfur only to infected plants listed in package instructions. |
| Powdery black or brown dusting on foliage and blossoms; leaves may drop. | Leaf spot; fungal disease. Common in low-light, crowded plantings. | Remove shading foliage, increase air circulation; spray with sulfur fungicide. |
| Light powdery dusting of gray or white on leaves and flowers; deformed new growth; stunting; loss of vigor. | Powdery mildew; fungal disease. Common if humid, warm days and cool nights alternate. | Remove shading foliage, increase air circulation; spray affected plants with solution of 1 Tbsp. (15 ml) baking soda and 3 Tbsp. (44 ml) horticultural oil to 1 gallon (4 l) water; dust with sulfur. |
| Raised humps of usually brown, orange, or yellow, sometimes purple, powder on leaf undersides join to coat their surface. Leaves yellow, then drop. | Rust; fungal disease. Many different fungi specific to ornamental plants; infection of a species usually remains on plants of that species. Spores overwinter in fallen leaves. | Space resistant cultivars and divide plantings for good air circulation. Water soil only; avoid wetting foliage. Remove leaf debris from garden in autumn; avoid composting it. Spray sulfur fungicide on infected plants listed in package directions. |
| Wilting leaves become yellow or pink, wither, and drop. Stem centers appear dark when cut. | Verticillium wilt; fungal disease. Long-lived spores overwinter in fallen leaves and soil. Water splashes them on foliage or insects carry spores to plants. Enters plants through wounds. | Plant resistant cultivars and divide plantings for good air circulation. Water soil only; avoid wetting foliage. Remove leaf debris from garden. Limit water to infected plants, then water deeply. Prune off infected foliage; clean tools between cuts. |

Control pest infestations and disease infections as directed [see Flower Pests and Organic Cures, pg. 139, and Flower Diseases and Organic Cures, opposite pg.]. Identify the problem as one caused by a pest or a plant disease, choose the control method required, and follow the steps shown for either condition.

> ### WARNING
> Follow package label instructions exactly when applying garden chemicals. Read and heed all safety warnings and cautions. Match plants to the control agent. Clean and store all implements and protective clothing carefully. Reserve them for use when applying garden chemicals.

## Pesticidal Soap

**1** Identify the specific pest causing the damage to your flowers. Use hand picking and other non-pesticidal methods first. Confirm that the specific pest is listed on the soap label and that it is approved for use on your plant. If uncertain, avoid harming your plants by testing a leaf and waiting several days before applying soap to other leaves.

**2** Wear protective gloves, measure the concentrate carefully, and mix it with water before pouring it into a hand sprayer. Clean up any spills.

**3** On a cool, calm day, apply the soap solution directly to the insect pests. Avoid areas that are pest-free. Spray the leaf undersides where pests are found, as well as their tops, moving from the center stem outward to the leaves.

**4** Dispose of extra solution and empty containers in accordance with the directions given on the label.

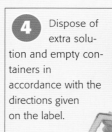

## Fungicidal Sprays

**1** Identify the specific disease. Select a control that both lists the disease condition and is approved for your plants. Follow the package directions for setting the applicator's rate of flow and dilution.

**2** In the morning on a cool, calm day, apply fungicidal spray directly on the infested foliage, avoiding healthy areas. Spray tops and undersides of affected leaves, stems, and flower buds.

**3** Wash the applicator in soapy water and rinse. Clean up any spills, and dispose of extra solution and empty containers in accordance with the directions given on the package label.

# encyclopedia of flowers

YOU WILL BE MOST LIKELY TO SUCCEED AT FLOWER GARDENING IF YOU ARE KNOWLEDGE-ABLE about the flowers you wish to grow. This comprehensive encyclopedia of 480 flowering plants lists groups of plants—annuals, perennials, bulbs, shrubs, succulents and cacti, aquatic plants, and ornamental grasses—so you can zero in on your particular favorites. It lists all the planting and care data you need to grow and enjoy a wide variety of plants. While every flower is listed by its scientific name, its common names accompany it and can also be found in the plant index at the back of the book. Each plant has a close-up color photograph to help you identify it as well as choose new cultivars.

Each listing includes a description of a plant, including its foliage and flowers as well as its bloom time, hardiness range, soil requirements, and information about planting and caring for it. The soil section notes the ideal type of soil for each plant, its moisture, drainage requirements, and preferred pH. In the section on blooms, you'll discover when that particular plant actually flowers and the size, shape, and colors of the blooms. You'll also learn the plant's hardiness potential—important information if a plant is tender and you live in an area that gets hard frost all winter long. You'll learn which plants have the potential to naturalize or self-seed on your site. You will also find suggestions for how to use the plant, whether it is good in borders, hanging baskets, or containers, for instance, and for all of the types of gardens in which it best fits.

Ensure you have healthy plants and long-lasting blooms by using the information in this encyclopedia as you select, plant, and care for flowers. Within its pages, you'll discover new options, find many appealing features of the plants that catch your eye, and be able to weigh all the facts you should consider as you select and plant them in your garden.

# Special Needs of Annuals

Use colorful annuals for quick color and to fill spaces between shrubs and perennials before and after they bloom.

Massed plantings of annual sunflowers in bloom add cheer and are reminiscent of the countryside in the South of France.

Annuals—those plants that germinate, grow shoots and leaves, flower, set seed, and die within a single season—grow so quickly they seem to change from day to day. Annuals will establish themselves quickly and set about the business of growing. It is common to go out to the garden in the morning and find that a vigorous annual such as garden nasturtium has taken over a nearby planter, or that a whole bed full of zinnias has gone from buds to blooms almost overnight. Compared to other ornamentals, annuals produce blooms fast—and for a minimal investment in terms of time and effort. Depending on where you live and the type of flower you select, annuals can also last in your garden for considerable lengths of time, sometimes for many months. And, although they finish after just one season, they often mature seed that will self-sow and reappear for years. Many annuals adapt to a wide range of climates. Snapdragons and pansies, for example, are just two of the many species able to grow throughout North America. In cold-winter climates, annuals provide fast color for the summer. Most garden centers carry these tender plants in spring.

Annuals do need a fair amount of attention to grow showy blooms. They require regular watering and feeding throughout their growth, formation of buds, and flowering. Mulching is also a good practice for annuals; it shades roots and keeps the soil moist longer, which encourages flowering. In warm climates, mulching winter annuals heavily will extend their bloom for several weeks longer into summer.

## Annuals Update and Refresh Your Garden

Annuals make the perfect replacement fillers for the landscape because they establish themselves quickly and burst into bloom, sometimes overnight but often within a week or two. Use annuals to fill in holes left by perennials and bulbs that have bloomed and finished their display. Once a foxglove is done for the season, for example, add color with a hardworking annual such as statice, sunflower, or zinnia. You can use annuals throughout the season to add a fresh spark to the garden. Change color palettes from pastels in spring to gold and bronze in autumn. Another place to use annuals is in the foreground of beds of taller flowering plants such as shrubs. Choose contrasting colors to add bright highlights or complementary colors to unify your plantings.

The planting times for annuals vary according to climate and specific plant. Cool-season annuals such as flossflower and sweet pea grow best when the soil and weather are cool. Many other annuals grow well in the warmer months and can be planted in spring and summer. In mild-winter climates, plant annuals in autumn for winter color or late in winter to have early-spring flowers.

The key to maintaining annuals is to keep them growing steadily, which will mean a lot of blooms for you. Before planting, mix a complete fertilizer such as 5–5–5 into the soil. It usually supplies annuals with enough food for roughly half of their growing period. Follow it with liquid organic fertilizer every two to four weeks during active growth, or less frequently if that is recommended for the species. A few species such as cosmos bloom best in nutrient-poor soils; avoid fertilizing them when planting.

Annuals are programmed to flower, set seed pods, and mature seed in short order. Deadhead them—snip off faded blossoms to make way for new ones—to prevent them from finishing earlier than you'd like. If you prune faded foliage as well, clip off just one-third of growth; otherwise you could shock the plant and cause it to take time recovering rather than blooming. Pinch foliage buds early in the growth cycle to keep the plant compact and dense. This is a particularly important care consideration in shade gardens, where plants seeking more light tend to be tall and rangy.

You can grow annuals from seed. In the case of plants that transplant with difficulty, sowing seed is the only way to grow the annuals you desire. Note which plants should be planted directly in garden soil. If you live in a climate that is slow to warm up in spring such as central Canada, the Great Plains, or the Northeast, start seed indoors in late winter and early spring and bring young plants out into the garden after danger of frost has passed and the soil has warmed. Shelter them for a few days before planting to harden them to outdoor conditions. If you plant nursery starts instead, start with the healthiest plants available. At the nursery or garden center, keep an eye out for those annuals that look healthy, stocky, and dense, and that have vibrant leaves. Choose plants with buds, but avoid those in full bloom that take longer to establish. Plants that are already full of flowers will soon fade, and you'll have to wait for another growth cycle. Seek plants that have healthy roots; rootbound specimens have used up a great deal of energy trying to grow in tight quarters and may be stunted, weak bloomers. It's easy to inspect their roots —just slip them out of their nursery container.

## What's Meant by...

**Few, Various, Numerous:** Categorical references for the relative number of commercially available cultivars of a plant species or genus.

**Hardiness:** Plant survival at minimum low temperature in combination with wind, heat, freezing, and snow cover; in annuals, survival of seed at minimum low temperatures.

**Languid:** Slow-growing.

**Zones:** The plants in this book are rated according to the coldest temperature they can survive, with zone 11 rated warmest and zone 1 coldest. See the zone map on end-sheets for the zone information for your area.

## Help Finding Your Other Favorite "Annuals"

Is your favorite bedding plant missing from the annuals listing? Plants commonly offered as annuals include many tender perennials, sub-shrubs, or bulbous plants, and a genus can contain both annual and perennial species. Find them in the quick reference list below or the complete plant index, beginning on pg. 282:

Garden centers usually group their plants into sections that include one with annuals.

*Antirrhinum majus*—snapdragon (pg. 163)
*Begonia grandis*—hardy begonia (pg. 216)
*Begonia* × *tuberhybrida*—tuberous begonia (pg. 216)
*Catharanthus roseus*—Madagascar periwinkle (pg. 170)
*Ipomoea* spp.—morning glory (pg. 186)
*Impatiens walleriana*—balsam (pg.186)
*Lobularia maritima*—sweet alyssum (pg. 189)

*Pelargonium peltatum*—trailing geranium (pg.196)
*Pelargonium* spp.—florist's geranium (pg.196)
*Petunia* spp.—Petunia (pg. 197)
*Salvia* spp.—Sage (pg. 203)
*Scaevola aemula*—fan flower (pg. 204)
*Scenecio* × *hybridus*—florist's cineraria (pg. 204)
*Verbena* × *hybrida*—verbena (pg. 209)

## *Ageratum houstonianum* ASTERACEAE (COMPOSITAE)

### Flossflower (Ageratum, Pussy-Foot)

**SHAPE:** Numerous mounded, erect annuals to 30″ (75 cm) tall. Woolly, heart-shaped, fine-toothed leaves to 5″ (13 cm) long.

**FLOWER:** Early-summer to autumn bloom. Clusters of tiny, fuzzy flowers to ¼″ (6 mm) wide. Choose from blue, pink, purple, violet, and white.

**HARDINESS:** Zones 4–11, may self-seed. Protect from hot sun.

**SOIL TYPE:** Loam. High moisture, good drainage, high fertility, 6.5–7.0 pH.

**PLANTING GUIDE:** Sow seed indoors and transplant, zones 2–9; sow outdoors, zones 10–11. Plant in full sun to partial shade, 6″–9″ (15–23 cm) apart.

**CARE TIPS:** Easy. Even moisture. Fertilize every 4 weeks. Extend bloom by deadheading. Propagate by seed.

**NOTES:** Thrives in beds, containers, edgings. Nice in cottage, formal, wildlife gardens. Cutting flower. Susceptible to mealybugs, orthegia, whiteflies, sclerotinia wilt.

## *Amaranthus caudatus* AMARANTHACEAE

### Love-Lies-Bleeding (Tassel Flower)

**SHAPE:** Various vertical, branched annuals, 36″–60″ (90–150 cm) tall. Alternate, smooth, oval, pointed, veined, edible leaves to 10″ (25 cm) long. See also *A. tricolor*, Joseph's-coat.

**FLOWER:** Summer to late-autumn bloom. Woolly or ropelike clusters of tiny, flute-shaped flowers, 18″–24″ (45–60 cm) long. Dark red.

**HARDINESS:** Zones 2–10, may self-seed.

**SOIL TYPE:** Loam. Average–low moisture, good drainage, high–medium fertility, 7.0–7.5 pH.

**PLANTING GUIDE:** Mid- to late spring, as soil warms. Plant in full sun, 24″ (60 cm) apart. Best sown in garden soil.

**CARE TIPS:** Easy. Water when soil dries 2″–3″ (50–75 mm) deep. Fertilize every 4 weeks. Tolerates heat and drought. Propagate by seed.

**NOTES:** Thrives in accents, backgrounds, beds, fence lines, walls. Nice in cottage, meadow, natural, wildlife gardens. Good for drying, salads, grain. Resists pests and diseases.

## *Amaranthus tricolor* AMARANTHACEAE

### Joseph's-Coat (Tampala)

**SHAPE:** Various branched, erect annuals, 12″–48″ (30–120 cm) tall. Alternate, smooth, oval, pointed, edible leaves to 4″ (10 cm) wide and 6″ (15 cm) long in tiers vertically along the stalk. See also *A. caudatus*, love-lies-bleeding.

**FLOWER:** Summer to autumn bloom. Grow for cream, red, yellow foliage bracts.

**HARDINESS:** Zones 2–10, may self-seed.

**SOIL TYPE:** Loam. Average–low moisture, good drainage, medium–low fertility, 5.5–7.0 pH.

**PLANTING GUIDE:** Spring, as soil warms. Plant in full sun, 18″ (45 cm) apart. Best sown outdoors.

**CARE TIPS:** Easy. Water when soil dries 2″–3″ (50–75 mm) deep. Fertilize sparingly. Tolerates heat and drought. Support with stakes. Propagate by seed.

**NOTES:** Thrives in accents, backgrounds, borders, containers, mixed plantings. Nice in cottage, formal, meadow gardens. Cutting material. Resists pests and diseases.

## *Brachyscome iberidifolia* ASTERACEAE (COMPOSITAE)

### Swan River Daisy

**SHAPE:** Various branched, mounded, erect annuals to 18″ (45 cm) tall. Alternate, plumelike, divided, deep-cut leaves to 3″ (75 mm) long.

**FLOWER:** Late-spring to early-summer bloom. Daisylike, fragrant flowers to 1″ (25 mm) wide. Choose from blue, pink, and white with yellow, buttonlike centers.

**HARDINESS:** Zones 5–10, may self-seed.

**SOIL TYPE:** Sandy loam. High moisture, good drainage, high fertility, 6.5–7.5 pH.

**PLANTING GUIDE:** Spring, when frost risk ends. Plant in full sun to partial shade, 6″–12″ (15–30 cm) apart. Plant 3-week successions.

**CARE TIPS:** Easy. Even moisture. Fertilize every 4 weeks. Pinch tips for bushy plants. Extend bloom by deadheading. Protect from hot sun, zones 9–11. Propagate by seed.

**NOTES:** Thrives in beds, borders, containers, edgings, massed plantings. Nice in cottage, formal, rock gardens. Resists pests and diseases.

## *Brassica oleracea* BRASSICACEAE (CRUCIFERAE)

### Ornamental Kale (Decorative Kale, Wild Cabbage)

**SHAPE:** Numerous short, open annuals to 20″ (50 cm) wide. Shiny or waxy, edible leaves to 12″ (30 cm) long in wavy whorls with fringed, feathered edges. Best color after frost.

**FLOWER:** Summer to autumn bloom. Erect, feathery plumes of tiny, 4-petaled flowers. Grow for cream, green, white, and yellow foliage.

**HARDINESS:** Zones 2–10, may self-seed. Hardy.

**SOIL TYPE:** Sandy loam. High moisture, good drainage, high–medium fertility, 6.5–7.5 pH.

**PLANTING GUIDE:** Spring, when frost risk ends. Plant in full sun, 12″–24″ (30–60 cm) apart. Start indoors for early bloom.

**CARE TIPS:** Easy. Even moisture. Fertilize every 4 weeks. Bolts in hot weather, zones 9–11. Propagate by seed.

**NOTES:** Thrives in accents, borders, containers, edgings. Nice in formal, small-space gardens. Good for geometric pattern plantings. Susceptible to caterpillars.

## *Calendula officinalis* ASTERACEAE (COMPOSITAE)

### Pot Marigold (Scot's Marigold)

**SHAPE:** Numerous erect, branched or mounded annuals to 24″ (60 cm) tall. Alternate, textured, oval, wavy-edged, sometimes toothed leaves to 1½″ (38 mm) long. Dwarf cultivars available. *Tagetes erecta*, marigold, is a close relative.

**FLOWER:** Spring to autumn bloom. Round, double, edible flowers to 4″ (10 cm) wide. Choose from deep orange and light or bright yellow.

**HARDINESS:** Zones 2–10, may self-seed.

**SOIL TYPE:** Loam. High moisture, good drainage, high–medium fertility, 6.5–7.5 pH.

**PLANTING GUIDE:** Spring, when frost risk ends. Plant in full sun, 6″–12″ (15–30 cm) apart. Start indoors for early bloom.

**CARE TIPS:** Easy. Even moisture. Fertilize every 6–8 weeks. Extend bloom by deadheading. Support with stakes. Propagate by seed.

**NOTES:** Thrives in beds, borders, containers. Nice in cottage, formal, small-space gardens. Cutting flower. Susceptible to spider mites, whiteflies.

## *Callistephus chinensis* ASTERACEAE (COMPOSITAE)

### China Aster (Annual Aster)

**SHAPE:** Numerous vertical or branched annuals, 8″–32″ (20–80 cm) tall. Oval or lancelike, toothed leaves to 5″ (13 cm) long. See also *Aster* spp., Aster.

**FLOWER:** Summer to autumn bloom. Lone round, often double flower, 2″–5″ (50–125 mm) wide. Choose from blue, pink, purple, red, white, and yellow.

**HARDINESS:** Zones 5–10, may self-seed.

**SOIL TYPE:** Loam. High moisture, good drainage, high fertility, 6.5–7.0 pH.

**PLANTING GUIDE:** Spring, as soil warms. Plant in full to filtered sun, 12″ (30 cm) apart.

**CARE TIPS:** Easy. Even moisture; avoid wetting foliage. Fertilize every 4 weeks. Pinch tips for bushy plants. Extend bloom by deadheading. Rotate plantings each year. Propagate by seed.

**NOTES:** Thrives in beds, borders, containers. Nice in cottage, formal, shade gardens. Cutting flower. Susceptible to root aphids, blister beetles, leafhoppers, aster wilt, aster yellows.

## *Celosia* spp. AMARANTHACEAE

### Woolflower (Cockscomb)

**SHAPE:** Nearly 60 mounded, vigorous annuals, 10″–36″ (25–90 cm) tall. Alternate, usually variegated, lancelike leaves to 2″ (50 mm) long. Dwarf cultivars available.

**FLOWER:** Summer to autumn bloom. Upright plume- or crestlike clusters to 4″ (10 cm) tall of tiny, woolly, yarnlike flowers. Choose from gold, orange, purple, red, white, and yellow.

**HARDINESS:** Zones 2–11, may self-seed. Prefers hot-summer climates.

**SOIL TYPE:** Loam. High moisture, good drainage, high–low fertility, 6.5–7.5 pH.

**PLANTING GUIDE:** Spring, when frost risk ends. Plant in full sun, 9″–12″ (23–30 cm) apart.

**CARE TIPS:** Average. Even moisture. Fertilize every 10–12 weeks. Extend bloom by deadheading. Propagate by seed.

**NOTES:** Thrives in beds, borders, containers, edgings. Nice in cottage, formal, small-space gardens. Cutting flower. Resists pests and diseases.

## *Centaurea cyanus* ASTERACEAE (COMPOSITAE)

### Cornflower (Bachelor's-Button)

**SHAPE:** Numerous erect, slim annuals to 24″ (60 cm) tall. Hairy, slender, lancelike leaves to 3″ (75 mm) long with gray undersides. *C. cineraria*, dusty-miller, is a close relative.

**FLOWER:** Summer to autumn bloom. Lone round, narrow-petaled flower to 1½″ (38 mm) wide. Choose from blue, pink, purple, red, and white.

**HARDINESS:** Zones 3–9, may self-seed. Tolerates light frost.

**SOIL TYPE:** Sandy loam. High moisture, good drainage, medium–low fertility, 6.5–7.0 pH.

**PLANTING GUIDE:** Spring, when frost risk ends. Plant in full sun, 8″–12″ (20–30 cm) apart. Best sown in garden soil. Plant 2-week successions.

**CARE TIPS:** Easy. Even moisture. Fertilize every 4 weeks. Extend bloom by deadheading. Propagate by seed.

**NOTES:** Thrives in beds, borders, edgings, massed plantings. Nice in cottage, formal, small-space, wildlife gardens. Resists pests and diseases.

## *Chrysanthemum multicaule* ASTERACEAE (COMPOSITAE)

### Annual Chrysanthemum

**SHAPE:** Numerous short and flat, succulent annuals to 12″ (30 cm) tall. Smooth, oval or spoonlike, succulent, usually coarse-toothed or plumelike leaves to 3″ (75 mm) long.

**FLOWER:** Summer to autumn bloom. Daisylike flowers to 2½″ (63 mm) wide. Choose from gold and yellow with gold, yellow centers.

**HARDINESS:** Zones 4–10, may self-seed.

**SOIL TYPE:** Loam. High moisture, good drainage, high–medium fertility, 6.5–7.5 pH.

**PLANTING GUIDE:** Spring, when frost risk ends. Plant in full sun to partial shade, 12″–24″ (30–60 cm) apart. Plant successions.

**CARE TIPS:** Average. Even moisture. Avoid wetting foliage. Fertilize every 4 weeks. Pinch tips for bushy plants. Propagate by seed.

**NOTES:** Thrives in beds, containers, edgings, ground covers. Nice in cottage, formal, rock, small-space gardens. Cutting flower. Susceptible to aphids, midges, rust.

## *Clarkia amoena* ONAGRACEAE

### Satin Flower (Clarkia, Farewell-to-Spring, Godetia)

**SHAPE:** Various erect or sprawling annuals, 6″–24″ (15–60 cm) tall. Alternate, smooth, lancelike, tapering leaves, 1½″–3″ (38–75 mm) long.

**FLOWER:** Spring to early-summer bloom. Simple, 4-petaled, cup-shaped flowers, 2″–3″ (50–75 mm) wide. Choose from lavender and pink, often with contrasting edges and centers.

**HARDINESS:** Zones 2–10, may self-seed. Prefers mild-summer climates.

**SOIL TYPE:** Loam. High–average moisture, good drainage, medium fertility, 7.0 pH.

**PLANTING GUIDE:** Spring, as soil becomes workable. Plant in full sun to partial shade, 8″–10″ (20–25 cm) apart. Best sown in garden soil.

**CARE TIPS:** Easy. Water when soil dries 2″ (50 mm) deep. Fertilize every 10–12 weeks. Pinch tips for bushy plants. Propagate by seed.

**NOTES:** Thrives in beds, borders, edgings. Nice in cottage, rock, seaside, woodland gardens. Resists pests and diseases.

## *Cleome hasslerana* CAPPARACEAE

### Spider Flower

**SHAPE:** Numerous vertical, branched or shrubby annuals to 5′ (1.5 m) tall. Smooth, divided, pointed, fragrant leaves, each with 5–7 leaflets, 2″–3″ (50–75 mm) long. *C. spinosa*, spiny spider flower, is a close relative.

**FLOWER:** Summer to autumn bloom. Ball-like clusters to 6″ (15 cm) wide of 4-petaled flowers with threadlike stamens. Purple.

**HARDINESS:** Zones 2–11, may self-seed.

**SOIL TYPE:** Loam. High moisture, good drainage, high–medium fertility, 6.0–7.0 pH.

**PLANTING GUIDE:** Spring or earlier for long-season areas. Plant in full sun to partial shade, 18″–24″ (45–60 cm) apart. Start indoors for early bloom.

**CARE TIPS:** Average. Even moisture. Fertilize every 6–8 weeks. Support with stakes. Shelter from wind. Propagate by seed.

**NOTES:** Thrives in accents, backgrounds, borders. Nice in cottage, natural, wildlife gardens. Cutting flower. Resists pests and diseases.

## *Consolida ambigua* RANUNCULACEAE

### Rocket Larkspur (Annual Delphinium, Rocket)

**SHAPE:** Numerous vertical, slender annuals, 12″–60″ (30–150 cm) tall. Smooth, plumelike, divided, deep-toothed leaves to 4″ (10 cm) long.

**FLOWER:** Spring to early-summer bloom, zones 8–10; summer, zones 4–7. Erect stalks with tiers of 7-petaled flowers to 1½″ (38 mm) wide. Choose from blue, pink, rose, violet, and white.

**HARDINESS:** Zones 4–10, may self-seed.

**SOIL TYPE:** Loam. High moisture, good drainage, high fertility, 7.0–7.5 pH.

**PLANTING GUIDE:** Spring, zones 4–7; late summer, zones 8–10. Plant in full sun to partial shade, 8″–15″ (20–38 cm) apart. Best sown in garden soil.

**CARE TIPS:** Average. Even moisture. Fertilize every 4 weeks. Support with stakes. Shelter from wind. Propagate by seed.

**NOTES:** Thrives in beds, borders, fence lines, massed plantings. Nice in cottage, formal, shade, woodland gardens. Cutting flower. Resists pests and diseases.

## *Convolvulus tricolor* CONVOLVULACEAE

### Dwarf Morning-Glory

**SHAPE:** Numerous erect, sprawling or dangling annuals to 12″ (30 cm) tall. Smooth, lancelike, pointed leaves to 3″ (75 mm) long. See also *Ipomoea* spp., morning glory.

**FLOWER:** Spring to summer bloom. Round, open, deep-throated flowers to 1½″ (38 mm) wide, often as triplets. Choose from bright blue, pink, purple with white and yellow centers.

**HARDINESS:** Zones 2–10, usually self-seeds.

**SOIL TYPE:** Sandy soil. Average–low moisture, good drainage, medium–low fertility, 6.5–7.5 pH.

**PLANTING GUIDE:** Spring, as soil warms. Plant in full sun, 12″ (30 cm) apart. Start indoors for early bloom.

**CARE TIPS:** Easy. Water when soil dries 4″–6″ (10–15 cm) deep. Fertilize sparingly. Propagate by seed.

**NOTES:** Thrives in borders, containers, edgings. Nice in arid, casual, cottage, heritage, rock, seaside gardens. Aggressive. Resists pests and diseases.

## *Coreopsis tinctoria* ASTERACEAE (COMPOSITAE)

### Calliopsis (Coreopsis, Tickseed)

**SHAPE:** Numerous erect, branched, slender annuals, 18″–36″ (45–90 cm) tall. Opposite, smooth, divided, plumelike leaves to 6″ (15 cm) long with narrow, cosmos-like leaflets.

**FLOWER:** Spring to early-autumn bloom. Daisylike or saucer-shaped, single or double flowers to 2″ (50 mm) wide. Choose from brown, gold, red, and yellow with brown or deep red centers.

**HARDINESS:** Zones 4–9, may self-seed.

**SOIL TYPE:** Sandy soil. Average–low moisture, good drainage, medium fertility, 6.5–7.5 pH.

**PLANTING GUIDE:** Spring, when frost risk ends. Plant in full sun, 6″–12″ (15–30 cm) apart.

**CARE TIPS:** Easy. Water when soil dries 4″–6″ (10–15 cm) deep. Tolerates drought. Fertilize every 10–12 weeks. Extend bloom by deadheading. Propagate by seed.

**NOTES:** Thrives in accents, beds, borders, walls. Nice in arid, cottage, meadow, seaside, wildlife gardens. Cutting flower. Resists pests and diseases.

## *Cosmos bipinnatus* ASTERACEAE (COMPOSITAE)

### Cosmos

**SHAPE:** Numerous erect, branched or bush-like annuals, 7′–10′ (2.2–3 m) tall. Shiny, divided leaves to 5″ (13 cm) long, each with thread-like leaflets.

**FLOWER:** Summer to autumn bloom. Flat-faced flowers, 2″–3″ (50–75 mm) wide, with scalloped petals. Choose from pink, red, and violet with bright yellow centers.

**HARDINESS:** Zones 5–11, may self-seed.

**SOIL TYPE:** Sandy soil. Average–low moisture, good drainage, medium–low fertility, 7.0–7.5 pH. Blooms best in poor soil.

**PLANTING GUIDE:** Spring, as soil warms. Plant in full to filtered sun, 12″ (30 cm) apart.

**CARE TIPS:** Easy. Water when soil dries 4″–6″ (10–15 cm) deep. Fertilize sparingly. Support with stakes. Propagate by seed.

**NOTES:** Thrives in backgrounds, beds, borders. Nice in arid, cottage, wildlife gardens. Cutting flower. Resists pests and diseases.

## *Diascia barberae* SCROPHULARIACEAE

### Twinspur

**SHAPE:** Numerous vertical, sprawling annuals to 12″ (30 cm) tall and 18″ (45 cm) wide. Opposite, textured, oval, pointed, deep-toothed leaves to 1½″ (38 mm) long.

**FLOWER:** Summer to late-autumn bloom. Spiking clusters of flared, spurred, or horned flowers to ½″ (12 mm) wide. Choose from peach, pink, and rose.

**HARDINESS:** Zones 7–9, may self-seed.

**SOIL TYPE:** Loam; pond shorelines. High moisture, good drainage, high fertility, 6.5–7.5 pH.

**PLANTING GUIDE:** Spring, when frost risk ends. Plant in full sun to partial shade, 6″ (15 cm) apart. Start indoors for early bloom.

**CARE TIPS:** Easy. Water when soil dries 2″–3″ (50–75 mm) deep. Fertilize every 4 weeks. Remove spent stalks. Propagate by seed.

**NOTES:** Thrives in borders, containers, foregrounds. Nice in cottage, rock gardens. Resists pests and diseases.

## *Dimorphotheca pluvialis* and hybrids ASTERACEAE (COMPOSITAE)

### Cape Marigold

**SHAPE:** Numerous vertical, branched annuals to 16″ (40 cm) tall. Hairy, oval, usually divided leaves, 2″–3½″ (50–90 mm) long.

**FLOWER:** Early to late-summer bloom, zones 2–7; winter to early spring, zones 8–10. Daisylike flowers to 2″ (50 mm) wide. Choose from orange, pink, white, and yellow with light blue, cream, green, or purple undersides.

**HARDINESS:** Zones 2–10, may self-seed.

**SOIL TYPE:** Loam. Average–low moisture, good drainage, medium fertility, 6.5–7.5 pH.

**PLANTING GUIDE:** Spring, when frost risk ends. Plant in full sun, 12″ (30 cm) apart.

**CARE TIPS:** Easy. Water when soil dries 4″–6″ (10–15 cm) deep. Fertilize only in spring. Extend bloom by deadheading. Propagate by seed.

**NOTES:** Thrives in banks, borders, containers, massed plantings. Nice in cottage, meadow gardens and roadside plantings. Resists pests. Susceptible to fungal diseases.

## *Euphorbia marginata* EUPHORBIACEAE

### Snow-on-the-Mountain (Ghostweed)

**SHAPE:** Various vertical, branched annuals, usually 24″–48″ (60–120 cm) tall and 12″–24″ (30–60 cm) wide. Shiny, oval, pointed leaves to 3″ (75 mm) long. Pale green to white markings on upper leaves.

**FLOWER:** Summer to autumn color. Grow for variegated and spotted foliage.

**HARDINESS:** Zones 2–10, may self-seed.

**SOIL TYPE:** Loam. Most moistures, good drainage, medium–low fertility, 6.5–7.5 pH.

**PLANTING GUIDE:** Early spring, as soil becomes workable. Plant in full sun to open shade, 9″–18″ (23–45 cm) apart.

**CARE TIPS:** Easy. Water when soil dries 4″–6″ (10–15 cm) deep. Fertilize sparingly. Pinch to direct growth. Propagate by seed.

**NOTES:** Thrives in accents, beds, borders. Nice in formal, shade, woodland gardens. Cutting flower. Causes skin irritations; wear gloves when cutting. Resists pests and diseases.

## *Gaillardia pulchella* ASTERACEAE (COMPOSITAE)

### Blanket Flower

**SHAPE:** Numerous vertical, bushlike annuals to 36″ (90 cm) tall. Alternate, hairy, textured, lancelike leaves, 3″–6″ (75–150 mm) long.

**FLOWER:** Summer to autumn bloom. Single or double flowers, 3″–4″ (75–100 mm) wide. Choose from gold, red, and yellow, with center contrasts.

**HARDINESS:** Zones 5–9, may self-seed. Protect from frost.

**SOIL TYPE:** Sandy loam. Average–low moisture, good drainage, medium–low fertility, 6.0–7.5 pH.

**PLANTING GUIDE:** Spring, as soil becomes workable. Plant in full sun, 10″–15″ (25–38 cm) apart.

**CARE TIPS:** Easy. Water when soil dries 4″–6″ (10–15 cm) deep. Fertilize sparingly. Extend bloom by deadheading. Support with stakes. Propagate by seed.

**NOTES:** Thrives in beds, borders, slopes. Nice in cottage, meadow, wildlife gardens. Cutting flower. Susceptible to aphids, leaf spot, powdery mildew.

## *Gomphrena globosa* AMARANTHACEAE

### Globe Amaranth

**SHAPE:** Numerous erect, branched annuals, 9″–24″ (23–60 cm) tall. Alternate, opposite, hairy, oval to lancelike leaves, 2″–3½″ (50–90 mm) long. Dwarf cultivars available.

**FLOWER:** Summer bloom. Lone round, cloverlike compound flower, ½″–1″ (12–25 mm) wide. Choose from lavender, pink, purple, red, and white.

**HARDINESS:** Zones 3–11, may self-seed.

**SOIL TYPE:** Loam. Average moisture, good drainage, medium fertility, 6.5–7.5 pH.

**PLANTING GUIDE:** Spring. Plant in full sun, 9″–12″ (23–30 cm) apart. Start indoors for early bloom.

**CARE TIPS:** Easy. Water when soil dries 4″–6″ (10–15 cm) deep. Fertilize every 10–12 weeks. Propagate by seed.

**NOTES:** Thrives in beds, borders, containers, edgings. Nice in cottage, meadow, small-space gardens. Everlasting if dried. Cutting flower. Resists pests and diseases.

## *Gypsophila elegans* CARYOPHYLLACEAE

### Annual Baby's-Breath

**SHAPE:** Various open, mounded annuals, 8″–20″ (20–50 cm) tall. Lancelike, succulent leaves, 1″–2″ (25–50 mm) long. See also *G. paniculata*, perennial baby's-breath.

**FLOWER:** Late-spring to summer bloom. Masses of tiny 5-petaled flowers, ¼″–1″ (6–25 mm) wide. Choose from pink, purple, and white.

**HARDINESS:** Zones 3–9, may self-seed.

**SOIL TYPE:** Loam. Average–low moisture, good drainage, medium–low fertility, 7.0–8.0 pH.

**PLANTING GUIDE:** Spring, when frost risk ends. Plant in full sun, 12″–18″ (30–45 cm) apart. Start indoors for early bloom. Plant successions.

**CARE TIPS:** Easy. Water when soil dries 4″–6″ (10–15 cm) deep. Fertilize only in spring. Propagate by seed.

**NOTES:** Thrives in borders, containers, fillers, foregrounds. Nice in cottage, formal, rock, small-space gardens. Cutting flower. Resists diseases. Susceptible to gophers, slugs, snails.

## *Helianthus annuus* ASTERACEAE (COMPOSITAE)

### Common Sunflower (Cut-and-Come-Again, Mirasol)

**SHAPE:** Numerous erect, slender annuals to 10′ (3 m) tall. Usually alternate, textured, oval, coarse-toothed leaves to 12″ (30 cm) long. See also *Helianthus* spp., perennial sunflower.

**FLOWER:** Summer to autumn bloom. Round, single or double flowers, 6″–12″ (15–30 cm) wide, alone or in clusters, with edible seed. Choose from gold, orange, white, and yellow.

**HARDINESS:** Zones 4–9, may self-seed.

**SOIL TYPE:** Loam. High moisture, good drainage, medium fertility, 5.0–7.0 pH.

**PLANTING GUIDE:** Spring. Plant in full sun to partial shade, 18″–36″ (45–90 cm) apart.

**CARE TIPS:** Easy. Even moisture. Fertilize every 6–8 weeks. Support with stakes. Propagate by seed.

**NOTES:** Thrives in borders, fence lines, massed plantings. Nice in cottage, meadow, small-space, wildlife gardens. Cutting flower. Susceptible to stalk borers, sunflower maggots, sunflower moth larvae, powdery mildew, rust.

## *Helipterum roseum* ASTERACEAE (COMPOSITAE)

### Everlasting (Strawflower)

**SHAPE:** Numerous erect, branched annuals to 24″ (60 cm) tall. Alternate, lancelike, narrow leaves to 2½″ (63 mm) long.

**FLOWER:** Summer to early-autumn bloom. Lone daisylike, very double flower to 2″ (50 mm) wide with papery rays. Choose from orange, rose, and white.

**HARDINESS:** Zones 3–10, may self-seed.

**SOIL TYPE:** Sandy loam. Average moisture, good drainage, high–low fertility, 7.0–7.5 pH.

**PLANTING GUIDE:** Spring, when frost risk ends. Plant in full sun, 12″ (30 cm) apart. Start indoors for early bloom.

**CARE TIPS:** Easy. Water when soil dries 4″–6″ (10–15 cm) deep. Tolerates drought. Fertilize every 10–12 weeks. Propagate by seed.

**NOTES:** Thrives in beds, borders, containers, foregrounds. Nice in cottage, meadow, small-space gardens. Everlasting if dried. Cutting flower. Resists pests and diseases.

## *Iberis umbellata* BRASSICACEAE (CRUCIFERAE)

### Globe Candytuft

**SHAPE:** Numerous bushlike, branched annuals to 16″ (40 cm) tall. Shiny, lancelike, slender leaves to 3½″ (90 mm) long. See also *I. sempervirens*, candytuft.

**FLOWER:** Late-spring to autumn bloom. Round, globelike clusters of 4-petaled flowers to 3″ (75 mm) wide. Choose from lavender, pink, purple, red, and white.

**HARDINESS:** Zones 3–10, may self-seed.

**SOIL TYPE:** Loam. High moisture, good drainage, high fertility, 6.5–7.5 pH.

**PLANTING GUIDE:** Spring, when frost risk ends. Plant in full sun, 12″–15″ (30–38 cm) apart. Start indoors for early bloom. Plant successions.

**CARE TIPS:** Easy. Water when soil dries 2″–3″ (50–75 mm) deep. Fertilize every 4 weeks. Extend bloom by deadheading. Propagate by seed.

**NOTES:** Thrives in beds, borders, containers, massed plantings. Nice in cottage, rock gardens. Tolerates smog. Resists pests and diseases.

## *Lathyrus odoratus* FABACEAE (LEGUMINOSAE)

### Sweet Pea (Vetchling)

**SHAPE:** Numerous bushlike or climbing annuals to 36″ (90 cm) tall or to 6′ (1.8 m) long. Alternate, paired, smooth, lance- or oval-shaped leaves to 2″ (50 mm) long.

**FLOWER:** Spring to summer bloom. Pealike fragrant flowers to 2″ (50 mm) wide. Choose from pink, purple, red, violet, and white. Mixed colors on single plants. Forms pods with pealike seed.

**HARDINESS:** Zones 2–10, may self-seed.

**SOIL TYPE:** Loam. High moisture, good drainage, high fertility, 7.0–7.5 pH.

**PLANTING GUIDE:** Spring, as soil becomes workable. Plant in full sun, 6″–12″ (15–30 cm) apart.

**CARE TIPS:** Average. Even moisture. Fertilize every 4 weeks. Extend bloom by deadheading. Support with stakes. Shelter from wind. Propagate by seed.

**NOTES:** Thrives in accents, arbors, edgings, fence lines, massed plantings, trellises. Nice in cottage, formal, small-space gardens. Cutting flower. Resists diseases. Susceptible to slugs, snails.

## *Lavatera trimestris* MALVACEAE

### Tree Mallow

**SHAPE:** Numerous branched, bushlike annuals, 36″–60″ (90–150 cm) tall. Alternate, hairy, heart- or maple-shaped leaves to 2″ (50 mm) long.

**FLOWER:** Summer to late-autumn bloom. Satiny, saucer-shaped flowers to 4″ (10 cm) wide. Choose from pink, red, and white.

**HARDINESS:** Zones 2–10, may self-seed.

**SOIL TYPE:** Loam. High–average moisture, good drainage, high–medium fertility, 6.5–7.5 pH.

Tolerates salt and seashore conditions.

**PLANTING GUIDE:** Early spring, when frost risk ends. Plant in full sun, 24″ (60 cm) apart. Best sown in garden soil.

**CARE TIPS:** Average. Water when soil dries 4″–6″ (10–15 cm) deep. Fertilize every 4 weeks. Extend bloom by deadheading. Propagate by seed.

**NOTES:** Thrives in accents, beds, borders, fence lines. Nice in cottage, meadow, rock gardens. Resists pests. Susceptible to rust.

## *Limonium sinuatum*

### Florist's Statice

**SHAPE:** Few hairy, bushlike, shrubby annuals to 18″ (45 cm) tall. Woolly, harp-shaped, lobate leaves to 6″ (15 cm) long, in basal rosettes.

**FLOWER:** Summer to late-autumn bloom. Branched, winged stalks with open clusters of tiny cup-shaped flowers to 6″ (15 cm) wide. Choose from blue, lavender, white, and yellow.

**HARDINESS:** Zones 5–11, may self-seed. Protect from frost.

**SOIL TYPE:** Sandy loam. High moisture, good drainage, medium–low fertility, 6.0–8.0 pH.

**PLANTING GUIDE:** Early spring, as soil warms. Plant in full sun, 18″ (45 cm) apart.

**CARE TIPS:** Average to difficult. Water when soil dries 4″–6″ (10–15 cm) deep. Fertilize only in spring. Shelter from wind. Support with stakes. Propagate by seed.

**NOTES:** Thrives in beds, borders, edgings. Nice in cottage, wildlife gardens. Drying flower. Resists pests. Susceptible to rust.

## *Linaria maroccana* SCROPHULARIACEAE

### Toadflax (Baby Snapdragon, Spurred Snapdragon)

**SHAPE:** Few vertical, slender annuals, 18″–24″ (45–60 cm) tall. Whorls of smooth, lancelike, narrow leaves to 1″ (25 mm) long. *L. purpurea* and *L. reticulata* are close relatives.

**FLOWER:** Summer bloom, zones 3–7; winter to early spring, zones 8–10. Spiking clusters of snapdragon-like, spurred flowers to 1½″ (38 mm) wide. Choose from gold, pink, purple, red, tan, violet, and multicolored.

**HARDINESS:** Zones 3–10, may self-seed.

**SOIL TYPE:** Sandy loam. High moisture, good drainage, high–medium fertility, 6.5–7.5 pH

**PLANTING GUIDE:** Spring, zones 3–7; autumn, zones 8–10. Plant in full to filtered sun, 6″–10″ (15–25 cm) apart.

**CARE TIPS:** Easy. Tolerates drought when established. Fertilize every 6–8 weeks. Propagate by seed.

**NOTES:** Thrives in borders, containers, massed plantings. Nice in cottage, meadow, rock gardens. Resists pests and diseases.

## *Linum grandiflorum* LINACEAE

### Flowering Flax

**SHAPE:** Numerous erect, branched, slender annuals, 12″–24″ (30–60 cm) tall. Alternate, smooth, lancelike leaves to 1″ (25 mm) long. See also *L. perenne*, perennial flax.

**FLOWER:** Late-spring to late-summer bloom. Lone simple, 5-petaled flower to 1¼″ (32 mm) wide. Choose from pink, red, and white. Last one day.

**HARDINESS:** Zones 2–9, may self-seed.

**SOIL TYPE:** Sandy loam. Average moisture, good drainage, high–medium fertility, 6.5–7.5 pH.

**PLANTING GUIDE:** Early spring. Plant in full sun to open shade, 4″–6″ (10–15 cm) apart. Best sown in garden soil. Plant successions.

**CARE TIPS:** Easy. Water when soil dries 6″–10″ (15–25 cm) deep. Tolerates drought. Fertilize every 10–12 weeks. Propagate by seed.

**NOTES:** Thrives in accents, beds, borders, foregrounds, massed plantings. Nice in cottage, meadow, rock, shade gardens. Resists pests and diseases.

## *Matthiola longipetala* BRASSICACEAE (CRUCIFERAE)

### Evening Stock (Evening Scented Stock, Perfume Plant)

**SHAPE:** Few vertical, branched, open annuals to 18″ (45 cm) tall. Smooth, lancelike leaves to 3½″ (90 mm) long.

**FLOWER:** Summer bloom. Low spikes of horned, fragrant flowers to ¾″ (19 mm) wide. Choose from pink, purple, and yellow. Open at evening.

**HARDINESS:** Prefers mild-summer climates. Protect from frost.

**SOIL TYPE:** Sandy loam. High moisture, good drainage, high–medium fertility, 6.5–7.5 pH.

**PLANTING GUIDE:** Spring, zones 2–7, when frost risk ends; autumn, zones 8–11. Plant in full sun to partial shade, 12″ (30 cm) apart.

**CARE TIPS:** Easy. Water when soil dries 2″–3″ (50–75 mm) deep. Avoid wetting foliage. Fertilize every 4 weeks. Support with stakes. Shelter from wind. Propagate by seed.

**NOTES:** Thrives in backgrounds, beds, borders, containers. Nice in cottage, meadow, shade gardens. Cutting flower. Resists pests and diseases.

## *Moluccella laevis* LAMIACEAE (LABIATAE)

### Bells-of-Ireland (Shellflower)

**SHAPE:** Various vertical, slender annuals to 36″ (90 cm) tall. Opposite, smooth, oval to circular, fine-toothed leaves to 2″ (50 mm) long.

**FLOWER:** Summer bloom. Whorled stalks of tiny, tubular flowers to ¾″ (19 mm) long, borne within a showy, cup- or bell-shaped, veined calyx. Green; may turn white.

**HARDINESS:** Zones 2–10, may self-seed.

**SOIL TYPE:** Loam. High moisture, good drainage, high–medium fertility, 6.5–7.5 pH.

**PLANTING GUIDE:** Early spring, zones 2–8; autumn, zones 9–10. Plant in full sun, 9″ (23 cm) apart.

**CARE TIPS:** Easy. Water when soil dries 2″–3″ (50–75 mm) deep. Fertilize every 4 weeks. Extend bloom by deadheading. Support with stakes. Propagate by seed.

**NOTES:** Thrives in accents, backgrounds, beds, borders. Nice in cottage, rock gardens. Cutting flower. Protect from rain, wind. Resists pests and diseases.

### *Nemesia strumosa* and hybrids SCROPHULARIACEAE

#### Pouch Nemesia (Bluebird)

**SHAPE:** Various vertical, bushlike annuals, 6″–24″ (15–60 cm) tall. Usually alternate, lancelike, toothed leaves, 2″–4″ (50–100 mm) long. *N. caerulea* is a close relative.

**FLOWER:** Late-spring bloom. Branching clusters of lobed flowers to 1″ (25 mm) wide with fan-shaped upper and liplike lower petals. Choose from orange, pink, purple, red, white, and yellow.

**HARDINESS:** Zones 3–10, may self-seed. Prefers mild-summer climates.

**SOIL TYPE:** Loam. High moisture, good drainage, high fertility, 6.5–7.0 pH.

**PLANTING GUIDE:** Spring, when frost risk ends. Plant in full to filtered sun, 6″ (15 cm) apart. Start indoors for early bloom.

**CARE TIPS:** Easy. Even moisture. Fertilize every 4 weeks. Protect from hot sun. Propagate by seed.

**NOTES:** Thrives in hanging baskets, beds, borders, containers. Nice in cottage, heritage, rock gardens. Cutting flower. Resists pests and diseases.

### *Nemophila maculata* HYDROPHYLLACEAE

#### Five-Spot

**SHAPE:** Few short, mounded, sprawling or dangling annuals to 12″ (30 cm) tall and wide. Opposite, hairy, plumelike, divided leaves to 4″ (10 cm) long with 5–9 leaflets. See also *N. menziesii*, baby-blue-eyes.

**FLOWER:** Spring bloom. Simple, cup-shaped flowers, 1½″–2″ (38–50 mm) wide. Choose from white, striped, or with purple spots at the petal tips.

**HARDINESS:** Zones 7–9, may self-seed. Best in mild, dry climates.

**SOIL TYPE:** High humus. High moisture, good drainage, high fertility, 6.0–7.5 pH.

**PLANTING GUIDE:** Spring, zones 3–6, as soil becomes workable; autumn, zones 7–9. Plant in full sun to partial shade, 9″–12″ (23–30 cm) apart.

**CARE TIPS:** Easy. Even moisture. Fertilize every 4 weeks. Propagate by seed.

**NOTES:** Thrives in beds, borders, containers, edgings, walls. Nice in cottage, formal, natural gardens. Resists diseases. Susceptible to slugs, snails.

### *Nemophila menziesii* HYDROPHYLLACEAE

#### Baby-Blue-Eyes

**SHAPE:** Numerous short or sprawling annuals to 12″ (30 cm) tall. Opposite, smooth, plumelike, divided leaves to 2″ (50 mm) long with 5–9 leaflets. See also *N. maculata*, five-spot.

**FLOWER:** Early-summer to autumn bloom. Simple 5-petaled, open flowers, 1″–1½″ (25–38 mm) wide. Choose from blue, purple, violet, and white.

**HARDINESS:** Zones 2–10, may self-seed. Best in cool, dry climates.

**SOIL TYPE:** High humus. High moisture, good drainage, high–medium fertility, 6.5–7.0 pH.

**PLANTING GUIDE:** Spring, zones 2–6, as soil becomes workable; autumn, zones 7–10. Plant in full sun to partial shade, 9″–12″ (23–30 cm) apart.

**CARE TIPS:** Easy. Even moisture. Fertilize every 4 weeks. Apply mulch containing leaf mold. Propagate by seed.

**NOTES:** Thrives in beds, borders, containers, edgings. Nice in cottage, natural, rock gardens. Resists pests and diseases.

### *Nigella damascena* RANUNCULACEAE

#### Love-in-a-Mist (Fennel Flower, Wild Fennel)

**SHAPE:** Numerous vertical, branched, slender annuals to 18″ (45 cm) tall and 10″ (25 cm) wide. Smooth, divided leaves to 2″ (50 mm) long with 8–12 opposed, narrow leaflets.

**FLOWER:** Spring to summer bloom. Lone simple to double flower to 1½″ (38 mm) wide, a seed-pod at center, and edible seed. Choose from blue, pink, purple, rose, and white.

**HARDINESS:** Zones 2–10, may self-seed.

**SOIL TYPE:** Sandy loam. High moisture, good drainage, high–medium fertility, 6.5–7.5 pH.

**PLANTING GUIDE:** Spring, zones 2–8, as soil becomes workable; spring or autumn, zones 9–10. Plant in full sun, 12″ (30 cm) apart.

**CARE TIPS:** Easy. Water when soil dries 2″ (50 mm) deep. Fertilize every 6–8 weeks. Extend bloom by deadheading. Protect from hot sun. Propagate by seed.

**NOTES:** Thrives in beds, borders. Nice in cottage, natural gardens. Resists pests and diseases.

## *Papaver rhoeas* PAPAVERACEAE

### Flanders Poppy (Field Poppy, Shirley Poppy)

**SHAPE:** Numerous vertical, branched annuals to 36″ (90 cm) tall with hirsute stems. Shiny, hirsute, divided leaves to 6″ (15 cm) long.

**FLOWER:** Spring to summer bloom. Lone or pairs of bowl-shaped, single or double flowers to 3″ (75 mm) wide. Choose from pink, purple, red, white, and bicolored.

**HARDINESS:** Zones 5–10, may self-seed. Protect from frost.

**SOIL TYPE:** Sandy loam. High–average moisture, good drainage, high–medium fertility, 6.5–7.0 pH.

**PLANTING GUIDE:** Early spring, zones 2–7, as soil becomes workable; autumn or early spring, zones 8–10. Plant in full sun, 12″ (30 cm) apart.

**CARE TIPS:** Easy. Water when soil dries 4″–6″ (10–15 cm) deep. Fertilize every 6–8 weeks. Extend bloom by deadheading. Propagate by seed.

**NOTES:** Thrives in beds, borders, massed plantings. Nice in cottage, meadow, natural gardens. Cutting flower. Susceptible to aphids, blight.

## *Phlox drummondii* POLEMONIACEAE

### Annual Phlox (Drummond Phlox)

**SHAPE:** Numerous bushlike, mounded annuals to 20″ (50 cm) tall with hairy stems. Alternate, paired, lancelike, narrow or oval, pointed leaves to 2″ (50 mm) long.

**FLOWER:** Summer to autumn bloom. Tight clusters of star-shaped flowers to 1″ (25 mm) wide. Choose from cream, pink, purple, red, and white.

**HARDINESS:** Zones 3–10, may self-seed.

**SOIL TYPE:** Loam. Most moistures, good drainage, high–medium fertility, 6.5–7.0 pH.

**PLANTING GUIDE:** Sow seed indoors and transplant as soil warms, zones 3–6; sow outdoors, zones 7–10. Plant in full sun, 10″–12″ (25–30 cm) apart.

**CARE TIPS:** Easy. Even moisture. Fertilize every 4 weeks. Pinch tips for bushy plants. Propagate by seed.

**NOTES:** Thrives in beds, borders, containers, edgings, ground covers. Nice in cottage, meadow, shade, wildlife gardens. Susceptible to phlox bugs, spider mites, powdery mildew.

## *Portulaca grandiflora* PORTULACACEAE

### Moss Rose (Eleven-O'Clock, Rose Moss, Sun Plant)

**SHAPE:** Numerous short, sprawling annuals to 8″ (20 cm) tall and 18″ (45 cm) wide with succulent, branched stems. Alternate, smooth, succulent, needlelike leaves to 1″ (25 mm) long.

**FLOWER:** Spring to late-summer bloom. Roselike, single or double flowers to 1″ (25 mm) wide. Choose from orange, pink, red, white, and yellow.

**HARDINESS:** Zones 9–11, may self-seed. Protect from frost

**SOIL TYPE:** Sandy loam. Average moisture, good drainage, medium–low fertility, 6.5–7.0 pH.

**PLANTING GUIDE:** Spring, when frost risk ends. Plant in full sun, 6″–8″ (15–20 cm) apart.

**CARE TIPS:** Easy. Water when soil dries 4″–6″ (10–15 cm) deep. Fertilize sparingly. Tolerates hot sun. Propagate by cuttings, seed.

**NOTES:** Thrives in banks, beds, containers, edgings, ground covers, massed plantings, slopes. Nice in arid, cottage, heritage, rock gardens. Resists pests and diseases.

## *Sanvitalia procumbens* ASTERACEAE (COMPOSITAE)

### Creeping Zinnia (Trailing Sanvitalia)

**SHAPE:** Numerous short, branched or sprawling annuals to 6″ (15 cm) tall and 18″ (45 cm) wide. Opposite, hairy, oval, pointed leaves to 2½″ (63 mm) long.

**FLOWER:** Summer to autumn bloom. Lone daisy-like, single or double flower, ¾″–1″ (19–25 mm) wide. Choose from orange and yellow with large, purple-brown centers.

**HARDINESS:** Zones 2–11, may self-seed.

**SOIL TYPE:** Loam. High–average moisture, good drainage, medium–low fertility, 7.0–7.5 pH.

**PLANTING GUIDE:** Late spring, when frost risk ends. Plant in full sun, 6″–12″ (15–30 cm) apart. Best sown in garden soil.

**CARE TIPS:** Easy. Water when soil dries 2″–3″ (50–75 mm) deep. Fertilize every 10–12 weeks. Propagate by seed.

**NOTES:** Thrives in banks, borders, containers, fillers, ground covers. Nice in cottage, meadow, natural, rock gardens. Resists pests and diseases.

## *Scabiosa atropurpurea* (*S. grandiflora*) DIPSACACEAE

### Pincushion Flower (Mourning-Bride, Sweet Scabious)

**SHAPE:** Various vertical, slender annuals to 24″ (60 cm) tall and 12″ (30 cm) wide. Opposite, smooth, plumelike, fine-cut or lobate leaves, 2″–3″ (50–75 mm) long.

**FLOWER:** Summer to autumn bloom. Lone irregular, ruffled flower to 2″ (50 mm) wide with tubular and flat petals and raised centers. Choose from pink, light to deep purple, rose, and white.

**HARDINESS:** Zones 4–11, may self-seed.

**SOIL TYPE:** Loam. High–average moisture, good drainage, high–medium fertility, 7.0–8.0 pH.

**PLANTING GUIDE:** Early spring, as soil becomes workable. Plant in full sun, 12″ (30 cm) apart.

**CARE TIPS:** Easy. Even moisture until established; tolerates drought thereafter. Fertilize every 2 months. Extend bloom by deadheading. Propagate by seed.

**NOTES:** Thrives in beds, borders, massed plantings. Nice in cottage, formal, meadow, rock gardens. Cutting flower. Resists pests and diseases.

## *Schizanthus pinnatus* SOLANACEAE

### Poor-Man's Orchid (Butterfly Flower)

**SHAPE:** Few erect, branched annuals to 24″ (60 cm) tall. Alternate, plumelike, fine-cut leaves to 5″ (13 cm) long.

**FLOWER:** Summer to autumn bloom. Branched clusters of orchidlike flowers, 1″–1½″ (25–38 mm) wide. Choose from pink, purple, white, and yellow, with bright yellow contrasts.

**HARDINESS:** Zones 3–10, may self-seed. Prefers cool-summer climates. Protect from frost.

**SOIL TYPE:** Sandy loam. High moisture, good drainage, high fertility, 6.5–7.5 pH.

**PLANTING GUIDE:** Sow seed indoors and transplant when frost risk ends, zones 3–8; sow in garden as soil warms, zones 9–10. Plant in full sun to partial shade, 12″ (30 cm) apart.

**CARE TIPS:** Average. Even moisture. Fertilize every 4 weeks. Shelter from wind. Propagate by seed.

**NOTES:** Thrives in beds, borders, containers. Nice in cottage, small-space gardens. Cutting flower. Resists pests and diseases.

## *Silene coeli-rosa* (*Lychnis coeli-rosa, Agrostemma coeli-rosa*) CARYOPHYLLACEAE

### Rose-of-Heaven (Viscaria)

**SHAPE:** Few erect, compact, branched annuals to 20″ (50 cm) tall. Textured, lancelike, pointed, gray-green, wavy edged leaves to 2″ (50 mm) long.

**FLOWER:** Summer bloom. Open clusters of round, saucer-shaped flowers, 1″ (25 mm) wide. Choose from blue, lavender, pink, rose, and white, with center contrasts.

**HARDINESS:** Zones 5–10, may self-seed.

**SOIL TYPE:** Sandy loam. Average–low moisture, good drainage, medium fertility, 6.5–8.0 pH.

**PLANTING GUIDE:** Spring, zones 2–8; autumn, zones 9–11. Plant in full sun to partial shade, 6–8″ (15–20 cm) apart.

**CARE TIPS:** Easy. Water when soil dries 2″ (50 mm) deep. Fertilize only in spring. Propagate by seed.

**NOTES:** Thrives in accents, banks, beds, borders, containers. Nice in cottage, meadow, natural, seaside, small-space, wildlife gardens. Cutting flower. Resists pests and diseases.

## *Tagetes erecta* ASTERACEAE (COMPOSITAE)

### Marigold (African Marigold, Aztec Marigold, French Marigold)

**SHAPE:** Numerous mounded, bushlike annuals, 6″–36″ (15–90 cm) tall. Opposite, smooth, plumelike, lobate, toothed, fragrant leaves to 3″ (75 mm) long.

**FLOWER:** Summer to autumn bloom. Round, wavy-fringed flowers to 2½″ (63 mm) wide. Choose from cream, gold, white, and yellow.

**HARDINESS:** Zones 3–10, may self-seed.

**SOIL TYPE:** Loam. High moisture, good drainage, medium fertility, 6.5–7.0 pH.

**PLANTING GUIDE:** Spring, when frost risk ends. Plant in full sun, 8″–16″ (20–40 cm) apart. Start indoors for early bloom.

**CARE TIPS:** Easy. Even moisture. Fertilize every 4 weeks. Extend bloom by deadheading. Propagate by seed.

**NOTES:** Thrives in beds, borders, containers. Nice in cottage, formal, small-space, wildlife gardens. Susceptible to aphids, leafhoppers, powdery mildew.

## *Torenia fournieri* SCROPHULARIACEAE

### Wishbone Flower (Blue Torenia, Bluewings)

**SHAPE:** Few branched annuals to 12″ (30 cm) tall and wide. Opposite, textured, oval, toothed leaves to 2″ (50 mm) long.

**FLOWER:** Summer to late-autumn bloom. Irregular, 5-petaled flowers to 1¼″ (32 mm) wide. Choose from purple, violet, white, yellow, and multicolored.

**HARDINESS:** Zones 8–11, may self-seed. Tropical. Protect from frost.

**SOIL TYPE:** High humus. High moisture, good drainage, high fertility, 6.5–7.5 pH.

**PLANTING GUIDE:** Spring, when frost risk ends. Plant in partial to full shade, 6″–8″ (15–20 cm) apart. Start indoors for early bloom.

**CARE TIPS:** Average. Even moisture. Fertilize every 4 weeks. Pinch tips for bushy plants. Propagate by seed.

**NOTES:** Thrives in accents, borders, hanging baskets, containers, edgings. Nice in rock, shade, tropical gardens. Resists pests and diseases.

## *Tropaeolum majus* TROPAEOLACEAE

### Garden Nasturtium (Common Nasturtium)

**SHAPE:** Numerous upright, mounded or trailing succulent annuals to 36″ (90 cm) tall and wide. Shiny, circular leaves to 3″ (75 mm) wide.

**FLOWER:** Summer to autumn bloom. Deep-throated, edible, fragrant flowers to 2½″ (63 mm) wide. Choose from orange, pink, red, white, yellow, and multicolored.

**HARDINESS:** Zones 6–10, may self-seed.

**SOIL TYPE:** Sandy loam. High moisture, good drainage, high–low fertility, 6.5–7.0 pH.

**PLANTING GUIDE:** Spring, when frost risk ends. Plant in full to filtered sun, 8″–12″ (20–30 cm) apart.

**CARE TIPS:** Easy. Even moisture. Fertilize sparingly. Extend bloom by deadheading. Support with stakes. Propagate by seed.

**NOTES:** Thrives in hanging baskets, borders, containers, edgings. Nice in cottage, formal, small-space, wildlife gardens. Aggressive. Susceptible to aphids, leaf miners, fusarium wilt.

## *Zinnia angustifolia* ASTERACEAE (COMPOSITAE)

### Narrow-Leaved Zinnia

**SHAPE:** Various vertical, thick-growing annuals to 15″ (38 cm) tall and wide. Opposite, smooth, lancelike, narrow, pointed leaves, 2½″–3″ (63–75 mm) long.

**FLOWER:** Summer to late-autumn bloom. Round, daisylike, open flowers to 1½″ (38 mm) wide. Choose from orange, white, and yellow with green undersides and brown or orange centers.

**HARDINESS:** Zones 8–11, may self-seed. Protect from frost.

**SOIL TYPE:** High humus. High moisture, good drainage, high fertility, 6.0–7.0 pH.

**PLANTING GUIDE:** Spring, as soil warms. Plant in full sun, 6″–8″ (15–20 cm) apart.

**CARE TIPS:** Easy. Even moisture. Fertilize every 4 weeks. Propagate by seed.

**NOTES:** Thrives in beds, borders, containers, massed plantings. Nice in cottage, natural, wildlife gardens. Cutting flower. Susceptible to Japanese beetles, borers, slugs, snails, powdery mildew.

## *Zinnia elegans* and hybrids ASTERACEAE (COMPOSITAE)

### Garden Zinnia (Common Zinnia, Youth-and-Old-Age)

**SHAPE:** Numerous bushlike annuals, 12″–48″ (30–120 cm) tall. Opposite, textured, lancelike or oval, pointed leaves to 5″ (13 cm) long.

**FLOWER:** Summer to autumn bloom. Round, double, quilled, or crested flowers, 1″–7″ (25–180 mm) wide. Choose from green, orange, pink, purple, red, and yellow.

**HARDINESS:** Zones 4–11, may self-seed.

**SOIL TYPE:** Loam. High moisture, good drainage, high–medium fertility, 7.0–7.5 pH.

**PLANTING GUIDE:** Spring, as soil warms. Plant in full sun, 6″–12″ (15–30 cm) apart.

**CARE TIPS:** Easy. Even moisture; avoid wetting foliage. Fertilize every 10–12 weeks. Extend bloom by deadheading. Propagate by seed.

**NOTES:** Thrives in accents, beds, borders, containers, edgings. Nice in cottage, formal, meadow, natural, wildlife gardens. Cutting flower. Susceptible to Japanese beetles, borers, slugs, snails, powdery mildew.

# Perennials and Biennials

Meet the special care needs of these long-lived flowering plants and they will reward you season after season.

Mixed plantings of layered perennials are marked by varied foliage texture and profuse color.

Perennial plants live three years or more and include trees and shrubs as well as herbaceous perennials—plants with foliage that dies down at the end of each growing season and reappears at the start of the next. Flowers in this category include columbine, cyclamen, hosta, and peony. Other perennials keep low tufts of leaves throughout the winter in mild climates and burst forth with new growth in spring. These include plants such as coralbells, Shasta daisy, and yarrow. Still other plants such as kangaroo-paw (*Anigozanthus* spp.), lily-of-the-Nile (*Agapanthus africanus*), lily-of-the-Incas, golden marguerite, and thrift are either semi-evergreen or evergreen.

While many perennials live for a few years—or for many—biennials have a life cycle lasting two years. Foxglove, for instance, can be planted by seed in the early spring of one season and flowers in the spring of the next. Many garden centers offer second-year biennial stock in nursery containers. Other biennials are Canterbury-bells and sweet William.

Perennials and biennials have similar growing requirements, and you will find them listed together in this section of the Encyclopedia. First, it is essential that you plant them where they will have enough space as well as appropriate light and soil conditions so they have a chance to grow to their natural size without becoming crowded. Check for mature growth size and a general spacing recommendation. Specific cultivars may be genetic dwarfs, small-statured, or large-statured; follow the spacing recommendations on their care tags for best results. Plant care tags also tell you the special requirements a grower has found to be best for the cultivar.

**Care during Growth.** Routine watering works for most perennials and biennials, although some grow best when the soil is drier and others thrive when it is moist. Until their roots are established, younger plants typically require more frequent watering than older plants. Add a layer of mulch to conserve water and keep your perennials blooming by cooling their roots.

Proper fertilizing is another care consideration for perennial and biennial plants. When planting, feed both with a granular or liquid organic food high in phosphorus and potassium such as 2–5–5. Fertilize again in early spring when new seasonal growth begins and periodically at the intervals recommended in the plant listings.

Some perennials and biennials, including yarrow, monkshood (*Aconitum napellus*), bugloss, and false indigo (*Baptisia australis*), are naturally floppy-headed. Stake and support them to display their blooms and keep them from falling over on neighboring plants. Support individual flowers with a single stake and garden tape or twine. You'll need to tie groupings of flowers together to keep them upright. You will find supports at your garden center or nursery, or you can make your own.

**Preparing for Winter.** In late autumn or early winter before snow accumulates, perform a major cleanup. Remove dead foliage, flowers, and stems so the plants can put all of their resources into storing energy for next year's bloom. Some species should be sheared at this time. Use this opportunity to mulch the garden to insulate and protect plant roots.

Cleaning up your garden also helps prevent pests and diseases from wintering over with the decaying foliage. If you live in a cold-winter climate, mulch your perennials to protect them from freeze-thaw cycles that can damage their roots. The purpose of such a mulch is to keep the ground consistently frozen. Use a lightweight mulch that will insulate, such as salt hay, straw, or pine needles.

Divide perennials when they become crowded. Generally, divide spring-blooming plants in autumn and autumn-blooming plants in spring (or in late winter in mild-winter climates). Lift rhizomatous perennials as recommended for your zone. Pack the roots loosely in damp peat moss or straw and store them in an unheated garage or other structure with temperatures of 40°F (4°C). Depending on the species, you may either replant them in autumn or wait until the soil warms again to set them out in the garden.

**Saving Seed.** Autumn is also a good time collect seedpods and seed heads from your favorite perennial plants. Many old favorites will breed true from their seed; check the listings for recommendations. After you have cut off the pods or heads, put them in a sheltered, warm, dry spot to cure and thoroughly dry for a week or two. Winnow the seed from the husks and store it in a cool spot until it's time to plant again. The best spot for it is in the vegetable keeper of a household refrigerator.

## What's Meant by...

**Lone, Few, Various, Numerous:** Categorical references for the relative number of commercially available cultivars of a plant species or genus.

**Hardiness:** Plant survival at minimum low temperature in combination with wind, heat, freezing, and snow cover.

**Hirsute:** Hairy.

**Impermanent:** Short-lived.

**Languid:** Slow-growing.

**Zones:** The plants in this book are rated according to the coldest temperature they can survive, with zone 11 rated warmest and zone 1 coldest. See the zone map on end-sheets for the zone information for your area.

## *Acanthus mollis* ACANTHACEAE

### Bear's-Breech (Artist's Acanthus)

**SHAPE:** Various mounded, sprawling, deciduous perennials to 36″ (90 cm) tall and wide. Shiny, soft, oval, lobed, deep-cut, toothed leaves to 30″ (75 cm) long.

**FLOWER:** Summer bloom. Multiple stout spikes to 5′ (1.5 m) tall of tubular flowers to 2″ (50 mm) long with leaflike bracts between and beneath the flowers. Choose from pink, purple, and white.

**HARDINESS:** Zones 7–10. Protect from frost.

**SOIL TYPE:** Sandy loam; pond shorelines. High moisture, good drainage, medium fertility, 6.5–7.5 pH.

**PLANTING GUIDE:** Spring. Plant in full sun to partial shade, 36″ (90 cm) apart.

**CARE TIPS:** Easy. Even moisture. Fertilize only in spring. Propagate by division, seed.

**NOTES:** Thrives in accents, backgrounds. Nice in natural, shade, woodland gardens. Cutting flower. Resists diseases. Susceptible to slugs, snails.

## *Achillea spp.* ASTERACEAE (COMPOSITAE)

### Yarrow

**SHAPE:** Almost 100 erect, open, semi-deciduous perennials, 6″–54″ (15–135 cm) tall, 12″–18″ (30–45 cm) wide. Soft, fine-cut, often toothed, aromatic leaves to 8″ (20 cm) long.

**FLOWER:** Spring or continual bloom. Flat clusters, 3″–5″ (75–125 mm) wide, of many tiny flowers. Choose from pink, red, white, and yellow.

**HARDINESS:** Zones 3–11.

**SOIL TYPE:** Sandy loam. Low moisture, good drainage, medium–low fertility, 6.5–8.0 pH.

**PLANTING GUIDE:** Spring or autumn, zones 3–8; autumn, zones 9–11. Plant in full sun, 12″–24″ (30–60 cm) apart.

**CARE TIPS:** Easy. Even moisture; tolerates drought when established. Fertilize only in spring. Support with stakes. Propagate by cuttings, division.

**NOTES:** Thrives in accents, beds, massed plantings. Nice in cottage, natural, seaside, wildlife, woodland gardens. Cutting, drying flower. Resists pests. Susceptible to powdery mildew, stem rot.

## *Aconitum napellus* RANUNCULACEAE

### Garden Monkshood (Aconite, Helmet Flower)

**SHAPE:** Numerous erect, slender, deciduous perennials, 36″–48″ (90–120 cm) tall. Hairy, lobed, deep-toothed leaves, 2″–4″ (50–100 mm) wide.

**FLOWER:** Late-summer to autumn bloom. Spikes to 12″ (30 cm) tall with dense clusters of helmet-shaped flowers, 1″–2″ (25–50 mm) wide, with visorlike extensions. Choose from blue and violet.

**HARDINESS:** Zones 2–9.

**SOIL TYPE:** High humus. High moisture, good drainage, high fertility, 5.0–6.0 pH.

**PLANTING GUIDE:** Spring, zones 3–5; autumn, zones 6–11. Plant in partial shade, 18″ (45 cm) apart.

**CARE TIPS:** Easy. Even moisture; water when soil dries 2″–3″ (50–75 mm) deep. Apply mulch in autumn in cold-winter climates. Support with stakes. Propagate by division, seed.

**NOTES:** Thrives in backgrounds, beds, borders. Nice in country, natural, woodland gardens. Cutting flower. Resists pests and diseases.

## *Adenophora spp.* CAMPANULACEAE (LOBELIACEAE)

### Ladybells

**SHAPE:** About 40 erect, slender, deciduous perennials, 24″–36″ (60–90 cm) tall. Opposite, woolly, lancelike, fine-cut leaves to 3″ (75 mm) long. See also *Campanula* spp., Canterbury-bells and Serbian bellflower.

**FLOWER:** Summer to autumn bloom. Showy, nodding, tubular, flared flowers to 1″ (25 mm) long, usually in twins or triplets. Choose from blue, pink, and purple.

**HARDINESS:** Zones 3–9.

**SOIL TYPE:** Average moisture, good drainage, high–medium fertility, 6.5–7.5 pH.

**PLANTING GUIDE:** Spring. Plant in full sun to partial shade, 18″–24″ (45–60 cm) apart.

**CARE TIPS:** Easy. Water when soil dries 4″–6″ (10–15 cm) deep. Fertilize every 4 weeks. Avoid division or transplanting. Propagate by seed.

**NOTES:** Thrives in borders, containers, edgings. Nice in country, natural, wildlife, woodland gardens. Resists pests and diseases.

## *Aethionema* spp. BRASSICACEAE (CRUCIFERAE)

### Stone Cress

**SHAPE:** Numerous thick-growing, erect, circular, shrubby annuals or perennials to 10″ (25 cm) tall and wide. Dusky, wide, oval, sharp-tipped leaves to 1″ (25 mm) long.

**FLOWER:** Late-spring to summer bloom. Dense, round, terminal clusters of flowers to 4″ (10 cm) wide. Choose from pink, rose, white, and yellow.

**HARDINESS:** Zones 6–9.

**SOIL TYPE:** Sandy loam. Average–low moisture, good drainage, medium–low fertility, 7.0–8.0 pH. Tolerates salt.

**PLANTING GUIDE:** Spring. Plant in full sun, 12″ (30 cm) apart.

**CARE TIPS:** Easy. Even moisture. Fertilize sparingly. Apply mulch. Extend bloom by deadheading. Propagate by division, seed.

**NOTES:** Thrives in borders, containers, edgings, massed plantings. Nice in country, natural, rock, seaside gardens. Resists pests and diseases.

## *Agapanthus africanus* and hybrids *(A. umbellatus)* AMARYLLIDACEAE

### Lily-of-the-Nile (Harriet's Flower)

**SHAPE:** Few rhizomatous, clumping, deciduous or evergreen perennials, 12″–18″ (30–45 cm) tall. Swordlike, curved, thick, shiny, succulent leaves to 18″ (45 cm) long.

**FLOWER:** Summer bloom. Dense, spherical clusters to 8″ (20 cm) wide of multiple flared, tube-shaped flowers. Choose from blue, purple, and white.

**HARDINESS:** Zones 7–11. With protection, zone 6.

**SOIL TYPE:** Loam. High–average moisture, good drainage, medium fertility, 5.5–6.5 pH.

**PLANTING GUIDE:** Spring to autumn. Plant in full sun to partial shade, 12″–24″ (30–60 cm) apart, slightly below soil level.

**CARE TIPS:** Easy. Even moisture during growth. Fertilize every 6–8 weeks. Apply mulch, zones 6–8. Store in-ground. Propagate by division, seed.

**NOTES:** Thrives in beds, containers, massed plantings. Nice in cottage, woodland gardens. Cutting flower. Resists diseases. Susceptible to deer.

## *Agastache* spp. and hybrids LAMIACEAE (LABIATAE)

### Hyssop (Giant Hyssop, Hummingbird Mint)

**SHAPE:** About 30 branched, mounded, erect perennials, 24″–48″ (60–120 cm) tall. Opposite, oval, sharp-tipped, fine-toothed, veined, aromatic leaves to 3″ (75 mm) long.

**FLOWER:** Summer bloom. Conical spikes to 6″ (15 cm) tall of many tiny, mintlike, edible flowers, ¼″ (6 mm) wide. Choose from blue, orange, pink, and red.

**HARDINESS:** Most, zones 5–11; some, zones 3–4.

**SOIL TYPE:** Sandy loam. Average moisture, good drainage, high–medium fertility, 6.5–7.5 pH.

**PLANTING GUIDE:** Spring, as soil warms. Plant in full to filtered sun, 12″ (30 cm) apart.

**CARE TIPS:** Easy. Even moisture; water when soil dries 2″–3″ (50–75 mm) deep. Fertilize only in spring. Extend bloom by deadheading. Propagate by division, seed.

**NOTES:** Thrives in backgrounds, borders, edgings, fence lines. Nice in arid, country, natural, rock, wildlife gardens. Resists pests and diseases.

## *Ajuga reptans* LAMIACEAE (LABIATAE).

### Carpet Bugleweed (Ajuga)

**SHAPE:** Numerous vigorous, low, sprawling, stoloniferous, deciduous perennials, 4″–12″ (10–30 cm) tall. Opposite, shiny, textured, oval or circular, curly leaves to 4″ (10 cm) long. Turns colors in autumn.

**FLOWER:** Late-spring to early-summer bloom. Whorled, spikelike clusters to 6″ (15 cm) long of many tiny, tubular, 2-lipped flowers. Choose from blue, pink, purple, and white.

**HARDINESS:** Zones 3–9.

**SOIL TYPE:** High humus. High moisture, good drainage, high–medium fertility, 6.0–7.0 pH.

**PLANTING GUIDE:** Spring, as soil warms. Plant in filtered sun to full shade, 6″–18″ (15–45 cm) apart.

**CARE TIPS:** Easy. Even moisture. Fertilize every 8–10 weeks. Shear in spring. Propagate by division.

**NOTES:** Thrives in banks, borders, containers, paths. Nice in cottage, shade, rock gardens. Aggressive. Susceptible to slugs, snails, leaf burn, fungal diseases, crown rot.

## *Alcea rosea* (*Althaea rosea*) MALVACEAE

### Hollyhock

**SHAPE:** Upright, slender biennial or perennial to 9' (2.7 m) tall. Textured, circular leaves, 6"–8" (15–20 cm) wide, forming a basal rosette.

**FLOWER:** Summer to autumn bloom. Stalks with vertical, tiered clusters of showy, pompon or saucer-shaped flowers to 4" (10 cm) wide. Choose from maroon, pink, red, white, and yellow.

**HARDINESS:** Zones 3–11.

**SOIL TYPE:** Loam. High moisture, good drainage, medium fertility, 7.0–7.5 pH.

**PLANTING GUIDE:** Spring for annual cultivars; late summer for biennial cultivars. Plant in full sun to partial shade, 12" (30 cm) apart.

**CARE TIPS:** Easy. Even moisture. Fertilize only in spring. Support with stakes. Shelter from wind. Cut stalks when flowers fade. Propagate by division, seed.

**NOTES:** Thrives in accents, backgrounds, beds. Nice in cottage, formal, natural, wildlife gardens. Susceptible to slugs, snails, rust.

## *Alchemilla* spp. ROSACEAE

### Lady's-Mantle

**SHAPE:** Nearly 200 mostly short, sprawling, deciduous annuals or perennials, 6"–24" (15–60 cm) tall, with runnerlike stolons. Soft, often fringed, circular or heart-shaped, deeply lobate leaves, 2"–5" (50–125 mm) wide.

**FLOWER:** Summer bloom. Terminal branching clusters to 2"–3" (50–75 mm) wide of many tiny flowers. Choose from green and yellow.

**HARDINESS:** Zones 3–9. Prefers cool climates.

**SOIL TYPE:** Loam. High moisture, good drainage, medium fertility, 6.0–7.0 pH.

**PLANTING GUIDE:** Spring. Plant in full to filtered sun, 12"–18" (30–45 cm) apart.

**CARE TIPS:** Easy. Even moisture. Fertilize every 4 weeks. Protect from hot sun. Propagate by division, runners, seed.

**NOTES:** Thrives in accents, edgings, foregrounds, ground covers. Nice in cottage, natural, shade, woodland gardens. Cutting flower. Resists pests and diseases.

## *Alstroemeria* spp. LILIACEAE

### Lily-of-the-Incas (Peruvian Lily)

**SHAPE:** About 50 rhizomatous or tuberous, deciduous or evergreen perennials, 18"–48" (45–120 cm) tall. Alternate, lancelike leaves to 4" (10 cm) long, on leafy stems.

**FLOWER:** Late-spring to summer bloom. Radiating clusters of multiple flared, trumpet-shaped, often fragrant, long-lasting flowers to 2" (50 mm) wide. Choose from purple, red, white, yellow, and bicolored.

**HARDINESS:** Zones 7–11.

**SOIL TYPE:** High humus. High moisture, good drainage, high fertility, 6.0–7.0 pH.

**PLANTING GUIDE:** Spring. Plant in full sun to partial shade, 12" (30 cm) apart, 6"–8" (15–20 cm) deep.

**CARE TIPS:** Average. High moisture during growth. Fertilize every 6–8 weeks. Apply mulch. Lift and store, zone 7. Propagate by division, seed.

**NOTES:** Thrives in beds, borders, containers. Nice in casual gardens. Cutting flower. Naturalizes. Resists diseases. Susceptible to deer, rodents.

## *Amsonia tabernaemontana* APOCYNACEAE

### Bluestar

**SHAPE:** Various languid, durable, erect, slim, shrubby, deciduous perennials to 42" (1.1 m) tall, 18"–24" (45–60 cm) wide. Dull, lancelike or willowlike leaves to 9" (23 cm) long. Turns colors in autumn.

**FLOWER:** Late-spring to early-summer bloom. Terminal clusters to 6" (15 cm) wide of star-shaped flowers. Choose from gray blue or steel gray with light blue centers.

**HARDINESS:** Zones 4–9.

**SOIL TYPE:** Loam. Average moisture, good drainage, high–medium fertility, 6.5–7.0 pH.

**PLANTING GUIDE:** Spring, zones 4–7; autumn, zones 8–9. Plant in full sun to partial shade, 6"–9" (15–23 cm) apart.

**CARE TIPS:** Easy. Even moisture. Tolerates drought. Fertilize every 4 weeks. Propagate by cuttings, division, seed.

**NOTES:** Thrives in borders. Nice in natural, wildlife gardens. Cutting flower. Resists pests and diseases.

## *Anchusa* spp. BORAGINACEAE

### Bugloss (Alkanet, Cape Forget-Me-Not)

**SHAPE:** About 35 vertical or sprawling annuals or perennials, 36″–60″ (90–150 cm) tall. Alternate, hirsute, textured, oval, sharp-tipped leaves, 3″–4″ (75–100 mm) long.

**FLOWER:** Summer bloom. Drooping, terminal clusters to 6″ (15 cm) wide of forget-me-not-like, 5-petaled flowers, ½″ (12 mm) wide. Choose from bright blue, violet, and white.

**HARDINESS:** Zones 3–8. Prefers low humidity.

**SOIL TYPE:** Sandy loam. High moisture, good drainage, medium–low fertility, 6.0–7.5 pH.

**PLANTING GUIDE:** Spring. Plant in full sun to partial shade, 18″–30″ (45–75 cm) apart.

**CARE TIPS:** Easy. Even moisture. Fertilize sparingly. Support with stakes. Shelter from wind. Propagate by cuttings, seed.

**NOTES:** Thrives in backgrounds, accents, borders, fence lines. Nice in formal, natural, woodland gardens. Cutting flower. Susceptible to leafhoppers, crown rot.

## *Anigozanthos* spp. and hybrids HAEMODORACEAE

### Kangaroo-Paw

**SHAPE:** About 10 species of rhizomatous, evergreen, herbaceous perennials, 18″–48″ (45–120 cm) tall. Smooth, straplike leaves to 20″ (50 cm) long.

**FLOWER:** Winter to spring bloom. Fanlike clusters of multiple slender, cylinder-shaped flowers, ¾″–3″ (19–75 mm) long. Choose from green, orange, pink, red, and yellow.

**HARDINESS:** Zones 9–11.

**SOIL TYPE:** Sandy loam. High moisture, good drainage, high fertility, 6.0–6.5 pH.

**PLANTING GUIDE:** Spring or early-autumn. Plant in full sun, 24″ (60 cm) apart.

**CARE TIPS:** Average. Even moisture during growth. Fertilize until buds form. Deadhead flowers. Lift and store. Propagate by division.

**NOTES:** Thrives in backgrounds, beds, borders, containers. Nice in arid, rock, wildlife gardens and greenhouses. Cutting flower. Susceptible to deer, slugs, snails.

## *Anthemis tinctoria* ASTERACEAE (COMPOSITAE)

### Golden Marguerite

**SHAPE:** Various impermanent, shrubby, semi-evergreen biennials or perennials, 24″–36″ (60–90 cm) tall. Smooth, deep-cut, aromatic leaves to 3″ (75 mm) long.

**FLOWER:** Summer to autumn bloom. Masses of daisylike, multirayed, upturned flowers, 1½″–2″ (38–50 mm) wide. Choose from gold, orange, white, and yellow with wide yellow centers.

**HARDINESS:** Zones 3–10. May self-seed.

**SOIL TYPE:** Sandy loam. Average–low moisture, good drainage, low fertility, 6.5–7.0 pH.

**PLANTING GUIDE:** Spring, as soil warms, or summer. Plant in full sun, 15″–18″ (38–45 cm) apart.

**CARE TIPS:** Easy. Water only when soil dries. Fertilize sparingly. Extend bloom by dead heading. Propagate by cuttings, division, seed.

**NOTES:** Thrives in accents, borders, containers. Nice in cottage, meadow, natural gardens. Cutting flower. Resists diseases. Susceptible to aphids.

## *Antirrhinum majus* SCROPHULARIACEAE

### Snapdragon (Garden Snapdragon)

**SHAPE:** Numerous upright, deciduous perennials to 36″ (90 cm) tall. Shiny, lancelike leaves to 3″ (75 mm) long.

**FLOWER:** Spring to early-summer bloom. Double-lipped or double flowers to 2″ (50 mm) long. Choose from orange, pink, red, white, yellow, and bicolored.

**HARDINESS:** Zones 8–11.

**SOIL TYPE:** High humus. High moisture, good drainage, high fertility, 6.5–7.0 pH.

**PLANTING GUIDE:** Spring, as soil becomes workable. Plant in full to filtered sun, 4″–6″ (10–15 cm) apart.

**CARE TIPS:** Easy. Even moisture; avoid wetting foliage. Fertilize every 3–4 weeks. Shear after bloom. Propagate by seed.

**NOTES:** Thrives in beds, borders, edgings, fence lines. Nice in cottage, formal, wildlife gardens. Cutting flower. Susceptible to aphids, leaf miners, whiteflies, rust.

## *Aquilegia* spp. RANUNCULACEAE

### Columbine

**SHAPE:** About 70 erect, open perennials, 12″–36″ (30–90 cm) tall. Fine-textured, divided, cut or lobed leaves to 8″ (20 cm) wide.

**FLOWER:** Early-summer bloom. Cup-and-saucer-shaped flowers, 1½″–2″ (38–50 mm) wide and to 2″ (50 mm) long, with dangling spurs. Choose from blue, white, rose, yellow, and bicolored.

**HARDINESS:** Zones 3–10.

**SOIL TYPE:** Sandy loam. High moisture, very good drainage, high–medium fertility, 6.5–7.5 pH.

**PLANTING GUIDE:** Spring, as soil warms. Plant in full sun to partial shade, 12″–24″ (30–60 cm) apart.

**CARE TIPS:** Easy. Even moisture during growth; limit thereafter. Fertilize every 2 weeks. Propagate by division, seed.

**NOTES:** Thrives in borders, containers, massed plantings. Nice in natural, wildlife, woodland gardens. Susceptible to aphids, leaf miners, powdery mildew, rust, wilt.

## *Arctotis venusta* and hybrids (*A. stoechadifolia*) ASTERACEAE

### African Daisy

**SHAPE:** Numerous erect, branched, or mounded, deciduous perennials to 24″ (60 cm) tall. Hairy, textured, lobate leaves, 3″–4″ (75–100 mm) long. See also *Dimorphotheca pluvialis*.

**FLOWER:** Late-spring to summer bloom. Daisy-like, double flowers, 2″–3″ (50–75 mm) wide. Choose from pink, purple, red, white, and yellow.

**HARDINESS:** Zones 8–10. Protect from frost. Prefers cool, coastal areas.

**SOIL TYPE:** Sandy loam. High moisture, good drainage, high fertility, 6.5–7.5 pH.

**PLANTING GUIDE:** Spring, if grown as an annual; autumn, zones 8–10. Plant in full sun, 6″–12″ (15–30 cm) apart.

**CARE TIPS:** Easy. Water only when soil dries. Fertilize every 4 weeks. Extend bloom by deadheading. Propagate by cuttings, division, seed.

**NOTES:** Thrives in beds, borders, containers. Nice in cottage, natural, woodland gardens. Cutting flower. Resists pests and diseases.

## *Aristea* spp. IRIDACEAE

### Aristea

**SHAPE:** About 50 species of rhizomatous or fibrous-rooted, tropical, deciduous perennials to 24″ (60 cm) tall. Straplike, shiny leaves to 24″ (60 cm) long, in basal rosettes.

**FLOWER:** Late-spring to autumn bloom. Branching sprays of single, 6-petaled flowers, ¾″–1″ (19–25 mm) wide. Choose from blue and violet.

**HARDINESS:** Zones 8–10.

**SOIL TYPE:** Loam. High moisture, good drainage, medium fertility, 6.0–7.0 pH.

**PLANTING GUIDE:** Autumn. Plant in full sun to partial shade, 10″–12″ (25–30 cm) apart, 2″–3″ (50–75 mm) deep.

**CARE TIPS:** Easy. Even moisture during growth. Fertilize in spring. Extend bloom by deadheading. Store in-ground. Propagate by division, seed.

**NOTES:** Thrives in beds, borders, containers, mixed plantings. Nice in woodland gardens. Aggressive, self-sowing. Resists pests and diseases.

## *Armeria maritima* PLUMBAGINACEAE.

### Thrift (Common Thrift, Sea Pink)

**SHAPE:** Numerous, mounded or bunching, evergreen perennials to 6″ (15 cm) tall and 12″ (30 cm) wide. Shiny, very slender, grasslike leaves, 4″–6″ (10–15 cm) long.

**FLOWER:** Spring to summer bloom. Wiry stems, 10″–12″ (25–30 cm) tall, with showy, ball-shaped clusters to ¾″ (19 mm) wide of tiny flowers. Choose from pink, purple, red, and white.

**HARDINESS:** Zones 3–11. May self-seed. Prefers arid, mild-winter climates; tolerates heat.

**SOIL TYPE:** Sandy loam. Average–low moisture, good drainage, medium fertility, 6.5–8.0 pH.

**PLANTING GUIDE:** Spring, as soil warms. Plant in full sun, 12″ (30 cm) apart.

**CARE TIPS:** Easy. Water when soil dries 4″–6″ (10–15 cm) deep. Fertilize only in spring. Propagate by cuttings, division, seed.

**NOTES:** Thrives in borders, containers, edgings. Nice in cottage, rock, seaside, Xeriscape gardens. Cutting flower. Resists pests and diseases.

## *Aruncus dioicus* (A. sylvester) ROSACEAE

### Goatsbeard

**SHAPE:** Various mounded, deciduous perennials to 6′ (1.8 m) tall, 4′ (1.2 m) wide. Deeply textured, oval, divided leaves to 12″ (30 cm) long with coarse-toothed, oval leaflets, on radiating stalks.

**FLOWER:** Late-spring to early-summer bloom. Plumelike, often nodding, terminal clusters to 18″ (45 cm) long of many tiny flowers. Choose from cream and white.

**HARDINESS:** Zones 3–9.

**SOIL TYPE:** Sandy loam; pond shorelines. High moisture, good drainage, high fertility, 6.0–8.0 pH. Tolerates salt.

**PLANTING GUIDE:** Spring. Plant in full sun to partial shade, 18″–24″ (45–60 cm) apart.

**CARE TIPS:** Easy. Even moisture. Fertilize only in spring. Propagate by division, seed.

**NOTES:** Thrives in beds, borders. Nice in shade, woodland gardens and ponds. Drying flower. Resists pests and diseases.

## *Asclepias tuberosa* ASCLEPIADACEAE

### Milkweed (Butterfly Weed, Indian Paintbrush)

**SHAPE:** Various erect and branched, hirsute perennials, 24″–36″ (60–90 cm) tall, 12″–18″ (30–45 cm) wide. Smooth, lancelike leaves to 4½″ (11 cm) long, in spirals or clusters.

**FLOWER:** Summer bloom. Broad, flat, mounded clusters of showy, starlike flowers to ⅓″ (8 mm) wide. Choose from orange, red, yellow. Forms pods bearing thread-covered seed, in autumn.

**HARDINESS:** Zones 3–9.

**SOIL TYPE:** Sandy loam. Average–low moisture, good drainage, low fertility, 6.5–7.0 pH.

**PLANTING GUIDE:** Early spring when frost risk ends, zones 3–6; autumn, zones 7–9. Plant in full sun, 12″–18″ (30–45 cm) apart.

**CARE TIPS:** Easy. Water only when soil dries. Fertilize sparingly. Propagate by division, seed.

**NOTES:** Thrives in accents, beds, borders, containers. Nice in natural, meadow, wildlife gardens. Cutting flower. Somewhat aggressive. Resists pests and diseases.

## *Aster spp.* ASTERACEAE (COMPOSITAE)

### Aster

**SHAPE:** More than 600 bushlike, erect, usually shrubby, deciduous, herbaceous perennials, 4″–60″ (10–150 cm) tall and wide. Hairy, lancelike leaves, 3″–5″ (75–125 mm) long.

**FLOWER:** Late-summer to autumn bloom. Tall stalks of showy, daisylike flowers to 2½″ (63 mm) wide. Choose from blue, pink, purple, red, and white.

**HARDINESS:** Zones 2–9.

**SOIL TYPE:** Sandy loam. High moisture, good drainage, high–medium fertility, 6.0–7.0 pH.

**PLANTING GUIDE:** Spring, as frost risk ends and soil becomes workable. Plant in full to filtered sun, 36″–48″ (90–120 cm) apart.

**CARE TIPS:** Easy. Even moisture. Fertilize every 4 weeks. Extend bloom by deadheading. Propagate by cuttings, division.

**NOTES:** Thrives in accents, backgrounds, containers, massed plantings. Nice in cottage, formal, natural, wildlife gardens. Aggressive. Susceptible to aphids, mildew, aster yellow.

## *Astilbe spp.* SAXIFRAGACEAE

### Astilbe (False Spiraea, Meadow Sweet)

**SHAPE:** Few low, mounded, perennials, 8″–36″ (20–90 cm) tall, 12″–24″ (30–60 cm) wide. Shiny, neatly formed, plumelike, finely divided, toothed leaves to 3″ (75 mm) long.

**FLOWER:** Summer bloom. Slender, stiff stalks form fluffy plumes to 12″ (30 cm) tall of many tiny flowers. Choose from pink, deep red, white.

**HARDINESS:** Zones 4–11.

**SOIL TYPE:** Sandy loam; pond shorelines. High moisture, good drainage, high–medium fertility, 5.5–7.0 pH.

**PLANTING GUIDE:** Spring. Plant in full sun to full shade, 12″–24″ (30–60 cm) apart.

**CARE TIPS:** Easy to average. Even moisture. Fertilize only in spring. Apply mulch. Shear in winter. Propagate by division, seed.

**NOTES:** Thrives in borders, containers, ground covers. Nice in bog, cottage, shade gardens and ponds. Cutting flower. Susceptible to Japanese beetles, slugs, snails, powdery mildew.

## *Astrantia major* APIACEAE (UMBELLIFERAE)

### Masterwort

**SHAPE:** Various mounded, deciduous perennials, 24″–36″ (60–90 cm) tall. Textured, often variegated, palm-shaped, 5-lobed leaves to 12″ (30 cm) wide.

**FLOWER:** Late-spring bloom. Clusters of flowers, 2″–3″ (50–75 mm) wide. Choose from cream with green, pink or purple centers and purple leaf bracts.

**HARDINESS:** Zones 6–9.

**SOIL TYPE:** Sandy loam; pond shorelines. High moisture, good drainage, medium fertility, 6.5–7.0 pH.

**PLANTING GUIDE:** Early spring, zone 6; autumn, zone 7–9. Plant in full sun to partial shade, 18″ (45 cm) apart.

**CARE TIPS:** Easy. Even moisture. Apply mulch. Propagate by division, seed.

**NOTES:** Thrives in backgrounds, borders. Nice in bog, natural, woodland gardens. Cutting flower. Resists pests and diseases.

## *Baptisia australis* FABACEAE (LEGUMINOSAE)

### False Indigo (Blue False Indigo, Wild Indigo)

**SHAPE:** Various erect, bunching, deciduous perennials, 24″–72″ (60–180 cm) tall. Dull, oval leaves, 2½″ (63 mm) long, in 3-leaflet groups.

**FLOWER:** Early-summer bloom. Long terminal racemes of pealike flowers to 1″ (25 mm) wide. Blue. Forms beanlike seedpods in autumn.

**HARDINESS:** Zones 3–9.

**SOIL TYPE:** Loam. Average–low moisture, good drainage, medium–low fertility, 6.5–7.0 pH.

**PLANTING GUIDE:** Spring, zones 3–7; autumn, zones 8–9. Plant in full sun to partial shade, 24″–36″ (60–90 cm) apart.

**CARE TIPS:** Easy. Even moisture; water when soil dries 2″–3″ (50–75 mm) deep. Tolerates drought. Fertilize sparingly. Stake to support. Protect from wind. Propagate by division, seed.

**NOTES:** Thrives in accents, backgrounds, borders, massed plantings, screens. Nice in cottage, meadow gardens. Cutting flower. Resists deer, pests, and diseases.

## *Begonia* × *semperflorens-cultorum* hybrids BEGONIACEAE

### Bedding Begonia (Wax Begonia)

**SHAPE:** Numerous vigorous, bushlike, erect, succulent, fibrous-rooted perennials, 8″–12″ (20–30 cm) tall. Smooth, shiny, sometimes variegated leaves to 1″ (25 mm) wide.

**FLOWER:** Spring to autumn bloom. Fleshy stems with round clusters of waxy, single flowers to 1″ (25 mm) wide. Choose from pink, red, and white.

**HARDINESS:** Zones 8–11. Protect from frost.

**SOIL TYPE:** High humus. High moisture, good drainage, high fertility, 6.5–7.5 pH.

**PLANTING GUIDE:** Spring. Plant in filtered sun to partial shade, 8″–10″ (20–25 cm) apart.

**CARE TIPS:** Easy. Even moisture. Fertilize every 4 weeks. Apply mulch. Pinch tips for bushy plants. Propagate by cuttings, seed.

**NOTES:** Thrives in hanging baskets, beds, borders, containers, foregrounds, window boxes. Nice in formal, shade gardens. Susceptible to mealybugs, whiteflies, leaf spot.

## *Belamcanda chinensis* IRIDACEAE

### Blackberry Lily (Leopard Flower)

**SHAPE:** Few rhizomatous, deciduous perennials, 24″–48″ (60–120 cm) tall. Narrow, swordlike, erect or curved leaves to 16″ (41 cm) long.

**FLOWER:** Late-summer to early-autumn bloom. Open, star-shaped flowers, 2″–3″ (50–75 mm) wide. Orange with red speckles. Forms black, berrylike, clustered seed in autumn.

**HARDINESS:** Zones 6–11. Protect from frost.

**SOIL TYPE:** Sandy loam. High moisture, good drainage, high–medium fertility, 6.5–7.0 pH.

**PLANTING GUIDE:** Spring. Plant in full sun to partial shade, 10″–12″ (25–30 cm) apart, slightly below soil level.

**CARE TIPS:** Easy. Even moisture during growth. Fertilize until buds form. Lift and store. Propagate by division, seed.

**NOTES:** Thrives in backgrounds, borders, fence lines. Nice in cottage, shade gardens. Dry berries. Resists deer and rodents. Susceptible to mosaic virus.

## *Bellis perennis* ASTERACEAE (COMPOSITAE)

### English Daisy

**SHAPE:** Various open and mounding, evergreen perennials to 8″ (20 cm) tall. Smooth to woolly, spoon-shaped, toothed leaves, 1″–2″ (25–50 mm) wide, in basal rosettes.

**FLOWER:** Spring to early-summer bloom. Stiff stalks of daisylike, flat, open, single or double flowers to 2″ (25 mm) wide. Choose from pink, rose, and white.

**HARDINESS:** Zones 3–8. Protect from hot sun. Prefers mild-summer climates.

**SOIL TYPE:** High humus. High moisture, good drainage, high–medium fertility, 6.5–7.5 pH.

**PLANTING GUIDE:** Spring. Plant in full sun to partial shade, 8–10″ (20–25 cm) apart.

**CARE TIPS:** Easy. Even moisture; water when soil dries 2–4″ (50–100 mm) deep. Fertilize every 6–8 weeks. Propagate by division.

**NOTES:** Thrives in beds, borders, edgings, ground covers. Nice in natural, woodland gardens. Resists pests and diseases.

## *Bergenia cordifolia* SAXIFRAGACEAE

### Heartleaf Bergenia

**SHAPE:** Various open and sprawling, rhizomatous, semi-evergreen perennials to 18″ (45 cm) tall. Hairy, shiny, heart-shaped or circular, wavy-edged leaves, 6″–10″ (15–25 cm) wide, in basal rosettes. Creeping, spreading rootstock.

**FLOWER:** Early-spring bloom. Clusters to 16″ (40 cm) tall of showy, nodding, 5-petaled flowers, ¾″ (19 mm) wide. Choose from deep pink, purple, red, and white.

**HARDINESS:** Zones 3–8. Very cold tolerant.

**SOIL TYPE:** Loam. High moisture, good drainage, medium–low fertility, 6.0–7.5 pH.

**PLANTING GUIDE:** Spring. Plant in partial to full shade, 12″ (30 cm) apart.

**CARE TIPS:** Easy. Even moisture; tolerates drought when established. Fertilize every 10–12 weeks. Propagate by division, seed.

**NOTES:** Thrives in borders, edgings, ground covers. Nice in natural, shade, woodland gardens. Susceptible to nematodes, slugs.

## *Browallia speciosa* SOLANACEAE

### Bush Violet (Amethyst Flower, Lovely Browallia)

**SHAPE:** Numerous mounded, circular, shrubby deciduous perennials to 24″ (60 cm) tall. Hairy, slender, oval, sharp-tipped leaves to 2½″ (63 mm) long.

**FLOWER:** Spring to summer bloom. Lone 5-petaled flowers to 2″ (50 mm) wide. Choose from blue, violet, and white with contrasting centers.

**HARDINESS:** Zones 9–11. Protect from frost. Prefers hot, humid climates.

**SOIL TYPE:** High humus. High moisture, good drainage, high fertility, 6.5–7.5 pH.

**PLANTING GUIDE:** Spring, as soil warms, zones 4–9; autumn, zones 10–11. Plant in partial to full shade, 12″ (30 cm) apart.

**CARE TIPS:** Easy. Even moisture. Fertilize sparingly. Apply mulch in full sun. Pinch tips for bushy plants. Propagate by cuttings, seed.

**NOTES:** Thrives in beds, borders, containers. Nice in country, shade gardens. Cutting flower. Resists pests and diseases.

## *Brunnera macrophylla* BORAGINACEAE

### Siberian Bugloss (Heartleaf Brunnera)

**SHAPE:** Various bushlike, short, deciduous perennials, 18″–24″ (45–60 cm) tall. Alternate, hirsute, variegated, heart-shaped leaves to 4″ (10 cm) wide and 6″–8″ (15–20 cm) long.

**FLOWER:** Spring to summer bloom. Wiry, slightly hirsute stems to 6″ (15 cm) tall with open, branching clusters of many tiny, delicate flowers to ¼″ (6 mm) wide. Blue with contrasting yellow centers.

**HARDINESS:** Zones 3–10.

**SOIL TYPE:** High humus. High moisture, good drainage, high fertility, 6.5–7.0 pH.

**PLANTING GUIDE:** Autumn. Plant in partial shade, 12″ (30 cm) apart.

**CARE TIPS:** Easy. Even moisture. Fertilize only in spring. Apply mulch. Propagate by cuttings, division, seed.

**NOTES:** Thrives in borders, edgings, fillers, ground covers. Nice in shade, woodland gardens. Self-sows. Resists pests and diseases.

### *Calamintha nepeta* (*C. nepetoides*) LAMIACEAE (LABIATAE)

#### Calamint (Calamint Savory)

**SHAPE:** Various short, mounded, rhizomatous, deciduous perennials to 2″ (60 cm) tall. Opposite, oval, sharp-tipped, fine-toothed, very aromatic leaves to ¾″ (19 mm) long.

**FLOWER:** Summer bloom. Clusters of 2-part flowers to ¾″ (19 mm) long, bearing prominent stamens. Choose from lavender, white.

**HARDINESS:** Zones 5–9.

**SOIL TYPE:** Loam. High moisture, good drainage, medium fertility, 6.5–7.0 pH.

**PLANTING GUIDE:** Spring. Plant in full sun to partial shade, 15″–18″ (38–45 cm) apart.

**CARE TIPS:** Average. Even moisture. Fertilize every 10–12 weeks. Apply mulch in winter, zones 5–6. Pinch tips or shear for bushy plants. Propagate by cuttings, division.

**NOTES:** Thrives in hanging baskets, beds, borders, containers, entries, ground covers. Nice in natural, small-space, wildlife, woodland gardens. Aggressive. Resists pests and diseases.

### *Calceolaria* spp. and hybrids SCROPHULARIACEAE

#### Slipper Flower (Pocketbook Plant, Slipperwort)

**SHAPE:** Numerous branched, shrubby, deciduous perennials, 6″–72″ (15–180 cm) tall. Textured, oval, toothed leaves to 3″ (75 mm) long.

**FLOWER:** Spring to early-summer bloom. Open clusters of pouchlike flowers, ½″–1″ (12–25 mm) long. Choose from bronze, maroon, pink, red, and yellow, with green or purple markings.

**HARDINESS:** Zones 8–11. Protect from frost.

**SOIL TYPE:** High humus. High moisture, good drainage, high–medium fertility, 7.0 pH.

**PLANTING GUIDE:** Spring, when frost risk ends. Plant in full to filtered sun, 6″–12″ (15–30 cm) apart. Start indoors, zones 2–7.

**CARE TIPS:** Average. Water when soil dries 4″–6″ (10–15 cm) deep. Fertilize every 4 weeks. Extend bloom by deadheading. Propagate by cuttings, seed.

**NOTES:** Thrives in beds, borders, containers. Nice in country, shade, woodland gardens. Susceptible to spider mites.

### *Calibrachoa* spp. SOLANACEAE

#### Million Bells

**SHAPE:** Various short and trailing or mounded, deciduous perennials to 24″ (60 cm) tall and 36″ (90 cm) wide. Textured, oval, sharp-tipped, toothed leaves to 1″ (25 mm) long, on slender, flexible stems.

**FLOWER:** Summer bloom. Showy, petunia-like flowers to 1″ (25 mm) wide. Choose from blue, pink, purple, red, and violet.

**HARDINESS:** Zones 8–11. Protect from frost.

**SOIL TYPE:** Sandy loam. High moisture, good drainage, high–medium fertility, 6.5–8.0 pH.

**PLANTING GUIDE:** Spring, as soil warms. Plant in full to filtered sun, 18″ (45 cm) apart.

**CARE TIPS:** Average. Water when soil dries 4″–6″ (10–15 cm) deep. Fertilize every 4 weeks. Avoid deadheading; pinch tips for bushy plants. Propagate by cuttings, seed.

**NOTES:** Thrives in beds, borders, containers. Nice in formal, country gardens. Resists pests. Susceptible to fungal diseases.

### *Campanula medium* CAMPANULACEAE

#### Canterbury-Bells

**SHAPE:** Numerous erect, biennials, 24″–36″ (60–90 cm) tall. Alternate, rough-textured, oval, sharp-tipped leaves to 10 in (25 cm) long on hirsute stalks.

**FLOWER:** Spring to early-summer bloom. Vertical tiers of bell-shaped, often double flowers to 2″ (50 mm) long with reflexed petals. Choose from violet blue, pink, and white.

**HARDINESS:** Zones 4–8.

**SOIL TYPE:** Loam. High moisture, good drainage, high fertility, 7.0–7.5 pH.

**PLANTING GUIDE:** Early spring, as soil warms. Plant in partial shade, 12″ (30 cm) apart.

**CARE TIPS:** Average. Even moisture. Fertilize every 4 weeks. Extend bloom by deadheading. Support with stakes. Propagate by seed.

**NOTES:** Thrives in accents, backgrounds, borders. Nice in cottage, meadow, shade, woodland gardens. Cutting flower. Resists diseases. Susceptible to spider mites, slugs, snails.

## *Campanula poscharskyana* CAMPANULACEAE

### Serbian Bellflower

**SHAPE:** Various vigorous, low, crawling, sprawling, or dangling perennials to 12″ (30 cm) tall and 36″–48″ (90–120 cm) wide. Smooth, textured, heart- or kidney-shaped, veined leaves to 1½″ (38 mm) long, on jointed stems.

**FLOWER:** Late-spring to autumn bloom. Bell- or star-shaped flowers, ½″–1″ (12–25 mm) wide. Pale lavender and blue, often with light blue, deep-throated centers.

**HARDINESS:** Zones 3–7.

**SOIL TYPE:** High humus. Average moisture, good drainage, medium fertility, 6.5–7.0 pH.

**PLANTING GUIDE:** Spring, when frost risk ends. Plant in full sun, 12″–18″ (30–45 cm) apart.

**CARE TIPS:** Easy. Even moisture. Fertilize only in spring. Extend bloom by deadheading. Propagate by cuttings, division, seed.

**NOTES:** Thrives in accents, beds, borders, walls. Nice in cottage, rock, wildlife gardens. Susceptible to spider mites, slugs, snails.

## *Canna* spp. and hybrids CANNACEAE

### Canna (Indian-Shot)

**SHAPE:** Few rhizomatous, semi-evergreen, perennials, 4′–16′ (1.2–4.9 m) tall. Showy, large, long, wide, sometimes variegated, usually fringed leaves to 20″ (51 cm) long.

**FLOWER:** Summer to autumn bloom. Terminal clusters of flowers to 6″ (15 cm) wide. Choose from orange, pink, red, white, yellow, and bicolor.

**HARDINESS:** Zones 8–11. Protect from frost.

**SOIL TYPE:** High humus–sandy loam mix; pond shorelines. High moisture, good drainage, high fertility, 6.0–7.0 pH.

**PLANTING GUIDE:** Spring, zones 3–7, autumn, zones 8–11. Plant in full sun, 12″–24″ (30–60 cm) apart, slightly below soil level.

**CARE TIPS:** Easy. Even moisture during growth. Fertilize until buds form. Apply mulch. Lift and store. Propagate by division.

**NOTES:** Thrives in accents, borders, containers. Nice in tropical, wildlife gardens and ponds. Susceptible to slugs, snails.

## *Capsicum annuum* SOLANACEAE

### Ornamental Pepper (Christmas Pepper)

**SHAPE:** Numerous branched, shrubby, deciduous perennials, 12″–48″ (30–120 cm) tall and to 36″ (90 cm) wide. Shiny, oval, sharp-tipped leaves to 3″ (75 mm) long.

**FLOWER:** Summer bloom. Tiny, star-shaped flowers to ½″ (12 mm) wide. White with yellow centers. Forms colorful seed-filled, edible fruit in late summer to late autumn.

**HARDINESS:** Zones 9–11. Protect from frost.

**SOIL TYPE:** Sandy loam. High moisture, good drainage, high fertility, 6.5–7.0 pH.

**PLANTING GUIDE:** Spring, once soil has warmed. Plant in full sun, 6″–12″ (15–30 cm) apart.

**CARE TIPS:** Easy. Even moisture; water when soil dries 2″–3″ (50–75 mm) deep. Fertilize every 4 weeks. Propagate by seed.

**NOTES:** Thrives in accents, borders, containers, edgings. Nice in arid, desert, rock gardens. Cut seedpods. Resists diseases. Susceptible to aphids, cutworms, weevils, whiteflies.

## *Catananche caerulea* ASTERACEAE (COMPOSITAE)

### Cupid's-Dart

**SHAPE:** Various impermanent, erect, mounded perennials to 18″ (45 cm) tall and 12″ (30 cm) wide. Alternate, woolly, slender, grasslike, toothed leaves to 12″ (30 cm) long.

**FLOWER:** Summer to autumn bloom. Daisylike flowers to 2″ (50 mm) wide with toothed petals. Choose from blue, violet, and white with dark centers.

**HARDINESS:** Zones 3–9. May self-seed.

**SOIL TYPE:** Sandy loam. Average–low moisture, good drainage, medium fertility, 6.5–8.0 pH.

**PLANTING GUIDE:** Spring, when frost risk ends. Plant in full sun, 12″ (30 cm) apart.

**CARE TIPS:** Average. Light moisture during growth; limit thereafter. Fertilize every 6–8 weeks. Propagate by division, seed.

**NOTES:** Thrives in borders, containers, edgings. Nice in cottage, formal, seaside, Xeriscape gardens. Cutting flower. Resists pests. Susceptible to fungal diseases.

## *Catharanthus roseus* (Vinca rosea) APOCYNACEAE

### Periwinkle (Madagascar Periwinkle)

**SHAPE:** Various erect, crawling or sprawling, perennials to 20″ (50 cm) tall and 18″ (45 cm) wide. Opposite, shiny, oval, sharp-tipped leaves to 2″ (50 mm) long.

**FLOWER:** Spring to autumn bloom. Single, 5-petaled flowers to 1½″ (38 mm) wide. Choose from rose pink, rose, and white with contrasting centers.

**HARDINESS:** Zones 9–11. Protect from frost. Protect from frost. May self-seed.

**SOIL TYPE:** Sandy loam. High moisture, good drainage, high fertility, 6.5–7.5 pH.

**PLANTING GUIDE:** Spring, as soil warms. Plant in full sun to partial shade, 9″–12″ (23–30 cm) apart. Start indoors for early bloom.

**CARE TIPS:** Very easy. Even moisture. Fertilize every 4 weeks. Shear in late autumn. Propagate by seed.

**NOTES:** Thrives in beds, borders, containers, edgings, ground covers. Nice in arid, formal, shade, woodland gardens. Resists diseases. Susceptible to slugs, snails.

## *Centaurea* spp. ASTERACEAE (COMPOSITAE)

### Knapweed (Dusty-Miller)

**SHAPE:** Numerous bushlike, circular annuals, biennials, or perennials, 12″–60″′ (30–150 cm) tall. Woolly, needlelike, usually deep-cut leaves to 12″ (30 cm) long. See also *C. cyanus*, cornflower.

**FLOWER:** Spring to summer bloom. Lone or clusters of fringed, tubular, thistlelike, tufted flowers, 2″–3″ (50–75 mm) wide. Choose from blue, lavender, pink, and yellow.

**HARDINESS:** Zones 3–9.

**SOIL TYPE:** Loam. High moisture, good drainage, medium fertility, 6.5–8.0 pH. Tolerates salt.

**PLANTING GUIDE:** Early spring, when frost risk ends, zones 3–7; autumn, zones 8–9. Plant in full to filtered sun, 12″–24″ (30–60 cm) apart.

**CARE TIPS:** Easy. Even moisture. Fertilize only in spring. Stake to support. Propagate by division, seed.

**NOTES:** Thrives in accents, backgrounds, beds. Nice in arid, formal, rock gardens. Cutting flower. Resists diseases. Susceptible to aphids.

## *Centranthus ruber* (Valeriana rubra) VALERIANACEAE

### Red Valerian (Jupiter's-Beard)

**SHAPE:** Various bushlike, deciduous perennials to 36″ (90 cm) tall. Opposite, shiny, oval, sharp-tipped leaves to 4″ (10 cm) long.

**FLOWER:** Spring to summer bloom. Spiked clusters of tubular, flared flowers to 3″ (75 mm) tall and ½″–1½″ (12–38 mm) wide. Choose from blue, pink, red, and white.

**HARDINESS:** Zones 4–11. May self-seed.

**SOIL TYPE:** Loam. High moisture, good drainage, medium–low fertility, 6.5–8.0 pH.

**PLANTING GUIDE:** Spring. Plant in full sun, 24″–36″ (60–90 cm) apart, as soil becomes workable.

**CARE TIPS:** Easy. Even moisture; tolerates drought when established. Fertilize sparingly. Extend bloom by deadheading. Propagate by division, seed.

**NOTES:** Thrives in accents, backgrounds, beds, borders, massed plantings. Nice in arid, meadow, natural, rock, seaside gardens. Aggressive. Resists pests and diseases.

## *Cephalaria gigantea* (Scabiosa gigantea) DIPSACACEAE

### Cephalaria

**SHAPE:** Few coarse, vertical, branched, hirsute perennials to 8′ (2.4 m) tall and 36″ (90 cm) wide. Opposite, plumelike, divided, deeply cut leaves to 16″ (40 cm) long, with lancelike leaflets.

**FLOWER:** Late-summer bloom. Branched clusters of ball-shaped, often fringed flowers to 2½″ (64 mm) wide. Choose from cream and light yellow. Forms seeds in autumn.

**HARDINESS:** Zones 3–9.

**SOIL TYPE:** Loam. Average moisture, good drainage, medium fertility, 6.5–7.5 pH.

**PLANTING GUIDE:** Spring. Plant in full sun, 4′ (1.2 m) apart, as soil becomes workable.

**CARE TIPS:** Easy. Even moisture; tolerates drought when established. Fertilize every 10–12 weeks. Propagate by division, seed.

**NOTES:** Thrives in accents, backgrounds, edgings. Nice in meadow, natural, rock, wildlife gardens. Resists pests and diseases.

## *Cerastium tomentosum* CARYOPHYLLACEAE

### Snow-in-Summer

**SHAPE:** Few low, flat perennials, 4″–8″ (10–20 cm) tall and 36″ (90 cm) wide. Opposite, woolly, lancelike, sharp-tipped leaves to 1″ (25 mm) long.

**FLOWER:** Spring to early-summer bloom. Erect branching stems to 12″ (30 cm) long with many tiny, divided- and 5-petaled flowers. Bright white.

**HARDINESS:** Zones 1–11.

**SOIL TYPE:** Sandy loam or high humus. High–average moisture, good drainage, medium–low fertility, 6.0–7.0 pH.

**PLANTING GUIDE:** Spring, as soil becomes workable. Plant in full to filtered sun, 18″ (45 cm) apart.

**CARE TIPS:** Easy. Water when soil dries 4″–6″ (10–15 cm) deep. Tolerates drought. Fertilize only in spring. Shear after bloom. Propagate by cuttings, division, seed.

**NOTES:** Thrives in accents, banks, containers, edgings, paths. Nice in cottage, meadow, rock, Xeriscape gardens. Resists pests and diseases.

## *Ceratostigma plumbaginoides* PLUMBAGINACEAE

### Dwarf Plumbago (Chinese Plumbago)

**SHAPE:** Various mounding or spreading, semi-evergreen, stoloniferous perennials, 8″–12″ (20–30 cm) tall. Alternate, shiny, oval, hirsute leaves to 3½″ (89 mm) long in tufted bunches.

**FLOWER:** Late-summer to early-autumn bloom. Wiry, hirsute stems hold clusters of open, phlox-like flowers to 1″ (25 mm) wide. Bright blue.

**HARDINESS:** Zones 5–9. Protect from hot sun, zones 9–11.

**SOIL TYPE:** Sandy loam. High–average moisture, good drainage, medium–low fertility, 6.5–7.5 pH.

**PLANTING GUIDE:** Spring. Plant in full to filtered sun, 12″–18″ (30–45 cm) apart.

**CARE TIPS:** Easy. Even moisture. Fertilize only in spring. Apply mulch, zones 8–11. Shear after frost. Propagate by cuttings, division.

**NOTES:** Thrives in borders, containers, ground covers, paths. Nice in cottage, natural, woodland gardens. Aggressive. Resists diseases. Susceptible to slugs, snails.

## *Chrysanthemum* spp. ASTERACEAE (COMPOSITAE)

### Chrysanthemum

**SHAPE:** Numerous bushlike or erect, semi-evergreen, annuals or perennials, 12″–60″ (30–150 cm) tall. Leathery or shiny, slender or oval, deep-cut leaves to 3″ (75 mm) long. See also *C. maximum*, Shasta daisy, and *C. × morifolium*, florist's mum.

**FLOWER:** Summer to autumn bloom. Usually double, fragrant flowers, 1″–6″ (25–150 mm) wide. Choose from lilac, pink, red, and white.

**HARDINESS:** Zones 6–11.

**SOIL TYPE:** High humus. High moisture, good drainage, high fertility, 6.0–7.0 pH.

**PLANTING GUIDE:** Spring. Plant in full sun to partial shade, 18″ (45 cm) apart.

**CARE TIPS:** Easy. Even moisture. Fertilize every 4 weeks during growth. Apply mulch, zones 6–8. Pinch tips for bushy plants. Shear after frost. Propagate by cuttings, division, seed.

**NOTES:** Thrives in borders, containers. Nice in formal, small-space gardens. Susceptible to aphids, borers, slugs, snails, root gall.

## *Chrysanthemum frutescens* (*Argyranthemum frutescens*) ASTERACEAE (COMPOSITAE)

### Marguerite (Paris Daisy, White Marguerite)

**SHAPE:** Various bushlike, woody perennials, 36″–48″ (90–120 cm) tall. Alternate, oval, featherlike, deep-cut, sharp-tipped leaves, 2″–4″ (50–100 mm) long.

**FLOWER:** Late-spring to autumn bloom. Daisylike, single or double flowers to 2″ (50 mm) wide. Choose from white and yellow.

**HARDINESS:** Zones 7–11.

**SOIL TYPE:** Sandy loam. High moisture, good drainage, high–medium fertility, 5.5–7.0 pH.

**PLANTING GUIDE:** Spring, when frost risk ends. Plant in full sun, 4′–5′ (1.2–1.5 m) apart.

**CARE TIPS:** Average. Even moisture. Fertilize every 6–8 weeks. Extend bloom by deadheading. Prune to shape. Propagate by cuttings, seed.

**NOTES:** Thrives in backgrounds, beds, borders, containers, massed plantings, paths. Nice in cottage, formal, meadow, seaside gardens. Resists diseases. Susceptible to leaf miners, nematodes, thrips, root gall.

## *Chrysanthemum maximum* *(Leucanthemum × superbum, C. × superbum)* ASTERACEAE (COMPOSITAE)

### Shasta Daisy

**SHAPE:** Numerous erect, mounded, deciduous perennials, 24″–36″ (60–90 cm) tall. Leathery to shiny, textured, oval to lancelike, coarse-toothed leaves to 12″ (30 cm) long.

**FLOWER:** Late-spring to autumn bloom. Usually double, fringed, frilly, or quilled flowers, 2″–6″ (50–150 mm) wide. Choose from cream, white with gold centers. Long blooming.

**HARDINESS:** Zones 4–11.

**SOIL TYPE:** Loam. High–average moisture, good drainage, high–medium fertility, 7.0 pH.

**PLANTING GUIDE:** Spring. Plant in full sun to partial shade, 24″ (60 cm) apart.

**CARE TIPS:** Easy. Even moisture; tolerates drought when established. Fertilize only in spring. Support with stakes. Protect from hot sun. Propagate by division, seed.

**NOTES:** Thrives in backgrounds, beds, borders. Nice in cottage, natural gardens. Cutting flower. Susceptible to nematodes, slugs, snails, root gall.

## *Chrysanthemum × morifolium* ASTERACEAE (COMPOSITAE)

### Florist's Chrysanthemum

**SHAPE:** Numerous varied, erect, mounded, deciduous perennials, 12″–72″ (30–180 cm) tall. Leathery, textured, thick, oval to lancelike, coarse-toothed, aromatic leaves to 12″ (30 cm) long.

**FLOWER:** Summer to autumn bloom. Anemone-like, dahlialike, pompon, quilled, reflexed, spiderlike, or spooned flowers, 2″–6″ (50–150 mm) wide. Choose from bronze, cream, orange, pink, purple, white, and multicolored. Long blooming.

**HARDINESS:** Zones 4–11.

**SOIL TYPE:** High humus. High–average moisture, good drainage, high–medium fertility, 7.0 pH.

**PLANTING GUIDE:** Spring. Plant in full sun to partial shade, 24″–48″ (60–120 cm) apart.

**CARE TIPS:** Easy. Even moisture. Fertilize every 4 weeks. Support with stakes. Protect from hot sun. Propagate by division, seed.

**NOTES:** Thrives in beds, borders. Nice in cottage, natural gardens. Cutting flower. Resists diseases. Susceptible to aphids, borers, slugs, snails.

## *Chrysanthemum parthenium* *(Tanacetum ptarmiciflorum)* ASTERACEAE (COMPOSITAE)

### Feverfew (Tansy)

**SHAPE:** Various vigorous, erect, bushlike, dense, deciduous perennials, 12″–36″ (30–90 cm) tall. Feathery or lobed, textured, broadly oval, hirsute, aromatic leaves to 3″ (75 mm) long.

**FLOWER:** Summer bloom. Daisylike, circular, open or ball-shaped flowers, ¾″–1″ (19–25 mm) wide. Choose from white and yellow. Long blooming.

**HARDINESS:** Zones 4–11. May self-seed.

**SOIL TYPE:** High humus. High–average moisture, good drainage, high–medium fertility, 6.5–7.5 pH.

**PLANTING GUIDE:** Spring. Plant in full sun, 24″–48″ (60–120 cm) apart.

**CARE TIPS:** Easy. Even moisture. Fertilize every 4 weeks. Support with stakes. Pinch tips for bushy plants. Propagate by cuttings, division, seed.

**NOTES:** Thrives in beds, borders, containers. Nice in cottage, herb, meadow, natural, small-space gardens. Cutting, drying, medicinal flower. Resists diseases. Susceptible to aphids, nematodes, slugs, snails, root gall.

## *Chrysogonum virginianum* ASTERACEAE (COMPOSITAE)

### Goldenstar

**SHAPE:** Few low, mounding or branched, hirsute, deciduous perennials, 10″–12″ (25–30 cm) tall and to 16″ (40 cm) wide. Stems of opposite, heart-shaped, textured, toothed leaves, 1″–3″ (25–75 mm) long.

**FLOWER:** Spring to summer bloom. Radiating, open, round, 5-petaled, bristly, flowers to 1½″ (38 mm) long. Yellow.

**HARDINESS:** Zones 6–11.

**SOIL TYPE:** High humus. High moisture, good drainage, high fertility, 6.0–6.5 pH.

**PLANTING GUIDE:** Spring, as soil warms. Plant in partial shade, 12″–16″ (30–40 cm) apart.

**CARE TIPS:** Easy. Even moisture. Fertilize every 4 weeks. Pinch tips for bushy plants. Propagate by division, seed.

**NOTES:** Thrives in beds, borders, containers, foregrounds, ground covers. Nice in cottage, natural, wildlife, woodland gardens. Resists pests and diseases.

## *Cimicifuga* spp. RANUNCULACEAE

### Bugbane (Rattletop, Snakeroot)

**SHAPE:** About 15 slender, erect, deciduous perennials, 30″–96″ (75–240 cm) tall. Shiny, plume-like, toothed, veined leaves to 10″ (25 cm) long divided into leaflets 1″–3″ (25–75 mm) long.

**FLOWER:** Summer to early-autumn bloom. Slim, wandlike spikes to 4′ (1.2 m) tall of many tiny, bristly, horned, fragrant flowers. Choose from cream and white.

**HARDINESS:** Zones 3–9.

**SOIL TYPE:** High humus. High moisture, good drainage, high fertility, 6.0–6.5 pH.

**PLANTING GUIDE:** Early spring, as frost risk ends. Plant in filtered sun to partial shade, 24″ (60 cm) apart.

**CARE TIPS:** Easy. Even moisture. Fertilize every 4 weeks. Pinch tips for bushy plants. Propagate by division, seed.

**NOTES:** Thrives in backgrounds, beds, borders. Nice in cottage, woodland gardens. Resists pests and diseases.

## *Clematis* spp. and hybrids RANUNCULACEAE

### Clematis

**SHAPE:** Numerous twining, herbaceous or woody vines to 20′ (6 m) long with clinging leafstalks. Opposite, smooth or velvety, divided leaves, with veined leaflets, 2″–3″ (50–75 mm) long.

**FLOWER:** Spring–autumn bloom, or remontant. Branching clusters of open, round, reflexed, sepals, 2″–10″ (50–250 mm) wide, with tiny true flowers. Choose from blue, gray, pink, purple, rose, silver, white, and yellow.

**HARDINESS:** Most, zones 7–10; some, zones 2–6.

**SOIL TYPE:** Loam. High moisture, good drainage, high–medium fertility, 7.0–8.0 pH.

**PLANTING GUIDE:** Spring. Plant in full sun to partial shade, 12″–18″ (30–45 cm) apart.

**CARE TIPS:** Average. Even moisture. Fertilize every 6–8 weeks. Support with stakes. Prune after flowering. Propagate by cuttings, seed.

**NOTES:** Thrives in arbors, trellises, walls. Nice in cottage, seaside, woodland gardens. Susceptible to clematis borers, leaf spot.

## *Convallaria majalis* LILIACEAE

### Lily-of-the-Valley (Muget)

**SHAPE:** Few rhizomatous perennials to 8″ (20 cm) tall. Broad, sometimes variegated or ribbed, sharp-tipped leaves to 6″ (15 cm) long.

**FLOWER:** Spring bloom. Multiple clusters of nodding, bell-shaped, fragrant flowers, ¼″–½″ (6–12 mm) wide. Choose from pink and white. Forms red, berrylike fruit in autumn.

**HARDINESS:** Zones 2–7. Prefers cold-winter climates.

**SOIL TYPE:** High humus. High–average moisture, good drainage, high–medium fertility, 5.5–6.5 pH.

**PLANTING GUIDE:** Autumn or early spring. Plant in partial to full shade, 12″–24″ (30–60 cm) apart, 1½″–3″ (38–75 mm) deep.

**CARE TIPS:** Average. Even moisture. Fertilize only in spring during growth. Apply mulch. Propagate by division, pips.

**NOTES:** Thrives in containers, ground covers. Nice in cottage, small-space, woodland gardens. Cutting flower. Naturalizes. Resists deer and rodents. Susceptible to mealybugs.

## *Convolvulus sabatius* (*C. mauritanicus*) CONVOLVULACEAE

### Ground Morning Glory (Bindweed)

**SHAPE:** Various open, sprawling or trailing, evergreen perennials to 36″ (90 cm) tall. Woolly, circular to oval leaves to 1½″ (38 mm) long. See also *Ipomoea* spp., morning glory vine.

**FLOWER:** Late-spring to summer bloom. Clusters of one to six, open, bell-shaped flowers, 1″–2″ (25–50 mm) wide. Choose from blue, pink, purple, and white with blue or violet centers.

**HARDINESS:** Zones 7–11. May self-seed.

**SOIL TYPE:** Sandy loam. Average–low moisture, good drainage, medium fertility, 6.0–8.0 pH.

**PLANTING GUIDE:** Spring. Plant in full sun to partial shade, 36″ (90 cm) apart.

**CARE TIPS:** Easy. Even moisture; tolerates drought when established. Shear in late winter. Propagate by cuttings, division, seed.

**NOTES:** Thrives in arbors, containers, edgings, ground covers, trellises. Nice in natural, cottage, rock, seaside gardens. Aggressive. Resists pests and diseases.

## *Coreopsis* spp. ASTERACEAE (COMPOSITAE)

### Tickseed

**SHAPE:** Numerous slender, erect annuals or perennials, 6″–36″ (15–90 cm) tall. Shiny, strap-like, toothed or lobed leaves to 3″ (75 mm) long.

**FLOWER:** Summer to autumn bloom. Daisylike flowers to 3″ (75 mm) wide. Choose from brownish orange, rose, yellow, and bicolored with contrasting centers.

**HARDINESS:** Zones 4–11. May self-seed.

**SOIL TYPE:** Sandy loam. Average moisture, good drainage, high–low fertility, 5.0–6.0 pH.

**PLANTING GUIDE:** Spring, as soil warms, zones 4–8; autumn, zones 9–11. Plant in full sun, 12″ (30 cm) apart.

**CARE TIPS:** Very easy. Water only when soil dries. Fertilize only in spring. Extend bloom by dead-heading. Propagate by cuttings, division, seed.

**NOTES:** Thrives in borders, edgings, foregrounds. Nice in cottage, formal, natural, wildlife gardens. Cutting flower. Susceptible to chewing insects, leaf spot, powdery mildew, rust.

## *Coreopsis verticillata* ASTERACEAE (COMPOSITAE)

### Threadleaf Coreopsis

**SHAPE:** Various bunching, erect perennials, 24″–36″ (60–90 cm) tall. Shiny, slender, fine-cut, fine-toothed leaves to 2″ (50 mm) long.

**FLOWER:** Summer to autumn bloom. Daisylike flowers to 2″ (50 mm) wide. Choose from gold, and bright yellow with dark yellow centers.

**HARDINESS:** Zones 4–11. May self-seed.

**SOIL TYPE:** Sandy loam. Average moisture, good drainage, medium–low fertility, 6.5–7.5 pH.

**PLANTING GUIDE:** Spring, as soil warms, zones 4–8; autumn, zones 9–11. Plant in full to filtered sun, 12″ (30 cm) apart.

**CARE TIPS:** Very easy. Water when soil dries 4″–6″ (10–15 cm) deep. Tolerates drought. Fertilize only in spring. Extend bloom by deadheading. Propagate by cuttings, division, seed.

**NOTES:** Thrives in borders, edgings, massed plantings. Nice in cottage, formal, natural, wildlife gardens. Cutting flower. Susceptible to chewing insects, leaf spot, powdery mildew, rust.

## *Crambe* spp. BRASSICACEAE (CRUCIFERAE)

### Colewort (Sea Kale)

**SHAPE:** About 20 mounded, usually slender, deciduous annuals or perennials, 36″–84″ (90–215 cm) tall. Smooth, succulent, divided, deep-cut and lobate, wavy-edged leaves to 36″ (90 cm) long.

**FLOWER:** Summer bloom. Profuse, branching clusters of fragrant, round, 4-petaled flowers, ¼″–½″ (6–12 mm) wide. Choose from cream, green, and white. Dormant after bloom.

**HARDINESS:** Zones 4–9.

**SOIL TYPE:** Sandy loam. High moisture, good drainage, high fertility, 6.5–7.5 pH.

**PLANTING GUIDE:** Spring. Plant in full to filtered sun, 18″–24″ (45–60 cm) apart.

**CARE TIPS:** Easy. Even moisture. Fertilize every 4 weeks. Shear after flowering. Propagate by seed.

**NOTES:** Thrives in accents. Nice in cottage, natural gardens. Good for early spring color. Resists diseases. Susceptible to cabbage loopers.

## *Cuphea ignea* LYTHRACEAE

### Cigar Flower (Firecracker Plant, Red-White-and-Blue Flower)

**SHAPE:** Few erect, branched, bushlike, shrubby perennials, 12″–36″ (30–90 cm) tall. Smooth, lancelike, slender, sharp-tipped leaves to 1½″ (38 mm) long in whorled clusters.

**FLOWER:** Summer to autumn bloom. Shiny, narrow, tubular flowers to 1½″ (38 mm) long with protruding stamens. Orange red with brown tips.

**HARDINESS:** Zones 10–11. Protect from frost. Tolerates heat and humidity.

**SOIL TYPE:** Sandy loam. High moisture, good drainage, high–medium fertility, 7.0–7.5 pH.

**PLANTING GUIDE:** Sow seed indoors and transplant as soil warms, zones 3–8; sow in garden, zones 9–11. Plant in full sun, 9″ (23 cm) apart.

**CARE TIPS:** Easy. Even moisture. Fertilize every 2 weeks. Pinch tips for bushy plants. Propagate by cuttings, seed.

**NOTES:** Thrives in borders, containers, massed plantings. Nice in cottage, wildlife gardens. Resists diseases. Susceptible to spider mites.

## *Delphinum* spp. RANUNCULACEAE

### Delphinium (Scarlet or Candle Larkspur)

**SHAPE:** Numerous erect or branched, slender annuals, biennials, or perennials, 12″–96″ (30–240 cm) tall. Textured, fanlike, lobate, deep-toothed leaves to 8″ (20 cm) wide.

**FLOWER:** Summer bloom. Spiking clusters of starlike flowers to 3″ (75 mm) wide. Choose from blue, cream, pink, purple, white, and bicolored with contrasting centers.

**HARDINESS:** Zones 3–10.

**SOIL TYPE:** Sandy loam. High moisture, good drainage, high fertility, 6.5–7.0 pH.

**PLANTING GUIDE:** Spring, as soil becomes workable. Plant in full sun, 18″–36″ (45–90 cm) apart.

**CARE TIPS:** Easy to average. Even moisture. Fertilize every 4 weeks. Apply mulch. Extend bloom by deadheading. Stake to support. Propagate by cuttings, division, seed.

**NOTES:** Thrives in backgrounds. Nice in cottage, wildlife gardens. Cutting flower. Susceptible to aphids, slugs, snails, fungal diseases.

## *Dianthus* × *allwoodii* hybrids *(D. 'Allwoodii')* CARYOPHYLLACEAE

### Cottage Pink (Allwood Pink)

**SHAPE:** Numerous short, sprawling, evergreen perennials, 8″–16″ (20–40 cm) tall, 24″–36″ (60–90 cm) wide. Shiny, slender leaves to 2″ (50 mm) long in spreading, tufted, mats.

**FLOWER:** Spring to summer bloom. Pairs of showy, very fragrant flowers, ½″–1″ (12–25 mm) wide. Choose from crimson, pink, rose, and white.

**HARDINESS:** Zones 3–9.

**SOIL TYPE:** High humus. Average moisture, good drainage, high fertility, 7.0–8.5 pH.

**PLANTING GUIDE:** Spring, when frost risk ends. Plant in full sun, 12″–18″ (30–45 cm) apart.

**CARE TIPS:** Easy. Water only when soil dries. Apply mulch, zones 4–6. Pinch tips for bushy plants. Extend bloom by deadheading. Propagate by cuttings, division, layering, seed.

**NOTES:** Thrives in accents, borders, containers, edgings, foregrounds. Nice in cottage, formal, wildlife gardens. Cutting flower. Susceptible to rust, fusarium wilt.

## *Dianthus barbatus* CARYOPHYLLACEAE

### Sweet William

**SHAPE:** Numerous erect, bushlike biennials, 12″–24″ (30–60 cm) tall. Shiny, lancelike, slender leaves, 1″–2½″ (25–63 mm) long.

**FLOWER:** Summer to early-autumn bloom. Clusters of saucer-shaped, sometimes fragrant flowers to ⅓″ (8 mm) wide with bearded petals. Choose from pink, purple, red, white, and bicolored.

**HARDINESS:** Zones 5–11. May self-seed.

**SOIL TYPE:** Sandy loam. High moisture, good drainage, high fertility, 7.0–7.5 pH.

**PLANTING GUIDE:** Late spring. Plant in filtered sun to partial shade, 12″–36″ (30–90 cm) apart.

**CARE TIPS:** Easy. Even moisture; water when soil dries 2″–3″ (50–75 mm) deep. Fertilize every 4 weeks. Propagate by seed.

**NOTES:** Thrives in accents, beds, borders, containers, edgings, massed plantings. Nice in cottage, formal, heritage, shade gardens. Cutting flower. Susceptible to spider mites, rust, mosaic virus, fusarium wilt.

## *Dianthus caryophyllus* CARYOPHYLLACEAE

### Carnation (Border Carnation, Florist's Carnation, Pink)

**SHAPE:** Numerous either dense and short or bushlike and erect, semi-evergreen perennials to 12″ (30 cm) tall. Shiny, usually slender, grasslike leaves to 2″ (50 mm) long.

**FLOWER:** Spring to summer bloom. Lacy, fragrant flowers, 1″–1½″ (25–38 mm) wide. Choose from pink, rose, white, yellow, and bicolored.

**HARDINESS:** Zones 4–11.

**SOIL TYPE:** Sandy loam. Average moisture, good drainage, high fertility, 7.0–8.0 pH.

**PLANTING GUIDE:** Spring, when frost risk ends. Plant in full sun, 12″–15″ (30–38 cm) apart.

**CARE TIPS:** Easy. Water when soil dries 4″–6″ (10–15 cm) deep. Apply light mulch, zones 4–6. Propagate by cuttings, division, layering, seed.

**NOTES:** Thrives in accents, beds, borders, containers, edgings, foregrounds, mixed plantings. Nice in cottage, formal, heritage, seaside, wildlife gardens. Cutting flower. Susceptible to rust, fusarium wilt.

## *Dianthus chinensis* CARYOPHYLLACEAE

### Pink (China Pink)

**SHAPE:** Numerous erect, mounded, evergreen, biennials or perennials to 24″ (60 cm) tall. Shiny, slender, grasslike leaves to 2″ (50 mm) long.

**FLOWER:** Spring to summer bloom. Lacy, fragrant flowers, 1″–1½″ (25–38 mm) wide. Choose from pink, rose, white, yellow, and bicolored.

**HARDINESS:** Zones 8–11. Protect from frost. May self-seed.

**SOIL TYPE:** Sandy loam. Average moisture, good drainage, high fertility, 7.0–8.0 pH.

**PLANTING GUIDE:** Spring, when frost risk ends, zones 2–7; late summer, zones 8–11. Plant in full sun, 12″–15″ (30–38 cm) apart.

**CARE TIPS:** Easy. Water only when soil dries. Apply mulch, zones 4–6. Propagate by cuttings, division, layering, seed.

**NOTES:** Thrives in beds, borders, containers. Nice in cottage, heritage, wildlife gardens. Cutting flower. Resists pests. Susceptible to rust, fusarium wilt.

## *Dictamnus albus* RUTACEAE

### Gas Plant (Burning Bush, Dittany, Fraxinella)

**SHAPE:** Various erect, mounded, herbaceous perennials, 30″–36″ (75–90 cm) tall. Alternate, shiny, textured, thick-growing, oval, toothed, aromatic leaves to 3″ (75 mm) long.

**FLOWER:** Late-spring to summer bloom. Loose, upright spikes to 12″ (30 cm) tall of star-shaped flowers with prominent pistils. Choose from rose pink, purple, and white. Forms pods bearing seed in autumn.

**HARDINESS:** Zones 3–8.

**SOIL TYPE:** High humus. High moisture, good drainage, high fertility, 6.5–7.5 pH.

**PLANTING GUIDE:** Spring. Plant in full sun to partial shade, 36″ (90 cm) apart.

**CARE TIPS:** Easy. Even moisture; allow soil to dry between waterings. Tolerates drought. Fertilize every 10–12 weeks. Propagate by division, seed.

**NOTES:** Thrives in backgrounds, beds, borders. Nice in cottage, shade, woodland gardens. Resists pests and diseases.

## *Digitalis* spp. SCROPHULARIACEAE

### Foxglove

**SHAPE:** Various erect, slim biennials or perennials, 24″–60″ (60–150 cm) tall. Hairy, oval or lance-like, sharp-tipped leaves to 8″ (20 cm) long.

**FLOWER:** Summer bloom. Spikes of showy, nodding, bell-shaped flowers, 2″ (50 mm) long. Choose from pink, purple, white, and yellow with marked or spotted centers.

**HARDINESS:** Zones 3–9.

**SOIL TYPE:** High humus. High moisture, good drainage, high fertility, 6.5–7.0 pH.

**PLANTING GUIDE:** Spring, zones 3–7; autumn, zones 8–9. Plant in filtered sun to partial shade, 15″–18″ (38–45 cm) apart.

**CARE TIPS:** Easy. Even moisture. Fertilize only in spring. Remove spent stalks. Apply mulch, zones 3–5. Propagate by division, seed.

**NOTES:** Thrives in accents, backgrounds, fence lines. Nice in cottage, heritage, shade, wildlife, woodland gardens. Susceptible to Japanese beetles, leaf spot.

## *Digitalis grandiflora* (*D. ambigua*) SCROPHULARIACEAE

### Yellow Foxglove

**SHAPE:** Various erect, slender, herbaceous biennials or perennials, 24″–36″ (60–90 cm) tall. Conical spikes of alternate, opposite, hirsute, oval to lancelike leaves to 8″ (20 cm) long.

**FLOWER:** Summer bloom. Spiking stalks with tiers of flutelike, nodding flowers, 1″–2″ (25–50 mm) long. Creamy yellow, speckled with brown spots.

**HARDINESS:** Zones 4–9. May self-seed.

**SOIL TYPE:** High humus. High moisture, good drainage, high fertility, 6.5–7.0 pH.

**PLANTING GUIDE:** Autumn. Plant in partial shade, 15″–18″ (38–45 cm) apart.

**CARE TIPS:** Easy. Even moisture. Fertilize every 4 weeks. Propagate by seed.

**NOTES:** Thrives in backgrounds, beds, borders, fence lines, paths. Nice in cottage, shade, woodland gardens. Cutting flower. Foliage yields digitalis, a medicinal extract. Resists pests. Susceptible to leaf spot.

## *Doronicum* spp. ASTERACEAE (COMPOSITAE)

### Leopard's-Bane

**SHAPE:** Various short, mounded, rhizomatous, deciduous perennials to 24″ (60 cm) tall. Smooth, heart-shaped to circular, toothed or lobate leaves to 3″ (75 mm) long. Semi-dormant in summer.

**FLOWER:** Spring bloom. Long stems of lone, daisy-like, sometimes double flowers to 2″ (50 mm) wide. Choose from gold and yellow.

**HARDINESS:** Zones 3–9. Prefers cool-summer climates.

**SOIL TYPE:** Loam. High moisture, good drainage, high fertility, 6.5–7.5 pH.

**PLANTING GUIDE:** Spring or autumn. Plant in full to filtered sun, 12″–24″ (30–60 cm) apart.

**CARE TIPS:** Easy. Even moisture until buds form; limit thereafter. Fertilize only in spring. Apply mulch. Shear after bloom. Propagate by division, seed.

**NOTES:** Thrives in borders, beds, containers. Nice in cottage, natural, woodland gardens. Cutting flower. Resists pests and diseases.

## *Echinacea purpurea* ASTERACEAE (COMPOSITAE)

### Purple Coneflower

**SHAPE:** Numerous erect, sprawling, herbaceous perennials, 24″–48″ (60–120 cm) tall and wide. Alternate, textured, oval to bladelike leaves, 4″–8″ (10–20 cm) long.

**FLOWER:** Summer bloom. Tall stalks of showy flat or drooping flowers, 3″–6″ (75–150 mm) wide. Choose from pink, purple, red, white with dark, button- or conelike centers

**HARDINESS:** Zones 3–11.

**SOIL TYPE:** Loam. Average–low moisture, good drainage, medium fertility, 6.5–7.5 pH.

**PLANTING GUIDE:** Spring, as soil warms. Plant in full sun to partial shade, 18″–24″ (45–60 cm) apart.

**CARE TIPS:** Easy. Even moisture. Fertilize every 10–12 weeks. Apply mulch. Propagate by division, seed.

**NOTES:** Thrives in beds, borders. Nice in cottage, natural, wildlife gardens. Good for windy sites. Susceptible to Japanese beetles, mites, southern blight, downy and powdery mildew, rust.

## *Echinops* spp. ASTERACEAE (COMPOSITAE)

### Globe Thistle

**SHAPE:** About 100 sprawling, erect biennials or perennials, 36″–48″ (90–120 cm) tall. Spiny, hirsute, coarse-textured, thistlelike, toothed leaves to 12″ (30 cm) long.

**FLOWER:** Summer to autumn bloom. Dense globe-shaped clusters, 2″–3″ (50–75 mm) wide, of tiny, spiny flowers. Choose from pink, purple, red, white, and yellow.

**HARDINESS:** Zones 3–9.

**SOIL TYPE:** Sandy loam. Average moisture, good drainage, high–medium fertility, 5.0–6.0 pH.

**PLANTING GUIDE:** Spring. Plant in full to filtered sun, 18″–24″ (45–60 cm) apart.

**CARE TIPS:** Easy to average. Even moisture; water when soil dries 2″–3″ (50–75 mm) deep. Tolerates drought. Fertilize only in spring. Stake to support. Thin. Propagate by cuttings, division, seed.

**NOTES:** Thrives in accents, backgrounds. Nice in natural, rock, wildlife, woodland gardens. Cutting flower. Resists pests and diseases.

## *Epimedium* spp. BERBERIDACEAE

### Barrenwort (Bishop's-Hat, Longspur)

**SHAPE:** Various low and sprawling, rhizomatous perennials, 6″–12″ (15–30 cm) tall. Wiry stems of smooth or leathery, heart-shaped, divided or lobed, toothed leaves to 3″ (75 mm) long, usually in basal rosettes. Turns colors in autumn.

**FLOWER:** Spring bloom. Clusters of flat, 4-petaled, hooded or spurred flowers, ¾″–2″ (19–50 mm) wide. Choose from pink, red, white, and yellow.

**HARDINESS:** Zones 3–9.

**SOIL TYPE:** High humus. High–low moisture, good drainage, high–medium fertility, 5.0–6.5 pH.

**PLANTING GUIDE:** Spring. Plant in full sun to partial shade, 18″–24″ (45–60 cm) apart.

**CARE TIPS:** Easy. Even moisture; water when soil dries 4″–6″ (10–15 cm) deep. Fertilize every 4–6 weeks. Shear in winter. Propagate by division.

**NOTES:** Thrives in accents, containers, ground covers. Nice in natural, rock, shade, woodland gardens. Resists pests and diseases.

## *Erigeron* spp. ASTERACEAE (COMPOSITAE)

### Fleabane

**SHAPE:** Numerous branched, bushlike, erect, deciduous annuals, biennials, but usually perennials to 24″ (60 cm) tall. Alternate, slender, lancelike leaves, 2″–4″ (50–100 mm) long.

**FLOWER:** Spring to autumn bloom. Single or branched clusters of single or semi-double flowers, 1½″–2″ (38–50 mm) wide, with threadlike petals. Choose from pink, purple, white, and yellow with yellow centers.

**HARDINESS:** Zones 3–11. Tolerates heat.

**SOIL TYPE:** Sandy loam. High moisture, good drainage, medium–low fertility, 6.5–7.5 pH.

**PLANTING GUIDE:** Early to midspring. Plant in full sun to partial shade, 18″ (45 cm) apart.

**CARE TIPS:** Easy. Even moisture. Fertilize only in spring. Extend bloom by deadheading. Propagate by cuttings, division, seed.

**NOTES:** Thrives in beds, borders, edgings. Nice in meadow, natural, rock, seaside, wildlife, woodland gardens. Resists pests and diseases.

## *Erodium reichardii* (*E. chamaedryoides*) GERANIACEAE

### Alpine Geranium (Crane's-Bill, Heron's-Bill, Sea Holly)

**SHAPE:** Various short, sprawling or trailing, deciduous perennials to 4″ (10 cm) tall. Shiny, textured, oval, sharp-tipped, wavy-edged leaves to ⅜″ (9 mm) long.

**FLOWER:** Spring to autumn bloom. Single, round-petaled flowers, ½″ (12 mm) wide. Choose from pink, white, and yellow with contrasting-veined petals.

**HARDINESS:** Zones 6–9. May self-seed.

**SOIL TYPE:** Sandy loam. Average–low moisture, good drainage, medium–low fertility, 6.5–8.0 pH.

**PLANTING GUIDE:** Spring. Plant in full sun to partial shade, 12″ (30 cm) apart.

**CARE TIPS:** Easy. Even moisture; tolerates drought when established. Fertilize only in spring. Shear in autumn. Propagate by division, seed.

**NOTES:** Thrives in borders, edgings, ground covers. Nice in natural, rock, seaside gardens. Aggressive in mild climates. Resists pests and diseases.

## *Eryngium* spp. APIACEAE (UMBELLIFERAE)

### Sea Holly (Rattlesnake-Master, Sea Holm)

**SHAPE:** Nearly 200 bushlike, erect, herbaceous perennials, 12″–72″ (30–180 cm) tall. Fleshy, hirsute, spiny, sharp-tipped, 3-lobed, deep-cut leaves to 2″ (50 mm) long.

**FLOWER:** Summer bloom. Thistlelike flowers, 1″–2″ (25–50 mm) wide, on tall, thick stems above leaflike, spiny bracts. Choose from light blue, yellow green, and white.

**HARDINESS:** Zones 4–9. May self-seed.

**SOIL TYPE:** Sandy loam. Most moistures, good drainage, medium–low fertility, 6.5–7.5 pH.

**PLANTING GUIDE:** Spring. Plant in full sun, 12″ (30 cm) apart. Best sown in garden soil.

**CARE TIPS:** Easy. Even moisture; tolerates drought when established. Fertilize only in spring. Propagate by division, seed.

**NOTES:** Thrives in beds, borders, edgings. Nice in natural, rock, seaside, wildlife gardens. Cutting flower. Aggressive. Resists diseases. Susceptible to slugs, snails.

## *Erysimum cheiri* (*Cheiranthus cheiri*) BRASSICACEAE (CRUCIFERAE)

### Wallflower

**SHAPE:** Numerous erect, branched biennials or perennials, 12″–30″ (30–75 cm) tall. Shiny, lancelike, slender, sharp-tipped leaves to 3″ (75 mm) long.

**FLOWER:** Spring to early-summer bloom. Spiking clusters of single or double, fragrant flowers to 1″ (25 mm) wide. Choose from apricot, cream, pink, purple, red, white, and yellow.

**HARDINESS:** Zones 7–9. May self-seed. Protect from hot sun.

**SOIL TYPE:** Loam. High moisture, good drainage, high–low fertility, pH 7.0–7.5.

**PLANTING GUIDE:** Spring, when frost risk ends. Plant in partial shade, 6″–12″ (15–30 cm) apart.

**CARE TIPS:** Easy. Even moisture. Fertilize every 10–12 weeks. Propagate by seed.

**NOTES:** Thrives in beds, borders, containers, edgings, foregrounds. Nice in cottage, formal, rock, shade, woodland gardens. Cutting flower. Resists pests and diseases.

## *Eschscholzia californica* PAPAVERACEAE

### California Poppy

**SHAPE:** Various mounded, herbaceous perennials, 6″–24″ (15–60 cm) tall. Dull, fine-cut, lobate, plumelike leaves to 4″ (10 cm) long.

**FLOWER:** Spring to summer bloom. Flexible stems of cup-shaped, poppylike, 4-petaled flowers to 2½″ (63 mm) wide. Choose from gold, red, yellow, and variegated.

**HARDINESS:** Zones 8–10. Protect from frost. May self-seed.

**SOIL TYPE:** Sandy soil. Average–low moisture, good drainage, medium–low fertility, 7.0–7.5 pH.

**PLANTING GUIDE:** Spring. Plant in full sun, 6″–8″ (15–20 cm) apart. Best sown in garden soil.

**CARE TIPS:** Easy. Even moisture; tolerates drought when established. Fertilize sparingly. Extend bloom by deadheading. Propagate by seed.

**NOTES:** Thrives in accents, beds, borders, edgings. Nice in arid, cottage, meadow, natural, rock, seaside, wildflower, wildlife gardens. Resists pests and diseases.

## *Eupatorium coelestinum* (*Conoclinium coelestinum*) ASTERACEAE (COMPOSITAE)

### Mist Flower (Boneset, Hardy Ageratum)

**SHAPE:** Various mounded, shrubby, rhizomatous perennials to 36″ (90 cm) tall. Opposite or clustered, usually hirsute, triangular to oval, toothed, coarse leaves to 3″ (75 mm) long. See also *E. purpureum*, Joe-Pye weed.

**FLOWER:** Summer to autumn bloom. Dense clusters of open, flat or dome-shaped, fluffy, tubular, fuzzy flowers, ½″ (12 mm) wide. Choose from blue, purple, violet, white, and yellow.

**HARDINESS:** Zones 6–10.

**SOIL TYPE:** Sandy loam. High moisture, good drainage, medium fertility, 6.5–7.5 pH.

**PLANTING GUIDE:** Spring. Plant in full sun to partial shade, 12″ (30 cm) apart.

**CARE TIPS:** Easy. Even moisture. Pinch tips for bushy plants. Propagate by cuttings, division, seed.

**NOTES:** Thrives in accents, borders, edgings, fence lines. Nice in meadow, natural, rock, wildlife gardens. Aggressive. Resists diseases. Susceptible to aphids.

## *Eupatorium purpureum* ASTERACEAE (COMPOSITAE)

### Joe-Pye Weed (Green-Stemmed Joe-Pye Weed)

**SHAPE:** Various mounded, shrubby, rhizomatous perennials to 10′ (3 m) tall. Opposite or clustered, usually hirsute, triangular to oval, toothed, coarse leaves to 4″ (10 cm) long. See also *E. coelestinum*, mist flower.

**FLOWER:** Autumn bloom. Clusters of open, flat or dome-shaped, tubular flowers, ½″ (12 mm) wide. Choose from pink, purple, white, and yellow.

**HARDINESS:** Zones 6–10.

**SOIL TYPE:** Sandy loam. High moisture, good drainage, medium fertility, 6.5–7.5 pH.

**PLANTING GUIDE:** Spring. Plant in full sun to partial shade, 4′–6′ (1.2–1.8 m) apart.

**CARE TIPS:** Easy. Even moisture. Prune to shape. Extend bloom by deadheading. Propagate by cuttings, division, seed.

**NOTES:** Thrives in dividers, fence lines. Nice in natural, rock, wildlife gardens. Aggressive. Culture may be prohibited in some areas. Resists pests and diseases.

## *Eustoma grandiflorum* (*Lisianthus russellianus*) GENTIANACEAE

### Prairie Gentian (Lisianthus, Texas Bluebell, Tulip Gentian)

**SHAPE:** Various mounded, deciduous annuals or biennnials to 36″ (90 cm) tall. Opposite, dusky, textured, oval to lancelike leaves to 3″ (75 mm) long with gray undersides. Dwarf cultivars available.

**FLOWER:** Summer bloom. Showy, swirled-trumpet-shaped, deep-throated, single or double flowers to 3″ (75 mm) wide. Choose from blue, cream, pink, purple, red, and white.

**HARDINESS:** Zones 3–9.

**SOIL TYPE:** High humus. High moisture, good drainage, high fertility, 6.0–7.0 pH.

**PLANTING GUIDE:** Spring, when soil warms. Plant in full to filtered sun, 36″ (90 cm) apart.

**CARE TIPS:** Average. Even moisture; water when soil dries 2″–3″ (50–75 mm) deep. Extend bloom by deadheading. Propagate by seed.

**NOTES:** Thrives in beds, borders, containers. Nice in cottage, formal gardens. Cutting flower. Resists pests and diseases.

## *Exacum affine* GENTIANACEAE

### Persian Violet

**SHAPE:** Various branched, bushlike annuals or biennials to 24″ (60 cm) tall. Opposite, shiny, oval, sharp-tipped leaves to 1½″ (38 mm) long.

**FLOWER:** Summer to early-autumn bloom. Single 5-petaled, fragrant flowers to ½″ (12 mm) wide. Choose from blue violet and white with bright yellow stamens.

**HARDINESS:** Zones 9–11. Protect from frost.

**SOIL TYPE:** High humus. High moisture, good drainage, high fertility, 6.5–7.5 pH.

**PLANTING GUIDE:** Spring. Plant in partial shade, 6″–8″ (15–20 cm) apart, on top of soil. Start indoors for early bloom.

**CARE TIPS:** Average. Even moisture. Tolerates drought. Fertilize every 2 weeks. Extend bloom by deadheading. Propagate by seed.

**NOTES:** Thrives in beds, borders, containers, edgings. Nice in fragrance, shade, small-space, tropical gardens and greenhouses. Susceptible to aphids, fungal diseases.

## *Filipendula rubra* ROSACEAE

### Queen-of-the-Prairie (Meadowsweet)

**SHAPE:** Various erect, slender, deciduous perennials to 8′ (2.4 m) tall, 24″–48″ (60–120 cm) wide. Smooth, deep-cut and toothed, plumelike leaves, 4″–8″ (10–20 cm) wide. Dwarf cultivars available.

**FLOWER:** Summer to autumn bloom. Plumed, branching clusters, 4″–6″ (10–15 cm) wide, of many tiny flowers. Choose from pink, purple, deep red, and white.

**HARDINESS:** Zones 3–9. Prefers cool climates.

**SOIL TYPE:** High humus; pond margins. High moisture, good drainage, high fertility, 6.0–8.0 pH. Tolerates salt.

**PLANTING GUIDE:** Spring. Plant in full sun to partial shade, 12″–36″ (30–90 cm) apart.

**CARE TIPS:** Average. Even moisture. Fertilize every 4 weeks. Apply mulch. Propagate by division, seed.

**NOTES:** Thrives in backgrounds, fence lines. Nice in cottage, natural, woodland gardens and ponds. Resists pests. Susceptible to powdery mildew.

## *Fragaria* spp. ROSACEAE

### Ornamental Strawberry (Beach Strawberry, Fraise du Bois, Woodland Strawberry)

**SHAPE:** About 12 short, sprawling, stoloniferous, evergreen perennials to 8″ (20 cm) tall. Leathery, oval, toothed leaves to 5″ (13 cm) wide with 3-lobed leaflets to 2″ (50 mm) long.

**FLOWER:** Spring bloom. Single, 5-petaled flowers to 1″ (25 mm) wide. Choose from pink, red, and white. Forms semi-edible pseudoberries covered with seedlike achenes in summer.

**HARDINESS:** Zones 3–10. Protect flowers from frost.

**SOIL TYPE:** Sandy loam. High moisture, good drainage, high–medium fertility, 6.0–8.0 pH. Tolerates salt.

**PLANTING GUIDE:** Early spring. Plant in full sun, 12″–30″ (30–75 cm) apart.

**CARE TIPS:** Average. Even moisture. Fertilize every 4 weeks. Propagate by division, offsets, runners, seed.

**NOTES:** Thrives in accents, banks, ground covers, massed plantings. Nice in natural, wildlife, woodland gardens. Resists pests and diseases.

## *Gaillardia* spp. ASTERACEAE (COMPOSITAE)

### Blanket Flower

**SHAPE:** Various bushlike, erect annuals, biennials, or perennials, 24″–36″ (60–90 cm) tall. Alternate, hirsute, textured, lancelike leaves, 3″–6″ (75–150 mm) long.

**FLOWER:** Summer to autumn bloom. Flat flowers, 3″–4″ (75–100 mm) wide. Choose from gold, deep red, or yellow with contrasting centers and tips.

**HARDINESS:** Zones 3–9. May self-seed.

**SOIL TYPE:** Sandy loam. Average–low moisture, good drainage, medium–low fertility, 6.0–7.5 pH.

**PLANTING GUIDE:** Early spring. Plant in full sun, 10″–15″ (25–38 cm) apart.

**CARE TIPS:** Easy. Water when soil dries 4″–6″ (10–15 cm) deep. Fertilize sparingly. Extend bloom by deadheading. Stake to support. Propagate by cuttings, division, seed.

**NOTES:** Thrives in banks, beds, borders, hillsides. Nice in cottage, formal, meadow, wildlife gardens. Cutting flower. Susceptible to aphids, leaf spot, powdery mildew.

## *Galium odoratum* (*Asperula odorata*) RUBIACEAE

### Sweet Woodruff

**SHAPE:** Various vigorous, crawling or sprawling perennials to 6″ (15 cm) tall and 36″–48″ (90–120 cm) wide. Smooth, lancelike, fine-toothed, aromatic leaves to 1½″ (38 mm) long armed with bristles on the leaf tips.

**FLOWER:** Late-spring to summer bloom. Branched, clusters to 1½″ (38 mm) wide of star-shaped, 4-petaled, flat flowers to ¼″ (6 mm) wide. White.

**HARDINESS:** Zones 4–9. May self-seed.

**SOIL TYPE:** Loam. Average–low moisture, good drainage, high–medium fertility, 7.0–7.5 pH.

**PLANTING GUIDE:** Spring. Plant in partial to full shade, 12″ (30 cm) apart.

**CARE TIPS:** Easy. Water when soil dries 4″–6″ (10–15 cm) deep. Fertilize sparingly. Propagate by division, seed.

**NOTES:** Thrives in accents, mixed-shrub plantings. Nice in natural, shade gardens. Cutting flower. Aggressive; plant in buried containers. Resists pests and diseases.

## *Gaura lindheimeri* ONAGRACEAE

### White Gaura

**SHAPE:** Various upright perennials to 4′ (1.2 m) tall. Alternate, textured, lancelike leaves, 1″–3½″ (25–90 mm) long.

**FLOWER:** Late-spring to autumn bloom. Branched spikes of 4-petaled flowers to 1″ (25 mm) long. Choose from gold, pink, and white turning pink.

**HARDINESS:** Zones 5–9. May self-seed. Tolerates hot sun.

**SOIL TYPE:** Sandy loam; pond margins. Average–low moisture, good drainage, medium–low fertility, 6.0–7.5 pH.

**PLANTING GUIDE:** Early spring. Plant in full to filtered sun, 18″–32″ (45–80 cm) apart.

**CARE TIPS:** Easy. Water when soil dries 4″–6″ (10–15 cm) deep. Fertilize every 10–12 weeks. Extend bloom by deadheading. Propagate by seed.

**NOTES:** Thrives in accents, beds, borders, containers. Nice in cottage, meadow, wildlife, woodland gardens and ponds. Cutting flower. Resists pests and diseases.

## *Gazania* spp. and hybrids ASTERACEAE (COMPOSITAE)

### Treasure Flower (Gazania)

**SHAPE:** Various round, shrubby or dangling, rhizomatous, evergreen, usually perennials, 10″–18″ (25–45 cm) tall. Woolly, slender, lance-like, wavy-edged leaves to 4″ (10 cm) long.

**FLOWER:** Late-spring to summer bloom. Upright stems of daisylike flowers, 2″–4″ (50–100 mm) wide. Choose from bronze, copper, orange, pink, red, white, yellow, and variegated.

**HARDINESS:** Zones 8–10. Tolerates hot sun.

**SOIL TYPE:** Sandy loam. Average–low moisture, good drainage, medium fertility, 5.5–7.0 pH.

**PLANTING GUIDE:** Spring. Plant in full to filtered sun, 18″ (45 cm) apart.

**CARE TIPS:** Easy. Even moisture. Fertilize every 10–12 weeks. Extend bloom by deadheading. Propagate by seed.

**NOTES:** Thrives in accents, beds, containers, driveways, slopes. Nice in formal, meadow, seaside, wildlife gardens. Resists diseases. Susceptible to slugs, snails.

## *Geranium maculatum* GERANIACEAE

### Wild Geranium (Spotted Cranesbill, Wild Cranesbill)

**SHAPE:** Various round, shrubby, herbaceous, semi-evergreen perennials, 12″–24″ (30–60 cm) tall and wide. Textured, circular, sharp-tipped, 3–7-lobed leaves to 5″ (13 cm) wide.

**FLOWER:** Spring to summer bloom. Upright stems of 5-petaled, open flowers, 1″–1½″ (25–38 mm) wide. Choose from pink, violet, and white.

**HARDINESS:** Zones 4–8. Prefers cool-summer climates.

**SOIL TYPE:** Loam. High moisture, good drainage, high fertility, 6.0–7.0 pH.

**PLANTING GUIDE:** Spring. Plant in filtered sun to partial shade, 10″–15″ (25–38 cm) apart.

**CARE TIPS:** Easy. Even moisture. Fertilize every 4 weeks. Extend bloom by deadheading. Propagate by division, seed.

**NOTES:** Thrives in accents, hanging baskets, borders, edgings, foregrounds. Nice in cottage, natural, rock, wildflower, woodland gardens. Aggressive. Resists pests and diseases.

## *Geranium pratense* GERANIACEAE

### Meadow Cranesbill

**SHAPE:** Numerous mounded, sprawling, rhizomatous perennials, 18″–24″ (45–60 cm) tall. Hirsute, maplelike, lobed, deep-cut leaves to 6″ (15 cm) long. See also *Pelargonium × hortorum*, florist's geranium.

**FLOWER:** Spring to summer bloom. Lone 5-petaled flowers to 1″ (25 mm) wide. Choose from blue and white with red, purple veins.

**HARDINESS:** Zones 4–9. May self-seed.

**SOIL TYPE:** Sandy loam. High moisture, good drainage, medium fertility, 6.0–8.0 pH.

**PLANTING GUIDE:** Spring, as soil warms. Plant in full to filtered sun, 18″ (45 cm) apart.

**CARE TIPS:** Easy to average. Even moisture. Fertilize only in spring. Renew bloom by shearing when flowers fade. Propagate by division, seed.

**NOTES:** Thrives in accents, borders, edgings, filler, foregrounds, ground covers. Nice in cottage, natural, rock, wildflower, woodland gardens. Resists pests and diseases.

## *Gerbera jamesonii* ASTERACEAE (COMPOSITAE)

### Transvaal Daisy

**SHAPE:** Numerous mounded perennials, 12″–18″ (30–45 cm) tall and 24″–32″ (60–75 cm) wide. Hairy, lancelike, lobate leaves to 10″ (25 cm) long with pale undersides.

**FLOWER:** Summer to autumn bloom. Single or double, daisylike flowers, 2″–5″ (50–125 mm) wide. Choose from cream, orange, pink, purple, red, white, yellow, and multicolored.

**HARDINESS:** Zones 8–11.

**SOIL TYPE:** High humus. High moisture, good drainage, high fertility, 6.0–7.0 pH.

**PLANTING GUIDE:** Spring, as soil warms. Plant in full sun to partial shade, 6″–12″ (15–30 cm) apart.

**CARE TIPS:** Easy. Even moisture. Fertilize every 10–12 weeks. Apply mulch. Extend bloom by deadheading. Propagate by cuttings, division, seed.

**NOTES:** Thrives in containers, ground covers. Nice in cottage, seaside gardens. Cutting flower. Susceptible to slugs, snails, fungal diseases.

## *Geum spp.* ROSACEAE

### Avens

**SHAPE:** Numerous durable, mounded, semi-evergreen perennials, 12″–24″ (30–60 cm) tall. Smooth, divided, irregular and wavy-edged, veined, toothed leaves, 2″–4″ (50–100 mm) long.

**FLOWER:** Late-spring to summer bloom. Branched stems of single, semi-double, or double roselike flowers to 1½″ (38 mm) wide. Choose from orange, bright red, and yellow.

**HARDINESS:** Zones 3–7. Prefers cold-winter, cool-summer climates.

**SOIL TYPE:** High humus. High moisture, good drainage, high fertility, 7.0–8.0 pH. Tolerates salt.

**PLANTING GUIDE:** Spring, as soil warms. Plant in full sun to partial shade, 12″–18″ (30–45 cm) apart.

**CARE TIPS:** Easy. Even moisture. Fertilize every 4 weeks. Apply mulch. Propagate by division, seed.

**NOTES:** Thrives in accents, island beds, edgings. Nice in shade, rock, woodland gardens. Cutting flower. Resists pests. Susceptible to downy mildew.

## *Gypsophila paniculata* CARYOPHYLLACEAE

### Baby's-Breath

**SHAPE:** Various branched, mounded, erect, rhizomatous perennials to 36″ (90 cm) tall and wide. Smooth, graceful, lancelike, fine-toothed leaves to 3″ (75 mm) long.

**FLOWER:** Summer bloom. Lone or branched stems with dense clusters of semi-double flowers, ¹⁄₁₆″–⅛″ (1.5–3 mm) wide. Choose from pink and white.

**HARDINESS:** Zones 4–9.

**SOIL TYPE:** Sandy loam. High moisture, good drainage, medium–low fertility, 7.0–8.0 pH.

**PLANTING GUIDE:** Early spring. Plant in full sun, 24″–30″ (60–75 cm) apart. Best sown in garden soil.

**CARE TIPS:** Easy. Even moisture. Fertilize only in spring. Support with stakes. Propagate by cuttings, division, seed.

**NOTES:** Thrives in accents, borders. Nice in cottage, rock, rose gardens. Cutting flower. Resists diseases. Susceptible to leafhoppers, slugs, snails.

## *Hedychium* spp. ZINGIBERACEAE

### Ginger Lily (Garland Lily)

**SHAPE:** Nearly 50 arched or erect, rhizomatous, semi-evergreen, tropical perennials, 36″–84″ (90–215 cm) tall and wide. Opposite, shiny, oval, sharp-tipped, veined leaves to 24″ (60 cm) long.

**FLOWER:** Summer to autumn bloom. Spiking clusters to 12″ (30 cm) high of tubular, very fragrant flowers, 2″–3″ (50–75 mm) long, with leafy basal bracts. Choose from pink, red, white, and yellow.

**HARDINESS:** Zones 8–11.

**SOIL TYPE:** High humus; pond shorelines or margins. High moisture, good drainage, high fertility, 6.0–7.0 pH.

**PLANTING GUIDE:** Spring. Plant in full sun, 4′–6′ (1.2–1.8 m) apart.

**CARE TIPS:** Average. Even moisture. Fertilize every 4 weeks. Apply mulch. Propagate by division.

**NOTES:** Thrives in borders, containers, fence lines. Nice in seaside, shade, tropical gardens and ponds. Cutting flower. Resists pests and diseases.

## *Helenium* spp. and hybrids *(H. autumnale)* ASTERACEAE (COMPOSITAE)

### Sneezeweed

**SHAPE:** More than 40 erect, deciduous, usually perennials, 24″–60″ (60–150 cm) tall. Alternate, opposite, shiny, willowlike, lancelike, fine-toothed leaves to 4″ (10 cm) long.

**FLOWER:** Late-summer to autumn bloom. Terminal clusters to 5′ (1.5 m) high of daisylike, sometimes reflexed flowers, 2″–3″ (50–75 mm) wide. Choose from bronze, brown, copper, orange, red, yellow, and multicolored.

**HARDINESS:** Zones 3–9.

**SOIL TYPE:** Sandy loam. High moisture, good drainage, high fertility, 6.5–7.5 pH.

**PLANTING GUIDE:** Spring, as soil warms. Plant in full sun, 8″–16″ (20–40 cm) apart.

**CARE TIPS:** Easy. Even moisture. Fertilize only in spring. Support with stakes. Propagate by cutting, division, seed.

**NOTES:** Thrives in backgrounds, beds, borders. Nice in cottage, natural, wildlife gardens. Cutting flower. Resists pests and diseases.

## *Helianthus* spp. ASTERACEAE (COMPOSITAE)

### Perennial Sunflower

**SHAPE:** Various erect, slender or bushlike, deciduous, annuals or perennials, 36″–84″ (90–215 cm) tall. Alternate, hirsute, textured, coarse-toothed leaves. See also *H. annuus*, annual sunflower.

**FLOWER:** Summer to autumn bloom. Lone or clustered, single or double, round flowers, 3″–12″ (75–305 mm) wide. Yellow with brown centers.

**HARDINESS:** Zones 4–8.

**SOIL TYPE:** Sandy loam. High moisture, good drainage, medium fertility, 5.0–7.0 pH.

**PLANTING GUIDE:** Spring, as soil warms. Plant in full sun to partial shade, 18″–36″ (45–90 cm) apart.

**CARE TIPS:** Easy. Even moisture. Fertilize every 2 weeks. Stake to support. Propagate by division, seed.

**NOTES:** Thrives in borders, containers, massed plantings. Nice in cottage, wildlife gardens. Cutting flower. Susceptible to stalk borers, sunflower maggots, sunflower moth larvae, powdery mildew, rust.

## *Helichrysum* spp. ASTERACEAE (COMPOSITAE)

### Strawflower (Curry Plant, Everlasting, Immortelle, Licorice Plant)

**SHAPE:** Numerous erect or trailing, slender, shrubby, deciduous annuals and perennials, 18″–36″ (45–90 cm) tall. Woolly or smooth, lance- or straplike leaves, 1″–5″ (25–125 mm) long.

**FLOWER:** Summer to early-autumn bloom. Lone or clustered, single or double, round, papery, flowerlike bracts, ½″–2½″ (12–63 mm) wide, with tiny true flowers. Choose from orange, pink, red, white, and yellow with contrasting centers.

**HARDINESS:** Zones 7–11.

**SOIL TYPE:** Sandy loam. Average moisture, good drainage, high–low fertility, 7.0–7.5 pH.

**PLANTING GUIDE:** Spring, as soil warms. Plant in full sun, 12″–24″ (30–60 cm) apart.

**CARE TIPS:** Easy. Even moisture. Fertilize every 2 weeks. Stake to support. Propagate by seed.

**NOTES:** Thrives in accents, beds, borders, containers, paths. Nice in cottage, formal, meadow, wildlife gardens. Cutting, drying flower. Resists pests and diseases.

## *Heliconia bihai* (H. humilis) HELICONIACEAE

### Lobster-Claw (False Bird-of-Paradise)

**SHAPE:** Numerous rhizomatous, evergreen perennials to 4′ (1.2 m) tall. Spoonlike, long leaves to 36″ (90 cm) long.

**FLOWER:** Summer to autumn bloom. Stalks with vertical tiers of multiple, lobster-claw-like flowers, 5″–10″ (13–25 cm) long. Choose from orange, red, and yellow.

**HARDINESS:** Zones 10–11.

**SOIL TYPE:** Sandy loam. High moisture, good drainage, high fertility, 6.0–6.5 pH.

**PLANTING GUIDE:** Spring to autumn. Plant in partial shade, 36″ (90 cm) apart, as deep as the soil level in the nursery container.

**CARE TIPS:** Average. Even moisture during growth. Fertilize every 4 weeks. Shelter from wind. Store in-ground. Propagate by division.

**NOTES:** Thrives in accents, borders, containers, paths. Nice in tropical, woodland gardens and greenhouses. Cutting flower. Resists pests and diseases.

## *Heliopsis helianthoides* ASTERACEAE (COMPOSITAE)

### False Sunflower (Oxeye)

**SHAPE:** Few vigorous, upright perennials to 5′ (1.5 m) tall and 36″ (90 cm) wide. Opposite, oval to lancelike, toothed leaves to 4½″ (114 mm) long.

**FLOWER:** Summer to autumn bloom. Long stems of daisylike flowers to 2½″ (63 mm) wide. Choose from gold and bright yellow.

**HARDINESS:** Zones 3–11.

**SOIL TYPE:** Loam. Average–low moisture, good drainage, medium–low fertility, 6.5–7.5 pH.

**PLANTING GUIDE:** Spring, as soil warms. Plant in full sun, 9″–12″ (23–30 cm) apart.

**CARE TIPS:** Easy. Water only when soil dries. Drought tolerant. Fertilize every 10–12 weeks. Pinch tips for bushy plants. Extend bloom by deadheading. Propagate by division.

**NOTES:** Thrives in accents, backgrounds, borders, containers, massed plantings. Nice in cottage, formal, meadow, natural, wildlife gardens. Cutting flower. Resists pests and diseases.

## *Heliotropium arborescens* BORAGINACEAE

### Common Heliotrope (Cherry-Pie)

**SHAPE:** Numerous erect, slender, shrubby, evergreen perennials, 24″–48″ (60–120 cm) tall. Shiny, textured, oval, sharp-tipped leaves to 3″ (75 mm) long with prominent veins.

**FLOWER:** Summer bloom. Broad, mounded or branched clusters to 5″ (13 cm) wide of tiny 5-petaled, fragrant flowers to ¼″ (6 mm) wide. Choose from blue, purple, violet, and white.

**HARDINESS:** Zones 10–11. Protect from frost.

**SOIL TYPE:** Sandy loam. High moisture, good drainage, high fertility, 6.5–7.5 pH.

**PLANTING GUIDE:** Spring, as soil warms. Plant in filtered sun to partial shade, 12″–16″ (30–40 cm) apart.

**CARE TIPS:** Easy to average. Even moisture. Fertilize every 4 weeks. Apply mulch in winter. Propagate by cuttings, layering, seed.

**NOTES:** Thrives in borders, containers. Nice in cottage, natural, shade, woodland gardens. Resists pests and diseases.

## *Helleborus spp.* RANUNCULACEAE

### Lenten Rose (Hellebore, Christmas Rose)

**SHAPE:** Various erect, mounded, rhizome-rooted, deciduous or evergreen perennials, 12″–24″ (30–60 cm) tall. Shiny, hand-shaped, lobate, toothed or scalloped leaves to 16″ (40 cm) wide.

**FLOWER:** Late-winter to spring bloom. Nodding, pendulous stalks of showy, cup- or bell-shaped flowers to 3″ (75 mm) wide. Choose from cream, green, lavender, pink, and white.

**HARDINESS:** Zones 4–9.

**SOIL TYPE:** High humus. High moisture, good drainage, high fertility, 6.0–7.0 pH.

**PLANTING GUIDE:** Early spring, as soil becomes workable. Plant in partial to full shade, 18″–24″ (45–60 cm) apart.

**CARE TIPS:** Average to difficult. Even moisture. Fertilize every 4 weeks. Apply mulch. Propagate by division, seed.

**NOTES:** Thrives in beds, borders, containers. Nice in cottage, shade, woodland gardens. Resists pests. Susceptible to leaf spot, slugs, snails.

## *Hemerocallis* spp. LILIACEAE

### Daylily

**SHAPE:** About 15 bunching, fiberous or tuberous, deciduous or evergreen perennials to 6′ (1.8 m) tall. Slender, swordlike, arched basal leaves, 8″–24″ (20–60 cm) long.

**FLOWER:** Late-spring to autumn bloom. Flared, trumpet-shaped, flowers to 6″ (15 cm) wide. Choose from orange, pink, purple, and yellow.

**HARDINESS:** Zones 3–10.

**SOIL TYPE:** Sandy loam. High moisture, good drainage, medium–low fertility, 5.0–7.0 pH.

**PLANTING GUIDE:** Spring, zones 3–6; autumn, zones 7–10. Plant in full sun to partial shade, 15″–24″ (38–60 cm) apart, slightly below soil level.

**CARE TIPS:** Easy. Even moisture during growth. Fertilize sparingly. Apply mulch. Propagate by division. Store in damp peat moss, 40°–50°F (4°–10°C).

**NOTES:** Thrives in beds, borders. Nice in cottage gardens. Resists insect pests and diseases. Susceptible to deer, rodents.

## *Heuchera sanguinea* SAXIFRAGACEAE

### Coralbells (Alumroot)

**SHAPE:** Bushy perennial, 12″–24″ (30–60 cm) tall and wide, with tall flower stems above foliage. Hairy, textured, circular to heart-shaped, 5–9-lobed, evergreen leaves to 2″ (50 mm) long.

**FLOWER:** Summer to autumn bloom. Nodding, bell-shaped flowers, 2″–4″ (50–100 mm) wide. Choose from green, pink, red, and white.

**HARDINESS:** Zones 4–9.

**SOIL TYPE:** High humus. High moisture, good drainage, high fertility, 6.0–7.0 pH.

**PLANTING GUIDE:** Early spring, after frost hazard has passed, zones 4–6; autumn, zones 7–9. Plant in partial to full shade, 9″–15″ (23–38 cm) apart.

**CARE TIPS:** Easy. Even moisture. Fertilize only in spring. Apply mulch in winter. Propagate by division, seed.

**NOTES:** Thrives in borders, edgings, foregrounds, paths. Nice in cottage, wildlife, woodland gardens. Susceptible to mealybugs, nematodes, root weevils, stem rot.

## *Hosta* spp. and hybrids LILIACEAE

### Plantain Lily (Daylily, Hosta)

**SHAPE:** Numerous mounded, sprawling, rhizomatous perennials, 8″–36″ (20–90 cm) tall and to 5′ (1.5 m) wide. Shiny or smooth, fringed, variegated or scallop-edged, overlapping, oval leaves, 6″–12″ (15–30 cm) long.

**FLOWER:** Summer bloom. Succulent or woody stalks with drooping clusters of nodding, lilylike, tubular, sometimes fragrant flowers, 1½″ (38 mm) long. Choose from cream, mauve, purple, and white.

**HARDINESS:** Zones 2–10.

**SOIL TYPE:** High humus. High moisture, good drainage, high–low fertility, 5.5–7.0 pH.

**PLANTING GUIDE:** Spring. Plant in partial to full shade, 12″–60″ (30–150 cm) apart.

**CARE TIPS:** Easy. Even moisture. Fertilize every 4–6 weeks. Apply mulch in winter. Shear in autumn. Propagate by division.

**NOTES:** Thrives in borders, ground covers. Nice in shade, woodland gardens. Susceptible to slugs, snails, crown rot.

## *Iberis sempervirens* BRASSICACEAE (CRUCIFERAE)

### Candytuft

**SHAPE:** Numerous dense, short, sprawling or shrubby, evergreen perennials, 8″–12″ (20–30 cm) tall. Shiny, slender, oval, sharp-tipped leaves to 1½″ (38 mm) long.

**FLOWER:** Early-spring to summer bloom; 'Autumn Snow' remontant in autumn. Round or flat clusters to 4″ (10 cm) wide of tiny, 4-petaled flowers to ⅝″ (16 mm) wide. White.

**HARDINESS:** Zones 3–10.

**SOIL TYPE:** High humus. High moisture, good drainage, high fertility, 6.0–7.0 pH.

**PLANTING GUIDE:** Spring. Plant in full to filtered sun, 6″–12″ (15–30 cm) apart.

**CARE TIPS:** Very easy. Even moisture. Fertilize every 4 weeks. Deadhead. Pinch tips for bushy plants. Propagate by cuttings, division, seed.

**NOTES:** Thrives in accents, borders, containers, edgings. Nice in cottage, formal, rock gardens. Cutting flower. Resists diseases. Susceptible to slugs, snails.

## *Impatiens wallerana* and hybrids *(I. holstii)* BALSAMINACEAE

### Balsam (Busy Lizzie, Impatiens)

**SHAPE:** Numerous dense, short, sprawling, succulent, deciduous perennials, 8″–24″ (20–60 cm) tall. Shiny, slender, oval, sharp-tipped leaves to 1½″–4″ (38–100 mm) long.

**FLOWER:** Summer to early-autumn bloom. Single, 5-petaled flowers, 1″–2″ (25–50 mm) wide. Choose from brown, cream, orange, pink, purple, red, tan, white, variegated, and fringed.

**HARDINESS:** Zones 9–11. Protect from frost. May self-seed.

**SOIL TYPE:** Sandy loam. High moisture, good drainage, high fertility, 6.5–7.5 pH.

**PLANTING GUIDE:** Spring. Plant in filtered sun to full shade, 10″–12″ (25–30 cm) apart.

**CARE TIPS:** Very easy. Even moisture. Fertilize every 4 weeks. Propagate by cuttings, seed.

**NOTES:** Thrives in accents, beds, borders, containers, edgings, massed plantings. Nice in cottage, formal, small-space, rock gardens. Resists diseases. Susceptible to aphids.

## *Incarvillea arguta* *(I. delavayi)* BIGNONIACEAE

### Hardy Gloxinia

**SHAPE:** Few nearly stemless, erect, arching, woody-rooted, deciduous perennials to 5′ (1.5 m) tall. Shiny, divided, oval leaves to 12″ (30 cm) long with paired leaflets to 2″ (50 mm) long.

**FLOWER:** Spring to summer bloom. Stalks with clusters of irregular, trumpet-shaped, 5-petaled flowers to 3″ (75 mm) wide. Choose from mauve, pink and white, with yellow or purple throats.

**HARDINESS:** Zones 6–10.

**SOIL TYPE:** Sandy loam. High moisture, good drainage, high fertility, 6.5–7.5 pH.

**PLANTING GUIDE:** Spring. Plant in filtered sun to partial shade, 4′–5′ (1.2–1.5 m) apart.

**CARE TIPS:** Moderate. Even moisture. Fertilize every 4 weeks. Protect from hot sun. Mulch in autumn. Support with stakes. Propagate by division, seed.

**NOTES:** Thrives in backgrounds, borders, edgings, fence lines, paths. Nice in cottage, shade gardens. Resists diseases. Susceptible to slugs, snails.

## *Ipomoea spp.* CONVOLVULACEAE

### Morning Glory

**SHAPE:** About 500 vigorous, twining, annual or perennial vines, 6′–15′ (1.8–4.5 m) long. Alternate, smooth, heart-shaped or 3-lobed leaves, 3″–8″ (75–200 mm) long.

**FLOWER:** Summer bloom. Lone, funnel-shaped flowers, 2″–6″ (50–150 mm) wide. Choose from blue, red, white, and variegated.

**HARDINESS:** Zones 3–10. May self-seed.

**SOIL TYPE:** Loam. High–average moisture, good drainage, high–medium fertility, 6.5–7.5 pH.

**PLANTING GUIDE:** Spring. Plant in full sun to partial shade, 36″–60″ (90–150 cm) apart.

**CARE TIPS:** Easy. Water when soil dries 4″–6″ (10–15 cm) deep. Fertilize every 10–12 weeks. Support with stakes. Propagate by seed.

**NOTES:** Thrives in arbors, banks, screens, trellises. Nice in cottage, meadow, tropical gardens. Cutting flower. Aggressive, depending on species. Resists diseases. Susceptible to aphids, tortoise beetles, cutworms, sweet-potato weevils.

## *Iris cristata* IRIDACEAE

### Crested Iris

**SHAPE:** Few rhizomatous, deciduous perennials, 8″–10″ (20–25 cm) tall. Narrow, flat, straplike leaves to 12″ (30 cm) long.

**FLOWER:** Spring bloom. Stalks of fragrant flowers to 2½″ (63 mm) wide with graceful segmented falls and raised, crestlike centers. Choose from blue, lilac, and white with yellow.

**HARDINESS:** Zones 4–9.

**SOIL TYPE:** High humus. High moisture, good drainage, high–medium fertility, 6.0–7.0 pH.

**PLANTING GUIDE:** Autumn. Plant in open to partial shade, 6″–12″ (15–30 cm) apart, 2″ (50 mm) deep, rhizome slightly above soil level.

**CARE TIPS:** Easy. Even moisture during growth. Fertilize until established. Lift and store. Propagate by division, seed.

**NOTES:** Thrives in borders, containers, drifts, edgings, ground covers, slopes. Nice in meadow, natural, rock, woodland gardens. Susceptible to slugs, snails.

## *Iris × germanica* hybrids IRIDACEAE

### German Bearded Iris

**SHAPE:** Numerous rhizomatous, deciduous perennials to 30″ (75 cm) tall. Swordlike, erect or curved leaves to 36″ (90 cm) long.

**FLOWER:** Summer bloom; some remontant. Upright stalks of multiple, fleur-de-lis–shaped flowers to 3″ (75 mm) wide with erect petals and drooping, bearded falls. Choose from most colors, bicolors, and blends.

**HARDINESS:** Zones 5–10.

**SOIL TYPE:** High humus. High moisture, good drainage, medium fertility, 6.0–7.0 pH.

**PLANTING GUIDE:** Autumn, zones 8–10; late summer, zones 4–7. Plant in full sun to partial shade, 12″–24″ (30–60 cm) apart, 2″ (50 mm) deep.

**CARE TIPS:** Easy. Even moisture during growth; reduce water thereafter. Fertilize in spring. Apply mulch. Lift and store. Propagate by division.

**NOTES:** Thrives in edgings, massed plantings. Nice in shade gardens. Cutting flower. Susceptible to deer, rodents, iris borers, soft rot.

## *Iris versicolor* IRIDACEAE

### Blue Flag Iris (Wild Iris)

**SHAPE:** Numerous rhizomatous, deciduous perennials, 30″ (75 cm) tall. Strap- or swordlike, erect or curved leaves to 36″ (90 cm) long.

**FLOWER:** Summer. Lone or multiple fleur-de-lis–shaped flowers to 3″ (75 mm) wide with erect petals and drooping, beardless falls. Choose from blue, lavender, and white.

**HARDINESS:** Zones 3–9.

**SOIL TYPE:** High humus; pond margins. High moisture, average drainage, medium fertility, 6.0–7.0 pH.

**PLANTING GUIDE:** Autumn. Plant in full sun to partial shade, 12″–24″ (30–60 cm) apart, 2″ (50 mm) deep.

**CARE TIPS:** Easy. Even moisture. Fertilize only in spring. Apply mulch. Propagate by division.

**NOTES:** Thrives in edgings, foregrounds. Nice in natural, woodland gardens and ponds. Cutting flower. Susceptible to deer, rodents, iris borers, soft rot.

## *Kirengeshoma palmata* HYDRANGEACEAE (SAXIFRAGACEAE)

### Yellow Waxbells

**SHAPE:** Few low or erect, rhizomatous, deciduous perennials, 2′–4′ (60–120 cm) tall. Opposite, shiny, maplelike, toothed leaves to 8″ (20 cm) long, on purple leaf stalks.

**FLOWER:** Late-summer to autumn bloom. Branched stalks with nodding clusters of bell-shaped, deep-throated flowers, 1″–1½″ (25–38 mm) wide. Light yellow.

**HARDINESS:** Zones 4–9.

**SOIL TYPE:** High humus. High moisture, good drainage, high fertility, 6.0–7.0 pH.

**PLANTING GUIDE:** Spring. Plant in partial to full shade, 4′–5′ (1.2–1.5 m) apart.

**CARE TIPS:** Easy. Even moisture. Fertilize every 4 weeks. Protect from hot sun. Mulch in autumn. Propagate by division, seed.

**NOTES:** Thrives in accents, backgrounds, borders, edgings, fence lines. Nice in cottage, casual, shade gardens. Resists diseases. Susceptible to slugs, snails.

## *Kniphofia uvaria* LILIACEAE

### Torch Lily (Red-Hot-Poker)

**SHAPE:** Numerous rhizomatous, deciduous or semi-evergreen perennials to 4′ (1.2 m) tall and 24″ (60 cm) wide. Broad, grasslike or straplike, arching or upright leaves, 24″–48″ (60–120 cm) long.

**FLOWER:** Summer. Succulent stalks with vertical tiers of radiating, tubular flowers, 1″ (25 mm) long. Choose from orange, red, and yellow.

**HARDINESS:** Zones 6–10. Protect from frost.

**SOIL TYPE:** Sandy loam. High moisture, good drainage, medium–low fertility, 5.5–6.5 pH.

**PLANTING GUIDE:** Spring. Plant in full sun, 18″ (45 cm) apart, barely covered.

**CARE TIPS:** Average. Even moisture during growth. Fertilize in spring. Apply mulch. Lift and store. Propagate by division, offsets, seed.

**NOTES:** Thrives in mixed plantings. Nice in tropical, wildlife gardens. Cutting flower. Evergreen in warm-winter climates. Susceptible to slugs, snails.

## *Lathyrus latifolius* FABACEAE (LEGUMINOSAE)

### Perennial Sweet Pea (Everlasting Sweet Pea)

**SHAPE:** Various upright, climbing and twining perennials to 9′ (2.7 m) tall or long. Supported by tendrils. Paired, oval or lancelike leaves to 4″ (10 cm) long.

**FLOWER:** Spring to summer bloom. Pealike fragrant flowers to 1½″ (38 mm) wide. Choose from pink, purple, red, and white. Forms flat pods with round, pealike seed.

**HARDINESS:** Zones 4–10. May self-seed.

**SOIL TYPE:** Sandy loam. Average moisture, good drainage, medium fertility, 7.0–8.0 pH. Tolerates salt.

**PLANTING GUIDE:** Spring, as soil warms. Plant in full sun, 6″–12″ (15–30 cm) apart.

**CARE TIPS:** Average. Even moisture. Fertilize every 10–12 weeks. Extend bloom by deadheading. Support with stakes. Propagate by division, seed.

**NOTES:** Thrives in arbors, banks, fence lines, ground covers. Nice in cottage, natural gardens. Cutting flower. Resists diseases. Susceptible to slugs, snails.

## *Lavandula* spp. LAMIACEAE (LABIATAE)

### Lavender

**SHAPE:** About 20 bushy, erect, semi-evergreen perennials and shrubs, 12″–48″ (30–120 cm) tall. Woolly, matte, needlelike leaves to 2″ (50 mm) long.

**FLOWER:** Summer bloom. Dense, plumelike clusters to 10″ (25 cm) long of many tiny, fragrant flowers. Choose from blue, pink, and purple.

**HARDINESS:** Zones 4–10.

**SOIL TYPE:** Sandy loam. Average–low moisture, good drainage, low fertility, 6.5–7.5 pH.

**PLANTING GUIDE:** Spring, when frost risk ends. Plant in full sun, 12″–18″ (30–45 cm) apart.

**CARE TIPS:** Easy. Water when soil dries 4″–6″ (10–15 cm) deep. Fertilize sparingly. Apply inorganic mulch in winter, zones 7–8. Prune after flowering. Propagate by cuttings, division.

**NOTES:** Thrives in accents, borders, containers, hedges, paths. Nice in cottage, country, natural, rock gardens. Cutting, drying flower. Resists pests and diseases.

## *Lewisia cotyledon* PORTULACACEAE

### Broad-leaved Lewisia (Bitterroot)

**SHAPE:** Various mounded, evergreen perennials to 12″ (30 cm) tall. Soft, succulent, slender, oval, sometimes scallop-edged leaves to 3″ (75 mm) wide. Turns color in autumn.

**FLOWER:** Early-spring to summer bloom. Succulent stalks to 10″ (25 cm) tall with loose clusters of showy, star-shaped, open, 9-petaled flowers to 1″ (25 mm) wide. Choose from pink, purple, orange, white, and yellow.

**HARDINESS:** Zones 3–9.

**SOIL TYPE:** Sandy loam. Average–low moisture, good drainage, medium–low fertility, 6.0–7.0 pH.

**PLANTING GUIDE:** Spring. Plant in full sun to partial shade, 12″ (30 cm) apart.

**CARE TIPS:** Difficult. Even moisture. Fertilize sparingly. Propagate by division, seed.

**NOTES:** Thrives in accents, beds, containers, edgings, foregrounds. Nice in natural, rock, seaside, woodland, Xeriscape gardens. Resists pests and diseases.

## *Linum perenne* LINACEAE

### Perennial Flax

**SHAPE:** Numerous impermanent, branched, open, erect, deciduous perennials, 18″–24″ (45–60 cm) tall. Hirsute, branched stems with alternate, lancelike leaves, 1″–1½″ (25–38 mm) long. See also *L. grandiflorum*, annual flax.

**FLOWER:** Spring to summer bloom. Open, simple, 5-petaled flowers, 1″–1¾″ (25–44 mm) wide. Choose from blue and white. Last one day.

**HARDINESS:** Zones 4–10. May self-seed.

**SOIL TYPE:** Sandy loam. Average moisture, good drainage, medium–low fertility, 6.5–7.5 pH.

**PLANTING GUIDE:** Spring, as soil warms, or summer. Plant in full sun, 18″ (45 cm) apart.

**CARE TIPS:** Easy to average. Even moisture. Fertilize every 4 weeks. Apply mulch in winter. Propagate by cuttings, division, seed.

**NOTES:** Thrives in accents, beds, borders, foregrounds, massed plantings. Nice in cottage, natural, rock gardens. Cutting flower. Resists pests and diseases.

## *Lobelia erinus* CAMPANULACEAE (LOBELIACEAE)

### Edging Lobelia (Indian Pink)

**SHAPE:** Numerous short, sprawling or trailing perennials to 9″ (23 cm) tall. Shiny, gold-tinged, oval or lancelike to needle-shaped leaves, ½″–1″ (12–25 mm) long.

**FLOWER:** Early-summer to autumn bloom. Open, 5-petaled flowers to ¾″ (19 mm) wide. Choose from blue, pink, purple, and white with white and yellow centers.

**HARDINESS:** Zones 9–10. Protect from frost. May self-seed.

**SOIL TYPE:** High humus. High moisture, good drainage, high fertility, 6.5–7.5 pH.

**PLANTING GUIDE:** Spring, when frost risk ends. Plant in full to filtered sun, 12″ (30 cm) apart.

**CARE TIPS:** Easy. Even moisture. Fertilize every 4 weeks. Apply mulch. Protect from hot sun. Propagate by seed.

**NOTES:** Thrives in hanging baskets, beds, borders, containers, edgings, hedges. Nice in cottage, formal gardens. Resists pests and diseases.

## *Lobularia maritima* BRASSICACEAE (CRUCIFERAE)

### Sweet Alyssum

**SHAPE:** Numerous short, branched, sprawling, fine-textured perennials to 12″ (30 cm) tall. Smooth, lancelike leaves to 2″ (50 mm) long.

**FLOWER:** Late-spring to late-autumn bloom. Clusters of tiny, simple, 4-petaled flowers to ¼″ (6 mm) wide. Choose from pink, purple, and white

**HARDINESS:** Zones 7–11. Protect from frost. May self-seed.

**SOIL TYPE:** Loam. High moisture, good drainage, medium fertility, 6.5–7.0 pH.

**PLANTING GUIDE:** Early spring, as soil becomes workable. Plant in full sun to partial shade, 6″ (15 cm) apart. Start indoors for early bloom.

**CARE TIPS:** Easy. Even moisture. Fertilize sparingly. Extend bloom by deadheading and shearing. Propagate by seed.

**NOTES:** Thrives in hanging baskets, borders, containers, edgings, foregrounds. Nice in cottage, meadow, rock gardens. Resists diseases. Susceptible to slugs, snails.

## *Lupinus* spp. and hybrids FABACEAE (LEGUMINOSAE)

### Lupine

**SHAPE:** About 200 erect or bushlike annual or perennials, 36″–60″ (90–150 cm) tall. Woolly, frondlike, deeply lobate leaves to 4″ (10 cm) long. Dwarf cultivars available.

**FLOWER:** Spring to summer bloom. Spikes to 24″ (60 cm) long with vertical tiers of of pealike flowers. Choose from blue, cream, orange, pink, purple, red, white, yellow, and bicolored.

**HARDINESS:** Zones 4–9. May self-seed.

**SOIL TYPE:** Sandy loam. Average–low moisture,

good drainage, high–low fertility, 6.0–7.0 pH.

**PLANTING GUIDE:** Spring, as soil warms. Plant in full to filtered sun, 24″–36″ (60–90 cm) apart.

**CARE TIPS:** Easy. Water only when soil dries. Fertilize only in spring. Extend bloom by deadheading. Shelter from wind. Propagate by division, seed.

**NOTES:** Thrives in accents, backgrounds, beds, borders, paths. Nice in meadow, natural, wildlife, woodland gardens. Resists diseases. Susceptible to lupine aphids.

## *Lupinus texensis* (*L. subcarnosus*) FABACEAE (LEGUMINOSAE)

### Texas Bluebonnet (Lupine)

**SHAPE:** Various erect or bushlike annual or perennials, 12″–16″ (30–40 cm) tall and 12″ (30 cm) wide. Woolly, frondlike, deeply lobate leaves to 4″ (10 cm) long with lancelike, sharp-tipped leaflets.

**FLOWER:** Spring to summer bloom. Spikes to 12″ (30 cm) long of pealike flowers. Choose from deep blue, cream, white, and bicolored.

**HARDINESS:** Zones 4–10. May self-seed.

**SOIL TYPE:** Sandy loam. Average–low moisture,

good drainage, high–low fertility, 6.0–7.0 pH.

**PLANTING GUIDE:** Spring, when frost risk ends. Plant in full to filtered sun, 8″–12″ (20–30 cm) apart.

**CARE TIPS:** Easy. Water only when soil dries. Fertilize only in spring. Extend bloom by deadheading. Shelter from wind. Propagate by division, seed.

**NOTES:** Thrives in backgrounds, beds, borders, massed plantings. Nice in cottage, meadow, natural, wildlife gardens. Resists diseases. Susceptible to lupine aphids.

## *Lychnis chalcedonica* or *L. coronaria* CARYOPHYLLACEAE

### Maltese-Cross (Scarlet-Lightning)

**SHAPE:** Various slender, open or dense, deciduous perennials to 36″ (90 cm) tall. Oval, tapered, hirsute leaves to 1″ (25 mm) long.

**FLOWER:** Summer bloom. Spiking half-circular clusters to 3″ (75 mm) wide, of star-shaped, lobate, deep-cut flowers to ½″ (12 mm) wide. Choose from red, salmon, scarlet, and white.

**HARDINESS:** Zones 2–10. Prefers cold-winter climates.

**SOIL TYPE:** Loam. High moisture, good drainage, medium fertility, 5.5–7.0 pH.

**PLANTING GUIDE:** Spring. Plant in full to filtered sun, 24″–32″ (60–80 cm) apart.

**CARE TIPS:** Easy. Even moisture. Fertilize every 10–12 weeks. Protect from hot sun. Propagate by division, seed.

**NOTES:** Thrives in accents, borders, containers, edgings, massed plantings. Nice in cottage, formal, heritage, meadow, natural, rock gardens. Resists pests and diseases.

## *Lythrum virgatum* and hybrids LYTHRACEAE

### Purple Loosestrife

**SHAPE:** Various erect perennials to 36″ (90 cm) tall. Usually alternate, woolly, lancelike leaves to 4″ (10 cm) long.

**FLOWER:** Summer to autumn bloom. Cone-shaped, spiking clusters to 5′ (1.5 m) tall of star-shaped flowers, ½″–¾″ (12–19 mm) wide. Choose from pink, purple, and red.

**HARDINESS:** Zones 3–9. Prefers cool, moist climates.

**SOIL TYPE:** High humus. High moisture, good drainage, high fertility, 5.5–7.0 pH.

**PLANTING GUIDE:** Summer. Plant in full sun, 24″ (60 cm) apart.

**CARE TIPS:** Easy. Even moisture. Fertilize every 4 weeks. Apply mulch. Support with stakes. Propagate by division.

**NOTES:** Thrives in accents, backgrounds, fence lines, walls. Nice in cottage, formal, meadow, natural gardens. Very invasive; culture may be prohibited in some areas. Resists pests and diseases.

## *Macleaya* spp. *(Bocconia* spp.*)* PAPAVERACEAE

### Plume Poppy

**SHAPE:** Few erect, open, shrubby, stoloniferous, deciduous perennials to 5′ (1.5 m) tall and wide. Tall central spike with stiff, radiating leaf stalks and shiny, circular, deeply lobate, upturned leaves to 8″ (20 cm) long.

**FLOWER:** Late-spring to summer bloom. Dense terminal clusters to 8″ (20 cm) long of many tiny, frothlike flowers. Choose from cream, pink, tan, and white.

**HARDINESS:** Zones 4–9.

**SOIL TYPE:** High humus. High moisture, good drainage, high–medium fertility, 6.0–7.0 pH.

**PLANTING GUIDE:** Spring, as soil warms. Plant in full to filtered sun, 5′ (1.5 m) apart.

**CARE TIPS:** Easy. Even moisture. Fertilize every 4 weeks. Apply mulch. Support with stakes. Propagate by division, suckers.

**NOTES:** Thrives in accents, backgrounds, fence lines, screens, walls. Nice in cottage, natural, tropical gardens. Aggressive. Resists pests and diseases.

## *Malva alcea* MALVACEAE

### Hollyhock Mallow

**SHAPE:** Various short-lived, erect, branched, bush-like or slender perennials, 36″–48″ (90–120 cm) tall. Textured, circular, plumelike, cut, lobate leaves to 5″ (13 cm) long.

**FLOWER:** Late-spring to autumn bloom. Showy, open, 4-petaled flowers, 1″–2″ (25–50 mm) wide. Choose from gold, pink, and white.

**HARDINESS:** Zones 4–10. May self-seed.

**SOIL TYPE:** Sandy loam. Average–low moisture, good drainage, medium fertility, 7.0–7.5 pH.

**PLANTING GUIDE:** Spring, as soil warms. Plant in filtered sun to partial shade, 12″–24″ (30–60 cm) apart.

**CARE TIPS:** Easy. Even moisture. Fertilize every 4 weeks. Support with stakes. Propagate by division, seed.

**NOTES:** Thrives in accents, backgrounds, borders, edgings, fence lines. Nice in cottage, formal, meadow, natural, shade gardens. Resists diseases. Susceptible to aphids, root borers.

## *Matthiola incana* BRASSICACEAE (CRUCIFERAE)

### Stock (Gillyflower, Imperial Stock)

**SHAPE:** Numerous erect, slender biennials or perennials to 30″ (75 cm) tall and 18″–24″ (45–60 cm) wide. Usually alternate, smooth, oval to lancelike, round-tipped leaves to 4″ (10 cm) long.

**FLOWER:** Spring to summer bloom. Tall spikes of single or double, fragrant flowers to 1″ (25 mm) wide. Choose from blue, cream, pink, purple, red, and yellow.

**HARDINESS:** Zones 7–9. May self-seed.

**SOIL TYPE:** Sandy loam. High moisture, good drainage, high–medium fertility, 6.5–7.5 pH.

**PLANTING GUIDE:** Spring, zones 2–7; autumn, zones 8–9. Plant in full sun to partial shade, 12″ (30 cm) apart.

**CARE TIPS:** Easy. Even moisture. Fertilize every 4 weeks. Stake to support. Propagate by seed.

**NOTES:** Thrives in beds, borders, containers. Nice in cottage, shade gardens. Cutting flower. Resists pests and diseases.

## *Mazus reptans* SCROPHULARIACEAE

### Mazus

**SHAPE:** Various low, sprawling, tufted, herbaceous semi-evergreen perennials to 2″ (50 mm) tall and 12″ (30 cm) wide. Prostrate stems of broadly oval to lancelike, toothed leaves to 1″ (25 mm) long.

**FLOWER:** Late-spring bloom. Clusters of irregular, arrowhead-shaped, lipped flowers to ¾″ (19 mm) wide. Purple blue with spotted lips.

**HARDINESS:** Zones 3–9.

**SOIL TYPE:** Sandy loam. High moisture, good drainage, high fertility, 6.5–7.5 pH.

**PLANTING GUIDE:** Spring, zones 3–7; autumn, zones 8–9. Plant in full sun to partial shade, 12″ (30 cm) apart.

**CARE TIPS:** Easy. Even moisture. Fertilize every 4 weeks. Mulch in autumn. Shear to renew. Propagate by division, seed.

**NOTES:** Thrives in beds, borders, containers, ground covers, paths. Nice in cottage, rock, shade gardens. Resists pests and diseases.

## *Meconopsis cambrica* PAPAVERACEAE

### Welsh Poppy

**SHAPE:** Various erect, branched perennials to 24″ (60 cm) tall. Hairy, plumelike, toothed leaves to 4″ (10 cm) long.

**FLOWER:** Late-spring to early-autumn bloom. Slim, branched stems of showy, flat- or cup-faced, 4-petaled, papery flowers, 2″–3″ (50–75 mm) wide. Choose from orange and yellow.

**HARDINESS:** Zones 4–8. May self-seed.

**SOIL TYPE:** High humus. High moisture, good drainage, high fertility, 6.0–7.0 pH.

**PLANTING GUIDE:** Early spring, zones 4–6; autumn, zones 7–8. Plant in partial to full shade, 12″–18″ (30–45 cm) apart.

**CARE TIPS:** Average. Even moisture. Fertilize every 4 weeks until flowers fade. Protect from hot sun, wind. Propagate by seed.

**NOTES:** Thrives in backgrounds, beds, borders, containers, foregrounds. Nice in cottage, rock, shade, woodland gardens. Cutting flower. Resists pests and diseases.

## *Melampodium leucanthum* ASTERACEAE (COMPOSITAE)

### Blackfoot Daisy

**SHAPE:** Various short-lived, thick-growing, mounded, semi-evergreen perennials, 6″–12″ (15–30 cm) tall, with deep taproots. Usually alternate, smooth, oval leaves, 2″–3″ (50–75 mm) long.

**FLOWER:** Late-spring to autumn bloom. Daisylike, flat-faced, fragrant flowers, ½″–1″ (12–25 mm) wide. White with yellow centers and purple veins on their undersides.

**HARDINESS:** Zones 4–9. May self-seed.

**SOIL TYPE:** Sandy loam. Average–low moisture, good drainage, medium–low fertility, 5.5–6.5 pH.

**PLANTING GUIDE:** Spring. Plant in full sun, 12″–24″ (30–60 cm) apart. Best sown in garden soil.

**CARE TIPS:** Easy. Water when soil dries 4″–6″ (10–15 cm) deep. Fertilize only in spring. Prune in autumn. Propagate by seed.

**NOTES:** Thrives in banks, beds, borders. Nice in cottage, meadow, rock, Xeriscape gardens. Resists pests and diseases.

## *Mentha spp.* LAMIACEAE (LABIATAE)

### Mint

**SHAPE:** Various erect, mounded or trailing, stoloniferous, deciduous perennials to 36″ (90 cm) tall. Usually alternate, hirsute, textured, sometimes variegated, oval, fine-toothed, aromatic leaves, 1″–4″ (25–100 mm) long.

**FLOWER:** Summer bloom. Insignificant fragrant flowers. Purple-tinged white. Grow for foliage.

**HARDINESS:** Zones 5–9.

**SOIL TYPE:** Loam. High moisture, good drainage, high–medium fertility, 6.5–7.5 pH.

**PLANTING GUIDE:** Spring. Plant in full sun to full shade, 36″ (90 cm) apart.

**CARE TIPS:** Easy. Even moisture. Fertilize only in spring. Pinch tips for bushy plants. Propagate by cuttings, division, seed.

**NOTES:** Thrives in beds, borders, containers, ground covers. Nice in cottage, natural, shade, wildlife, woodland gardens. Pineapple-flavored cooking garnish, herb. Aggressive. Resists most pests. Susceptible to rust.

## *Mertensia pulmonarioides* (*M. virginica*) BORAGINACEAE

### Virginia Bluebells (Bluebells, Cowslip)

**SHAPE:** Various erect, tuberous or rhizomatous perennials, 12″–36″ (30–90 cm) tall and to 18″ (45 cm) wide. Alternate, smooth or textured, oval or lancelike, sharp-tipped leaves, 3″–7″ (75–180 mm) long.

**FLOWER:** Early-spring bloom. Nodding clusters of drooping, bell- or trumpet-shaped, deep-throated flowers to 1″ (25 mm) long. Pink turning blue. Semi-dormant after bloom.

**HARDINESS:** Zones 3–10.

**SOIL TYPE:** High humus. High moisture, good drainage, high fertility, 6.5–7.0 pH.

**PLANTING GUIDE:** Spring, when frost risk ends and soil becomes workable, or autumn. Plant in full sun to partial shade, 12″ (30 cm) apart.

**CARE TIPS:** Easy. Even moisture during growth; limit water thereafter. Propagate by division, seed.

**NOTES:** Thrives in accents, borders. Nice in cottage, natural, shade, wildlife, woodland gardens. Resists pests. Susceptible to fungal diseases.

## *Mimulus × hybridus* SCROPHULARIACEAE

### Monkey Flower

**SHAPE:** Numerous impermanent, erect, mounded perennials, 12″–18″ (30–45 cm) tall. Smooth, oval, toothed, paired leaves to 2″ (50 mm) long.

**FLOWER:** Summer to autumn bloom. Irregular, 5-petaled flowers, 2″–2½″ (50–63 mm) wide, with reflexed upper petals, 3 lower petals, and tonguelike centers. Choose from brown, cream, orange, red, yellow, and multicolored.

**HARDINESS:** Zones 9–11. Protect from frost.

**SOIL TYPE:** High humus; pond shorelines. High moisture, good drainage, high fertility, 6.5–7.5 pH.

**PLANTING GUIDE:** Spring, zones 3–7; late winter, zones 8–11. Plant in partial to full shade, 6″ (15 cm) apart. Start indoors for early bloom.

**CARE TIPS:** Average. Even moisture. Fertilize every 4 weeks. Propagate by seed.

**NOTES:** Thrives in beds, borders, containers. Nice in rock, shade gardens and ponds. Resists pests and diseases.

## *Monarda didyma* LAMIACEAE (LABIATAE)

### Bee Balm (Oswego Tea)

**SHAPE:** Various erect, bushlike and upright or mounded, perennials to 4′ (1.2 m) tall. Textured, oval to lancelike, toothed, aromatic leaves, 3″–6″ (75–150 mm) long.

**FLOWER:** Summer bloom. Erect, woody stems of irregular, single or double, whorled, tubular, lipped flowers to 2″ (50 mm) long with papery bracts. Choose from pink, red, and white.

**HARDINESS:** Zones 4–9. Protect from hot sun. Prefers cold-winter climates.

**SOIL TYPE:** High humus. High moisture, good drainage, medium fertility, 6.5–7.0 pH.

**PLANTING GUIDE:** Spring, as soil warms. Plant in full sun to partial shade, 24″ (60 cm) apart.

**CARE TIPS:** Easy. Even moisture during growth. Fertilize sparingly. Propagate by division, seed.

**NOTES:** Thrives in backgrounds, borders, massed plantings. Nice in meadow, natural, wildlife, woodland gardens. Resists pests. Susceptible to powdery mildew, rust.

## *Morina longifolia* MORINACEAE

### Whorlflower

**SHAPE:** Various erect, thistlelike perennials, 4′ (1.2 m) tall. Textured, slender, lancelike, ribbed, toothed, armored leaves to 12″ (30 cm) long, in a basal rosette.

**FLOWER:** Summer bloom. Spiking vertical tiers of whorled clusters with nodding, tubular, fluted flowers to 1½″ (38 mm) long. White turning first pink, then crimson red.

**HARDINESS:** Zones 5–10. May self-seed.

**SOIL TYPE:** Loam. Average moisture, average drainage, medium fertility, 6.5–7.5 pH.

**PLANTING GUIDE:** Spring, as soil becomes workable. Plant in full to filtered shade, 16″ (40 cm) apart.

**CARE TIPS:** Easy. Even moisture; water only when soil dries. Fertilize every 10–12 weeks. Propagate by division, seed.

**NOTES:** Thrives in accents, backgrounds, borders, containers, edgings, fence lines. Nice in natural, rock, wildlife, woodland gardens. Resists pests and diseases.

## *Myosotis scorpioides* BORAGINACEAE

### Perennial Forget-Me-Not (Water Forget-Me-Not)

**SHAPE:** Numerous short, mounded, stoloniferous, rhizomatous, deciduous perennials, 12″–36″ (30–90 cm) tall and 32″–48″ (75–120 cm) wide. Shiny, oval to lancelike, ribbed leaves to 2″ (50 mm) long. See also *M. sylvatica*, garden forget-me-not.

**FLOWER:** Early-summer bloom. Clusters of open flowers, ¼″–½″ (6–12 mm) wide. Blue with central eyes of pink, white, yellow.

**HARDINESS:** Zones 5–10. May self-seed.

**SOIL TYPE:** Dense clay; pond shorelines or margins. High moisture, average drainage, medium fertility, 6.0–8.0 pH. Tolerates salt.

**PLANTING GUIDE:** Late spring. Plant in full sun to full shade, 12″–24″ (30–60 cm) apart.

**CARE TIPS:** Easy. Even moisture. Fertilize every 4 weeks. Propagate by cuttings, division, seed.

**NOTES:** Thrives in accents, borders, edgings. Nice in natural, shade, woodland gardens and ponds. Aggressive. Resists pests and diseases.

## *Myosotis sylvatica* (*M. alpestris*) BORAGINACEAE

### Garden Forget-Me-Not (Woodland Forget-Me-Not)

**SHAPE:** Numerous erect, branched annuals or biennials, 6″–24″ (15–60 cm) tall. Hairy or sticky, oval leaves, 2″–4″ (50–100 mm) long.

**FLOWER:** Spring to autumn bloom. Open, circular clusters of many tiny, flowers, ⅛″–¼″ (3–6 mm) wide. Choose from pink, purple, and white.

**HARDINESS:** Zones 5–8. May self-seed.

**SOIL TYPE:** High humus; pond shorelines. High moisture, good drainage, high–medium fertility, 6.5–7.5 pH.

**PLANTING GUIDE:** Early spring. Plant in filtered sun to partial shade, 6″–8″ (15–20 cm) apart. Sow seed for flowers the following season or plant second-year nursery stock.

**CARE TIPS:** Easy. Even moisture. Fertilize every 4 weeks. Propagate by division, seed.

**NOTES:** Thrives in beds, borders, containers, edgings. Nice in cottage, formal, rock, shade, woodland gardens and ponds. Aggressive. Resists diseases. Susceptible to slugs, snails.

## *Nicotiana* spp. and hybrids SOLANACEAE

### Flowering Tobacco (Nicotiana)

**SHAPE:** Numerous erect, branched, open perennials, 36″–48″ (90–120 cm) tall. Alternate, broadly lancelike, sticky leaves, 4″–6″ (10–15 cm) long, forming a basal rosette.

**FLOWER:** Early-summer to early-autumn bloom. Clusters of open or tubular, 5-petaled, fragrant flowers to 3″ (75 mm) wide, flaring into trumpets. Choose from green, pink, red, and white.

**HARDINESS:** Zones 9–10. Protect from frost. May self-seed.

**SOIL TYPE:** High humus. High moisture, good drainage, medium fertility, 6.5–7.5 pH.

**PLANTING GUIDE:** Spring, when frost risk ends. Plant in full sun to partial shade, 12″–24″ (30–60 cm) apart. Start indoors for early bloom.

**CARE TIPS:** Easy. Even moisture. Fertilize every 4 weeks. Support with stakes. Propagate by seed.

**NOTES:** Thrives in beds, borders, containers. Nice in cottage, heritage, shade, woodland gardens. Resists pests and diseases.

## *Nierembergia caerulea* (N. hippomanica) SOLANACEAE

### Cupflower

**SHAPE:** Various mounded, sprawling perennials to 12″ (30 cm) tall and wide. Alternate, spoon- or plumelike leaves to ¾″ (19 mm) long.

**FLOWER:** Summer to early-autumn bloom. Cup-shaped, 5-petaled flowers, 1″–2″ (25–50 mm) wide. Choose from purple, violet, and white with yellow throats.

**HARDINESS:** Zones 7–10.

**SOIL TYPE:** High humus. High moisture, good drainage, high fertility, 6.5–7.5 pH.

**PLANTING GUIDE:** Late winter to early spring, as soil becomes workable. Plant in filtered sun to partial shade, 6″ (15 cm) apart.

**CARE TIPS:** Easy. Even moisture. Fertilize every 4 weeks. Prune or shear after flowering. Propagate by cuttings, division, seed.

**NOTES:** Thrives in accents, borders, containers, edgings, ground covers. Nice in cottage, meadow, natural, rock, shade, woodland gardens. Resists pests and diseases.

## *Oenothera spp.* ONAGRACEAE

### Evening Primrose (Sundrops)

**SHAPE:** About 80 erect, sprawling, often rhizomatous, deciduous annuals, biennials, or usually perennials, 6″–24″ (15–60 cm) tall. Hairy or woolly, lancelike, lobate or toothed, scallop-edged leaves, 3″–4″ (75–100 mm) long.

**FLOWER:** Late-spring to summer bloom. Showy, broad, saucer-shaped, 4-petaled, fragrant flowers to 5″ (13 cm) wide. Choose from pink, white, and yellow.

**HARDINESS:** Zones 4–11.

**SOIL TYPE:** Sandy loam. Average–low moisture, good drainage, medium–low fertility, 6.5–7.5 pH.

**PLANTING GUIDE:** Late spring to early summer. Plant in full sun, 18″–24″ (45–60 cm) apart.

**CARE TIPS:** Very easy. Water when soil dries 4″–6″ (10–15 cm) deep. Fertilize only in spring. Propagate by division, seed.

**NOTES:** Thrives in backgrounds, fence lines, paths. Nice in cottage, fragrance gardens. Cutting flower. Resists pests. Susceptible to fungal diseases.

## *Omphalodes spp.* BORAGINACEAE

### Navelwort (Blue-Eyed Mary, Creeping Forget-Me-Not, Navelseed)

**SHAPE:** About 24 short, mounded, sprawling or trailing, semi-evergreen annual or perennials, 6″–18″ (15–45 cm) tall and 24″–36″ (60–90 cm) wide. Alternate, smooth or finely hirsute, oval leaves, 3″–4″ (75–100 mm) long.

**FLOWER:** Spring bloom. Branched sprays of open, 5-petaled flowers to ½″ (12 mm) wide. Choose from blue and white.

**HARDINESS:** Zones 5–10.

**SOIL TYPE:** Loam. High moisture, good drainage, medium fertility, 6.5–7.5 pH.

**PLANTING GUIDE:** Early spring. Plant in partial to full shade, 12″ (30 cm) apart.

**CARE TIPS:** Very easy. Even moisture; water when soil dries 2″–3″ (50–75 mm) deep. Fertilize every 4 weeks. Propagate by division, seed.

**NOTES:** Thrives in accents, ground covers, massed plantings. Nice in cottage, meadow, natural, shade, woodland gardens. Resists deer, pests, and diseases.

## *Origanum laevigatum* LAMIACEAE (LABIATAE)

### Ornamental Marjoram

**SHAPE:** Few erect, arching, or sprawling, rhizomatous, deciduous perennials, 24″ (60 cm) tall. Opposite, textured, broadly oval, sharp-pointed, toothed, fragrant leaves, 1″–1½″ (25–38 mm) long, in a basal clump.

**FLOWER:** Late-spring to autumn bloom. Spiking clusters of irregular, tubular flowers to ½″ (12 mm) wide. Choose from pink and purple with thready, purple bracts.

**HARDINESS:** Zones 7–11. May self-seed.

**SOIL TYPE:** Sandy loam. Average–low moisture, good drainage, medium fertility, 6.5–8.0 pH.

**PLANTING GUIDE:** Spring. Plant in full to filtered sun, 24″ (60 cm) apart.

**CARE TIPS:** Easy. Water only when soil dries. Fertilize only in spring. Protect from hot sun. Shear in autumn. Propagate by division, seed.

**NOTES:** Thrives in accents, bed, borders, containers, edgings, paths. Nice in arid, rock, seaside, wildlife gardens. Resists pests and diseases.

## *Paeonia* hybrids PAEONIACEAE

### Peony

**SHAPE:** More than 30 circular, shrubby, often rhizomatous or tuberous, herbaceous becoming woody-stemmed perennials, 18″–60″ (45–150 cm) tall; trees to 6′ (1.8 m) tall. Hirsute, lobate leaves, 3″–6″ (75–150 mm) long.

**FLOWER:** Spring to summer bloom. Single or double, papery, aromatic flowers, 2″–10″ (50–250 mm) wide. Choose from pink, purple, white, yellow.

**HARDINESS:** Zones 5–10. Protect from hot sun.

**SOIL TYPE:** Loam. High moisture, good drainage, high fertility, 5.5–6.5 pH.

**PLANTING GUIDE:** Late summer to autumn. Plant in full sun to partial shade, 48″ (120 cm) apart.

**CARE TIPS:** Very easy. Even moisture, fertilize during growth. Mulch in winter, zones 5–8; in summer, zones 9–10. Propagate by division. Store in sawdust, 40°–50°F (4°–10°C).

**NOTES:** Thrives in backgrounds, paths. Nice in heritage gardens. Cutting flower. Susceptible to ants, slugs, snails, botrytis, phytophthora blight.

## *Osteospermum* spp. and hybrids ASTERACEAE (COMPOSITAE)

### African Daisy (Freeway Daisy)

**SHAPE:** More than 70 mounded or trailing, stoloniferous, semi-evergreen annuals or perennials, usually 6″–12″ (15–30 cm) tall. Alternate, smooth, lancelike, usually toothed leaves, 2″–4″ (50–100 mm) long.

**FLOWER:** Late-spring to early-autumn bloom. Showy, daisylike, open flowers to 3″ (75 mm) wide. Choose from blue, pink, purple, white, and yellow.

**HARDINESS:** Zones 7–10. Protect from hot sun.

**SOIL TYPE:** Sandy loam. High moisture, good drainage, medium–low fertility, 6.5–8.0 pH.

**PLANTING GUIDE:** Spring; winter in arid climates. Plant in full sun, 18″ (45 cm) apart.

**CARE TIPS:** Easy. Water only when soil dries. Fertilize only in spring. Extend bloom by deadheading. Shear in autumn. Propagate by division, seed.

**NOTES:** Thrives in containers, ground covers, paths. Nice in arid, rock, seaside gardens. Resists diseases. Susceptible to slugs, snails.

## *Papaver nudicaule* PAPAVERACEAE

### Iceland Poppy

**SHAPE:** Numerous mounded, deciduous perennials to 12″ (30 cm) tall. Hairy, plumelike, lobate and cut leaves, 3″–4″ (75–100 mm) long.

**FLOWER:** Early-spring to-early summer bloom. Wiry stems with single or double, papery, fragrant flowers, 2″–3″ (50–75 mm) wide. Choose from cream, orange, pink, white, and yellow with dark or light, blending or contrasting centers.

**HARDINESS:** Zones 3–9.

**SOIL TYPE:** Loam. High moisture, good drainage, medium fertility, 6.5–7.0 pH.

**PLANTING GUIDE:** Early spring, as soil becomes workable. Plant in full to filtered sun, 12″ (30 cm) apart.

**CARE TIPS:** Easy. Even moisture. Fertilize every 4 weeks. Extend bloom by deadheading. Protect from hot sun. Propagate by seed.

**NOTES:** Thrives in accents, beds, borders, paths. Nice in cottage, formal, natural gardens. Cutting flower. Resists pests and diseases.

## *Papaver orientale* PAPAVERACEAE

### Oriental Poppy

**SHAPE:** Numerous mounded, deciduous perennials, 24″–48″ (60–120 cm) tall and to 24″ (60 cm) wide. Hairy, plumelike, cut, toothed leaves, 10″–12″ (25–30 cm) long.

**FLOWER:** Summer to autumn bloom. Wiry stems of single or double, crepe-paper-like, cup-shaped, frilly flowers, 4″–6″ (10–15 cm) wide. Choose from cream, orange, pink, purple, red, and white.

**HARDINESS:** Zones 3–7. Prefers cold-winter climates.

**SOIL TYPE:** Loam. High moisture, good drainage, high–medium fertility, 6.5–7.5 pH.

**PLANTING GUIDE:** Autumn. Plant in full sun to partial shade, 15″–20″ (38–50 cm) apart.

**CARE TIPS:** Easy to average. Even moisture. Fertilize only in spring. Apply mulch. Protect from hot sun. Propagate by division, seed.

**NOTES:** Thrives in accents, beds, borders. Nice in cottage, natural gardens. Cutting flower. Susceptible to aphids, nematodes, blight, downy mildew.

## *Passiflora* spp. and hybrids PASSIFLORACEAE

### Passion Vine (Passionflower)

**SHAPE:** About 400 vigorous, woody, evergreen vines, 25′–30′ (7.5–9 m) long, with tendrils. Alternate, smooth, oval or lancelike, circular or lobed, veined leaves to 6″ (15 cm) long.

**FLOWER:** Summer to autumn bloom. Round, double, overlapping-petaled, fragrant flowers, 3″–5″ (75–125 mm) wide, Forms round fruit. Choose from blue, pink, purple, violet, and white.

**HARDINESS:** Zones 9–11. Protect from frost.

**SOIL TYPE:** Sandy loam. High–average moisture, good drainage, high fertility, 5.5–7.0 pH.

**PLANTING GUIDE:** Spring. Plant in full to filtered sun, 8′–10′ (2.4–3 m) apart.

**CARE TIPS:** Average. Even moisture. Fertilize every 4 weeks. Support with stakes. Prune in spring. Shelter from wind. Propagate by cuttings, seed.

**NOTES:** Thrives in arbors, fences, trellises, walls. Nice in arid, seaside, tropical, wildlife gardens. Cutting flower. Aggressive. Resists diseases. Susceptible to nematodes.

## *Patrinia* spp. VALERIANACEAE

### Patrinia (Golden-Lace)

**SHAPE:** About 15 erect, branched, rhizomatous or stoloniferous perennials, 24″–60″ (60–150 cm) tall. Opposite, smooth or textured, divided or whole, deeply lobate and cut, toothed leaves, 3″–6″ (75–150 mm) long.

**FLOWER:** Late-summer to autumn bloom. Profuse, branching clusters of many tiny, sometimes spurred flowers, ⅛″–¼″ (3–6 mm) wide. Choose from white and yellow.

**HARDINESS:** Zones 4–10. May self-seed.

**SOIL TYPE:** High humus. High moisture, good drainage, high fertility, 6.5–7.5 pH.

**PLANTING GUIDE:** Spring, as soil warms. Plant in full to filtered sun, 36″ (90 cm) apart.

**CARE TIPS:** Easy. Even moisture. Fertilize every 4 weeks. Extend bloom by deadheading. Support with stakes. Propagate by division, seed.

**NOTES:** Thrives in backgrounds, borders. Nice in meadow, rock, wildlife gardens. Resists pests and diseases.

## *Pelargonium* spp. *(P. × hortorum)* GERANIACEAE

### Florist's Geranium

**SHAPE:** Numerous mounded annuals or perennials and shrubs to 4′ (1.2 m) tall and 36″–48″ (90–120 cm) wide. Hirsute, textured, circular, lobate leaves to 5″ (13 cm) wide.

**FLOWER:** Spring to summer bloom. Star- or butterfly-shaped fragrant flowers to 4″ (10 cm) wide. Choose from orange, pink, purple, red, and white.

**HARDINESS:** Zones 8–10. Protect from frost.

**SOIL TYPE:** High humus. High moisture, good drainage, medium fertility, 7.0–7.5 pH.

**PLANTING GUIDE:** Spring, as soil warms. Plant in full sun, 18″ (46 cm) apart.

**CARE TIPS:** Easy. Water only when soil dries. Fertilize every 4 weeks. Extend bloom by deadheading. Lift and store, zones 3–7; shear in autumn, zones 8–10. Propagate by cuttings, division, seed.

**NOTES:** Thrives in beds, containers, massed plantings. Nice in cottage, formal, rock, wildlife gardens. Susceptible to aphids, spider mites, whiteflies, mildew.

## *Pelargonium peltatum* GERANIACEAE

### Trailing Geranium (Ivy Geranium, Storksbill Geranium)

**SHAPE:** Numerous upright or trailing, succulent, evergreen perennials to 36″ (90 cm) tall or long. Shiny, usually fringed, maplelike, lobate leaves to 3″ (75 mm) wide, on dangling stems.

**FLOWER:** Summer to autumn bloom. Star-shaped, single or double, fragrant flowers to 2″ (50 mm) wide. Choose from pink, red, and white.

**HARDINESS:** Zones 8–10. Protect from frost.

**SOIL TYPE:** High humus. High moisture, good drainage, medium fertility, 7.0–7.5 pH.

**PLANTING GUIDE:** Spring, zones 3–8; autumn, zones 9–10. Plant in full sun, 15″ (38 cm) apart.

**CARE TIPS:** Easy. Even moisture. Water only when soil dries; avoid wetting foliage. Fertilize every 4 weeks. Extend bloom by deadheading. Propagate by cuttings, seed.

**NOTES:** Thrives in accents, beds, borders, containers, walls, window boxes. Nice in cottage, formal, small-space gardens. Susceptible to aphids, spider mites, slugs, snails.

## *Penstemon* spp. SCROPHULARIACEAE

### Beard-Tongue

**SHAPE:** About 250 erect or round perennials or deciduous woody shrubs, 24″–36″ (60–90 cm) tall. Opposite, usually shiny, lancelike leaves, 2″–4″ (50–100 mm) long, in whorls.

**FLOWER:** Spring to summer bloom. Hirsute, tubular or trumpet-shaped flowers, 1″–1½″ (25–38 mm) long. Choose from blue, pink, purple, red, white, and bicolored with spotted throats.

**HARDINESS:** Zones 3–10.

**SOIL TYPE:** Sandy loam. Average moisture, good drainage, medium fertility, 5.5–6.5 pH.

**PLANTING GUIDE:** Spring, as soil warms. Plant in full sun to partial shade, 12″–18″ (30–45 cm) apart.

**CARE TIPS:** Easy. Water only when soil dries. Fertilize every 4 weeks. Extend bloom by deadheading. Protect from hot sun. Propagate by cuttings, division, seed.

**NOTES:** Thrives in beds, borders, edgings, paths. Nice in cottage, rock, wildlife, woodland gardens. Resists pests and diseases.

## *Perovskia* spp. and hybrids LAMIACEAE (LABIATAE)

### Russian Sage

**SHAPE:** Few erect, branched or sprawling, woody-stalked, stoloniferous, deciduous perennials, 36″–48″ (90–120 cm) tall. Opposite, soft, oval, cut, toothed leaves to 2″ (50 mm) long.

**FLOWER:** Late-spring to autumn bloom. Erect, conical, plumelike clusters, 1″–4″ (25–100 mm) long, of tiny, fragrant flowers, ½″ (12 mm) long. Choose from blue and lavender.

**HARDINESS:** Zones 3–7. Prefers cold-winter, hot-summer climates.

**SOIL TYPE:** Loam. High moisture, good drainage, medium fertility, 6.5–7.5 pH.

**PLANTING GUIDE:** Spring. Plant in full sun, 24″–36″ (60–90 cm) apart.

**CARE TIPS:** Easy. Even moisture. Tolerates drought. Fertilize only in spring. Extend bloom by deadheading. Propagate by cuttings, seed.

**NOTES:** Thrives in accents, borders, massed plantings. Nice in cottage, meadow, rock gardens. Aggressive. Resists pests and diseases.

## *Petunia* × *hybrida* SOLANACEAE

### Petunia (Common Garden Petunia)

**SHAPE:** Numerous hybrid bushlike, mounded, or sprawling annual or perennials to 12″ (30 cm) tall. Sticky, oval leaves to 2″ (50 mm) long.

**FLOWER:** Late-spring to early-autumn bloom. Open, flared, trumpetlike, 5-petaled flowers, 1″–5″ (25–125 mm) wide, often with ruffled edges. Choose from blue, pink, purple, red, white, bicolored, and striped.

**HARDINESS:** Zones 8–10. May self-seed.

**SOIL TYPE:** Loam. High–average moisture, good drainage, high–medium fertility, 6.5–7.5 pH.

**PLANTING GUIDE:** Spring, when frost risk ends. Plant in full sun to partial shade, 7″–10″ (18–25 cm) apart. Start indoors for early bloom, zones 3–8.

**CARE TIPS:** Easy. Even moisture. Fertilize every 10–12 weeks. Propagate by cuttings, seed.

**NOTES:** Thrives in beds, borders, containers, edgings, ground covers, massed plantings. Nice in cottage, formal gardens. Susceptible to tobacco budworms, botrytis, smog.

## *Phlox paniculata* POLEMONIACEAE

### Garden Phlox (Perennial Phlox)

**SHAPE:** Various erect, mounded or bunching perennials, 24″–72″ (60–180 cm) tall. Smooth, slender, oval to lancelike, sharp-tipped, veined leaves, 3″–6″ (75–150 mm) long.

**FLOWER:** Spring to summer bloom. Round or cone-shaped clusters, 10″–14″ (25–36 cm) wide, of 5-petaled, fragrant flowers to 1″ (25 mm) wide. Choose from blue, lavender, pink, red, and white.

**HARDINESS:** Zones 3–10.

**SOIL TYPE:** Loam; pond shorelines. High moisture, good drainage, high fertility, 6.5–7.5 pH.

**PLANTING GUIDE:** Spring. Plant in full sun to partial shade, 18″ (45 cm) apart.

**CARE TIPS:** Average. Even moisture. Fertilize every 4 weeks. Pinch tips for bushy plants. Support with stakes. Propagate by cuttings, division, seed.

**NOTES:** Thrives in accents, borders, containers. Nice in cottage, formal, natural, shade gardens and pond edges. Susceptible to spider mites, powdery mildew, rust.

## *Phlox stolonifera* POLEMONIACEAE

### Creeping Phlox

**SHAPE:** Few languid, hirsute, low, spreading or mounded, stoloniferous, evergreen perennials, 3″–12″ (75–300 mm) tall and to 24″ (60 cm) wide. Opposite, hirsute, oval to lancelike, sharp-tipped leaves to 4″ (10 cm) long.

**FLOWER:** Spring bloom. Branched stems of fragrant, 5-petaled, open, blunt flowers to 1″ (25 mm) wide. Choose from blue, lavender, pink, purple, violet, and white.

**HARDINESS:** Zones 4–9.

**SOIL TYPE:** High humus. High moisture, good drainage, high fertility, 5.5–7.5 pH.

**PLANTING GUIDE:** Spring. Plant in filtered sun to full shade, 12″–24″ (30–60 cm) apart.

**CARE TIPS:** Easy. Even moisture. Fertilize every 4 weeks. Shear in spring. Propagate by division.

**NOTES:** Thrives in accents, edgings, massed plantings beneath trees, walls. Nice in rock, shade, woodland gardens. Susceptible to spider mites, powdery mildew.

## *Physalis alkekengi* SOLANACEAE

### Chinese-Lantern Plant (Japanese-Lantern, Strawberry Tomato, Winter Cherry)

**SHAPE:** Numerous short-lived, erect, open, rhizomatous perennials to 24″ (60 cm) tall and wide, with shiny, oval, 3-lobed, sharp-tipped leaves, 2″–4″ (50–100 mm) long. See also *Abutilon × hybridum*, Chinese-lantern.

**FLOWER:** Summer bloom. Tiny, star-shaped flowers form showy, nodding, pink, red, lantern-shaped, papery husks to 2″ (50 mm) long. White.

**HARDINESS:** Zones 2–10. May self-seed. Prefers cold-winter climates.

**SOIL TYPE:** Loam. High–average moisture, good drainage, medium fertility, 6.5–7.5 pH.

**PLANTING GUIDE:** Spring. Plant in full sun to partial shade, 12″–24″ (30–60 cm) apart.

**CARE TIPS:** Easy. Even moisture. Fertilize every 12 weeks. Propagate by cuttings, division, seed.

**NOTES:** Thrives in accents, containers, edgings, paths. Nice in cottage, formal, shade, woodland gardens. Cut and dry husks. Aggressive. Resists pests and diseases.

## *Physostegia virginiana* LAMIACEAE (LABIATAE)

### Obedience Plant (Obedient Plant, False Dragonhead)

**SHAPE:** Various erect, slender, rhizomatous, deciduous perennials to 4′ (1.2 m) tall. Lancelike, toothed leaves to 5″ (13 cm) long.

**FLOWER:** Early-spring to early-summer bloom; varies by region. Spikes with tiers of irregular, open, trumpet-shaped flowers to 1″ (25 mm) long. Choose from pink, rose, and white.

**HARDINESS:** Zones 2–9.

**SOIL TYPE:** Loam. High moisture, good drainage, high fertility, 6.0–6.5 pH.

**PLANTING GUIDE:** Spring, zones 2–7; autumn, zones 8–9. Plant in full sun to partial shade, 12″–24″ (30–60 cm) apart.

**CARE TIPS:** Very easy. Even moisture. Fertilize every 4 weeks. Pinch tips for bushy plants. Support with stakes. Propagate by division, seed.

**NOTES:** Thrives in backgrounds, beds, borders, containers, fence lines. Nice in cottage, formal, natural, shade, woodland gardens. Cutting flower. Aggressive. Resists pests and diseases.

## *Platycodon grandiflorus* CAMPANULACEAE (LOBELIACEAE)

### Balloon Flower

**SHAPE:** Few durable, erect, bunching perennials, 9″–30″ (23–75 cm) tall. Smooth, oval, toothed leaves, 1″–3″ (25–75 mm) long.

**FLOWER:** Summer to early-autumn bloom. Slim branching stalks with clusters of showy, single, bellflower-like, cup-shaped or sharp-tipped and star-shaped, open flowers to 3″ (75 mm) wide. Choose from deep to pale blue, pink, and white.

**HARDINESS:** Zones 3–9.

**SOIL TYPE:** Sandy loam. High moisture, good drainage, high fertility, 7.0–7.5 pH.

**PLANTING GUIDE:** Spring. Plant in full sun to partial shade, 12″–18″ (30–45 cm) apart.

**CARE TIPS:** Easy. Even moisture. Fertilize every 4 weeks. Extend bloom by deadheading. Propagate by division, seed.

**NOTES:** Thrives in beds, borders, fence lines. Nice in cottage, natural, shade, woodland gardens. Susceptible to gophers, nematodes, southern blight.

## *Polemonium caeruleum* (*P. reptans*) POLEMONIACEAE

### Jacob's-Ladder (Greek Valerian, Charity)

**SHAPE:** Various erect, sprawling or arching perennials, 12″–36″ (30–90 cm) tall and 12″–18″ (30–45 cm) wide. Divided, broadly oval, sharp-pointed leaves to 18″ (45 cm) long with alternate, narrow leaflets to 1″ (25 mm) long that resemble a flat ladder.

**FLOWER:** Spring to summer bloom. Panicles of cup-shaped, nodding flowers to 1″ (25 mm) wide. Choose from blue, lavender and white.

**HARDINESS:** Zones 3–10.

**SOIL TYPE:** Sandy loam. High moisture, good drainage, high fertility, 6.5–7.5 pH.

**PLANTING GUIDE:** Spring. Plant in full to filtered sun, 30″ (75 cm) apart.

**CARE TIPS:** Easy. Even moisture. Fertilize every 4 weeks. Protect from hot sun. Propagate by division, seed.

**NOTES:** Thrives in accents, beds, borders, mixed plantings. Nice in cottage, small-space gardens. Resists diseases. Susceptible to aphids.

## *Polianthes tuberosa* AGAVACEAE

### Tuberose

**SHAPE:** Few rhizomatous, herbaceous perennials to 42″ (1.1 m) tall. Narrow, grasslike leaves to 18″ (45 cm) long.

**FLOWER:** Summer to autumn bloom. Vertical tiers of single or double, tube-shaped, very fragrant flowers to 2½″ (63 mm) wide. White.

**HARDINESS:** Zones 9–11.

**SOIL TYPE:** High humus. High moisture, good drainage, high fertility, 6.0–6.5 pH.

**PLANTING GUIDE:** Spring. Plant in full sun, 6″–8″ (15–20 cm) apart, 2″–3″ (50–75 mm) deep.

**CARE TIPS:** Average to difficult. Even moisture during growth. Fertilize every 4 weeks with acidic fertilizer. Lift and store. Propagate by division, offsets, seed.

**NOTES:** Thrives in accents, beds, borders, mixed plantings. Nice in cottage, meadow, small-space gardens. Cutting flower. Naturalizes freely. Fragrance used in perfumes. Resists deer and rodents. Susceptible to aphids.

## *Polygonatum* spp. LILIACEAE

### Solomon's-Seal

**SHAPE:** Elegant, arched to erect, rhizomatous perennials, 24″–48″ (60–120 cm) tall, 18″–36″ (45–90 cm) wide. Alternate, oval, veined, leaves to 7″ (18 cm) long. See also *Smilacina racemosa*, false Solomon's-seal.

**FLOWER:** Spring bloom. Arching lone or clustered, nodding, bell-shaped flowers, ½″ (12 mm) long. Forms round fruit. Green and white.

**HARDINESS:** Zones 3–9.

**SOIL TYPE:** Loam. High moisture, good drainage, high fertility, 5.0–6.0 pH.

**PLANTING GUIDE:** Autumn. Plant in partial to full shade, 18″–36″ (45–90 cm) apart, 2″–3″ (50–75 mm) deep.

**CARE TIPS:** Easy to average. Even moisture during growth. Fertilize every 4 weeks. Apply mulch in summer. Lift and store. Propagate by division.

**NOTES:** Thrives in beds, borders, containers. Nice in natural, shade gardens. Use foliage in arrangements. Resists pests and diseases.

## *Potentilla neumanniana* (*P. tabernaemontani*) ROSACEAE

### Spring Cinquefoil

**SHAPE:** Few vigorous, low, flat, perennials, 3″–6″ (75–150 mm) tall and to 40″ (1 m) wide, with rooting stems. Alternate, smooth, frondlike, divided leaves with 5 oval, deep-toothed leaflets to ¾″ (19 mm) long.

**FLOWER:** Spring to summer bloom. Few saucer-shaped, 5-petaled, open flowers to ⅝″ (16 mm) wide. Choose from gold and yellow.

**HARDINESS:** Zones 5–9.

**SOIL TYPE:** Sandy loam. High–average moisture, good drainage, medium fertility, 6.5–7.0 pH.

**PLANTING GUIDE:** Spring, when frost risk ends. Plant in full sun to partial shade, 10″ (25 cm) apart.

**CARE TIPS:** Easy. Water only when soil dries. Fertilize every 10–12 weeks. Shear in spring. Propagate by division, seed.

**NOTES:** Thrives in borders, edgings, hedges, paths, massed plantings. Nice in natural, rock, shade, wildlife, woodland gardens. Aggressive. Resists pests and diseases.

## Pratia pedunculata *(Laurentia fluviatilis)* CAMPANULACEAE (LOBELIACEAE)

### Blue-Star Creeper (Isotoma)

**SHAPE:** Few short, mounded, sprawling, or dangling perennials, 3″–4″ (75–100 mm) tall and to 24″ (60 cm) wide with branched, rooting stems. Alternate, smooth, circular or lancelike leaves to ½″ (12 mm) long.

**FLOWER:** Early-summer bloom. Ball-shaped clusters of many tiny, star-shaped, 5-petaled flowers to ⅝″ (16 mm) wide. Choose from blue and white.

**HARDINESS:** Zones 7–10. Protect from frost.

**SOIL TYPE:** Loam. High moisture, good drainage, high–medium fertility, 7.0–7.5 pH.

**PLANTING GUIDE:** Spring, when frost risk ends. Plant in full sun to partial shade, 8″–12″ (20–30 cm) apart.

**CARE TIPS:** Easy. Even moisture; tolerates drought when established. Shear after flowering.

**NOTES:** Thrives in accents, hanging baskets, borders, containers, edgings, ground covers, paths. Nice in natural, rock gardens. Aggressive. Resists pests and diseases.

## Primula japonica PRIMULACEAE

### Japanese Primrose

**SHAPE:** Numerous erect, mounded perennials, 6″–30″ (15–75 cm) tall and 6″–12″ (15–30 cm) wide. Smooth or textured, circular or oval leaves, 7″–9″ (18–23 cm) wide.

**FLOWER:** Spring to early-summer bloom. Whorled clusters of single, open flowers to 1″ (25 mm) wide. Choose from pink, red, and white with gold centers.

**HARDINESS:** Zones 3–8. May self-seed.

**SOIL TYPE:** Sandy loam; pond shorelines. High moisture, good drainage, medium–low fertility, 6.0–6.5 pH.

**PLANTING GUIDE:** Spring. Plant in full sun to partial shade, 6″–12″ (15–30 cm) apart.

**CARE TIPS:** Easy. Even moisture. Fertilize every 4 weeks. Extend bloom by deadheading. Protect from hot sun. Propagate by division, seed.

**NOTES:** Thrives in borders, edgings. Nice in natural, shade, woodland gardens and ponds. Resists diseases. Susceptible to slugs, snails.

## Primula malacoides PRIMULACEAE

### Primrose (Baby Primrose, Fairy Primrose)

**SHAPE:** Numerous short-lived, mounded perennials, 4″–18″ (10–45 cm) tall and wide. Shiny, textured, oval, fine-toothed leaves to 10″ (25 cm) long on succulent stalks.

**FLOWER:** Spring bloom. Showy, open, saucer-shaped, 4-petaled flowers to ½″ (12 mm) wide. Choose from pink, light purple, and rose.

**HARDINESS:** Zones 7–10. Prefers mild climates. Protect from hot sun.

**SOIL TYPE:** High humus. High moisture, good drainage, high fertility, 6.5–7.0 pH.

**PLANTING GUIDE:** Spring, as soil warms. Plant in full sun to partial shade, 4″–6″ (10–15 cm) apart.

**CARE TIPS:** Easy. Even moisture. Fertilize every 4 weeks. Extend bloom by deadheading. Protect from hot sun. Propagate by seed.

**NOTES:** Thrives in beds, borders, containers, edgings. Nice in cottage, formal, shade, small-space, wildlife gardens. Resists diseases. Susceptible to slugs, snails.

## Primula × polyantha *(P. vulgaris)* **and hybrids** PRIMULACEAE

### English Primrose (Polyanth)

**SHAPE:** Numerous short, mounded, semi-evergreen perennials, 6″–9″ (15–23 cm) tall and to 12″ (30 cm) wide. Textured, oval, toothed leaves to 10″ (25 cm) long.

**FLOWER:** Spring to early-summer bloom. Open, deep-throated flowers to 2″ (50 mm) wide. Choose from blue, purple, red, white, and yellow.

**HARDINESS:** Zones 5–8.

**SOIL TYPE:** High humus. High moisture, good drainage, high fertility, 6.0–7.5 pH.

**PLANTING GUIDE:** Spring, zones 5–6; autumn, zones 7–8. Plant in full sun to partial shade, 6″–15″ (15–38 cm) apart.

**CARE TIPS:** Easy. Even moisture. Fertilize every 4 weeks. Apply mulch in winter. Extend bloom by deadheading. Propagate by division, seed.

**NOTES:** Thrives in accents, containers, massed plantings. Nice in formal, rock gardens. Susceptible to nematodes, slugs, snails, bacterial leaf spot, fungus leaf spot, root rot.

## *Prunella* spp. LAMIACEAE (LABIATAE)

### Self-Heal (Heal-All)

**SHAPE:** Few creeping, rhizomatous, deciduous perennials, 18″–24″ (45–60 cm) tall and wide. Opposite, textured, oval, sharp-tipped leaves, 1½″–2″ (38–50 mm) long, on square, self-rooting stems.

**FLOWER:** Summer bloom. Spiking clusters of hooded, lipped flowers, 1″–1½″ (25–38 mm) long. Choose from pink, purple, and white.

**HARDINESS:** Zones 3–10. May self-seed.

**SOIL TYPE:** Sandy loam. Average moisture, good drainage, medium fertility, 6.0–7.5 pH.

**PLANTING GUIDE:** Spring. Plant in full to filtered sun, 12″–18″ (30–45 cm) apart.

**CARE TIPS:** Easy. Light moisture. Fertilize only in spring. Extend bloom by deadheading. Shear in autumn. Propagate by division, seed.

**NOTES:** Thrives in banks, containers, foregrounds, ground covers. Nice in cottage, heritage, rock, shade, woodland gardens. Very aggressive; plant in buried containers. Resists pests and diseases.

## *Pulmonaria* spp. BORAGINACEAE

### Lungwort (Bethlehem Sage)

**SHAPE:** Few short, mounded, sprawling, hirsute, rhizomatous, deciduous perennials, 6″–18″ (15–45 cm) tall and wide. Smooth, variegated, broad, oval, sharp-tipped leaves, 3″–6″ (75–150 mm) long, usually marked with white.

**FLOWER:** Spring bloom. Showy, bell-shaped, deep-throated flowers, ¾″–1″ (19–25 mm) wide. Choose from blue, purple, red violet, and white.

**HARDINESS:** Zones 4–9.

**SOIL TYPE:** High humus. High moisture, good drainage, high fertility, 6.0–7.0 pH.

**PLANTING GUIDE:** Spring or autumn. Plant in filtered sun to full shade, 8″–12″ (20–30 cm) apart.

**CARE TIPS:** Easy. Even moisture. Fertilize every 4 weeks. Apply mulch in winter. Propagate by division.

**NOTES:** Thrives in beds, borders, containers, ground covers, massed plantings. Nice in cottage, shade, woodland gardens. Resists diseases. Susceptible to slugs, snails.

## *Pulsatilla vulgaris* *(P. patens, Anemone pulsatilla)* RANUNCULACEAE

### Pasque-Flower (Eastern Pasqueflower)

**SHAPE:** Various low, bunching, woody-rooted, perennials, 4″–6″ (10–15 cm) tall and 12″ (30 cm) wide. Feathery, divided and fine-cut, hirsute leaves to 12″ (30 cm) long in a basal rosette. May become dormant in summer.

**FLOWER:** Spring bloom. Stems of erect or drooping, cup-shaped flowers, 1″–3½″ (25–90 mm) wide. Choose from blue, mauve, pink, purple, red, and white. Forms woolly seedpods in summer.

**HARDINESS:** Zones 4–10. May self-seed.

**SOIL TYPE:** Sandy loam. High moisture, good drainage, medium fertility, 6.5–7.5 pH.

**PLANTING GUIDE:** Autumn. Plant in full to filtered sun, 12″ (30 cm) apart.

**CARE TIPS:** Easy. Even moisture. Fertilize in spring. Mulch in autumn. Lift and store, zones 2–4. Propagate by division, seed.

**NOTES:** Thrives in banks, containers, foregrounds, ground covers. Nice in cottage, heritage, meadow, rock, seaside gardens. Resists pests and diseases.

## *Rehmannia* spp. *(R. angulata)* GESNERIACEAE (SCROPHULARIACEAE)

### Chinese Foxglove

**SHAPE:** Various erect, hirsute, fibrous-rooted perennials to 36″ (90 cm) tall. Textured, broad, oval, lobate, toothed leaves to 10″ (25 cm) long with prominent veins.

**FLOWER:** Spring to summer bloom. Erect hollyhock-like spikes of showy, funnel-shaped, tubular, deep-throated flowers to 3″ (75 mm) wide. Choose from purple, red, and rose.

**HARDINESS:** Zones 8–10. Protect from frost.

**SOIL TYPE:** High humus. High moisture, good drainage, high fertility, 6.0–7.0 pH.

**PLANTING GUIDE:** Spring. Plant in full sun to partial shade, 8″–12″ (20–30 cm) apart.

**CARE TIPS:** Easy. Even moisture. Fertilize every 4 weeks. Apply mulch in winter. Propagate by cuttings, division, seed.

**NOTES:** Thrives in accents, borders, fence lines, paths. Nice in cottage, shade, woodland gardens. Cutting flower. Resists diseases. Susceptible to aphids.

## *Rodgersia* spp. SAXIFRAGACEAE

### Rodgersia

**SHAPE:** Few mounded, arched, rhizomatous perennials, 36″–72″ (90–180 cm) tall. Shiny, coarse-textured leaves to 24″ (60 cm) wide divided into lobed, fine-toothed leaflets.

**FLOWER:** Late-spring to summer bloom. Multiple branching clusters to 12″ (30 cm) tall and wide of many tiny, plumelike flowers. Choose from pink, rose, and white.

**HARDINESS:** Zones 5–9. Best in cool climates.

**SOIL TYPE:** High humus; pond shorelines.

High moisture, good drainage, high fertility, 6.0–8.0 pH. Tolerates salt.

**PLANTING GUIDE:** Spring. Plant in full sun to full shade, 30″ (75 cm) apart.

**CARE TIPS:** Easy. Even moisture. Fertilize every 4 weeks. Apply mulch. Protect from hot sun, wind. Propagate by division, seed.

**NOTES:** Thrives in accents, massed plantings. Nice in cottage, rock, shade, woodland gardens and ponds. Resists pests and diseases.

## *Romneya coulteri* PAPAVERACEAE

### Matilija Poppy (Sunny-Side-Up)

**SHAPE:** Lone rhizomatous, woody, deciduous perennial to 8′ (2.4 m) tall. Smooth, oak-leaf-shaped, deep-toothed, hirsute leaves to 4″ (10 cm) long in triplets along stalk.

**FLOWER:** Late-spring to summer bloom. Very showy, terminal, erect, open, cup-shaped, ruffled, crepelike flowers to 8″ (20 cm) wide. White with large, bright yellow centers.

**HARDINESS:** Zones 7–10.

**SOIL TYPE:** Loam. High moisture, good drainage,

medium–low fertility, 6.0–7.5 pH.

**PLANTING GUIDE:** Autumn. Plant in full sun, 3″–5″ (90–150 cm) apart, 4″–6″ (10–15 cm) deep for root divisions, 1″–2″ (25–50 mm) deep for seed.

**CARE TIPS:** Average. Even moisture during growth; limit thereafter. Fertilize only in spring. Store in-ground. Propagate by division, seed, suckers.

**NOTES:** Thrives in accents, backgrounds. Nice in arid, natural, rock gardens. Resists pests. Susceptible to fungal diseases.

## *Rudbeckia* spp. ASTERACEAE (COMPOSITAE)

### Black-Eyed Susan (Coneflower, Gloriosa Daisy)

**SHAPE:** Numerous high, erect, branched, annuals, biennials, or perennials, 24″–60″ (60–180 cm) tall. Textured, hirsute, lancelike, sometimes lobed leaves to 4″ (10 cm) long.

**FLOWER:** Summer to autumn bloom. Showy, lone, daisylike flowers, 2″–4″ (50–100 mm) wide. Orange-yellow blend with contrasting centers.

**HARDINESS:** Zones 3–10.

**SOIL TYPE:** Loam. High moisture, good drainage, medium fertility, 6.0–7.5 pH.

**PLANTING GUIDE:** Spring. Plant in full sun to partial shade, 12″ (30 cm) apart. Sow seed for flowers the following season or transplant second-year nursery stock.

**CARE TIPS:** Easy. Even moisture. Extend bloom by deadheading. Propagate by cuttings, division, seed.

**NOTES:** Thrives in accents, backgrounds, borders, fence lines, massed plantings. Nice in cottage, meadow, wildlife gardens. Cutting flower. Resists pests and diseases.

## *Salpiglossis* spp. SOLANACEAE

### Painted-Tongue (Velvet Flower)

**SHAPE:** Various erect, open perennials to 30″ (75 cm) tall. Sticky, oval, sharp-tipped, toothed leaves to 4″ (10 cm) long.

**FLOWER:** Late-spring to early-autumn bloom. Flared, trumpet-shaped flowers to 2″ (50 mm) wide. Choose from blue, orange, pink, red, yellow, multicolored, variegated, and patterned.

**HARDINESS:** Zones 8–10. Protect from frost. May self-seed.

**SOIL TYPE:** High humus. High moisture, good

drainage, high fertility, 6.5–7.5 pH.

**PLANTING GUIDE:** Spring, as soil warms. Plant in full sun, 8″–12″ (20–30 cm) apart. Start indoors for early bloom.

**CARE TIPS:** Easy. Even moisture. Fertilize every 4 weeks. Pinch tips for bushy, branching plants. Support with stakes. Propagate by seed.

**NOTES:** Thrives in backgrounds, borders, containers. Nice in cottage, small-space gardens. Cutting flower. Resists pests and diseases.

## *Salvia* spp., hybrids, and cultivars LAMIACEAE (LABIATAE)

### Sage (Ramona)

**SHAPE:** Over 900 annuals, biennials, perennials, or shrubs, with widely varied habits and usually aromatic, edible foliage.

**FLOWER:** Spring to autumn bloom. Spikes of diverse, showy to inconspicuous, 2-lipped, hooded flowers. Choose from blue, orange, pink, purple, red, white, and yellow.

**HARDINESS:** Zones 4–10.

**SOIL TYPE:** Sandy loam. Average moisture, good drainage, medium–low fertility, 6.0–7.5 pH.

**PLANTING GUIDE:** Spring, as soil becomes workable. Plant in full sun, 10″–24″ (25–60 cm) apart.

**CARE TIPS:** Easy. Even moisture; tolerates drought when established. Fertilize only in spring. Apply mulch, zones 4–6. Pinch tips for bushy plants. Propagate by cuttings, division, seed.

**NOTES:** Thrives in borders, edgings, mixed plantings. Nice in cottage, formal, herb, small-space, wildlife gardens. Resists diseases. Susceptible to scale, whiteflies, leaf spot, rust.

## *Sanguisorba* spp. ROSACEAE

### Burnet

**SHAPE:** Few erect, bunching or branched, rhizomatous, semi-evergreen perennial shrubs, 36″–72″ (90–180 cm) tall and 18″–36″ (45–90 cm) wide. Plumelike, oval to circular, toothed, sometimes divided leaves, 5″–20″ (13–50 mm) long with many edible leaflets.

**FLOWER:** Summer to autumn bloom. Slender spathes of tiny, tubular flowers to 1½″–8″ (38–203 mm) long. Pink, purple, red, and white.

**HARDINESS:** Zones 4–10. May self-seed.

**SOIL TYPE:** Loam. High moisture, good drainage, medium fertility, 6.0–7.5 pH.

**PLANTING GUIDE:** Spring. Plant in full to filtered sun, 36″ (90 cm) apart.

**CARE TIPS:** Easy. Even moisture. Fertilize every 4 weeks. Limit seed development by deadheading. Shear in autumn. Propagate by division, seed.

**NOTES:** Thrives in backgrounds, beds, borders, edgings, fence lines. Nice in cottage, wildlife, woodland gardens. Resists pests and diseases.

## *Santolina chamaecyparissus* (S. incana) ASTERACEAE (COMPOSITAE)

### Lavender Cotton

**SHAPE:** Various wide, mounded, branched, evergreen perennial shrubs to 24″ (60 cm) tall and 36″ (90 cm) wide. Dusky, coarsely textured, plumelike, lobate, fine-cut, aromatic leaves to 1¼″ (32 mm) long.

**FLOWER:** Summer bloom. Round-headed, fragrant flowers to ¾″ (19 mm) wide. Yellow.

**HARDINESS:** Zones 7–10. Protect from frost.

**SOIL TYPE:** Sandy loam. Average moisture, good drainage, medium–low fertility, 6.5–7.5 pH.

**PLANTING GUIDE:** Spring. Plant in full sun, 36″ (90 cm) apart.

**CARE TIPS:** Easy. Even moisture; tolerates drought when established. Fertilize only in spring. Extend bloom by deadheading. Pinch tips or shear for bushy plants. Propagate by cuttings.

**NOTES:** Thrives in banks, borders, edgings, foregrounds, ground covers. Nice in arid, coastal, cottage, meadow, wildlife gardens. Fire retardant. Resists deer, pests, and diseases.

## *Saxifraga stolonifera* (S. sarmentosa) SAXIFRAGACEAE

### Strawberry Geranium (Beefsteak Geranium, Mother-of-Thousands)

**SHAPE:** Various sprawling, stoloniferous perennials to 24″ (60 cm) tall. Shiny, textured, variegated, circular, sharp-tipped, veined leaves to 4″ (10 cm) wide, with pink undersides, forming a basal rosette.

**FLOWER:** Summer to autumn bloom. Wiry stems with tall, branching clusters of irregular flowers to 1″ (25 mm) wide. White.

**HARDINESS:** Zones 5–10. Protect from frost.

**SOIL TYPE:** Loam. High moisture, good drainage, high–medium fertility, 7.0–7.5 pH.

**PLANTING GUIDE:** Spring. Plant in filtered sun to partial shade, 8″–10″ (20–25 cm) apart.

**CARE TIPS:** Average. Even moisture; water when soil dries 2″–3″ (50–75 mm) deep. Fertilize every 4 weeks. Propagate by division, runners, seed.

**NOTES:** Thrives in accents, hanging baskets, borders, containers, edgings, ground covers. Nice in cottage, formal, natural gardens. Aggressive. Resists diseases. Susceptible to mealybugs.

## *Scabiosa caucasica* DIPSACACEAE

### Pincushion Flower

**SHAPE:** Various mounded or sprawling, semi-evergreen perennials, 18″–30″ (45–75 cm) tall, 12″–18″ (30–45 cm) wide. Opposite, smooth, fine-cut or toothed, leaves to 5″ (13 cm) long.

**FLOWER:** Summer bloom. Flexible, slender stalks of showy, ball-shaped, often fringed flowers, 2″–3″ (50–75 mm) wide. Choose from blue, pink, purple, red, and white.

**HARDINESS:** Zones 4–9. Prefers mild-summer, humid climates.

**SOIL TYPE:** Sandy loam. High moisture, good drainage, high fertility, 7.0–8.0 pH.

**PLANTING GUIDE:** Spring. Plant in full sun to partial shade, 12″–15″ (30–38 cm) apart.

**CARE TIPS:** Average. Even moisture. Fertilize every 4 weeks. Apply mulch. Propagate by division.

**NOTES:** Thrives in accents, beds, borders, edgings, ground covers, massed plantings. Nice in cottage, formal, shade gardens. Cutting flower. Resists pests. Susceptible to mildew, root rot.

## *Scaevola* spp. and hybrids GOODENIACEAE

### Scaevola (Beach Naupaka)

**SHAPE:** Various vertical, short and sprawling or trailing, semi-evergreen or evergreen perennials and shrubs, 6″–60″ (15–150 cm) tall. Fleshy, circular, oval leaves, 1″–6″ (25–150 mm) long.

**FLOWER:** Summer bloom. Showy, open, flat-faced flowers, 1″–3″ (25–75 mm) wide. Choose from blue, pink, purple, and white.

**HARDINESS:** Zones 9–11.

**SOIL TYPE:** Sandy loam. Average–low moisture, good drainage, medium fertility, 6.5–8.0 pH.

**PLANTING GUIDE:** Spring. Plant in full sun, 18″–24″ (45–60 cm) apart for low species, 6′ (1.8 m) apart for shrub species.

**CARE TIPS:** Easy. Even moisture; water when soil dries 2″–3″ (50–75 mm) deep. Tolerates drought, wind. Fertilize only in spring. Propagate by cuttings, division, seed.

**NOTES:** Thrives in accents, ground covers, paths. Nice in arid, natural, seaside gardens. Susceptible to slugs, snails, fungal diseases.

## *Senecio* × *hybridus* ASTERACEAE (COMPOSITAE)

### Florist's Cineraria

**SHAPE:** Dense or branched, evergreen perennials, 12″–36″ (30–90 cm) tall and 32″ (75 cm) wide. Heart-shaped, cut, aromatic leaves, 3″–5″ (75–125 mm) long.

**FLOWER:** Spring to early-summer bloom. Open, scalloped flowers, 3″–5″ (75–125 mm) wide. Choose from blue, pink, purple, red, violet, white, and multicolored.

**HARDINESS:** Zones 8–10. May self-seed.

**SOIL TYPE:** High humus. High moisture, good drainage, high fertility, 6.5–7.5 pH.

**PLANTING GUIDE:** Spring, as soil warms. Plant in full to filtered sun, 8″–10″ (20–25 cm) apart.

**CARE TIPS:** Easy. Water only when soil dries. Fertilize every 4 weeks. Pinch tips for bushy plants. Propagate by cuttings, division, seed.

**NOTES:** Thrives in accents, beds, borders, containers. Nice in cottage, formal, small-space gardens. Resists diseases. Susceptible to aphids, mealy-bugs, leaf miners, spider mites, slugs, snails.

## *Sidalcea* spp. and hybrids MALVACEAE

### Mallow (Checkerbloom, Checkermallow, Prairie Mallow)

**SHAPE:** About 20 vertical or sprawling, holly-hock-like, fibrous-rooted or rhizomatous annuals or perennials, 24″–48″ (60–120 cm) tall. Textured, circular, lobate leaves, 3″–8″ (75–200 mm) long.

**FLOWER:** Early-summer bloom. Round, 5-petaled, scalloped flowers, ¾″–2″ (19–50 mm) wide. Choose from pale to deep pink and purple.

**HARDINESS:** Zones 4–10.

**SOIL TYPE:** Loam. High moisture, good drainage, high–medium fertility, 6.5–7.5 pH.

**PLANTING GUIDE:** Spring, zones 4–7; autumn, zones 8–10. Plant in full sun to partial shade, 18″–24″ (45–60 cm) apart.

**CARE TIPS:** Easy. Even moisture. Fertilize every 10–12 weeks. Support with stakes. Propagate by division, seed.

**NOTES:** Thrives in accents, borders, massed plantings. Nice in cottage, meadow, natural gardens. Resists diseases. Susceptible to aphids.

## *Silene californica* CARYOPHYLLACEAE

### California Indian Pink (Wild Campion)

**SHAPE:** Various erect, branched, deciduous perennials, 24″–48″ (60–120 cm) tall and 36″ (90 cm) wide. Opposite, textured, slender, oval, sharp-tipped, wavy-edged leaves, 3″–4″ (75–100 mm) long.

**FLOWER:** Late-spring bloom. Stiff stalks with sparse to full clusters of showy, irregular, double, hirsute, fringed flowers 1½″ (38 mm) wide. Scarlet red.

**HARDINESS:** Zones 6–10.

**SOIL TYPE:** Sandy loam. Average–low moisture, good drainage, medium fertility, 6.5–8.0 pH. Tolerates salt.

**PLANTING GUIDE:** Spring. Plant in full sun to partial shade, 6″–8″ (15–20 cm) apart.

**CARE TIPS:** Easy. Water only when soil dries. Fertilize in spring. Propagate by cuttings, division, seed.

**NOTES:** Thrives in accents, banks, beds, borders. Nice in cottage, natural, seaside, wildlife gardens. Resists pests and diseases.

## *Smilacina racemosa* LILIACEA

### False Solomon's-Seal (False Spikenard)

**SHAPE:** Elegant, arched to erect, rhizomatous perennials, 24″–48″ (60–120 cm) tall, 18″–36″ (45–90 cm) wide. Alternate, oval, veined, leaves to 8″ (20 cm) long. See also *Polygonatum* spp., Solomon's-seal.

**FLOWER:** Spring bloom. Arching stalks with clusters of tiny, plumelike flowers, 3½″ (90 mm) long. White. Forms round, red, berrylike fruit.

**HARDINESS:** Zones 3–9.

**SOIL TYPE:** High humus. High moisture, good drainage, high fertility, 5.0–6.5 pH.

**PLANTING GUIDE:** Spring or autumn. Plant in partial to full shade, 18″–24″ (45–60 cm) apart.

**CARE TIPS:** Easy. Even moisture. Fertilize every 4 weeks. Apply mulch in summer. Shear in autumn. Protect from hot sun. Propagate by division, seed.

**NOTES:** Thrives in banks, beds, borders, containers. Nice in natural, shade, wildlife, woodland gardens. Resists pests and diseases.

## *Solidago* spp. and hybrids ASTERACEAE (COMPOSITAE)

### Goldenrod

**SHAPE:** Numerous erect, rhizomatous perennials to 36″ (90 cm) tall and wide. Hairy or shiny, slender, lancelike, usually toothed leaves to 6″ (15 cm) long.

**FLOWER:** Summer to autumn bloom. Tall, plume-like clusters to 10″ (25 cm) long of showy, tiny, hirsute flowers. Choose from cream, white, and bright yellow.

**HARDINESS:** Zones 2–10.

**SOIL TYPE:** Sandy loam. Average moisture, good drainage, medium–low fertility, 6.5–7.5 pH.

**PLANTING GUIDE:** Spring, as soil warms. Plant in full to filtered sun, 18″–24″ (45–60 cm) apart.

**CARE TIPS:** Easy. Water only when soil dries. Fertilize only in spring. Support with stakes. Propagate by division, seed.

**NOTES:** Thrives in backgrounds, beds. Nice in cottage, meadow, natural, wildlife, woodland gardens. Aggressive. False reputation for causing allergic reactions. Resists pests and diseases.

## *Stachys byzantina* LAMIACEAE (LABIATAE)

### Lamb's-Ears (Woolly Betony)

**SHAPE:** Various short, mounded or sprawling, stoloniferous perennials, 12″–36″ (30–90 cm) tall. Woolly or velvety, silvery, lamb's-ear-shaped leaves, 4″–6″ (10–15 cm) long.

**FLOWER:** Spring to early-autumn bloom. Tubular, flared-lipped or cottony, hirsute flowers to 1″ (25 mm) wide. Choose from pink and purple.

**HARDINESS:** Zones 4–10. Prefers cool, low-humidity climates.

**SOIL TYPE:** Sandy loam. Average moisture, good drainage, medium–low fertility, 6.5–7.5 pH.

**PLANTING GUIDE:** Early spring. Plant in full sun to partial shade, 10″–18″ (25–45 cm) apart.

**CARE TIPS:** Average. Water only when soil dries. Fertilize only in spring. Extend bloom by dead-heading. Propagate by division, seed.

**NOTES:** Thrives in accents, containers, edgings, ground covers, paths. Nice in cottage, formal, seaside, wildlife, woodland gardens. Resists pests and diseases.

## *Stokesia laevis* ASTERACEAE (COMPOSITAE)

### Stokes' Aster

**SHAPE:** Various erect, branched perennials, 18″–24″ (45–60 cm) tall. Smooth, lancelike, fine-toothed leaves, 2″–8″ (50–200 mm) long, forming a basal rosette.

**FLOWER:** Early-summer to mid-autumn bloom. Fringed, hirsute-centered flowers, 2″–5″ (50–125 mm) wide. Choose from blue, lavender, pink, and white.

**HARDINESS:** Zones 4–10. Tolerates hot sun.

**SOIL TYPE:** Sandy loam. High–average moisture, good drainage, medium fertility, 5.5–7.5 pH.

**PLANTING GUIDE:** Early spring. Plant in full sun, 12″–15″ (30–38 cm) apart.

**CARE TIPS:** Easy. Water when soil dries 4″–6″ (10–15 cm) deep. Tolerates drought. Fertilize only in spring. Extend bloom by deadheading. Propagate by cuttings, division, seed.

**NOTES:** Thrives in accents, borders, containers, edgings. Nice in arid, cottage, formal, meadow gardens. Cutting flower. Resists pests and diseases.

## *Tellima grandiflora* SAXIFRAGACEAE

### Fringecups

**SHAPE:** One mounded, rhizomatous, semi-evergreen perennial, 14″–18″ (45–45 cm) tall. Textured, triangular to circular, lobate, veined, hirsute leaves to 4″ (10 cm) wide, forming a basal rosette.

**FLOWER:** Late-spring bloom. Stalks with vertical tiers of drooping, cup-shaped, fringed flowers to ¼″ (6 mm) wide. Choose from green and white, may turn dark red.

**HARDINESS:** Zones 4–8.

**SOIL TYPE:** High humus. High moisture, good drainage, high fertility, 6.0–7.0 pH.

**PLANTING GUIDE:** Early autumn. Plant in partial to full shade, 12″–18″ (30–45 cm) apart.

**CARE TIPS:** Easy. Even moisture during growth; limit thereafter. Fertilize every 4 weeks. Shear in autumn. Propagate by division.

**NOTES:** Thrives in borders, containers, edgings, ground covers. Nice in natural, rock, shade, woodland gardens. Resists pests and diseases.

## *Thalictrum* spp. RANUNCULACEAE

### Meadow Rue

**SHAPE:** About 100 erect, bushlike or sprawling, open perennials, ranging from 8″–96″ (20–244 cm) tall. Shiny, textured, deep-cut and lobate, veined leaves to 6″ (15 cm) long in plumelike leaflets to 2″ (50 mm) wide.

**FLOWER:** Spring bloom. Erect, branching stems with round, powderpuff-like clusters of hirsute flowers to 2″ (50 mm) wide. Choose from cream, pink, purple, violet, and yellow.

**HARDINESS:** Zones 4–9.

**SOIL TYPE:** High humus. High moisture, good drainage, high fertility, 6.0–7.0 pH.

**PLANTING GUIDE:** Spring. Plant in filtered sun to partial shade, 12″–16″ (30–40 cm) apart.

**CARE TIPS:** Easy. Even moisture. Fertilize every 4 weeks. Stake to support. Shelter from hot sun, wind. Propagate by division, seed.

**NOTES:** Thrives in beds, borders, containers, fence lines. Nice in meadow, natural, shade, woodland gardens. Resists pests and diseases.

## *Thunbergia alata* ACANTHACEAE

### Black-Eyed Susan Vine (Canary-Flower Vine, Clock Vine)

**SHAPE:** Numerous vigorous, short-lived, upright or trailing, twining, perennials to 10′ (3 m) long or wide. Opposite, textured, triangular, sharp-tipped, veined leaves to 3″ (75 mm) long. See also *T. gregorii*, orange clock vine.

**FLOWER:** Summer bloom. Tubular, flared flowers to 1½″ (38 mm) wide, with square-tipped, divided petals. Choose from gold, orange, white, and yellow.

**HARDINESS:** Zones 9–11. Protect from frost.

**SOIL TYPE:** Sandy loam. High moisture, good drainage, high fertility, 6.5–7.5 pH.

**PLANTING GUIDE:** Spring, as soil warms. Plant in full sun to partial shade, 12″ (30 cm) apart.

**CARE TIPS:** Easy. Even moisture. Fertilize every 4 weeks. Support with stakes. Shear in autumn. Propagate by cuttings, layering, seed.

**NOTES:** Thrives in containers, fence lines, trellises. Nice in cottage, formal, shade, wildlife, woodland gardens. Resists pests and diseases.

## *Thunbergia gregorii* (T. gibsonii) ACANTHACEAE

### Orange Clock Vine

**SHAPE:** Few vigorous, durable, twining, perennials to 6′ (1.8 m) long. Opposite, textured, triangular, toothed, veined leaves to 3″ (75 mm) long. See also *T. alata*, black-eyed Susan vine.

**FLOWER:** Summer bloom, zones 3–8; year-round, zones 9–11. Long, hirsute stems of single, tubular, flared, square-tipped flowers to 2″ (50 mm) wide. Orange.

**HARDINESS:** Zones 8–11. Protect from frost.

**SOIL TYPE:** Sandy loam. High moisture, good drainage, high fertility, 6.5–7.5 pH.

**PLANTING GUIDE:** Spring, as soil warms. Plant in full to filtered sun, 6′ (1.8 m) apart.

**CARE TIPS:** Easy. Even moisture. Fertilize every 4 weeks. Support on stakes. Pinch tips for bushy plants. Shear in autumn. Propagate by cuttings, layering, seed.

**NOTES:** Thrives in containers, fence lines, trellises, walls. Nice in cottage, informal, tropical, wildlife gardens. Resists pests and diseases.

## *Thymophylla tenuiloba* (Dyssodia tenuiloba) ASTERACEAE (COMPOSITAE)

### Dahlberg Daisy (Golden-Fleece)

**SHAPE:** Numerous short-lived, mounded or sprawling perennials to 12″ (30 cm) tall and 18″ (45 cm) wide. Alternate, plumelike, divided, aromatic leaves to 3″ (75 mm) long with lance-like leaflets.

**FLOWER:** Summer to autumn bloom. Showy, daisy-like flowers to 1″ (25 mm) wide. Bright yellow.

**HARDINESS:** Zones 9–11. Protect from frost.

**SOIL TYPE:** Sandy loam. Average moisture, good drainage, medium fertility, 6.5–7.5 pH.

**PLANTING GUIDE:** Spring, as soil warms, zones 2–7; autumn, zones 8–11. Plant in full sun, 9″–12″ (23–30 cm) apart. Start indoors for early bloom.

**CARE TIPS:** Easy. Water only when soil dries. Fertilize every 10–12 weeks. Extend bloom by deadheading. Propagate by seed.

**NOTES:** Thrives in accents, borders, containers, massed plantings. Nice in cottage, formal, small-space, wildlife gardens. Cutting flower. Resists pests and diseases.

## *Thymus serpyllum* (T. praecox subsp. *arcticus*) LAMIACEAE (LABIATAE)

### Creeping Thyme (Mother-of-Thyme)

**SHAPE:** Numerous vigorous, low, flat, evergreen perennials, 3″–6″ (75–150 mm) tall and 36″ (90 cm) wide, with rooting stems. Opposite, smooth, circular or oval, aromatic leaves to ½″ (12 mm) long.

**FLOWER:** Summer to early-autumn bloom. Many tiny, 2-lipped flowers, ⅛″–¼″ (4–6 mm) wide. Choose from pink and purple.

**HARDINESS:** Zones 3–10.

**SOIL TYPE:** Sandy loam. Average moisture, good drainage, medium–low fertility, 6.5–7.5 pH.

**PLANTING GUIDE:** Spring, as soil warms. Plant in full to filtered sun, 12″–24″ (30–60 cm) apart.

**CARE TIPS:** Easy. Water when soil dries 4″–6″ (10–15 cm) deep. Fertilize sparingly. Pinch tips for bushy plants. Shear in spring. Propagate by cuttings, division.

**NOTES:** Thrives in edgings, paths, massed plantings. Nice in arid, natural, seaside, wildlife gardens. Resists diseases. Susceptible to slugs, snails.

## *Tiarella cordifolia* SAXIFRAGACEAE

### Foamflower

**SHAPE:** Various short, mounded, rhizomatous, evergreen perennials, 6″–12″ (15–30 cm) tall. Downy, textured, triangular to heart-shaped, toothed, lobate, veined leaves to 4″ (10 cm) long forming a basal rosette. Turns colors in autumn.

**FLOWER:** Spring to early-summer bloom. Cone-shaped clusters to 5″ (13 cm) tall of tiny, tubular flowers. Choose from pink and white.

**HARDINESS:** Zones 3–9.

**SOIL TYPE:** High humus. High moisture, good drainage, high fertility, 6.5–7.5 pH.

**PLANTING GUIDE:** Early autumn. Plant in partial to full shade, 12″–18″ (30–45 cm) apart.

**CARE TIPS:** Easy. Even moisture during growth; limit thereafter. Fertilize every 4 weeks. Propagate by division, seed.

**NOTES:** Thrives in borders, containers, ground covers. Nice in natural, rock, woodland gardens. Resists pests and diseases.

### *Tradescantia virginiana* COMMELINACEAE

## Spiderwort (Common Spiderwort, Widow's-Tears)

**SHAPE:** Few erect, bunching perennials, 12″–36″ (30–90 cm) tall. Smooth, grasslike, curved and folded leaves to 12″ (30 cm) long.

**FLOWER:** Late-spring to early-summer bloom. Varies by region. Dense clusters of open, 3-petaled flowers to 1″ (25 mm) wide. Choose from blue, pink, purple, and white. Flowers last one day.

**HARDINESS:** Zones 5–11. May self-seed.

**SOIL TYPE:** High humus. High moisture, good drainage, high–medium fertility, 6.0–7.0 pH.

**PLANTING GUIDE:** Spring, when soil warms. Plant in full sun to partial shade, 12″–24″ (30–60 cm) apart.

**CARE TIPS:** Easy. Even moisture; water when soil dries 2″–3″ (50–75 mm) deep. Fertilize only in spring. Propagate by cuttings, division, seed.

**NOTES:** Thrives in accents, borders, containers, ground covers, walls. Nice in natural, rock, shade, woodland gardens. Aggressive. Resists pests and diseases.

### *Tricyrtis hirta* LILIACEAE

## Toad Lily

**SHAPE:** Few rhizomatous, deciduous perennials, 24″–36″ (60–90 cm) tall. Alternate, broad, oval, erect, curved, hirsute, usually variegated leaves, 6″–8″ (15–20 cm) long.

**FLOWER:** Summer to autumn bloom. Lone or clustered orchidlike flowers to 1″ (25 mm) wide. Choose from purple, white, and yellow with distinctive spots.

**HARDINESS:** Zones 8–9. Protect from frost and hot sun.

**SOIL TYPE:** High humus; pond shorelines. High moisture, good drainage, high fertility, 5.0–6.0 pH.

**PLANTING GUIDE:** Spring. Plant in partial shade, 18″–24″ (45–60 cm) apart, 4″ (10 cm) deep.

**CARE TIPS:** Average. Even moisture. Fertilize every 4 weeks. Lift and store. Propagate by division, seed.

**NOTES:** Thrives in accents, containers, entrances, paths, tree planters. Nice in shade, tropical, woodland gardens and ponds. Cutting flower. Resists diseases. Susceptible to slugs, snails.

### *Trillium grandiflorum* LILIACEAE

## Snow Trillium (White Trillium)

**SHAPE:** Few rhizomatous perennials, 12″–18″ (30–45 cm) tall and 8″ (20 cm) wide. Oval or heart-shaped, smooth, veined leaves to 6″ (15 cm) long as a 3-leaf whorl. See also *Trillium* spp., wake-robin.

**FLOWER:** Spring bloom. Single or double, 3-part flowers, 2″–3″ (50–75 mm) wide. White, turning rose or purple.

**HARDINESS:** Zones 4–9. Protect roots from freeze-thaw cycles.

**SOIL TYPE:** High humus. High moisture, good drainage, high fertility, 6.5–7.0 pH.

**PLANTING GUIDE:** Spring. Plant in partial shade, 5″ (13 cm) apart, 4″ (10 cm) deep.

**CARE TIPS:** Easy. Even moisture. Fertilize only in spring. Apply mulch in winter. Store in-ground. Propagate by division, seed.

**NOTES:** Thrives in beds, borders, ground covers. Nice in natural, rock, shade, woodland gardens. Resists pests and diseases.

### *Trillium spp.* LILIACEAE

## Wake-Robin (Trillium)

**SHAPE:** About 30 rhizomatous, deciduous perennials, 6″–20″ (15–50 cm) tall. Oval leaves to 6″ (15 cm) long as a 3-leaf whorl. See also *T. grandiflorum*, snow trillium.

**FLOWER:** Spring bloom. Lone flowers, 2″–3″ (50–75 mm) wide, usually with three sharp-tipped petals. Choose from purple, white, and yellow.

**HARDINESS:** Zones 4–8. Protect roots from freeze-thaw cycles.

**SOIL TYPE:** High humus. High moisture, good drainage, high fertility, 6.0–7.0 pH.

**PLANTING GUIDE:** Autumn. Plant in partial to full shade, 6″–12″ (15–30 cm) apart, 4″ (10 cm) deep.

**CARE TIPS:** Average. Even moisture. Fertilize only in spring. Lift and store. Propagate by division, seed.

**NOTES:** Thrives in accents, borders, drifts, edgings, mounds. Nice in natural, rock, shade, wood-land gardens. Resists diseases. Susceptible to deer, rodents.

## *Trollius europaeus* and hybrids RANUNCULACEAE

### Globeflower

**SHAPE:** Various erect, mounded, open, fibrous-rooted perennials, 18″–24″ (45–60 cm) tall. Shiny, 3–5-lobed, fine-toothed leaves to 3″ (75 mm) long with gray undersides. See also *T. chinensis*, Chinese globeflower.

**FLOWER:** Late-spring to early-summer bloom. Round, ball-shaped flowers, 1″–2″ (25–50 mm) wide. Choose from yellow and green yellow.

**HARDINESS:** Zones 3–7. May self-seed.

**SOIL TYPE:** High humus; pond shorelines. High moisture, good drainage, high fertility, 5.5–7.0 pH.

**PLANTING GUIDE:** Spring or autumn. Plant in full sun to partial shade, 18″ (45 cm) apart.

**CARE TIPS:** Easy. Even moisture. Fertilize every 4 weeks. Apply mulch. Extend bloom by deadheading. Propagate by division, seed.

**NOTES:** Thrives in accents, beds, borders. Nice in bog, natural, shade gardens and ponds. Cutting flower. Resists diseases. Susceptible to aphids.

## *Valeriana officinalis* VALERIANACEAE

### Common Valerian (Garden Heliotrope)

**SHAPE:** Numerous erect, rhizomatous, deciduous perennials, 42″–60″ (1.1–1.5 m) tall. Textured, lacey, deep-cut, divided, toothed, aromatic leaves, 18″–24″ (45–60 cm) long with 7–10 paired leaflets.

**FLOWER:** Late-spring to summer bloom. Tall stems with flat, round clusters of funnel-shaped, very fragrant flowers, ⅛″–¼″ (3–6 mm) wide. Choose from pink, and white.

**HARDINESS:** Zones 3–10. May self-seed.

**SOIL TYPE:** Loam. High moisture, good drainage, high–medium fertility, 6.5–7.5 pH.

**PLANTING GUIDE:** Spring. Plant in full sun to partial shade, 24″–36″ (60–90 cm) apart.

**CARE TIPS:** Easy. Water only when soil dries. Fertilize every 4 weeks. Propagate by division, seed.

**NOTES:** Thrives in accents, containers, massed plantings. Nice in arid, meadow, woodland, wildlife gardens. Cutting flower. Attracts cats. Aggressive. Resists pests and diseases.

## *Verbascum* spp. and hybrids SCROPHULARIACEAE

### Mullein

**SHAPE:** About 250 erect, mounded, hirsute, often annuals or perennials but usually biennials, 4′–7′ (1.2–2.2 m) tall. Woolly, bluntly circular, paddle-shaped leaves, 10″–18″ (25–45 cm) long, forming a basal rosette.

**FLOWER:** Summer bloom. Tall, spiking clusters of showy, trumpet-shaped, fragrant flowers to 1″ (25 mm) wide. Choose from red, white, bright and lemon yellow, often with contrasting throats.

**HARDINESS:** Most, zones 5–9; some, zones 3–4. May self-seed.

**SOIL TYPE:** Sandy loam. Average–low moisture, good drainage, medium fertility, 6.5–7.5 pH.

**PLANTING GUIDE:** Spring. Plant in full sun, 12″–16″ (30–40 cm) apart.

**CARE TIPS:** Easy. Even moisture. Fertilize only in spring. Propagate by cuttings, division, seed.

**NOTES:** Thrives in accents, backgrounds. Nice in arid, meadow, seaside, wildlife gardens. Cutting flower. Aggressive. Resists pests and diseases.

## *Verbena* spp. and hybrids VERBENACEAE

### Verbena (Vervain)

**SHAPE:** About 200 varied, usually low and sprawling or trailing annuals, perennials, or shrubs, 2″–18″ (50–460 mm) tall. Opposite, hirsute, oval, toothed leaves to 4″ (10 cm) long.

**FLOWER:** Late-spring to autumn bloom. Clusters of broad, flat flowers, ½″ (12 mm) wide. Choose from pink, purple, red, white, and yellow.

**HARDINESS:** Zones 8–9. Protect from frost.

**SOIL TYPE:** Sandy loam. High moisture, good drainage, high–medium fertility, 6.5–7.0 pH.

**PLANTING GUIDE:** Spring, when frost risk ends. Plant in full sun, 12″–24″ (30–60 cm) apart.

**CARE TIPS:** Easy. Even moisture; avoid wetting foliage. Fertilize every 2 weeks. Propagate by cuttings, division.

**NOTES:** Thrives in accents, containers, edgings, ground covers. Nice in natural, wildlife gardens. Aggressive, zones 8–9. Susceptible to budworms, verbena leaf miners, woolly-bear caterpillars, powdery mildew.

## *Veronica* spp. and hybrids SCROPHULARIACEAE

### Speedwell (Brooklime)

**SHAPE:** About 250 vertical or short, bushlike annuals or perennials, 12″–48″ (30–120 cm) tall, 12″–18″ (30–45 cm) wide. Textured, lancelike, sharp-tipped leaves to 2″ (50 mm) long.

**FLOWER:** Late-spring to summer bloom. Spiking clusters to 24″ (60 cm) tall of tiny, tubular, lipped flowers. Choose from blue, pink, and white.

**HARDINESS:** Zones 3–8.

**SOIL TYPE:** Loam. High moisture, good drainage, medium–low fertility, 6.5–7.5 pH.

**PLANTING GUIDE:** Spring or autumn. Plant in full sun to partial shade, 12″–24″ (30–60 cm) apart.

**CARE TIPS:** Average. Even moisture. Fertilize only in spring during active growth. Mulch in winter, zones 3–5. Support with stakes. Propagate by cuttings, division, seed.

**NOTES:** Thrives in accents, beds, borders, containers, fence lines. Nice in cottage, formal, heritage, natural gardens. Resists pests. Susceptible to downy mildew, leaf spot.

## *Vinca* spp. APOCYNACEAE

### Periwinkle

**SHAPE:** About 10 short, bushlike, mounded, or trailing, evergreen perennial subshrubs, 6″–24″ (15–60 cm) tall and 12″–36″ (30–90 cm) wide. Opposite, shiny, oval or lancelike, sharp-tipped leaves to 2″ (50 mm) long.

**FLOWER:** Early-spring bloom. Single, rounded, 5-petaled flowers, 1″–2″ (25–50 mm) wide. Choose from blue, purple, and white.

**HARDINESS:** *V. major*, zones 8-11; *V. minor*, zones 3–11. Prefers mild-summer climates.

**SOIL TYPE:** Loam. Most moistures, good drainage, medium–low fertility, 6.0–8.0 pH. Tolerates salt.

**PLANTING GUIDE:** Spring. Plant in full sun to full shade, 18″–24″ (45–60 cm) apart.

**CARE TIPS:** Easy. Even moisture. Fertilize in spring. Shear in autumn. Propagate by cuttings, division.

**NOTES:** Thrives in banks, borders, containers, ground covers. Nice in natural, woodland gardens. Aggressive. Resists diseases. Susceptible to slugs, snails.

## *Viola cornuta* VIOLACEAE

### Viola (Horned Violet, Tufted Pansy)

**SHAPE:** Various short-lived, mounded perennials to 12″ (30 cm) tall and wide. Shiny, oval leaves to 1″ (25 mm) long with wavy or scalloped edges.

**FLOWER:** Late-spring to autumn bloom. Pansylike, spurred flowers to 1½″ (38 mm) wide. Choose from purple, white, and multicolored.

**HARDINESS:** Zones 3–9.

**SOIL TYPE:** Loam. High moisture, good drainage, high–medium fertility, 6.5–7.5 pH.

**PLANTING GUIDE:** Late spring, as soil warms. Plant in full sun to partial shade, 4″–6″ (10–15 cm) apart. Start indoors for early bloom.

**CARE TIPS:** Easy. Even moisture. Fertilize every 6–8 weeks. Extend bloom by deadheading. Propagate by division, seed.

**NOTES:** Thrives in accents, beds, borders, containers, edgings. Nice in cottage, formal, meadow, rock, shade, woodland gardens. Cutting flower. Susceptible to slugs, snails, violet sawfly larvae, anthracnose.

## *Viola odorata* and hybrids VIOLACEAE

### Sweet Violet (English Violet, Florist's Violet)

**SHAPE:** Numerous short, mounded, tufted perennials, 8″–24″ (20–60 cm) tall. Shiny, circular or kidney-shaped, fine-toothed leaves, 1″–2″ (25–50 mm) long.

**FLOWER:** Early-spring bloom. Single or double, spurred, fragrant flowers, ½″–⅞″ (12–22 mm) wide. Choose from blue, purple, violet, and white.

**HARDINESS:** Zones 4–10. May self-seed.

**SOIL TYPE:** Loam. High moisture, good drainage, high fertility, 5.5–6.5 pH.

**PLANTING GUIDE:** Spring, zones 2–5; late summer, zones 6–10. Plant in filtered sun to partial shade, 8″–12″ (20–30 cm) apart.

**CARE TIPS:** Easy. Even moisture. Fertilize every 4 weeks. Extend bloom by deadheading. Propagate by division, offsets, runners, seed.

**NOTES:** Thrives in containers, edgings. Nice in cottage, woodland gardens. Cutting flower. Aggressive. Resists diseases. Susceptible to spider mites.

## *Viola tricolor* and hybrids VIOLACEAE

### Johnny-Jump-Up (Field Pansy, Miniature Pansy)

**SHAPE:** Numerous short-lived, mounded, tufted perennials, 6″–12″ (15–30 cm) tall. Oval lobate leaves, 1″–2″ (25–50 mm) long.

**FLOWER:** Early-spring to summer bloom, zones 2–8; winter to spring, zones 9–10. Flat, single flowers, 1/2″–7/8″ (12–22 mm) wide. Choose from apricot, blue, lavender, orange, pink, purple, red, white, yellow, and multicolored.

**HARDINESS:** Zones 4–10. Protect foliage and flowers from frost. May self-seed.

**SOIL TYPE:** High humus. High moisture, good drainage, high–medium fertility, 6.5–7.5 pH.

**PLANTING GUIDE:** Spring, zones 2–8; autumn, zones 9–10. Plant in full sun to partial shade, 4″–8″ (10–20 cm) apart.

**CARE TIPS:** Easy. Even moisture. Fertilize every 4 weeks. Propagate by division, offsets, seed.

**NOTES:** Thrives in borders, containers, edgings. Nice in cottage, small-space, woodland gardens. Resists diseases. Susceptible to slugs, snails.

## *Viola* × *wittrockiana* VIOLACEAE

### Pansy (Garden Pansy, Heartsease, Ladies-Delight)

**SHAPE:** Numerous erect, mounded annuals or perennials, 6″–9″ (15–23 cm) tall. Shiny, oval to heart-shaped leaves to 2″ (50 mm) long with scalloped edges.

**FLOWER:** Spring or late-autumn bloom. Irregular, 5-petaled flowers, 2″–5″ (50–125 mm) wide. Choose from blue, brown, burgundy, lavender, red, violet, white, and yellow.

**HARDINESS:** Zones 5–9. Protect from frost. Best bloom in cool-summer climates.

**SOIL TYPE:** Loam. High moisture, good drainage, high–medium fertility, 6.5–7.5 pH.

**PLANTING GUIDE:** Late spring. Plant in full sun to partial shade, 6″–8″ (15–20 cm) apart.

**CARE TIPS:** Easy. Even moisture. Fertilize every 4 weeks. Propagate by division, seed.

**NOTES:** Thrives in borders, containers, massed plantings. Nice in cottage, formal, rock, shade, woodland gardens. Cutting flower. Susceptible to slugs, snails, sawfly larvae, anthracnose.

## *Zauschneria californica* (*Epilobium* spp.) ONAGRACEAE

### California Fuchsia

**SHAPE:** Few erect, branched, creeping, woody, perennials to 24″ (60 cm) tall. Alternate, lancelike, slender leaves to 1½″ (38 mm) long.

**FLOWER:** Late-summer to autumn bloom. Branched stems of showy, tubular, trumpet-shaped flowers, 1″–1½″ (25–38 mm) wide. Choose from orange, pink, and red.

**HARDINESS:** Zones 5–9. May self-seed.

**SOIL TYPE:** Sandy loam. Average–low moisture, good drainage, medium fertility, 6.5–8.0 pH.

Tolerates drought. Prefers low humidity.

**PLANTING GUIDE:** Spring. Plant in full sun, 18″–24″ (45–60 cm) apart.

**CARE TIPS:** Easy. Water only when soil dries. Fertilize only in spring. Pinch tips for bushy plants. Extend bloom by deadheading. Shear in autumn. Propagate by cuttings, division, seed.

**NOTES:** Thrives in banks, borders, containers, walls. Nice in cottage, rock, wildlife, woodland gardens. Resists pests and diseases.

## *Zingiber officinale* and hybrids ZINGIBERACEAE

### True Ginger

**SHAPE:** Numerous tuberous or rhizomatous, deciduous or evergreen perennials to 20″ (50 cm) tall, with edible roots. Shiny, lancelike leaves to 12″ (30 cm) long in tiers along stalk.

**FLOWER:** Summer bloom. Erect or drooping spikes of multiple trumpet-shaped, sometimes orchid-like flowers. Choose from orange, pink, white, and yellow, sometimes banded or edged.

**HARDINESS:** Zones 9–11. Protect from frost.

**SOIL TYPE:** High humus; pond shorelines.

High moisture, good drainage, high–medium fertility, 6.0–6.5 pH.

**PLANTING GUIDE:** Spring. Plant in open shade, 6″–12″ (15–30 cm) apart.

**CARE TIPS:** Average. Even moisture. Fertilize every 6–8 weeks. Lift and store. Propagate by division.

**NOTES:** Thrives in backgrounds, beds, borders, massed plantings. Nice in tropical, woodland gardens and ponds. Source of Asian cooking spice. Resists pests and diseases.

# Bulbs and Bulbous Plants

Understand the specialized requirements of spring, summer, and autumn bulbs to enjoy beautiful flower displays throughout the year.

Daffodils appear in mid- to late spring in cold-winter climates. In mild-winter areas, they may bloom as early as February.

Bulbous plants such as true bulbs, tubers, and corms are commonly grouped together even though they have highly varied growth habits and care needs. Some sources also include rhizomatous or fibrous perennials in this category, but you will find these plants in the perennials section of this book [see Perennials and Biennials, pg. 158].

Although they are somewhat different in their growth and reproductive habits, all of the bulbous plants grow from swollen underground structures that store needed nutrients. Most are dormant or semi-dormant through part of the gardening season or during winter. This dormancy is a natural part of their growth cycle. They have adapted to conditions found in their native environments—whether in a coastal location with warm and dry Mediterranean-like summers, an arid desert that receives all of its moisture in periodic rains that last a few short months, or a tropical rain forest subject to occasional droughts.

**Caring for Bulbs.** Bulbs need proper exposure, regular fertilizer, and adequate water during active growth. For many bulbous plants, this means watering them from the time their foliage first emerges from the soil until it dies back after flowering. For others, especially tropical bulbs, you'll need to water year-round but limit water for a month or two after the bulbs have bloomed.

When growth first begins, apply a high-nitrogen fertilizer such as 5–0–0 for the best flower production. Once flowering stops, much or all of a bulb's stored energy will have been spent. As long as its leaves are green and growing, the plant will continue to store energy for the next year's bloom, so it is important not to cut the leaves or lift the bulb until its foliage completely dies down. Help bulbs replenish nutrients for their next season by applying a complete fertilizer high in phosphorus and potassium such as 5–10–10 when the first flower buds begin to form.

Apply fertilizer near the root zone and water it in. Withhold all fertilizer after the flowers open. Most bulbs require a period without water after their foliage dies back. If your region receives heavy precipitation during the time the bulbs are dormant, lift and store them in a dark location as directed in the following pages. In some regions spring-blooming bulbs are

Mild-climate areas of the Pacific Coast of British Columbia and the United States have wet winters and nearly dry summers. There, spring bulbs such as tulip may remain in the ground year-round until they become crowded.

lifted for the summer and replanted in autumn. If you live in a frost-free area, store bulbs during the winter and plant them in spring when the soil warms. Also lift summer-blooming bulbs and store them for the winter; it's still important to allow them to complete their cycle of growth after flowering. Lift them when the first frosts kill their foliage.

In order to produce their flowers, bulbs such as narcissus and tulips require a period of winter chill. If you live in an area that receives little or no frost, you can simulate this natural chilling by placing them in your refrigerator for at least six weeks prior to planting. In mild-winter climates, bulbs may have been prechilled for immediate planting—check with the garden center or nursery staff.

**Naturalized Bulbs.** The best bulbs to grow are those that naturalize—grow in your garden year after year with little care. Rather than work against nature and grow bulbs that require a great deal of effort and attention, grow bulbs that you can plant and forget. Bulbs, corms, and tubers native to your area probably fall in this category. Bleeding heart

and Mariposa lily (*Calochortus* spp.) are examples of two plants that both naturalize easily and are native to specific regions of North America.

Naturalized flowers are a welcome surprise in the garden come spring, summer, or autumn. Visit public gardens and note what grows there to widen your acquaintance with bulbs that naturalize in your geographic area. Also consult with the staff of a local nursery or garden center for their recommendations of naturalizing bulbs.

The traditional method for naturalizing bulbs is to scatter them in the desired area and plant them where they fall. This simulates the way in which they would naturally disperse themselves in the wild; it is more random and casual than neat, patterned plantings. You can modify this technique somewhat to fit your flower scheme and plans. Some bulbs, even though naturalized, may need additional water if you have dry spells in the summer months. Coordinate the plantings of ground covers and grasses in the bed to match the dormancy needs of your naturalized bulbs. Xeriscape gardens are excellent covers for groups of naturalized bulbs.

### *Achimenes* spp. GESNERIACEAE

## Orchid Pansy (Mother's-Tears, Nut Orchid)

**SHAPE:** About 26 mounded, trailing, rhizomatous perennials, 12″–24″ (30–60 cm) tall. Oval, toothed, textured leaves to 5″ (13 cm) long.

**FLOWER:** Summer to autumn bloom. Flute-shaped flowers, 1″–2″ (25–50 mm) long. Choose from blue, orange, pink, purple, red, white, and yellow.

**HARDINESS:** Zones 9–11. Hardy. Protect from hot sun. Grow as annual, zones 4–8.

**SOIL TYPE:** High humus. Average moisture, good drainage, high fertility, 6.0–7.5 pH.

**PLANTING GUIDE:** Late spring to early summer. Plant in light shade 10″ (25 cm) apart, 1″ (25 mm) deep.

**CARE TIPS:** Easy. Even moisture. Fertilize during growth. Apply mulch. Support with stakes or allow to trail. Propagate by division. Store in damp peat moss, 50°–60°F (10°–16°C).

**NOTES:** Thrives in beds, borders, containers. Nice in cottage, formal gardens. Resists deer, rodents, diseases. Susceptible to spider mites, thrips.

### *Allium* spp. LILIACEAE

## Ornamental Onion (Allium)

**SHAPE:** About 700 aromatic, rhizomatous or bulbous perennials, 6″–60″ (15–150 cm) tall. Swordlike, hollow leaves to 4′ (1.2 m) long.

**FLOWER:** Spring to summer bloom. Clusters of star-shaped, often aromatic flowers, ¼″–1″ (6–25 mm) wide. Choose from blue, pink, red, violet, white, and yellow. Forms seed and bulbils.

**HARDINESS:** Zones 4–8. Hardy.

**SOIL TYPE:** High humus. High–average moisture, good drainage, medium fertility, 6.0–7.0 pH.

**PLANTING GUIDE:** Autumn. Plant in full sun to partial shade 12″ (30 cm) apart, 2″–8″ (50–200 mm) deep.

**CARE TIPS:** Easy. Even moisture. Fertilize during growth. Extend bloom by deadheading. Apply mulch. Propagate by bulbils, division, offsets, seed. Store in dry peat moss, 50°–60°F (10°–16°C).

**NOTES:** Thrives in borders, containers, edgings. Nice in cottage, formal, natural, woodland gardens. Naturalizes. Resists deer, rodents. Susceptible to onion maggots, thrips, mildew, rot.

### *Amaryllis belladonna* AMARYLLIDACEAE

## True Amaryllis (Belladonna Lily, Naked-Lady)

**SHAPE:** Lone arched, fanlike, bulbous perennials, 24″–36″ (60–90 cm) tall. Straplike leaves to 18″ (45 cm) long. See also *Hippeastrum* spp., florist's amaryllis.

**FLOWER:** Early-autumn bloom. Tall stalk with flared, trumpet-shaped, aromatic flowers to 4″ (10 cm) wide. Choose from pink, red, and white.

**HARDINESS:** Zones 8–11. Hardy.

**SOIL TYPE:** High humus. High–average moisture, good drainage, high fertility, 6.0–6.5 pH.

**PLANTING GUIDE:** Late spring to early summer. Plant in full sun, 8″–12″ (20–30 cm) apart, at soil level; in pots, slightly above soil level.

**CARE TIPS:** Average. Even moisture. Fertilize during growth. Propagate by division, offsets. Divide if crowded. Store in dry peat moss, 55°–70°F (13°–21°C).

**NOTES:** Thrives in beds, borders, containers. Nice in cottage, tropical gardens. Cutting flower. Resists deer, rodents, insect pests, diseases.

### *Anemone* spp. and hybrids RANUNCULACEAE

## Windflower (Lily-of-the-Field, Poppy Anemone)

**SHAPE:** About 120 mounded, rhizomatous or tuberous perennials, 2″–36″ (50–900 mm) tall. Plumelike, deep-toothed, lobate, hirsute leaves to 3″ (75 mm) long.

**FLOWER:** Late-winter to spring bloom. Succulent stems of poppylike flowers to 3″ (75 mm) wide. Choose from blue, pink, purple, red, and white.

**HARDINESS:** Zones 6–10. Hardy.

**SOIL TYPE:** High humus. High–average moisture, good drainage, high fertility, 6.0–7.5 pH.

**PLANTING GUIDE:** Autumn, zones 8–10; spring, zones 3–7. Plant in full sun to partial shade, 4″–12″ (10–30 cm) apart, 1″–2″ (25–50 mm) deep.

**CARE TIPS:** Easy. Even moisture. Fertilize during growth. Apply mulch. Propagate by division, seed. Store rhizomes in damp peat moss, 40°F (4°C); tuberous roots in dry peat moss, 50°F (10°C).

**NOTES:** Thrives in beds, containers, edgings. Nice in natural, woodland gardens. Cutting flower. Susceptible to birds, deer, rodents, fungal diseases.

## *Arisaema triphyllum* ARACEAE

### Jack-in-the-Pulpit

**SHAPE:** Few mounded, tuberous perennials to 24″ (60 cm) tall. Triplets of oval to lancelike, segmented basal leaves to 9″ (23 cm) long.

**FLOWER:** Spring to early-summer bloom. Succulent stalk with slender, hooded, striped spathe that protects the clublike central spadix to 5″ (13 cm) long. Choose from brown, green, and purple.

**HARDINESS:** Zones 4–9. Hardy.

**SOIL TYPE:** High humus. High moisture, good drainage, high–medium fertility, 5.5– 6.5 pH.

**PLANTING GUIDE:** Autumn. Plant in partial to full shade, 10″–12″ (25–30 cm) apart, 3″–4″ (75–100 mm) deep.

**CARE TIPS:** Average. Even moisture during growth. Fertilize every 4 weeks during growth. Apply mulch. Propagate by offsets, seed. Store in dry peat moss, 50°–60°F (10°–16°C).

**NOTES:** Thrives in beds, borders, containers. Nice in woodland gardens. Resists deer, rodents, insect pests, diseases.

## *Arum italicum* ARACEAE

### Lords-and-Ladies

**SHAPE:** Few varied, vertical, tuberous perennials to 18″ (45 cm) tall. Stems of heart-shaped, wavy basal leaves to 8″ (20 cm) long. See also *Arisaema triphyllum*, Jack-in-the-pulpit.

**FLOWER:** Spring bloom. Succulent stalk with red spathe that protects the spearlike central spadix to 8″ (20 cm) tall. Choose from green, purple, white, and yellow. Forms orange, red berries.

**HARDINESS:** Zones 5–10. Hardy.

**SOIL TYPE:** High humus. High moisture, good drainage, high–medium fertility, 6.5–7.5 pH.

**PLANTING GUIDE:** Autumn. Plant in partial to full shade, 12″ (30 cm) apart, 4″ (10 cm) deep.

**CARE TIPS:** Easy. Even moisture. Fertilize during growth. Apply mulch. Propagate by division in late summer–early autumn. Store in dry peat moss, 50°–60°F (10°–16°C).

**NOTES:** Thrives in beds, borders. Nice in woodland gardens and ponds. Cutting flower. Resists deer, rodents, insect pests, diseases.

## *Asparagus densiflorus* LILIACEAE

### Asparagus Fern (Ornamental Asparagus)

**SHAPE:** Several vertical, semi-tropical, tuberous ever-green shrubs, 18″–24″ (45–60 cm) tall. Branchlets of shiny, needle- or plumelike leaves to 2″ (50 mm) long. Related to the garden vegetable.

**FLOWER:** Spring bloom. Small, star-shaped, aromatic flowers. White. Forms shiny, red, berrylike fruit.

**HARDINESS:** Zones 9–11. Protect from frost.

**SOIL TYPE:** Sandy loam. High moisture, good drainage, high–medium fertility, 6.5–7.0 pH.

**PLANTING GUIDE:** Spring. Plant in full sun to partial shade, 24″–36″ (60–90 cm) apart, 6″–8″ (15–20 cm) deep.

**CARE TIPS:** Easy. Even moisture during growth. Fertilize only in spring. Apply mulch in winter. Propagate by division in autumn. Where hardy, store in ground year-round.

**NOTES:** Thrives in banks, beds, borders, containers, edgings. Nice in arid, rock, small-space, woodland gardens. Susceptible to asparagus beetles, spider mites, rust.

## *Babiana* spp. IRIDACEAE

### Baboon Flower

**SHAPE:** About 60 vertical perennials, 6″–12″ (15–30 cm) tall, from corms. Vertical, straplike, ribbed, hirsute leaves to 10″ (25 cm) long.

**FLOWER:** Late-spring to early-summer bloom. Star-shaped, aromatic flowers 1″–2″ (25–50 mm) wide. Choose from blue, purple, red, white, and yellow.

**HARDINESS:** Zones 9–10. Hardy.

**SOIL TYPE:** Sandy loam. High moisture, good drainage, medium fertility, 6.0–6.5 pH.

**PLANTING GUIDE:** Autumn, zones 9–10; spring, zone 8. Plant in full sun to partial shade, 2″–6″ (50–150 mm) apart, 2″–6″ (50–150 mm) deep; in pots, space 1″ (25 mm) apart, 1″ (25 mm) deep.

**CARE TIPS:** Average. Even moisture. Fertilize during growth. Shelter from wind. Propagate by bulbils, seed. Store in damp sawdust, 50°–60°F (10°–16°C).

**NOTES:** Thrives in beds, borders, containers, drifts. Nice in cottage, rock, shade gardens. Aggressive. Naturalizes. Resists pests and diseases.

## *Begonia grandis* BEGONIACEAE

### Hardy Begonia

**SHAPE:** Various vertical, succulent, tuberous perennials, 18″–36″ (45–90 cm) tall. Wing-shaped, veined leaves to 3″ (75 mm) wide.

**FLOWER:** Midsummer to autumn bloom. Clusters of irregular, drooping, aromatic flowers, 1″–1½″ (25–38 mm) wide. Choose from pink and white.

**HARDINESS:** Zones 6–9. Hardy.

**SOIL TYPE:** High humus. High moisture, good drainage, high fertility, 6.0–6.5 pH.

**PLANTING GUIDE:** Spring, zones 6–8; autumn, zone 9. Plant in partial shade, 8″–10″ (20–25 cm) apart, 4″ (10 cm) deep.

**CARE TIPS:** Easy. Even moisture. Fertilize during growth. Pinch buds for large flowers. Propagate by cuttings, dividing tubers. Store in dry peat moss, 50°–60°F (10°–16°C).

**NOTES:** Thrives in beds, borders, ground covers, mixed plantings. Nice in formal, hanging, small-space gardens. Susceptible to deer, rodents, slugs, snails.

## *Begonia* × *tuberhybrida* hybrids BEGONIACEAE

### Tuberous Begonia

**SHAPE:** Numerous short, vertical or dangling, tuberous perennials, 12″–36″ (30–90 cm) tall or long. Wing-shaped, textured, veined, toothed leaves to 5″ (13 cm) wide.

**FLOWER:** Summer to autumn bloom. Single, double, or very double, fringed or ruffled, aromatic flowers to 8″ (20 cm) wide. Choose from orange, pink, purple, red, white, yellow, and variegated.

**HARDINESS:** Zones 8–11. Hardy. Protect from frost and hot sun.

**SOIL TYPE:** High humus. High moisture, good drainage, high fertility, 5.5–6.5 pH.

**PLANTING GUIDE:** Spring. Plant in partial shade, 6″–12″ (15–30 cm) apart, at soil level.

**CARE TIPS:** Average. Even moisture. Fertilize during growth. Apply mulch. Propagate by division. Store in dry peat moss, 40°–50°F (4°–10°C).

**NOTES:** Thrives in beds, borders, containers. Nice in courtyard, small-space gardens. Susceptible to deer, rodents, slugs, snails.

## *Caladium* × *hortulanum* (*C. bicolor*) ARACEAE

### Fancy-Leaved Caladium (Mother-in-Law Plant, Elephant's-Ear)

**SHAPE:** Various mounded, tuberous perennials, 12″–36″ (30–90 cm) tall. Broad, heart-shaped, variegated, toothed, sharp-tipped, basal leaves, 2″–18″ (50–450 mm) long.

**FLOWER:** Insignificant flowers; grow for variegated foliage.

**HARDINESS:** Zones 9–11. Hardy. Protect from frost.

**SOIL TYPE:** Sandy loam. High moisture, good drainage, high fertility, 5.5–6.5 pH.

**PLANTING GUIDE:** Late spring. Plant in partial to full shade, 12″ (30 cm) apart, 1″–3″ (25–75 mm) deep.

**CARE TIPS:** Average. Even moisture during growth; limit water thereafter. Fertilize until buds form. Shelter from wind. Propagate by offsets. Store in dry peat moss, 50°–60°F (10°–16°C).

**NOTES:** Thrives in beds, borders, containers, edges, mixed plantings. Nice in shade, small-space, tropical gardens. Good with annual or perennial flowers. Resists deer, rodents. Susceptible to slugs, snails.

## *Calochortus* spp. LILIACEAE

### Mariposa Lily (Fairy Lantern, Star Tulip)

**SHAPE:** About 60 varied, bulbous perennials to 30″ (75 cm) tall. Grasslike, oval to lancelike basal leaves to 24″ (60 cm) long.

**FLOWER:** Late-spring to early-summer bloom. Erect or nodding, cup-shaped or globelike flowers, 1″–2″ (25–50 mm) wide, with spidery bracts. Choose from pink, purple, red, white, and yellow.

**HARDINESS:** Zones 6–8. Hardy.

**SOIL TYPE:** Loam. High moisture, good drainage, medium fertility, 5.5–6.5 pH.

**PLANTING GUIDE:** Autumn. Plant in full sun to partial shade, 18″ (45 cm) apart, 3″–5″ (75–125 mm) deep.

**CARE TIPS:** Average to difficult. Even moisture during growth; limit water thereafter. Fertilize first year. Apply mulch. Lift in humid climates. Propagate by offsets, seed. Store in sand, 60°F (16°C).

**NOTES:** Thrives in accents, containers, slopes. Nice in rock gardens. Cutting flower. Naturalizes. Susceptible to deer, rodents.

## *Camassia* spp. LILIACEAE

### Camass

**SHAPE:** Few bulbous perennials, 30″–48″ (75–120 cm) tall. Slender, strap- or grasslike basal leaves to 12″ (30 cm) long.

**FLOWER:** Late-spring bloom. Stalks with tiered clusters of multiple, star-shaped, often lightly aromatic flowers, 1″–2″ (25–50 mm) wide. Choose from blue, purple, and white.

**HARDINESS:** Zones 4–9. Hardy.

**SOIL TYPE:** High humus. High moisture, good drainage, high–medium fertility, 6.0–6.5 pH.

**PLANTING GUIDE:** Early autumn. Plant in full sun to partial shade, 6″–10″ (15–25 cm) apart, 4″–6″ (10–15 cm) deep.

**CARE TIPS:** Easy. Even moisture. Fertilize during growth. Propagate by division, seed. Leave bulbs undisturbed in garden soil unless crowded.

**NOTES:** Thrives in beds, borders, ground covers, mixed plantings. Nice in woodland gardens and ponds. Cutting flower. Naturalizes. Resists insect pests, diseases. Susceptible to deer, rodents.

## *Cardiocrinum giganteum* LILIACEAE

### Giant Lily

**SHAPE:** Few herbaceous, bulbous perennials to 12′ (3.7 m) tall. Oval, pointed, ribbed leaves to 18″ (45 cm) long, along stalk and in basal rosettes. Dies after fruiting; produces offsets.

**FLOWER:** Summer bloom in 3–7 years. Spiking clusters of up to 24 flute-shaped, aromatic flowers to 8″ (20 cm) long. White with red throats.

**HARDINESS:** Zones 6–9. Hardy. Protect from sun.

**SOIL TYPE:** High humus. High moisture, good drainage, high fertility, 6.0–6.5 pH.

**PLANTING GUIDE:** Autumn, zone 9; early spring, zones 6–8. Plant in partial shade, 36″ (90 cm) apart, at soil surface.

**CARE TIPS:** Difficult. Even moisture; avoid wetting foliage. Fertilize during growth. Mulch in summer. Propagate by offsets. Store in sawdust, 40°F (4°C).

**NOTES:** Thrives in accents. Nice in cottage gardens. Cutting flower. Susceptible to deer, rodents, lily beetles, leaf fungus, lily-mosaic virus.

## *Chionodoxa* spp. LILIACEAE

### Glory-of-the-Snow

**SHAPE:** Few bulbous perennials, 3″–6″ (75–150 mm) tall. Grasslike, slender, straight basal leaves to 4″ (10 cm) long.

**FLOWER:** Early-spring to summer bloom. Stalks with ascending, vertical-tiered or basal clusters of 6-pointed, star-shaped flowers to 1″ (25 mm) wide. Choose from blue, lavender, pink, and white.

**HARDINESS:** Zones 3–8. Hardy.

**SOIL TYPE:** High humus. High moisture, good drainage, high–medium fertility, 6.0–7.0 pH.

**PLANTING GUIDE:** Autumn. Plant in full sun to partial shade, 2″ (50 mm) apart, 4″ (10 cm) deep.

**CARE TIPS:** Easy. Even moisture. Fertilize during growth; limit water thereafter. Apply mulch, zones 7–8. Propagate by division, offsets, seed. Store in dry peat moss, 50°–60°F (10°–16°C).

**NOTES:** Thrives in borders, containers. Nice in cottage, rock, woodland gardens. Naturalizes. Resists pests and diseases.

## *Clivia* spp. AMARYLLIDACEAE

### Woodlily (Bush Lily)

**SHAPE:** Few bunching, tuberous evergreen perennials to 24″ (60 cm) tall. Straplike, arched leaves, 12″–60″ (30–150 cm) long.

**FLOWER:** Late-winter to spring bloom. Succulent stalk with branched clusters of flared, trumpet-shaped flowers to 2″ (50 mm) wide. Choose from orange, deep red, and yellow with light yellow centers.

**HARDINESS:** Zones 9–11. Hardy. Protect from frost.

**SOIL TYPE:** High humus. High moisture, good drainage, medium fertility, 6.5–7.0 pH.

**PLANTING GUIDE:** Autumn or spring. Plant in partial to full shade, 6″–12″ (15–30 cm) apart, slightly below soil level; transplants, 16″ (40 cm) apart.

**CARE TIPS:** Easy. Even moisture. Fertilize during growth; limit water thereafter. Apply mulch. Propagate by division, offsets, seed. Store in dry to slightly damp soil, 40°–60°F (4°–16°C).

**NOTES:** Thrives in beds, borders, containers. Nice in woodland gardens. Resists pests and diseases.

## *Colchicum autumnale* LILIACEAE

### Meadow Saffron (Autumn Crocus, Fall Crocus, Mysteria, Wonder Bulb)

**SHAPE:** Various perennials, 4″–12″ (10–30 cm) tall, from corms. Slim, straplike, leaves to 12″ (30 cm) long, after flowers fade.

**FLOWER:** Late-summer to early-autumn bloom. Multiple flared, crocuslike, single or double flowers to 4″ (10 cm) wide. Choose from pink, purple, rose, and white.

**HARDINESS:** Zones 4–9. Hardy.

**SOIL TYPE:** Loam. High moisture, good drainage, medium fertility, 6.0–7.5 pH.

**PLANTING GUIDE:** Summer. Plant in full sun, 6″–8″ (15–20 cm) apart, 3″–4″ (75–100 mm) deep.

**CARE TIPS:** Easy. Even moisture during winter. Fertilize during growth. Apply mulch, zones 5–7. Propagate by division, cormels in summer. Divide if crowded. Store in dry peat moss, 40°–50°F (4°–10°C).

**NOTES:** Thrives in borders. Nice in woodland gardens. Naturalizes. Resists deer, rodents, insect pests, diseases.

## *Corydalis* spp. FUMARIACEAE

### Fumaria (Fumewort)

**SHAPE:** About 300 rhizomatous or tuberous perennials, 6″–12″ (15–30 cm) tall. Plumelike, divided, lobate, toothed basal leaves to 2″ (50 cm) long.

**FLOWER:** Spring bloom. Clusters of nodding, tube-like flowers, ½″–1″ (12–25 mm) long. Choose from blue, pink, purple, red, white, and yellow.

**HARDINESS:** Zones 5–8. Hardy. May self-seed. Protect from hot sun.

**SOIL TYPE:** Sandy loam. High moisture, good drainage, medium fertility, 6.0–8.0 pH.

**PLANTING GUIDE:** Autumn; spring for transplants. Plant in partial to full shade, 6″ (15 cm) apart, 2″–4″ (50–100 mm) deep.

**CARE TIPS:** Easy. Even moisture. Fertilize during growth. Apply mulch. Propagate by division, seed. Store in damp sand, 50°–60°F (10°–16°C).

**NOTES:** Thrives in beds, borders. Nice in rock, shade, woodland gardens. Naturalizes. Resists deer, insect pests, diseases.

## *Cosmos atrosanguineus* ASTERACEAE (COMPOSITAE)

### Black Cosmos (Chocolate Cosmos)

**SHAPE:** Several branched, erect, tuberous perennials, 24″–96″ (60–240 cm) tall. Opposite divided, cut leaves to 6″ (15 cm) long with 5–7 threadlike segments. See also *C. bipinnatus. C. sulphureus* is a closely related annual.

**FLOWER:** Summer to autumn bloom. Wiry stems of daisylike, aromatic flowers to 2″ (50 mm) wide. Choose from chocolate and brown red.

**HARDINESS:** Zones 7–10. Hardy.

**SOIL TYPE:** Sandy soil. Average moisture, good drainage, high fertility, 5.0–8.0 pH.

**PLANTING GUIDE:** Spring, after soil warms. Plant in full sun, 18″ (45 cm) apart.

**CARE TIPS:** Easy. Even moisture. Fertilize during growth. Apply mulch. Extend bloom by dead-heading. Propagate by cuttings, division, seed. Store in dry peat moss, 50°–60°F (10°–16°C).

**NOTES:** Thrives in backgrounds, containers. Nice in cottage, formal gardens. Cutting flower. Resists diseases. Susceptible to aphids, spider mites.

## *Crocosmia × crocosmiiflora* IRIDACEAE

### Montebretia

**SHAPE:** Numerous branched perennials, 3′–4′ (90–120 cm) tall, from corms. Swordlike leaves, ¼″–1″ (6–25 mm) wide.

**FLOWER:** Summer bloom. Branched spiking stems with ascending tiers of tubular, trumpet-shaped flowers, 1½″–2″ (38–50 mm) wide. Choose from orange, red, and yellow.

**HARDINESS:** Zones 4–10. Hardy.

**SOIL TYPE:** Sandy loam. High moisture, good drainage, high–medium fertility, 5.5–6.5 pH.

**PLANTING GUIDE:** Spring. Plant in partial shade, 4″–6″ (10–15 cm) apart, 2″–4″ (50–100 mm) deep.

**CARE TIPS:** Easy. Even moisture during growth. Tolerates drought. Fertilize only in spring. Apply mulch, zones 6–7. Propagate by division, offsets, seed. Store in dry peat moss, 50°–60°F (10°–16°C).

**NOTES:** Thrives in accents, beds, borders, containers, drifts. Nice in cottage, formal, wildlife gardens. Naturalizes. Aggressive. Resists insect pests, diseases. Susceptible to slugs, snails.

## *Crocus* spp. IRIDACEAE

### Spring Crocus

**SHAPE:** About 80 perennials, 3″–6″ (75–150 mm) tall, from corms. Slender, grasslike leaves, 2″–4″ (50–100 mm) long.

**FLOWER:** Autumn or late-winter to early-spring bloom. Short stems of solitary, cup-shaped, often aromatic flowers, 1½″–3″ (38–75 mm) long. Choose from purple, white, yellow, and striped.

**HARDINESS:** Zones 3–8. Hardy.

**SOIL TYPE:** Sandy loam. High moisture, good drainage, medium fertility, 5.0–6.5 pH.

**PLANTING GUIDE:** Autumn. Plant in full sun to partial shade, 3″ (75 mm) apart, 4″ (10 cm) deep.

**CARE TIPS:** Easy. Even moisture. Fertilize during growth. Apply mulch, zones 3, 9–10. Propagate by division in autumn. Divide if crowded. Store in dry peat moss, 40°–50°F (4°–10°C).

**NOTES:** Thrives in beds, containers, edgings, massed plantings. Nice in cottage, meadow, woodland gardens. Naturalizes. Resists insect pests and diseases. Susceptible to deer, rodents.

## *Cyclamen persicum* PRIMULACEAE

### Florist's Cyclamen (Persian Violet)

**SHAPE:** Various mounded, tuberous perennials to 8″ (20 cm) tall. Shiny, heart-shaped, usually fine-toothed leaves to 6″ (15 cm) long and wide with contrasting, variegated markings, veins.

**FLOWER:** Winter to spring bloom. Multiple shooting-star-shaped, often aromatic flowers to 2″ (50 mm) long. Choose from pink, purple, red, and white.

**HARDINESS:** Zones 9–10.

**SOIL TYPE:** Sandy loam. High moisture, good drainage, high fertility, 6.0–6.5 pH.

**PLANTING GUIDE:** Spring, zones 5–8; autumn, zones 9–10. Plant in partial to full shade, 4″–6″ (10–15 cm) apart, at soil level.

**CARE TIPS:** Easy. Even moisture in winter. Fertilize during growth. Apply mulch. Propagate by division, seed. Leave undisturbed. Store in dry to slightly damp soil, 60°–70°F (16°–21°C).

**NOTES:** Thrives in beds, containers, drifts. Nice in rock, shade, gardens. Naturalizes. Resists insect pests. Susceptible to slugs, snails, fungal diseases.

## *Cyrtanthus* spp. AMARYLLIDACEAE

### Fire Lily (Miniature Amaryllis)

**SHAPE:** About 45 deciduous or evergreen, bulbous perennials to 18″ (45 cm) tall. Slender, erect, straplike, arched leaves to 24″ (60 cm) long.

**FLOWER:** Summer bloom. Basal stems of multiple flared, trumpet-shaped, amaryllis-like, aromatic flowers, 1″–1½″ (25–38 mm) long. Choose from orange, pink, red, white, and yellow.

**HARDINESS:** Zones 9–11. Hardy.

**SOIL TYPE:** High humus. Average moisture, good drainage, high fertility, 6.2–6.8 pH.

**PLANTING GUIDE:** Spring. Plant in full sun to partial shade, 6″–12″ (15–30 cm) apart, with neck at soil level.

**CARE TIPS:** Easy. Light moisture. Fertilize during growth; limit thereafter. Lift and store, zones 7–8. Propagate by division, offsets, seed. Store in sawdust, 55°–65°F (13°–18°C).

**NOTES:** Thrives in beds, borders, containers. Nice in cottage, indoor gardens. Cutting flower. Resists pests and diseases.

## *Dahlia* spp. and hybrids ASTERACEAE (COMPOSITAE)

### Dahlia

**SHAPE:** Numerous woody, tuberous perennials to 15′ (4.5 m) tall. Opposite, divided, toothed leaves to 12″ (30 cm) long.

**FLOWER:** Summer to autumn bloom. Circular, single, layered, pompon or cactuslike flowers, 2″–12″ (50–300 mm) wide. Choose from bronze, orange, pink, purple, red, white, yellow, and multicolored.

**HARDINESS:** Zones 9–11. Hardy.

**SOIL TYPE:** Light loam. High moisture, good drainage, high fertility, 6.5–7.0 pH.

**PLANTING GUIDE:** Autumn, zones 9–11; spring, zones 4–8. Plant in full sun, 24″–36″ (60–90 cm) apart, 6″ (15 cm) deep.

**CARE TIPS:** Average. Even moisture. Fertilize during growth. Apply mulch. Lift, zones 4–8. Support with stakes. Propagate by division in spring. Store in dry peat moss, 50°–60°F (10°–16°C).

**NOTES:** Thrives in beds. Nice in cottage gardens. Cutting flower. Resists insect pests. Susceptible to deer, rodents, slugs, snails, powdery mildew.

## *Dicentra* spp. FUMARIACEAE

### Bleeding-Heart

**SHAPE:** About 19 short-lived, vertical, arched, rhizomatous or tuberous perennials, 12″–30″ (30–75 cm) tall. Plumelike, heart-shaped, cut, toothed leaves to 6″ (15 cm) long.

**FLOWER:** Spring to early-summer bloom. Sprays of irregular, nodding flowers to 1½″ (38 mm) long. Choose from pink, purple, red, and white.

**HARDINESS:** Zones 3–9. Hardy.

**SOIL TYPE:** High humus. Average moisture, good drainage, high fertility, 7.0–8.0 pH.

**PLANTING GUIDE:** Early spring, as soil warms, zones 9–11; spring, zones 4–8. Plant in open to partial shade, 36″ (90 cm) apart.

**CARE TIPS:** Easy. Even moisture. Fertilize during growth. Apply mulch. Propagate by division, seed. Store in damp peat moss, 50°–60°F (10°–16°C).

**NOTES:** Thrives in accents, backgrounds, borders, edgings. Nice in cottage, heritage, shade, woodland gardens. Susceptible to aphids, stem rot, vascular wilt.

## *Dicentra cucullaria* FUMARIACEAE

### Dutchman's-Breeches

**SHAPE:** Various mounding or bushlike, tuberous perennials to 10″ (25 cm) tall. Plumelike, divided, deep-toothed, cut basal leaves to 4″ (10 cm) long.

**FLOWER:** Spring to summer bloom. Branched clusters of nodding or erect, pantaloon-shaped flowers to 2″ (50 mm) long. Choose from pink and white.

**HARDINESS:** Zones 4–9. Hardy. May self-seed. Protect from hot sun.

**SOIL TYPE:** High humus. High moisture, good drainage, high fertility, 5.5–6.5 pH.

**PLANTING GUIDE:** Autumn. Plant in partial shade, 12″–18″ (30–45 cm) apart, 2″ (50 mm) deep.

**CARE TIPS:** Average. Even moisture during growth. Fertilize until buds form. Apply mulch. Propagate by division in autumn, seed in spring. Store in dry peat moss, 50°–70°F (10°–21°C).

**NOTES:** Thrives in beds, borders. Nice in natural, rock gardens. Resists pests and diseases.

## *Dierama pulcherrimum* IRIDACEAE

### Wandflower (Fairy Wand)

**SHAPE:** Various erect, branched, arching, tropical, evergreen perennials to 6′ (1.8 m) tall, from corms. Fans of slender, swordlike, basal leaves to 36″ (90 cm) long.

**FLOWER:** Spring to summer bloom. Rodlike, arching stems of multiple, nodding, bell-shaped flowers to 1⅝″ (41 mm) long. Choose from pink, purple, violet, and white, often with creamy tips.

**HARDINESS:** Zones 7–11. Hardy.

**SOIL TYPE:** High humus. high moisture, good drainage, high fertility, 5.5–6.5 pH.

**PLANTING GUIDE:** Spring, as soil warms; start indoors, zones 5–8. Plant in full sun, 18″–24″ (45–60 cm) apart, 2″–3″ (50–75 mm) deep.

**CARE TIPS:** Difficult. Even moisture. Fertilize during growth. Lift in autumn. Apply mulch. Propagate by division. Store in sawdust at 50°F (10°C).

**NOTES:** Thrives in borders, foregrounds. Nice in tropical gardens and ponds. Resists pests and diseases.

## *Epipactis gigantea* ORCHIDACEAE

### Giant Helleborine (Stream Orchid, Chatterbox)

**SHAPE:** Few erect, rhizomatous perennials to 36″ (90 cm) tall. Oval or lancelike leaves to 8″ (20 cm) long.

**FLOWER:** Summer bloom. Spikes of multiple dangling, irregular, orchidlike flowers to 1″ (25 mm) long, with surrounding bracts. Choose from green, pink, and rose with purple veins.

**HARDINESS:** Zones 4–10. Hardy. Protect from sun.

**SOIL TYPE:** High humus; pond shorelines. High moisture, good drainage, high fertility, 6.0–6.5 pH.

**PLANTING GUIDE:** Spring. Plant in full sun, 24″–36″ (60–90 cm) apart, 4″–6″ (10–15 cm) deep. Plant in pots; sink in soil.

**CARE TIPS:** Average. Even moisture. Fertilize until buds form. Apply mulch. Propagate by cuttings, division, seed. Store in-ground year-round.

**NOTES:** Thrives in accents, borders. Nice in natural, rock gardens and ponds. Resists insect pests. Susceptible to slugs, snails, fungal diseases.

## *Eranthis hyemalis* RANUNCULACEAE

### Winter Aconite

**SHAPE:** Various low, tuberous perennials, 2″–6″ (50–150 mm) tall. Radiating, saucerlike clusters of narrow, divided, lobate leaves to 3″ (75 mm) long.

**FLOWER:** Winter to early-spring bloom. Terminal, cup-shaped, waxy flowers to 1½″ (38 mm) wide with collarlike bracts. Yellow.

**HARDINESS:** Zones 4–8. Hardy.

**SOIL TYPE:** High humus. High moisture, good drainage, high–medium fertility, 6.0–6.5 pH.

**PLANTING GUIDE:** Early autumn. Plant in full sun to partial shade, 3″ (75 mm) apart, 2″ (50 mm) deep.

**CARE TIPS:** Easy. Even moisture. Fertilize during growth; limit thereafter. Apply mulch. Propagate by division, seed. Store in damp peat moss, 40°–50°F (4°–10°C).

**NOTES:** Thrives in borders, containers, edgings, mixed plantings. Nice in natural, rock, shade, woodland gardens. Naturalizes. Resists deer, rodents, insect pests, diseases.

## *Erythronium* spp. LILIACEAE

### Dog-Tooth Violet (Trout Lily)

**SHAPE:** About 25 perennials, 4″–24″ (10–60 cm) tall, from corms. Pairs of opposite, tongue-shaped, prostrate, basal leaves.

**FLOWER:** Spring bloom. Usually clustered, nodding, star-shaped, reflexed flowers to 2″ (50 mm) wide. Choose from pink, purple, rose, white, and yellow.

**HARDINESS:** Zones 4–9. Hardy. May self-seed.

**SOIL TYPE:** Sandy loam. High moisture, good drainage, high fertility, 5.0–6.5 pH.

**PLANTING GUIDE:** Early autumn, zones 7–9; spring, zones 4–6. Plant in open to partial shade, 6″–8″ (15–20 cm) apart, 3″–4″ (75–100 mm) deep.

**CARE TIPS:** Average to difficult. Even moisture. Fertilize during growth. Apply mulch. Propagate by division, seed. Leave bulbs undisturbed in garden soil unless crowded. Store in damp peat moss, 50°–60°F (10°–16°C).

**NOTES:** Thrives in beds, borders, drifts, edges, mixed plantings. Nice in rock, shade, woodland gardens. Naturalizes. Resists pests and diseases.

## *Eucomis* spp. LILIACEAE

### Pineapple Lily

**SHAPE:** About 15 bunching bulbous perennials, 12″–30″ (30–75 cm) tall. Straplike, green leaves, often speckled and with ruffled edges.

**FLOWER:** Summer bloom. Spiking stalks with vertical tiers of star-shaped, often aromatic flowers, ½″–1¼″ (12–32 mm) long, with pineapple-like bracts. Choose from green, white and yellow.

**HARDINESS:** Zones 6–11. Hardy. Protect from hot sun.

**SOIL TYPE:** High humus. High moisture, good drainage, high fertility, 6.0–6.5 pH.

**PLANTING GUIDE:** Spring. Plant in partial shade, 6″–8″ (15–20 cm) apart, slightly below soil level.

**CARE TIPS:** Easy. Even moisture. Fertilize during growth. Apply mulch. Propagate by offsets, seed. Divide if crowded. Store in dry peat moss, 55°–65°F (13°–18°C).

**NOTES:** Thrives in beds, containers. Nice in shade, woodland gardens. Cutting flower. Resists insect pests and diseases. Susceptible to deer, rodents.

## *Freesia* spp. and hybrids IRIDACEAE

### Freesia

**SHAPE:** About 19 branched or bunched perennials to 18″ (45 cm) tall, from corms. Grasslike, veined leaves to 12″ (30 cm) long.

**FLOWER:** Spring bloom, zones 8–10; summer, zones 4–8. Flared, single or double, flutelike, aromatic flowers to 2″ (50 mm) long. Choose from blue, orange, pink, purple, red, white, and yellow.

**HARDINESS:** Zones 9–10. Hardy.

**SOIL TYPE:** Sandy loam. High moisture, good drainage, high–medium fertility, 6.5–7.5 pH.

**PLANTING GUIDE:** Autumn, zones 9–10; spring, zones 4–8. Plant in full sun, 3″–4″ (75–100 mm) apart, 1″–2″ (25–50 mm) deep.

**CARE TIPS:** Average. Even moisture. Fertilize until buds form. Extend bloom by deadheading. Apply mulch. Support with stakes. Propagate by offsets, seed. Store in dry peat moss, 50°–60°F (10°–16°C).

**NOTES:** Thrives in beds, borders, containers. Nice in beds, cottage gardens. Cutting flower. Naturalizes. Resists diseases. Susceptible to aphids.

## *Fritillaria meleagris* LILIACEAE

### Fritillary (Checkered Lily)

**SHAPE:** Numerous branched or bunched, bulbous perennials to 16″ (40 cm) tall. Few radiating, narrow, grasslike leaves.

**FLOWER:** Spring bloom. Spiking clusters of multiple nodding, bell-shaped, aromatic flowers, 2″–2½″ (50–63 mm) long. Choose from brown, pink, purple, violet, and white with variegated patterns.

**HARDINESS:** Zones 4–7. Hardy. Protect from hot sun.

**SOIL TYPE:** Sandy loam. High moisture, good drainage, medium fertility, 6.0–7.5 pH.

**PLANTING GUIDE:** Autumn, zones 4–9; spring, zones 2–3. Plant in full sun to partial shade, 6″–8″ (15–20 cm) apart, 4″–8″ (10–20 cm) deep.

**CARE TIPS:** Easy to average. Even moisture. Fertilize during growth. Apply mulch, zones 8–9. Propagate by offsets. Leave undisturbed. Store in dry peat moss, 40°–50°F (4°–10°C).

**NOTES:** Thrives in accents. Nice in woodland gardens. Resists deer, rodents, insect pests, diseases.

## *Galanthus* spp. AMARYLLIDACEAE

### Snowdrop

**SHAPE:** More than 15 low, bunched, bulbous perennials, 6″–12″ (15–30 cm) tall. Slender, straplike basal leaves to 10″ (25 cm) long.

**FLOWER:** Late-winter to early-spring bloom. Lone, nodding, circular, single, parasol-shaped flowers 1″–2″ (25–50 mm) wide. White.

**HARDINESS:** Zones 4–7. Hardy.

**SOIL TYPE:** High humus. High moisture, good drainage, high–medium fertility, 6.0–6.5 pH.

**PLANTING GUIDE:** Autumn. Plant in filtered sun to partial shade, 4″–6″ (10–15 cm) apart, 3″–4″ (75–100 mm) deep.

**CARE TIPS:** Easy. Even moisture. Fertilize during growth. Apply mulch. Propagate by division immediately after bloom. Store in dry peat moss, 40°–50°F (4°–10°C).

**NOTES:** Thrives in beds, borders, containers, edgings, mixed plantings, turfgrass. Nice in meadow, rock, woodland gardens. Naturalizes. Resists deer, rodents, insect pests, diseases.

## *Galtonia candicans* LILIACEAE

### Summer Hyacinth

**SHAPE:** Few bunched, bulbous perennials, 24″–48″ (60–120 cm) tall and to 10″ (25 cm) wide. Slender, straplike basal leaves, 24″–36″ (60–90 cm) long.

**FLOWER:** Late-summer to autumn bloom. Stalks with ascending vertical tiers of nodding, bell-shaped, aromatic flowers to 1½″ (38 mm) long. Choose from greenish white and white.

**HARDINESS:** Zones 7–10. Hardy.

**SOIL TYPE:** High humus. High moisture, good drainage, high–medium fertility, 5.5–6.5 pH.

**PLANTING GUIDE:** Autumn. Plant in full sun to partial shade, 8″–12″ (20–30 cm) apart, 6″ (15 cm) deep.

**CARE TIPS:** Average. Even moisture. Fertilize during growth. Mulch, zones 7–8. Propagate by offsets, seed. Store in sawdust, 50°–60°F (10°–16°C).

**NOTES:** Thrives in beds, containers. Nice in natural, woodland gardens. Cutting flower. Resists deer, rodents, insect pests. Susceptible to slugs, snails.

## *Gladiolus* spp. and hybrids IRIDACEAE

### Gladiolus (Corn Flag, Sword Lily)

**SHAPE:** About 300 erect perennials, 12″–72″ (30–180 cm) tall, from corms. Swordlike, veined leaves to 6′ (1.8 m) long.

**FLOWER:** Spring bloom, zones 7–11; summer, zones 3–6. One-sided spikes with tiers of tubular, flared, aromatic flowers, 1″–8″ (25–200 mm) wide. Choose from orange, pink, purple, red, white, yellow, multicolored, and striped.

**HARDINESS:** Most, zones 9–11; some, zones 7–11.

**SOIL TYPE:** Sandy loam. High moisture, good drainage, high–medium fertility, 6.0–6.5 pH.

**PLANTING GUIDE:** Spring to early summer, zones 3–8; year-round, zones 9–11. Plant in full sun, 4″–6″ (10–15 cm) apart, 4″–6″ (10–15 cm) deep.

**CARE TIPS:** Easy. Even moisture. Fertilize during growth. Apply mulch. Propagate by cormels, seed. Store in dry peat moss, 50°–60°F (10°–16°C).

**NOTES:** Thrives in beds, containers. Nice in cottage gardens. Cutting flower. Resists diseases. Susceptible to deer, rodents, thrips.

## *Gloriosa superba* LILIACEAE

### Gloriosa Lily (Climbing Lily)

**SHAPE:** Lone sprawling or vining, tuberous perennial vine to 8′ (2.4 m) tall. Opposite or whorled, oval or lancelike leaves, 5″–7″ (13–18 cm) long.

**FLOWER:** Spring to autumn bloom. Shooting-star-shaped flowers, 2″–3″ (50–75 mm) long, with frilly, reflexed petals. Choose from orange, red, and yellow, often with green, red, white, yellow edges and tips.

**HARDINESS:** Zones 9–11.

**SOIL TYPE:** High humus. High moisture, good drainage, high fertility, 6.0–6.5 pH.

**PLANTING GUIDE:** Late spring to summer. Plant in full sun, 12″–24″ (30–60 cm) apart, 2″ (50 mm) deep. Plant in pots; sink in soil.

**CARE TIPS:** Average. Even moisture. Fertilize during growth. Support with stakes. Propagate by division, offsets. Store in sawdust, 60°F (16°C).

**NOTES:** Thrives in containers, trellises. Nice in tropical gardens. Cutting flower. Resists insect pests and diseases. Susceptible to deer, rodents.

## *Hippeastrum* spp. and hybrids AMARYLLIDACEAE

### Florist's Amaryllis

**SHAPE:** About 80 deciduous or evergreen, bulbous perennials, 8″–24″ (20–60 cm) tall. Opposite, straplike, arched basal leaves to 20″ (50 cm) long.

**FLOWER:** Spring to summer bloom. Fleshy stalks with opposite, flared, aromatic flowers, 5″–10″ (13–25 cm) wide. Choose from orange, pink, red, and white.

**HARDINESS:** Zones 9–10.

**SOIL TYPE:** Loam. High moisture, good drainage, high fertility, 6.0–6.5 pH.

**PLANTING GUIDE:** Autumn to winter. Plant in full sun, 12″–24″ (30–60 cm) apart, slightly above soil level; in pots, one to a container.

**CARE TIPS:** Easy. Even moisture. Fertilize during growth. Extend bloom by deadheading. Apply mulch. Propagate by offsets, seed. Lift and cure. Store in sawdust, 50°–60°F (10°–16°C).

**NOTES:** Thrives in beds, containers. Nice in tropical gardens. Cutting flower. Resists insect pests and diseases. Susceptible to deer, rodents.

## *Hyacinthoides* spp. (*Endymion* spp., *Scilla* spp.) LILIACEAE

### Wood Hyacinth (English Bluebell, Spanish Bluebell)

**SHAPE:** Few bulbous perennials to 20″ (50 cm) tall. Slender, straplike, arched basal leaves to 24″ (60 cm) long.

**FLOWER:** Spring bloom. Lone stalks with vertical tiers of multiple, bell-shaped, aromatic flowers, ¾″ (19 mm) long. Choose from blue, pink, rose, and white.

**HARDINESS:** Zones 5–9. Hardy.

**SOIL TYPE:** High humus. High–average moisture, good drainage, high fertility, 6.0–7.0 pH.

**PLANTING GUIDE:** Autumn. Plant in full sun to partial shade, 4″–6″ (10–15 cm) apart, 3″–6″ (75–150 mm) deep.

**CARE TIPS:** Average. Even moisture. Fertilize during growth, limit water thereafter. Apply mulch, zones 5–7. Propagate by division, offsets. Store in sawdust, 40°–50°F (4°–10°C).

**NOTES:** Thrives in drifts. Nice in cottage, woodland gardens. Cutting flower. Naturalizes. Resists deer, rodents, insect pests, diseases.

## *Hyacinthus orientalis* LILIACEAE

### Hyacinth (Garden Hyacinth)

**SHAPE:** Three bulbous perennials to 12″ (30 cm) tall. Slender, straplike, wavy-edged basal leaves to 12″ (30 cm) long.

**FLOWER:** Spring bloom. Cone-shaped plumes of flared, trumpet-shaped, aromatic flowers to 1″ (25 mm) wide. Choose from apricot, blue, orange, pink, purple, red, white, and yellow.

**HARDINESS:** Zones 5–9. Hardy. Protect from sun.

**SOIL TYPE:** Sandy loam. High moisture, good drainage, high fertility, 5.0–6.5 pH.

**PLANTING GUIDE:** Autumn. Plant in full sun to partial shade, to 8″ (20 cm) apart, 5″–8″ (13–20 cm) deep.

**CARE TIPS:** Easy. Even moisture. Fertilize during growth. Apply mulch. Lift after bloom, zones 8–11. Propagate by offsets. Store in dry peat moss, 40°–50°F (4°–10°C).

**NOTES:** Thrives in beds, borders, containers. Nice in cottage, woodland gardens. Naturalizes. Resists deer, rodents, insect pests, diseases.

## *Hymenocallis* spp. AMARYLLIDACEAE

### Spider Lily (Crown-Beauty, Sea Daffodil)

**SHAPE:** More than 30 bulbous perennials, 10″–36″ (25–90 cm) tall. Usually slender, straplike basal leaves, 24″ (60 cm) long.

**FLOWER:** Summer bloom. Fleshy stalks of elegant, tubular, trumpet-like, aromatic flowers to 6″ (15 cm) wide with a radiating rosette of slim petal tendrils. Choose from ivory and white.

**HARDINESS:** Zones 8–10. Hardy.

**SOIL TYPE:** Sandy loam. High moisture, good drainage, high–medium fertility, 6.0–6.5 pH.

**PLANTING GUIDE:** Spring. Plant in full sun, 6″–18″ (15–45 cm) apart, slightly above soil level.

**CARE TIPS:** Easy. Even moisture. Fertilize during growth. Apply mulch, zones 6–8. Shelter from wind. Propagate by division, offsets, seed. Store in dry peat moss, 60°–70°F (16°–21°C).

**NOTES:** Thrives in accents, beds, borders, containers. Nice in small-space, tropical, water gardens. Cutting flower. Resists deer, rodents, insect pests, diseases.

## *Ipheion uniflorum* (*Brodiaea uniflora*, *Triteleia uniflora*) LILIACEAE

### Spring Starflower (Star Grass)

**SHAPE:** Few aromatic herbaceous, bulbous perennials, 6″–8″ (15–20 cm) tall. Fans of smooth, flat, slender, straplike, thin basal leaves to 8″ (15 cm) long.

**FLOWER:** Early-spring bloom. Terminal, single, star-shaped, often aromatic flowers to 1½″ (38 mm) wide. Choose from blue, white, and variegated.

**HARDINESS:** Zones 6–9. Hardy.

**SOIL TYPE:** Sandy loam. High moisture, good drainage, medium fertility, 6.0–7.0 pH.

**PLANTING GUIDE:** Autumn. Plant in full sun to partial shade, 4″ (10 cm) apart, 2″ (50 mm) deep.

**CARE TIPS:** Easy. Even moisture in winter. Fertilize during growth. Propagate by division, offsets. Divide if crowded. Store in dry peat moss, 40°–50°F (4°–10°C).

**NOTES:** Thrives in borders, containers, drifts, edgings, massed plantings. Nice in meadow, natural, rock, woodland gardens. Naturalizes. Resists deer, rodents, insect pests, diseases.

## *Iris reticulata* IRIDACEAE

### Reticulated Iris (Netted Iris)

**SHAPE:** Various vertical, bulbous perennials to 18″ (45 cm) tall. Flat, slender, straplike leaves to 6″ (15 cm) long, after blooms.

**FLOWER:** Early-spring bloom. Irregular, fragrant flowers to 3″ (75 mm) wide with erect standards and oval falls. Choose from blue, lavender, purple, and white with orange, yellow markings.

**HARDINESS:** Zones 3–8. Hardy.

**SOIL TYPE:** High humus. High moisture, good drainage, high–medium fertility, 6.5–7.5 pH.

**PLANTING GUIDE:** Autumn. Plant in full sun, 2″–3″ (50–75 mm) apart, 2″–3″ (50–75 mm) deep.

**CARE TIPS:** Easy. Even moisture. Fertilize during growth; limit thereafter. Propagate by division, seed. Divide if crowded. Store in dry peat moss, 40°–50°F (4°–10°C).

**NOTES:** Thrives in borders, containers, drifts, edgings, ground covers. Nice in natural, rock, woodland gardens. Resists insect pests and diseases. Susceptible to snails, slugs.

## *Ixia* spp. and hybrids IRIDACEAE

### Corn Lily

**SHAPE:** About 30 bunching perennials, 6″–36″ (15–90 cm) tall, from corms. Grasslike, sword-like basal leaves to 20″ (50 cm) long.

**FLOWER:** Late-spring to summer bloom. Clusters of open, 6-petaled, often aromatic flowers, ½″–1½″ (12–38 mm) wide. Choose from orange, pink, red, white, and yellow with contrasting dark centers.

**HARDINESS:** Zones 7–9. Hardy.

**SOIL TYPE:** Sandy loam. High moisture, good drainage, medium fertility, 6.5–7.0 pH.

**PLANTING GUIDE:** Autumn, zones 9–10; spring, zones 4–8. Plant in full sun, 3″–4″ (75–100 mm) apart, 2″–3″ (50–75 mm) deep.

**CARE TIPS:** Easy. Even moisture. Fertilize during growth. Mulch, zones 7–8. Propagate by cormels, seed. Store in dry soil, 50°–60°F (10°–16°C).

**NOTES:** Thrives in beds, containers, drifts. Nice in cottage, small-space gardens. Cutting flower. Naturalizes. Resists pests and diseases.

## Lachenalia spp. LILIACEAE

### Cape Cowslip (Leopard Lily)

**SHAPE:** About 90 sprawling, herbaceous, bulbous perennials, 6″–16″ (15–40 cm) tall. Pairs of slender, straplike, spotted basal leaves, 4″–8″ (10–20 cm) long.

**FLOWER:** Late-winter to spring bloom. Tiers of nodding, tubular flowers to 1½″ (38 mm) long. Choose from blue, pink, red, white, and yellow.

**HARDINESS:** Zones 9–10. Hardy. Protect from frost, hot sun.

**SOIL TYPE:** Sandy loam. High moisture, good drainage, high fertility, 6.0–6.5 pH.

**PLANTING GUIDE:** Autumn, zones 9–10; spring, zone 8. Plant in full sun, 4″–6″ (10–15 cm) apart, 2″–3″ (50–75 mm) deep.

**CARE TIPS:** Easy. Even moisture. Fertilize during growth. Propagate by bulbils, seed. Store in sawdust, 50°–60°F (10°–16°C).

**NOTES:** Thrives in beds, borders, containers. Nice in rock gardens. Cutting flower. Resists insect pests and diseases. Susceptible to slugs, snails.

## Leucojum spp. AMARYLLIDACEAE

### Snowflake

**SHAPE:** About 9 bunching, herbaceous, bulbous perennials to 16″ (40 cm) tall. Slim, strap- or threadlike basal leaves, 9″–18″ (23–45 cm) long.

**FLOWER:** Spring or autumn bloom. Loose clusters of nodding, bell-shaped flowers, ½″–1″ (12–25 mm) long. White with green, red, and yellow tints and spring green highlights.

**HARDINESS:** Zones 4–9.

**SOIL TYPE:** High humus. High–average moisture, good drainage, medium fertility, 6.0–6.5 pH.

**PLANTING GUIDE:** Autumn. Plant in full sun, 4″ (10 cm) apart, 4″ (10 cm) deep, or as recommended.

**CARE TIPS:** Easy. Even moisture. Fertilize during growth; limit water thereafter. Apply mulch. Propagate by bulblets, division. Leave undisturbed. Store in sawdust, 40°–60°F (4°–16°C).

**NOTES:** Thrives in beds, borders. Nice in natural, woodland gardens and ponds. Naturalizes. Resists deer, rodents, insect pests, diseases.

## Liatris spp. ASTERACEAE (COMPOSITAE)

### Blazing-Star (Gay-Feather)

**SHAPE:** Various erect herbaceous perennials to 5′ (1.5 m) tall, from corms or rhizomes. Columnar spikes with vertical tiers of alternate, needlelike leaves to 6″ (15 cm) long.

**FLOWER:** Late-summer to autumn bloom. Stalks with plumelike clusters to 12″ (30 cm) long of threadlike bracts. Choose from purple and white.

**HARDINESS:** Zones 4–9. Hardy.

**SOIL TYPE:** Sandy loam. High moisture, good drainage, medium fertility, 6.0–7.5 pH.

**PLANTING GUIDE:** Spring. Plant in full sun, 6″–8″ (15–20 cm) apart, 1″ (25 mm) deep.

**CARE TIPS:** Easy. Even moisture. Fertilize during growth. Extend bloom by deadheading. Apply mulch, zones 3–4. Support with stakes. Propagate by cormels, division, seed. Store in damp peat moss, 50°–60°F (10°–16°C).

**NOTES:** Thrives in beds, mixed plantings. Nice in meadow, wildlife gardens. Resists deer, rodents, insect pests, diseases.

## Lilium spp. and hybrids LILIACEAE

### Lily

**SHAPE:** Numerous herbaceous, bulbous perennials, 24″–72″ (60–180 cm) tall. Alternate, lancelike, ribbed leaves to 8″ (20 cm) long.

**FLOWER:** Summer bloom. Trumpet- or star-shaped, aromatic flowers, 4″–10″ (10–25 cm) wide, with prominent stamens and reflexed petals. Choose from orange, purple, red, white, and yellow.

**HARDINESS:** Zones 2–10. Hardy.

**SOIL TYPE:** Sandy loam. High moisture, good drainage, high fertility, 6.0–6.5 pH.

**PLANTING GUIDE:** Autumn or early spring. Plant in full sun to partial shade, 6″–12″ (15–30 cm) apart, 6″–12″ (15–30 cm) deep.

**CARE TIPS:** Easy. Even moisture; avoid wetting foliage. Fertilize during growth. Extend bloom by deadheading. Mulch in summer. Propagate by bulbils, offsets. Store in sawdust, 40°F (4°C).

**NOTES:** Thrives in accents, containers. Nice in cottage gardens. Cutting flower. Naturalizes. Susceptible to deer, rodents, beetles, leaf fungus, mosaic virus.

## *Liriope muscari* LILIACEAE

### Big Blue Lilyturf

**SHAPE:** Several bunching, tuberous, evergreen perennials, 18″–24″ (45–60 cm) tall and wide. Straplike leaves to 24″ (60 cm) long.

**FLOWER:** Late-summer to early-autumn bloom. Spiking stalks with whorled, tufted clusters to 10″ (25 cm) long of tiny, grape hyacinth-like flowers. Choose from purple, violet, and white.

**HARDINESS:** Zones 6–11.

**SOIL TYPE:** High humus; pond shorelines. High moisture, good drainage, medium fertility, 6.5–7.0 pH.

**PLANTING GUIDE:** Spring. Plant in filtered sun to full shade, 8″–12″ (20–30 cm) apart.

**CARE TIPS:** Easy. Even moisture. Fertilize during growth. Extend bloom by deadheading. Propagate by division. Store in damp sawdust, 50°F (10°C).

**NOTES:** Thrives in banks, borders, edgings. Nice in cottage, shade, small-space gardens or ponds. Cutting flower. Resists insect pests, diseases. Susceptible to slugs, snails.

## *Mirabilis jalapa* NYCTAGINACEAE

### Four-O'Clock (Marvel-of-Peru)

**SHAPE:** Various branched, tropical, bulbous, tuberous perennials to 36″ (90 cm) tall. Alternate, smooth, lancelike, wavy-edged leaves, 2″–5″ (50–125 mm) long.

**FLOWER:** Late-summer bloom. Flute-shaped, wavy-fringed, aromatic flowers to 2″ (50 mm) wide. Choose from pink, red, white, yellow, and variegated.

**HARDINESS:** Zones 8–11.

**SOIL TYPE:** Sandy loam. Average–low moisture, good drainage, high–medium fertility, 6.5–7.0 pH.

**PLANTING GUIDE:** Spring. Plant in full sun to partial shade, after soil warms, 12″–24″ (30–60 cm) apart, 2″–3″ (50–75 mm) deep.

**CARE TIPS:** Easy. Even moisture. Fertilize during growth. Propagate by cuttings, dividing tubers. Store in dry peat moss, 50°–60°F (10°–16°C).

**NOTES:** Thrives in accents, beds, borders, edgings, hedges. Nice in small-space, wildlife gardens and ponds. Resists pests, diseases, smog.

## *Muscari* spp. LILIACEAE

### Grape Hyacinth

**SHAPE:** About 40 bulbous perennials, 4″–12″ (10–30 cm) tall. Slim, grass- or straplike, basal leaves, 3″–10″ (75–255 mm) long.

**FLOWER:** Early-spring bloom. Wiry stalk with cone-shaped vertical tiers of multiple tube-shaped, aromatic flowers to ¼″ (6 mm) long. Choose from blue, purple, and white.

**HARDINESS:** Zones 3–9. Hardy.

**SOIL TYPE:** Sandy loam. High moisture, good drainage, medium fertility, 6.0–7.0 pH.

**PLANTING GUIDE:** Autumn. Plant in full sun to partial shade, 4″–6″ (10–15 cm) apart, 3″ (75 mm) deep.

**CARE TIPS:** Easy. Even moisture. Fertilize during growth, limit thereafter. Apply mulch. Propagate by offsets, seed. Store in sawdust, 40°–50°F (4°–10°C).

**NOTES:** Thrives in beds, borders, containers, edges, massed plantings. Nice in meadow, rock, woodland gardens. Cutting flower. Naturalizes. Resists deer, rodents, insect pests, diseases.

## *Narcissus* spp. AMARYLLIDACEAE

### Daffodil

**SHAPE:** About 26 erect, herbaceous, bulbous perennials, 4″–24″ (10–60 cm) tall. Slender, flat, straplike leaves, 3″–20″ (75–510 mm) long.

**FLOWER:** Late-winter to early-spring bloom. Lone or clustered, single or double, trumpet-shaped flowers, ½″–2″ (12–50 mm) wide, with smooth to ruffled cups. Choose from orange, peach, pink, red, white, yellow, and bicolored.

**HARDINESS:** Zones 4–9. Hardy.

**SOIL TYPE:** Sandy loam. High–average moisture, good drainage, high–medium fertility, 5.5–6.5 pH.

**PLANTING GUIDE:** Autumn. Plant in full sun to partial shade, 5″ (13 cm) apart, 5″–8″ (13–20 cm) deep.

**CARE TIPS:** Easy. Even moisture. Fertilize during growth. Propagate by division, offsets. Store in dry peat moss, 40°–50°F (4°–10°C).

**NOTES:** Thrives in beds, borders, containers, drifts, slopes. Nice in cottage, shade, woodland gardens. Cutting flower. Naturalizes. Resists deer, rodents, diseases. Susceptible to narcissus-bulb fly larvae.

## *Nerine* spp. AMARYLLIDACEAE

### Nerine (Guernsey Lily)

**SHAPE:** About 30 deciduous or semi-evergreen, herbaceous bulbous perennials to 36″ (90 cm) tall. Straplike basal leaves to 12″ (30 cm) long. Foliage withers before bloom.

**FLOWER:** Autumn bloom. Clusters of multiple, flared flowers, 2″–3″ (50–75 mm) wide. Choose from pink, red, and white. Long-lasting flowers.

**HARDINESS:** Zones 8–11. Hardy.

**SOIL TYPE:** Sandy loam. High moisture, good drainage, medium fertility, 6.0–7.0 pH.

**PLANTING GUIDE:** Late summer to autumn. Plant in full sun, 10″–12″ (25–30 cm) apart, at soil level.

**CARE TIPS:** Easy. Even moisture. Fertilize during growth; limit thereafter. Apply mulch. Propagate by offsets. Leave undisturbed. Store in dry peat moss, 50°–60°F (10°–16°C).

**NOTES:** Thrives in accents, backgrounds, beds, containers. Nice in cottage, small-space gardens. Cutting flower. Resists deer, rodents, insect pests, diseases.

## ORCHIDACEAE

### Orchid Family

**SHAPE:** Largest plant family. Varied deciduous or evergreen perennials, 4″–42″ (10–107 cm) tall or long. Mostly opposite, shiny or smooth, sword-shaped leaves, 3″–24″ (75–610 mm) long.

**FLOWER:** Year-round, summer, or autumn bloom. Showy to inconspicuous, irregular, often hirsute, lipped or lobate, deep-throated flowers, ¼″–6″ (6–150 mm) wide. Choose from most colors.

**HARDINESS:** Zones 3–11, depending on species.

**SOIL TYPE:** Bark chips or high humus; pond shorelines. High–average moisture, good drainage, high–low fertility, 6.0–7.0 pH.

**PLANTING GUIDE:** Autumn. Plant in partial to full shade, 12″–48″ (30–120 cm) apart.

**CARE TIPS:** Easy to average. Even moisture; limit water in semi-dormancy. Fertilize every 2 weeks. Propagate by division, seed. Store in damp peat moss, 50°–60°F (10°–16°C).

**NOTES:** Uses vary. Nice in tropical gardens or ponds. Susceptible to slugs, snails, fungal diseases.

## *Ornithogalum* spp. LILIACEAE

### Star-of-Bethlehem (Chincherinchee)

**SHAPE:** About 100 bulbous perennials, 12″–36″ (30–90 cm) tall. Shiny, straplike, arched basal leaves, 8″–20″ (20–50 cm) long.

**FLOWER:** Spring or summer bloom. Stalks with alternate, ascending vertical tiers of multiple, 6-petaled, star-shaped, often aromatic flowers, 2″–5″ (50–125 mm) wide. Choose from orange, green white, white, and yellow.

**HARDINESS:** Zones 4–10. Hardy.

**SOIL TYPE:** Sandy loam. High moisture, good drainage, high fertility, 6.0–7.0 pH.

**PLANTING GUIDE:** Autumn. Plant in full sun to partial shade, 6″–8″ (15–20 cm) apart, 3″–5″ (75–125 mm) deep.

**CARE TIPS:** Easy. Even moisture. Fertilize during growth. Mulch, zones 4–8. Propagate by offsets, seed. Store in sawdust, 50°–60°F (10°–16°C).

**NOTES:** Thrives in beds, borders, containers. Nice in woodland gardens. Cutting flower. Naturalizes. Resists deer, rodents, insect pests, diseases.

## *Oxalis* spp. OXALIDACEAE

### Wood Sorrel

**SHAPE:** Numerous bulbous, tuberous, or rhizomatous perennials, 4″–20″ (10–50 cm) tall. Cloverlike leaves to 1″ (25 mm) long.

**FLOWER:** Winter to summer bloom. Lone or multiple open or funnel-shaped flowers to 1″ (25 mm) wide. Choose from pink, rose, white, and yellow, often with contrasting centers.

**HARDINESS:** Zones 5–9. Hardy.

**SOIL TYPE:** High humus. High moisture, good drainage, high–medium fertility, 6.5–7.5 pH.

**PLANTING GUIDE:** Late summer to autumn. Plant in full sun to partial shade, 2″ (50 mm) apart, 1″–4″ (25–100 mm) deep.

**CARE TIPS:** Easy. Even moisture during growth. Fertilize only when planting. Apply mulch, zones 6–8. Propagate by division, offsets, seed in autumn. Store in sawdust, 50°–60°F (10°–16°C).

**NOTES:** Thrives in containers, ground covers. Nice in small-space, woodland gardens. Aggressive. Resists deer, rodents, insect pests, diseases.

## *Puschkinia scilloides* LILIACEAE

### Striped Squill

**SHAPE:** Few thick-growing, herbaceous, bulbous perennials to 6″ (15 cm) tall. Slender, straplike basal leaves to 6″ (15 cm) long.

**FLOWER:** Late-winter to spring bloom. Stalks with circular clusters of nodding, partly flared, star-shaped flowers, ½″ (12 mm) long. Choose from blue-white and white.

**HARDINESS:** Zones 4–8. Hardy. Protect from hot sun.

**SOIL TYPE:** Sandy loam. High moisture, good drainage, medium fertility, 6.0–7.5 pH.

**PLANTING GUIDE:** Autumn. Plant in partial shade, 2″–3″ (50–75 mm) apart, 2″–4″ (50–100 mm) deep.

**CARE TIPS:** Easy. Even moisture. Fertilize during growth, limit thereafter. Apply mulch. Propagate by offsets. Store in sawdust, 40°F (4°C).

**NOTES:** Thrives in borders, containers, drifts, edgings. Nice in meadow, natural gardens. Naturalizes. Resists deer, rodents, insect pests, diseases.

## *Ranunculus* spp. RANUNCULACEAE

### Buttercup (Crowfoot)

**SHAPE:** Numerous varied perennials to 36″ (90 cm) tall, from tubers or fibrous roots. Alternate, oval leaves to 6″ (15 cm) wide. See also *R. asiaticus*, Persian buttercup.

**FLOWER:** Spring to summer bloom. Circular, single, cup-shaped, erect flowers to ¾″ (19 mm) wide. Choose from orange, white, and yellow.

**HARDINESS:** Zones 3–9. Hardy.

**SOIL TYPE:** Loam; pond shorelines. High moisture, good drainage, medium fertility, 6.0–7.0 pH.

**PLANTING GUIDE:** Spring, zones 3–7; autumn, zones 8–9. Plant in partial to full shade at recommended spacing for cultivar. Soak before planting.

**CARE TIPS:** Easy. Even moisture. Fertilize during growth. Apply mulch, zones 4–8. Propagate by division. Store in sawdust, 50°–60°F (10°–16°C).

**NOTES:** Thrives in beds, drifts, ground covers. Nice in rock, shade gardens and ponds. Cutting flower. Resists deer, rodents, insect pests. Susceptible to slugs, snails.

## *Ranunculus asiaticus* and hybrids RANUNCULACEAE

### Persian Buttercup (Florist's Ranunculus)

**SHAPE:** Various erect, branched, tuberous perennials, 18″ (45 cm) tall. Plumelike, divided, toothed, leaves to 3″ (75 mm) wide.

**FLOWER:** Early-spring to summer bloom. Stems of terminal, circular, single or double, peony-like flowers, 1½″ (38 mm) wide. Choose from orange, pink, purple, red, white, and yellow.

**HARDINESS:** Zones 7–11.

**SOIL TYPE:** Sandy loam. High moisture, good drainage, medium–low fertility, 5.5–6.0 pH.

**PLANTING GUIDE:** Autumn, zones 9–11; spring, zones 7–8. Plant in full to filtered sun, 4″–6″ (10–15 cm) apart, 1″–2″ (25–50 mm) deep. Soak tubers for 24 hours before planting.

**CARE TIPS:** Easy. Even moisture. Fertilize during growth. Apply mulch, zones 4–8. Propagate by division. Store in sawdust, 50°–60°F (10°–16°C).

**NOTES:** Thrives in borders, drifts. Nice in cottage, rock gardens. Cutting flower. Resists deer, rodents, insect pests. Susceptible to slugs, snails.

## *Scadoxus* spp. (*Haemanthus* spp.) AMARYLLIDACEAE

### Blood Lily

**SHAPE:** About 9 herbaceous, bulbous perennials, 12″–24″ (30–60 cm) tall. Sparse, wide, swordlike, wavy-edged, sharp-pointed, veined basal leaves to 12″ (30 cm) long.

**FLOWER:** Spring to summer bloom. Ball-shaped clusters to 9″ (23 cm) wide of star-shaped, brush-like flowers to 1″ (25 mm) wide and long. Choose from coral, red, and white. Forms berrylike fruit.

**HARDINESS:** Zones 9–11. Protect from frost.

**SOIL TYPE:** High humus. High moisture, good drainage, high fertility, 5.5–6.5 pH.

**PLANTING GUIDE:** Spring. Plant in full sun to partial shade, 12″ (30 cm) apart, at soil level.

**CARE TIPS:** Average. Even moisture. Fertilize during growth. Propagate by offsets. Leave undisturbed. Store in dry peat moss, 50°–60°F (10°–16°C).

**NOTES:** Thrives in beds, containers, edgings. Nice in shade, small-space, tropical gardens. Cutting flower. Susceptible to rodent, slugs, snails, mosaic virus.

## *Scilla* spp. LILIACEAE

### Squill

**SHAPE:** About 90 herbaceous, bulbous perennials, 4″–18″ (10–45 cm) tall. Erect, slender, straplike basal leaves, 3″–12″ (75–305 mm) long.

**FLOWER:** Early-spring bloom. Lone short or tall stalks with tiered clusters of multiple star-shaped flowers to 1″ (25 mm) wide. Choose from blue, pink, purple, and white.

**HARDINESS:** Zones 3–10. Hardy.

**SOIL TYPE:** High humus. High moisture, good drainage, high fertility, 6.0–7.0 pH.

**PLANTING GUIDE:** Autumn. Plant in full sun to partial shade, 4″–6″ (10–15 cm) apart, 4″ (10 cm) deep.

**CARE TIPS:** Easy. Even moisture during growth. Fertilize every 4 weeks during growth. Apply mulch. Propagate by offsets, seed. Store in dry peat moss, 40°–50°F (4°–10°C).

**NOTES:** Thrives in borders, containers, edgings, massed plantings, paths. Nice in formal, small-space, woodland gardens. Cutting flower. Naturalizes. Resists pests, diseases.

## *Sinningia speciosa* **and hybrids** *(Gloxinia speciosa)* GESNERIACEAE

### Florist's Gloxinia

**SHAPE:** Various low, tropical, tuberous perennials to 12″ (30 cm) tall. Broad, oval, fine-toothed, hirsute leaves to 8″ (20 cm) long.

**FLOWER:** Summer bloom. Stalks of lone or clustered, nodding, funnel-shaped, often ruffled flowers to 5″ (13 cm) wide. Choose from blue, orange, pink, purple, red, white, and yellow, with contrasting bands or speckles.

**HARDINESS:** Zones 10–11. Hardy.

**SOIL TYPE:** High humus. High moisture, good drainage, high fertility, 6.0–6.5 pH.

**PLANTING GUIDE:** Early summer. Plant in partial shade, 12″ (30 cm) apart, 1″ (25 mm) deep; in pots, one to a container.

**CARE TIPS:** Easy. Even moisture. Fertilize during growth. Apply mulch. Shelter from rain, wind. Propagate by cuttings, division, seed. Store in sawdust, 60°F (16°C).

**NOTES:** Thrives in containers. Nice in tropical, small-space gardens. Resists pests, diseases.

## *Sparaxis* spp. IRIDACEAE

### Wandflower (Harlequin Flower)

**SHAPE:** Few herbaceous perennials to 24″ (60 cm) tall, from corms. Swordlike, arched leaves to 12″ (30 cm) long. See also *Ixia* spp., corn lily.

**FLOWER:** Spring to early-summer bloom. Cup- or star-shaped, flared flowers to 2″ (50 mm) wide with contrasting centers. Choose from orange, pink, purple, red, white, yellow, and bicolored.

**HARDINESS:** Zones 7–10. Hardy.

**SOIL TYPE:** Sandy loam. High moisture, good drainage, medium fertility, 6.0–7.0 pH.

**PLANTING GUIDE:** Autumn, zones 9–10; spring, zones 7–8. Plant in full sun, 3″–4″ (75–100 mm) apart, 2″–4″ (50–100 mm) deep.

**CARE TIPS:** Easy. Even moisture. Fertilize during growth. Mulch, zones 4–7. Propagate by cormels, offsets, seed. Store in sawdust, 50°F (10°C).

**NOTES:** Thrives in accents, beds, borders, containers, foregrounds. Nice in cottage, heritage gardens. Cutting flower. Naturalizes. Resists insect pests, diseases. Susceptible to deer, rodents.

## *Sternbergia lutea* AMARYLLIDACEAE

### Winter Daffodil (Lily-of-the-Field)

**SHAPE:** Few herbaceous, bulbous perennials to 12″ (30 cm) tall. Slender, straplike, basal leaves to 12″ (30 cm) long.

**FLOWER:** Autumn bloom. Low stalks of terminal, freesia-like, simple, waxy flowers to 1½″ (38 mm) wide. Bright yellow. Forms berrylike seed.

**HARDINESS:** Zones 7–9. Hardy.

**SOIL TYPE:** Sandy loam. High moisture, good drainage, high–medium fertility, 6.5–7.5 pH.

**PLANTING GUIDE:** Late summer. Plant in full sun, 4″–6″ (10–15 cm) apart, 4″–6″ (10–15 cm) deep; in pots, space 2″–3″ (50–75 mm) apart.

**CARE TIPS:** Easy. Even moisture during growth; limit water thereafter. Fertilize during growth. Apply mulch, zones 6–7. Propagate by division, offsets, seed. Store in dry peat moss, 40°–50°F (4°–10°C).

**NOTES:** Thrives in accents, beds, borders, containers, edgings. Nice in meadow, natural, rock gardens. Resists deer, rodents, diseases. Susceptible to spider mites.

## *Tigridia pavonia* IRIDACEAE

### Tiger Flower (Shell Flower, One-Day Lily)

**SHAPE:** Various erect, herbaceous perennials to 36″ (90 cm) tall, from corms. Swordlike, ribbed, slender, stiff leaves to 18″ (45 cm) long.

**FLOWER:** Summer to autumn bloom. Cup-shaped or open, triangular flowers to 3″ (75 mm) wide with curved inner petals. Choose from orange, pink, purple, red, white, and yellow with contrasts.

**HARDINESS:** Zones 7–11. Protect from frost, hot sun.

**SOIL TYPE:** Sandy loam. High moisture, good drainage, medium fertility, 6.0–7.0 pH.

**PLANTING GUIDE:** Late spring, zones 7–8; autumn, zones 9–11. Plant in full sun, 4″–6″ (10–15 cm) apart, 2″–3″ (50–75 mm) deep.

**CARE TIPS:** Average. Even moisture. Fertilize during growth. Mulch, lift, zones 7–8. Propagate by offsets, seed. Store in sawdust, 50°–60°F (10°–16°C).

**NOTES:** Thrives in beds, borders, containers, mixed plantings. Nice in tropical gardens. Resists diseases, Susceptible to deer, rodents, spider mites.

## *Tritonia* spp. IRIDACEAE

### Flame Freesia

**SHAPE:** About 50 herbaceous perennials to 18″ (45 cm) tall, from corms. Fans of straplike, arched basal leaves, 4″–8″ (10–20 cm) long. Foliage withers before bloom.

**FLOWER:** Early-summer to autumn bloom. Stalks with ascending clusters of cup-shaped flowers, 1″–2″ (25–50 mm) wide. Choose from orange, pink, red, white, and yellow.

**HARDINESS:** Zones 8–10. Hardy.

**SOIL TYPE:** Sandy loam. High moisture, good drainage, high–medium fertility, 6.0–7.0 pH.

**PLANTING GUIDE:** Autumn, zones 9–10; spring, zone 8. Plant in full sun, 6″–10″ (15–25 cm) apart, 3″–4″ (75–100 mm) deep.

**CARE TIPS:** Easy. Even moisture. Fertilize during growth; limit thereafter. Apply mulch. Propagate by division. Store in sawdust, 40°F (4°C).

**NOTES:** Thrives in beds, borders, containers. Nice in tropical gardens. Cutting flower. Naturalizes. Resists diseases. Susceptible to deer, rodents.

## *Tulbaghia violacea* AMARYLLIDACEAE

### Society Garlic

**SHAPE:** Various erect, evergreen, herbaceous, bulbous or rhizomatous perennials to 30″ (75 cm) tall. Slender, swordlike, aromatic leaves to 12″ (30 cm) long.

**FLOWER:** Late-spring to summer bloom. Slender stems with clusters of flared, tube-shaped, star-flared, aromatic flowers, ¾″–1″ (19–25 mm) long. Choose from lavender and white.

**HARDINESS:** Zones 7–11. Hardy. Protect blooms from frost.

**SOIL TYPE:** Sandy loam. High–average moisture, good drainage, medium fertility, 6.5–7.5 pH.

**PLANTING GUIDE:** Spring. Plant in full sun, 12″–18″ (30–45 cm) apart, 2″ (50 mm) deep.

**CARE TIPS:** Easy. Even moisture. Fertilize during growth. Apply mulch. Propagate by division, offsets, seed. Store in sawdust, 50°–60°F (10°–16°C).

**NOTES:** Thrives in accents, beds, borders, containers, edgings. Nice in meadow gardens. Cutting flower. Resists deer, rodents, insect pests, diseases.

## *Tulipa* spp. and hybrids LILIACEAE

### Tulip

**SHAPE:** Numerous herbaceous, bulbous perennials, 5″–24″ (13–60 cm) tall. Broad to straplike basal leaves to 12″ (30 cm) long.

**FLOWER:** Spring bloom. Single or double, egg-shaped, sometimes aromatic flowers to 4″ (10 cm) wide with circular, smooth, or fringed petals. Every color but blue; also multicolored.

**HARDINESS:** Zones 4–7. Hardy.

**SOIL TYPE:** Sandy loam. High moisture, good drainage, high–medium fertility, 5.5–6.5 pH.

**PLANTING GUIDE:** Autumn to winter. Plant in full sun to partial shade, 2″–4″ (50–100 mm) apart, 5″–8″ (13–20 cm) deep.

**CARE TIPS:** Easy. Even moisture. Fertilize during growth. Mulch, zones 8–10. Propagate by offsets in late summer. Store in sawdust, 40°F (4°C).

**NOTES:** Thrives in beds, containers, massed plantings, slopes. Nice in cottage, formal, meadow gardens. Cutting flower. Naturalizes. Resists diseases. Susceptible to deer, rodents, aphids.

## *Veltheimia capensis* HYACINTHACEAE

### Cape Hyacinth

**SHAPE:** Two mounding, bulbous perennials to 12″ (60 cm) tall. Broad, straplike, arched leaves, to 12″ (30 cm) long and 2″ (50 mm) wide, in a basal rosette.

**FLOWER:** Late-autumn bloom. Dense, spiking clusters of pendent, tubular, aromatic flowers to 1½″ (38 mm) long. Choose from apricot, pink, and rose with green and yellow tips.

**HARDINESS:** Zones 8–11. Protect from frost.

**SOIL TYPE:** Sandy loam. Average moisture, good drainage, high–medium fertility, 5.5–6.5 pH.

**PLANTING GUIDE:** Autumn. Plant in full sun, 8″ (20 cm) apart, with bulb partially exposed.

**CARE TIPS:** Easy. Even moisture during growth; limit in summer. Fertilize every 3–4 weeks. Mulch. Propagate by offsets, seed. Store in dry peat moss, 40°F (4°C).

**NOTES:** Thrives in accents, beds, containers. Nice in cottage, Xeriscape gardens. Resists diseases. Susceptible to slugs, snails.

## *Watsonia* spp. IRIDACEAE

### Watsonia (Bugle Lily)

**SHAPE:** About 60 erect, bunching, gladiolus-like, deciduous or evergreen perennials, 24″–72″ (60–180 cm) tall, from corms. Slender, swordlike, rigid leaves, 24″–32″ (60–80 cm) long.

**FLOWER:** Summer bloom. Spikes of alternate, tubular, flared, flute-shaped, aromatic flowers, 2½″–3″ (63–75 mm) wide. Choose from apricot, pink, red, rose, and white.

**HARDINESS:** Zones 7–11. Hardy. Protect from frost.

**SOIL TYPE:** Loam. High moisture, good drainage, high–medium fertility, 5.5–6.5 pH.

**PLANTING GUIDE:** Spring, zones 7–8; autumn, zones 9–11. Plant in full sun, 6″ (15 cm) apart, 4″ (10 cm) deep.

**CARE TIPS:** Easy. Even moisture. Fertilize every 6–8 weeks. Mulch. Propagate by division, offsets, seed. Store in dry peat moss, 40°–50°F (4°–10°C).

**NOTES:** Thrives in accents, beds, containers. Nice in cottage, heritage gardens. Cutting flower. Resists diseases. Susceptible to aphids, slugs, snails.

## *Zantedeschia* spp. ARACEAE

### Common Calla Lily (Arum Lily, Florist's Calla Lily, Garden Calla)

**SHAPE:** About 6 rhizomatous perennials, 12″–48″ (30–120 cm) tall. Fleshy stalks with shiny, heart-shaped or lancelike leaves to 18″ (45 cm) long, often with white speckles.

**FLOWER:** Summer to autumn bloom. Solitary petal-like spiral spathes and central spadixes form elegant flowers, 4½″–10″ (11–25 cm) long. Choose from pink, red, white, and yellow.

**HARDINESS:** Zones 8–10. Hardy.

**SOIL TYPE:** Sandy loam; pond margins or shorelines. Average moisture, good drainage, high fertility, 6.0–7.0 pH.

**PLANTING GUIDE:** Early autumn. Plant in full to filtered sun, 12″ (30 cm) apart, 4″ (10 cm) deep.

**CARE TIPS:** Easy. Even moisture year-round. Fertilize during growth. Apply mulch. Propagate by division, offsets, seed. Store in sawdust, 50°F (10°C).

**NOTES:** Thrives in borders, containers. Nice in indoor gardens or ponds. Cutting flower. Resists deer, rodents, diseases. Susceptible to spider mites.

## *Zephyranthes* spp. AMARYLLIDACEAE

### Zephyr Lily (Fairy Lily)

**SHAPE:** About 40 deciduous or semi-evergreen, bulbous perennials to 12″ (30 cm) tall. Grass-like, arched leaves, 4″–24″ (10–60 cm) long.

**FLOWER:** Summer to autumn bloom. Lone simple or lilylike flowers, 2″–4″ (50–100 mm) wide, with long, slender, radiating, flared, oval petals. Choose from pink, red, white, and yellow. Some species bloom at night.

**HARDINESS:** Zones 7–11. Hardy.

**SOIL TYPE:** Sandy loam. High moisture, good drainage, medium fertility, 6.0–7.0 pH.

**PLANTING GUIDE:** Spring. Plant in full sun, 4″ (10 cm) apart, 2″–4″ (50–100 mm) deep.

**CARE TIPS:** Easy. Even moisture; limit water for one month after bloom. Fertilize during growth. Mulch, zones 7–8. Propagate by offsets, seed. Store in dry peat moss, 50°–60°F (10°–16°C).

**NOTES:** Thrives in accents, containers, edges. Nice in natural, rock gardens. Naturalizes. Resists deer, rodents, pests, diseases.

# Flowering Shrubs and Vines

Choosing shrubs and vines as the foundation of your garden will provide you with blooms and greenery throughout the gardening season.

Throughout the entire coastal Pacific Northwest and much of the Mid-Atlantic seaboard, springtime is a time of colorful displays of azaleas and rhododendrons.

Flowering shrubs and vines are essential plants that are used to tie together various garden elements. Most are durable, woody-stemmed plants that will survive for years and may attain large size, so proper placement is critical. It is a challenge to successfully move a well-established shrub or vine, so be sure to choose the right home for yours right from the start.

**Selection.** When you're selecting a shrub, consider whether you prefer evergreen or deciduous plants; both have their own advantages. In some cases, you may want coverage from a shrub or vine year-round —for instance, to shroud a fence, screen your trash cans, or block an unwanted view. Evergreens are good choices for such duty. In other situations, you may

want to let in sun—with, for example, a shrub that provides seasonal shade to cool a window in summer but allows needed light in winter. Choose a deciduous species that will drop its leaves in autumn. A wisteria-covered arbor provides another example. It may be perfect for a deck that requires shade in hot, sunny months and warm winter sun during the cool season.

Give a flowering vine proper support from the start, once you choose a good location. Provide a structure that will support its growth, keeping in mind the vine's mature size. A support could be an existing sturdy fence, an arbor, a trellis, or a timber patio cover.

Take the growth habits of your shrubs into consideration when you make your selection. Keep in mind that the most attractive landscape plants are allowed to grow into their own natural shapes and forms without extensive pruning and shaping. Shrubs, as a rule, are self-supporting. While most grow into erect or vertical plants, others may tend to arch, sprawl, or spread horizontally over a wide area. Some deep-rooted cultivars are even useful as erosion-control measures for banks, as are those with creeping roots and stolons. It's best to find out before you plant how they will grow in your climate.

**PLANTING.** As a general rule, gardeners in temperate climates should plant shrubs and vines in spring or autumn; those in warmer regions can also plant in

close eye out for chlorosis—yellowing of leaves along the veins—in susceptible plants such as gardenia and azalea. Treat it by applying acidifying fertilizers containing iron sulfate and by mulching with pine needles.

Most shrubs and vines will require limited pruning. Again, the timing and degree will vary. Many shrub cultivars, including remontant roses, need regular pruning to continue producing blooms, while other shrubs and vines such as clematis only require pruning annually. Should a limb or branch break or become diseased, prune it away and remove it from the garden. Keep lanky shrubs compact by pinching growth tips, and improve air circulation in dense foliage by pruning crossing branches. Match your care to the particular shrub or vine.

OPPOSITE
Clematis requires supports to trail and vine down walls.

Camellia bloom very early in the season—in some areas, they flower during winter. Install path lighting or uplights to highlight their displays.

winter. Always avoid planting in the hottest months, when heat could stress the plant and cause it to get off to a slow start. Wait to acquire shrubs and vines until weather conditions are right for planting.

Most experts now suggest planting vines and shrubs in unamended garden soil to ensure that their roots will grow into the surrounding soil rather than becoming encircled within the planting hole. Spade the soil well and amend only to provide the recommended pH for the species rather than to provide nutrients.

**CARE.** Water newly planted shrubs and vines regularly. Keep the soil moist, but prevent it from becoming soggy. Mulch is always a good idea; keep it four to six inches (10 to 15 cm) away from the main stem. Many shrubs and vines will take a year or more to become established. For the largest species, the old rule, "a year to sleep, a year to creep, and a year to leap" is a good guide to follow when you gauge a plant's performance.

Watering and fertilizing established shrubs depend on the plant. Some are drought-tolerant once established, while others require continually moist soil to grow best. Vary feeding according to the plant species and your particular soil. Some vines and shrubs such as bougainvillea and rock rose (*Cistus albidus*) will do well with the nutrients found naturally in the soil, while others, including mandevilla and camellia, will require biannual feeding. Watch the shrubs and vines for signs that they require fertilizer. Look for weakening and yellowing in their foliage. Keep a

### *Abelia* × *grandiflora* CAPRIFOLIACEAE

#### Glossy Abelia

**SHAPE:** Various thick-growing, semi-evergreen shrubs, 6′–8′ (1.8–2.4 m) high and wide. Shiny, oval leaves. Turns colors in autumn. Dwarf hybrids available.

**FLOWER:** Summer to early-autumn bloom. Erect or pendulous clusters of trumpet-shaped, fluted flowers to ¾″ (19 mm) long. Choose from pink and white. Forms dry, berrylike, fruit with seed, in autumn.

**HARDINESS:** Zones 5–9.

**SOIL TYPE:** High humus. High moisture, good drainage, high-medium fertility, 5.5–6.5 pH.

**PLANTING GUIDE:** Spring, as soil warms, or autumn. Plant in full sun, 4′–6′ (1.2–1.8 m) apart.

**CARE TIPS:** Easy. Even moisture until established. Fertilize every 10–12 weeks. Prune sparingly in autumn. Shelter from wind. Propagate by cuttings.

**NOTES:** Thrives in accents, backgrounds, hedges. Nice in formal, woodland gardens. Resists pests, diseases.

### *Abutilon* × *hybridum* (A. hybrids) MALVACEAE

#### Chinese-Lantern (Chinese Bellflower, Flowering Maple, Indian Mallow)

**SHAPE:** Various vigorous, open, arched, deciduous shrubs, 36″–60″ (90–150 cm) high and wide. Alternate, smooth, maplelike, simple or lobate leaves, 2″–6″ (50–150 mm) long.

**FLOWER:** Spring to summer bloom. Branched clusters of bell-shaped, nodding flowers to 2″ (50 mm) long. Choose from orange, pink, red, white, and yellow. Forms dry fruit in autumn.

**HARDINESS:** Zones 9–11. Protect from hot sun, frost.

**SOIL TYPE:** High humus. High–average moisture, good drainage, high-medium fertility, 6.0–7.0 pH.

**PLANTING GUIDE:** Autumn. Plant in full sun to partial shade, 36″–60″ (90–150 cm) apart.

**CARE TIPS:** Average. Even moisture until established. Fertilize every 4 weeks. Prune in autumn. Propagate by cuttings, seed.

**NOTES:** Thrives in accents, containers, edgings. Nice in shade, small-space, woodland gardens. Susceptible to mealybugs, scale, whiteflies, verticillium wilt.

### *Aesculus parviflora* HIPPOCASTANACEAE

#### Bottlebrush Buckeye (Buckeye)

**SHAPE:** Various vigorous, open, sprawling, deciduous shrubs, 8′–12′ (2.4–3.7 m) high and wide. Textured, circular, 5–7-lobed leaves, 8″–11″ (20–28 cm) long. Turns colors in autumn.

**FLOWER:** Summer bloom. Erect, cone-shaped, showy spikes to 10″ (25 cm) long of tiny flowers. White. Forms leathery, round, scaly fruit to 2″ (50 mm) wide in autumn.

**HARDINESS:** Zones 4–10. Prefers long seasons.

**SOIL TYPE:** Sandy loam. High–average moisture, good drainage, high-medium fertility, 6.5–7.5 pH.

**PLANTING GUIDE:** Spring. Plant in full sun, 4′–6′ (1.2–1.8 m) apart.

**CARE TIPS:** Average. Even moisture until established. Fertilize every 12 weeks. Prune to shape. Drops flowers, fruit. Propagate by cuttings, grafting, seed.

**NOTES:** Thrives in accents, backgrounds, screens. Nice in cottage, meadow, wildlife, woodland gardens. Susceptible to Japanese beetles, tussock moths, anthracnose.

### *Bougainvillea* spp. and hybrids NYCTAGINACEAE

#### Bougainvillea

**SHAPE:** About 14 shrubby, twining, woody, evergreen shrubs, 20′–30′ (6–9 m) long, armed with sharp, thorny spines. Alternate, smooth, oval, folded leaves to 2½″ (63 mm) long.

**FLOWER:** Spring to autumn bloom. Insignificant flowers surrounded by showy, papery, petal-like bracts to 3″ (75 mm) wide. Choose from crimson, orange, pink, purple, and yellow.

**HARDINESS:** Zones 7–11. Protect from frost until established.

**SOIL TYPE:** Loam. Most moistures, good drainage, medium fertility, 6.5–7.5 pH.

**PLANTING GUIDE:** Spring, as soil warms. Plant in full to filtered sun, 4′–5′ (1.2–1.5 m) apart.

**CARE TIPS:** Average. Light moisture; tolerates drought. Fertilize every 10–12 weeks. Support. Prune in early spring. Propagate by cuttings.

**NOTES:** Thrives in arbors, trellises, walls, fence lines. Nice in seaside, tropical, wildlife gardens. Resists pests, diseases.

## *Brugmansia* × *candida* hybrids *(Datura meteloides, D. inoxia)* SOLANACEAE

### Angel's-Trumpet (Horn of Plenty, Trumpet Flower)

**SHAPE:** Various vigorous, mounded, semi-evergreen shrubs, 8′–12′ (2.4–3.7 m) high and wide. Woolly, oval, lobate, coarse-toothed leaves to 8″ (20 cm) long.

**FLOWER:** Summer to early-autumn bloom. Showy, musk-fragrant, trumpet-shaped, nodding flowers, 10″–12″ (25–30 cm) long. Choose from cream, pink, white, and yellow. Forms sparse fruit with large seed in late autumn.

**HARDINESS:** Zones 7–11. Protect from frost.

**SOIL TYPE:** Loam. High moisture, good drainage, high fertility, 6.5–7.5 pH.

**PLANTING GUIDE:** Spring. Plant in full to filtered sun, 24″–48″ (60–120 cm) apart.

**CARE TIPS:** Easy. Even moisture; water when soil dries 2″–3″ (50–75 mm) deep. Fertilize every 4 weeks. Propagate by cuttings, seed.

**NOTES:** Thrives in accents, fence lines, walls. Nice in rock, wildlife gardens and lath, shade structures. Resists pests, diseases.

## *Buddleia* spp. *(B. davidii)* BUDDLEIACEAE

### Butterfly Bush

**SHAPE:** More than 100 wide, willowlike, usually deciduous shrubs, 4′–15′ (1.2–4.5 m) high. Opposite, hirsute or feltlike, slender, oval leaves, 3″–5″ (75–125 mm) long.

**FLOWER:** Summer to autumn bloom. Arching spikes to 10″ (25 cm) long of small, aromatic, lilaclike flowers. Choose from orange, pink, purple, white, and yellow. Forms berrylike pods in autumn.

**HARDINESS:** Zones 5–10.

**SOIL TYPE:** Loam. Most moistures, good drainage, medium–low fertility, 6.5–7.5 pH.

**PLANTING GUIDE:** Spring. Plant in full sun to partial shade, 36″ (90 cm) apart.

**CARE TIPS:** Easy. Even moisture. Fertilize every 4 weeks. Extend bloom by deadheading. Prune in spring. Shear in cold-winter climates. Propagate by cuttings, seed.

**NOTES:** Thrives in backgrounds, borders. Nice in arid, cottage, tropical, wildlife gardens. Resists pests, diseases.

## *Callicarpa bodinieri* VERBENACEAE

### Beautyberry

**SHAPE:** Various arching, deciduous shrubs to 6′ (1.8 m) high and wide. Alternate, lancelike, toothed, veined leaves to 5″ (13 cm) long.

**FLOWER:** Summer bloom. Circular clusters to 3″ (75 cm) wide of tiny, aromatic, lilaclike flowers. Choose from lilac and pink. Forms clustered pink, purple, white, berrylike fruit in autumn to winter.

**HARDINESS:** Zones 6–10.

**SOIL TYPE:** Sandy loam. Average moisture, good drainage, high–medium fertility, 6.0–7.0 pH.

**PLANTING GUIDE:** Spring. Plant in full sun to partial shade, 6′–8′ (1.8–2.4 m) apart.

**CARE TIPS:** Easy. Even moisture. Fertilize every 8–10 weeks. Prune heavily in spring. Shear in cold-winter climates. Propagate by cuttings, layering, seed.

**NOTES:** Thrives in accents, backgrounds, borders. Nice in cottage, heritage, wildlife, woodland gardens. Resists pests, diseases.

## *Calluna vulgaris* and cultivars ERICACEAE

### Heather (Scot's Heather, Ling)

**SHAPE:** Numerous slow-growing, mounded or sprawling, evergreen shrubs to 36″ (90 cm) high. Overlapped, scaly leaves to ½″ (12 mm) long.

**FLOWER:** Summer to autumn bloom. Erect spikes to 10″ (25 cm) long of tiny, trumpet-shaped, double flowers. Choose from pink, purple, and white. Forms caplike seedpods in summer.

**HARDINESS:** Zones 4–7. Prefers cool, moist climates. Protect from hot sun.

**SOIL TYPE:** Loam. High moisture, good drainage, high-medium fertility, 5.5–6.5 pH.

**PLANTING GUIDE:** Spring. Plant in full sun to partial shade, 36″ (90 cm) apart.

**CARE TIPS:** Easy. Even moisture. Fertilize every 6 months. Apply mulch. Prune or shear after bloom. Shelter from wind. Propagate by cuttings, seed.

**NOTES:** Thrives in borders, edgings, ground covers, mixed plantings. Nice in cottage, rock, small-space, woodland gardens. Resists pests, diseases.

## *Calycanthus* spp. CALYCANTHACEAE

### Sweet Shrub (Spice Bush)

**SHAPE:** Few slow-growing, branched, deciduous shrubs, 6'–12' (1.8–3.7 m) high and wide. Shiny or textured, oval, veined, aromatic leaves, 5"–8" (13–20 cm) long. Turns colors in autumn.

**FLOWER:** Summer bloom. Aromatic, fountain-shaped, erect flowers to 2" (50 mm) long with straplike petals. Choose from brown and red brown. Forms urn-shaped fruit bearing many seed with dry, papery coverings, in late autumn.

**HARDINESS:** Zones 4–9.

**SOIL TYPE:** High humus. High moisture, good drainage, high fertility, 6.5–8.0 pH.

**PLANTING GUIDE:** Spring. Plant in full sun to partial shade, 4'–6' (1.2–1.8 m) apart.

**CARE TIPS:** Easy. Even moisture. Fertilize every 4 weeks. Prune for bushy plants. Propagate by division, layering, seed, suckers.

**NOTES:** Thrives in accents, borders, paths. Nice in cottage, meadow, shade, wildlife, woodland gardens. Drying flower. Resists pests, diseases.

## *Camellia japonica* THEACEAE

### Common Camellia

**SHAPE:** Over 200 slow-growing, bushlike, evergreen shrubs or small trees, 6'–45' (1.8–13.5 m) high. Shiny or waxy, oval leaves to 4" (10 cm) long. See also *Camellia sasanqua*, Sasanqua camellia.

**FLOWER:** Winter to spring bloom. Single to double, aromatic flowers, 2"–9" (50–228 mm) wide. Choose from pink, red, white, and multicolored. Forms capsule-shaped fruit in spring.

**HARDINESS:** Zones 7–10. Protect from hot sun, frost.

**SOIL TYPE:** High humus. High moisture, good drainage, high fertility, 6.0–6.5 pH.

**PLANTING GUIDE:** Spring. Plant in partial shade, 4'–5' (1.2–1.5 m) apart.

**CARE TIPS:** Easy. Even moisture. Fertilize every 6–8 weeks. Apply mulch. Prune after bloom. Propagate by cuttings.

**NOTES:** Thrives in containers, hedges, paths, screens. Nice in formal, shade, small-space gardens. Susceptible to mealybugs, scale, anthracnose, blight.

## *Camellia sasanqua* THEACEAE

### Sasanqua Camellia (Sasanqua)

**SHAPE:** Nearly 100 slow-growing, vertical, branched, evergreen shrubs to 12' (3.7 m) high and wide. Shiny or waxy, oval leaves to 2" (50 mm) long.

**FLOWER:** Autumn to winter bloom. Aromatic, single, semi-double, or double flowers to 2" (50 mm) wide. Choose from pink, red, rose, white, and multicolored. Forms capsule-shaped fruit in spring.

**HARDINESS:** Zones 8–10. Protect from hot sun, frost.

**SOIL TYPE:** High humus. High moisture, good drainage, high fertility, 6.5–7.0 pH.

**PLANTING GUIDE:** Spring. Plant in partial shade, 24"–36" (60–90 cm) apart.

**CARE TIPS:** Easy. Even moisture. Fertilize every 6–8 weeks. Apply mulch. Prune after bloom. Propagate by cuttings, grafting.

**NOTES:** Thrives in accents, containers, hedges, paths, screens. Nice in cottage, formal, shade, woodland gardens. Susceptible to mealybugs, scale, anthracnose, blight, canker.

## *Campsis radicans* BIGNONIACEAE

### Trumpet Vine (Trumpet Creeper)

**SHAPE:** Numerous vigorous, upright, twining, woody, deciduous vines, 30'–40' (9–12 m) long, with aerial rootlets. Opposite, shiny, divided, 9–11-lobed leaves with textured, oval, toothed, veined leaflets to 2½" (63 mm) long.

**BLOOM:** Summer bloom. Branching clusters of showy, trumpet-shaped, flared flowers to 3" (75 mm) long. Choose from orange and scarlet. Forms dry podlike fruit in autumn.

**HARDINESS:** Zones 5–10.

**SOIL TYPE:** High humus. Average moisture, good drainage, medium fertility, 6.5–7.0 pH.

**PLANTING GUIDE:** Spring. Plant in full to filtered sun, 4'–6' (1.2–1.8 m) apart.

**CARE TIPS:** Average. Light moisture. Fertilize every 12 weeks. Support. Prune in spring for bushy plants. Propagate by cuttings, layering, seed.

**NOTES:** Thrives in arbors, fence lines, trellises, walls. Nice in cottage, formal, wildlife gardens. Resists pests, diseases.

## *Caragana pygmaea* FABACEAE (LEGUMINOSAE)

### Dwarf Pea Shrub

**SHAPE:** Various vigorous, bushlike, spiny, deciduous small trees, 6′–20′ (1.8–6 m) high. Alternate, shiny, leaves to 3″ (75 mm) long with 3–6 paired, oval leaflets.

**FLOWER:** Late-spring bloom. Small clusters of pealike flowers to ⅞″ (22 mm) long. Yellow. Forms brown, bean- or pealike seedpods in spring.

**HARDINESS:** Zones 3–8.

**SOIL TYPE:** Sandy loam. High moisture, good drainage, medium to low fertility, 6.5–8.5 pH.

**PLANTING GUIDE:** Spring. Plant in full sun, 5′–6′ (1.5–1.8 m) apart.

**CARE TIPS:** Easy. Even moisture until established. Tolerates drought. Fertilize only in spring. Prune after bloom. Propagate by cuttings, division, grafting, layering, seed.

**NOTES:** Thrives in accents, barriers, borders, hedges, screens, windbreaks. Nice in arid, woodland gardens. Resists deer, rodents, insect pests, diseases.

## *Caryopteris* spp. and hybrids VERBENACEAE

### Bluebeard (Blue Mist, Blue Spiraea)

**SHAPE:** Few vigorous, erect, deciduous shrubs, 36″–48″ (90–120 cm) high. Opposite, textured, lancelike, often toothed, aromatic leaves, 2″–4″ (50–100 mm) long.

**FLOWER:** Late-summer bloom. Spiking stems with whorled clusters to 4″ (10 cm) wide of hirsute flowers to ¼″ (6 mm) long. Choose from blue, lavender, pink, and purple. Forms dry, segmented seedpods in autumn.

**HARDINESS:** Zones 7–10. Protect from frost.

**SOIL TYPE:** Sandy loam. High moisture, good drainage, high fertility, 6.5–7.0 pH.

**PLANTING GUIDE:** Spring. Plant in full sun, 24″ (60 cm) apart.

**CARE TIPS:** Easy. Even moisture. Fertilize every 6–8 weeks. Extend bloom by deadheading. Shear in spring. Propagate by cuttings, seed.

**NOTES:** Thrives in accents, backgrounds, borders, containers. Nice in cottage, formal gardens. Cutting flower. Resists pests, diseases.

## *Cestrum nocturnum* SOLANACEAE

### Night Jessamine (Night Jasmine)

**SHAPE:** Various bushlike, upright or sprawling, semi-evergreen tropical shrubs to 12′ (3.7 m) high. Shiny, oval, slender leaves, 4″–7″ (10–18 cm) long.

**FLOWER:** Summer bloom. Numerous aromatic, flute-shaped flowers to 1″ (25 mm) long. Choose from cream and white with green-tinged petals. Forms white berries in autumn.

**HARDINESS:** Zones 8–11. Protect from frost.

**SOIL TYPE:** High humus. High moisture, good drainage, Fertility: Rich. 6.0–7.0 pH.

**PLANTING GUIDE:** Spring, as soil warms. Plant in full sun, 8′–10′ (2.4–3 m) apart.

**CARE TIPS:** Average. Even moisture. Fertilize every 4 weeks during growth. Prune after bloom in late summer. Propagate by cuttings, seed.

**NOTES:** Thrives in accents, arbors, backgrounds, containers, fence lines, trellises. Nice in cottage, formal, fragrance, wildlife gardens. Cutting flower. Resists pests, diseases.

## *Chaenomeles speciosa* ROSACEAE

### Japanese Quince (Flowering Quince)

**SHAPE:** Numerous thick-growing, branched or sprawling, spiny, semi-evergreen shrubs, 6′–10′ (1.8–3 m) high and 8′–15′ (2.4–4.6 m) wide. Shiny, oval, finely toothed leaves to 3½″ (90 mm) long.

**FLOWER:** Early-spring bloom, before leaves. Clusters of dainty, single or double, waxy flowers to 2½″ (63 mm) wide. Choose from pink, red, and white. Forms green, pear-shaped fruit in autumn.

**HARDINESS:** Zones 5–9.

**SOIL TYPE:** Loam. High–average moisture, excellent drainage, medium fertility, 5.5–6.5 pH.

**PLANTING GUIDE:** Spring. Plant in full sun, 5′–6′ (1.5–1.8 m) apart.

**CARE TIPS:** Easy. Light moisture until established. Fertilize only in spring. Prune after bloom. Propagate by cuttings, grafting, layering, seed.

**NOTES:** Thrives in barriers, containers, walls. Nice in Asian, cottage, woodland gardens. Cutting flower. Susceptible to chlorosis, leaf spot.

## *Choisya ternata* RUTACEAE

### Mexican Orange

**SHAPE:** Few vigorous, vertical, branched or arched, evergreen shrubs, 5'–8' (1.5–2.4 m) high. Opposite, shiny, oval, divided leaves to 6" (15 cm) wide with fan-shaped groups of 3 leaflets, 2"–3" (50–75 mm) long.

**FLOWER:** Early-spring bloom. Profuse, mounded clusters of star-shaped, 4–5-petaled flowers to 1" (50 mm) wide. Choose from cream and white. Forms capsule-shaped fruit in early summer.

**HARDINESS:** Zones 7–11.

**SOIL TYPE:** High humus. Average–low moisture, good drainage, high fertility, 5.5–7.0 pH.

**PLANTING GUIDE:** Spring. Plant in full sun to partial shade, 5'–8' (1.5–2.4 m) apart.

**CARE TIPS:** Average. Light moisture. Tolerates drought. Fertilize every 6–8 weeks. Prune after bloom. Propagate by cuttings.

**NOTES:** Thrives in accents, containers, walls. Nice in arid, tropical, wildlife gardens. Susceptible to aphids, spider mites, chlorosis, fungal diseases.

## *Cistus albidus* CISTACEAE

### White-Leaved Rock Rose

**SHAPE:** Various vigorous, vertical, branched and open, evergreen shrubs to 8' (2.4 m) high and 4' (1.2 m) wide. Opposite, velvety, lancelike, aromatic leaves to 2½" (63 mm) long.

**FLOWER:** Summer bloom. Showy, flat, open flowers, 2"–3" (50–75 mm) wide. Choose from pink, white, and multicolored. Forms nutlike fruit to ½" (12 mm) wide in autumn.

**HARDINESS:** Zones 7–10. Protect from frost.

**SOIL TYPE:** Sandy loam. Average–low moisture, good drainage, medium–low fertility, 6.5–8.0 pH. Tolerates salt.

**PLANTING GUIDE:** Spring. Plant in full sun, 24"–48" (60–120 cm) apart.

**CARE TIPS:** Easy. Even moisture until established. Fertilize sparingly. Pinch tips for bushy plants. Prune sparingly. Propagate by cuttings, seed.

**NOTES:** Thrives in accents, banks, containers, paths. Nice in arid, natural, seaside, small-space gardens. Resists diseases. Susceptible to aphids.

## *Coleonema pulchrum* (*Diosma* spp.) RUTACEAE

### Breath of Heaven

**SHAPE:** Various graceful, branched, heathlike, evergreen shrubs to 5' (1.5 m) high and wide. Narrow, needlelike, aromatic leaves to 1½" (38 mm) long.

**FLOWER:** Winter to spring bloom. Tiny, single, 5-petaled flowers to ¾" (19 mm) wide. Choose from pink and red. Forms caplike seedpods in summer.

**HARDINESS:** Zones 8–10. Protect from frost.

**SOIL TYPE:** High humus. High moisture, good drainage, high fertility, 6.5–7.5 pH.

**PLANTING GUIDE:** Spring. Plant in full sun to partial shade, 6'–7' (1.8–2.2 m) apart.

**CARE TIPS:** Easy. Even moisture. Fertilize every 6–8 weeks. Apply mulch, zones 6–8. Prune or shear after bloom. Propagate by cuttings.

**NOTES:** Thrives in banks, backgrounds, borders, edgings, paths, slopes, walls. Nice in cottage, fragrance, meadow, natural, woodland gardens. Resists pests, diseases.

## *Corylopsis* spp. HAMAMELIDACEAE

### Winter Hazel

**SHAPE:** About 10 elegant, slow-growing, sprawling, open, deciduous shrubs, 6'–20' (1.8–6 m) high. Red-tinged buds turn to smooth, broad, oval, toothed leaves to 4" (10 cm) long. Turns colors in autumn.

**FLOWER:** Spring bloom, before leaves. Small, pendulous clusters of bell-shaped or tubular flowers to ¾" (19 mm) long. Yellow. Forms caplike seedpods in summer.

**HARDINESS:** Zones 6–9.

**SOIL TYPE:** Loam. High moisture, excellent drainage, high fertility, 5.5–6.5 pH.

**PLANTING GUIDE:** Spring. Plant in full sun to partial shade, 6'–10' (1.8–3 m) apart.

**CARE TIPS:** Easy. Even moisture. Fertilize only in spring. Apply mulch, zones 4–6. Prune after bloom. Propagate by cuttings, division, seed.

**NOTES:** Thrives in backgrounds, borders, walls. Nice in cottage, natural, woodland gardens. Resists pests, diseases.

## *Cotinus coggygria* ANACARDIACEAE

### Smoke Tree (Smokebush)

**SHAPE:** Various bushlike, open, deciduous shrubs to 15′ (4.5 m) high. Smooth, oval leaves to 5″ (13 cm) long. Turns colors in autumn. *C. obovatus*, American smoke tree, is a related native.

**FLOWER:** Early-summer bloom. Pendulous, branched clusters of tiny flowers, in yellow. Forms clouds of lavender, purple or red, hirsute panicles with small, berrylike, hard seed, in summer.

**HARDINESS:** Zones 4–9.

**SOIL TYPE:** Sandy loam. Low moisture, good drainage, medium–low fertility, 6.0–8.0 pH.

**PLANTING GUIDE:** Spring or autumn. Plant in full sun, 15′–20′ (4.5–6 m) apart.

**CARE TIPS:** Easy. Water until established when soil dries 2″–3″ (50–75 mm) deep. Tolerates drought. Fertilize, prune sparingly. Propagate by cuttings, layering, seed.

**NOTES:** Thrives in accents, hedges. Nice in arid, meadow, rock, small-space gardens. Tolerates smog. Resists pests, diseases.

## *Cotoneaster divaricatus* ROSACEAE

### Spreading Cotoneaster

**SHAPE:** Spiny deciduous shrub to 6′ (1.8 m) high and 10′ (3 m) wide. Shiny, smooth, oval, finely toothed leaves to ¾″ (19 mm) long with lighter undersides.

**FLOWER:** Spring bloom. Lone or clustered, roselike flowers to ½″ (12 mm) wide. Choose from pink and red. Forms red berries, ½″ (12 mm) wide, in autumn to winter.

**HARDINESS:** Zones 5–9. Protect from frost.

**SOIL TYPE:** Sandy loam. Average moisture, good drainage, medium–low fertility, 6.5–8.0 pH. Tolerates drought, salt.

**PLANTING GUIDE:** Spring, as soil warms. Plant in partial shade, 5′ (1.5 m) apart.

**CARE TIPS:** Easy. Even moisture until established. Fertilize every 4 weeks. Prune sparingly. Propagate by cuttings, seed.

**NOTES:** Thrives in barriers, espaliers, ground covers, hedges, paths. Nice in formal, natural, rock, wildlife gardens. Resists pests, diseases.

## *Daphne* spp. THYMELAEACEAE

### Daphne

**SHAPE:** About 50 slow-growing, sprawling, deciduous or evergreen shrubs to 4′ (1.2 m) high. Shiny, thick, oval leaves, 1″–3″ (25–75 mm) long.

**FLOWER:** Late-winter bloom. Clusters to 4″ (10 cm) long of small, fragrant, funnel-shaped, single, waxy flowers. Choose from pink, purple, and white. Forms red fruit in spring.

**HARDINESS:** Zones 4–9.

**SOIL TYPE:** High humus. High moisture, good drainage, high fertility, 6.5–7.0 pH.

**PLANTING GUIDE:** Spring. Plant in partial shade, 36″–60″ (90–150 cm) apart, rootball 1″ (25 mm) above surrounding soil.

**CARE TIPS:** Average to difficult. Even moisture until established. Fertilize only in winter. Apply mulch. Prune after bloom. Propagate by cuttings, grafting, layering, seed.

**NOTES:** Thrives in containers, edgings, paths. Nice in cottage, fragrance gardens. Cutting flower. Resists diseases. Susceptible to aphids.

## *Deutzia* spp. SAXIFRAGACEAE

### Deutzia

**SHAPE:** About 40 slow-growing, mounded or arched, usually deciduous shrubs, 6′–9′ (1.8–2.7 m) high and 5′–8′ (1.5–2.4 m) wide. Smooth, lancelike, fine-toothed leaves, 2″–5″ (50–125 mm) long.

**FLOWER:** Late-spring bloom. Arching clusters of star-shaped, single or double flowers to 1″ (25 mm) wide. Choose from pink, pale purple, and white. Forms many small seeds.

**HARDINESS:** Most, zones 6–9. Protect from frost.

**SOIL TYPE:** Sandy loam. High moisture, good drainage, medium fertility, 6.0–7.5 pH.

**PLANTING GUIDE:** Spring. Plant in full sun to partial shade, 5′–7′ (1.5–2.2 m) apart.

**CARE TIPS:** Easy. Even moisture. Fertilize every 10–12 weeks. Prune heavily after bloom. Propagate by cuttings, division, layering, seed.

**NOTES:** Thrives in backgrounds, borders, hedges, mixed plantings. Nice in cottage, natural, woodland gardens. Resists pests, diseases.

## *Erica* spp. ERICACEAE

### Heath

**SHAPE:** More than 500 slow-growing, branched or sprawling, evergreen shrubs or small trees, 12″–72″ (30–180 cm) high. Tiny, heatherlike needles or leaves. Dwarf cultivars available.

**FLOWER:** Late-winter, early-spring, summer to autumn bloom. Pendulous or erect clusters of irregular flowers to ⅛″ (3 mm) long. Choose from green, purple, rose, white, and yellow. Forms seed capsules in summer.

**HARDINESS:** Most, zones 4–10.

**SOIL TYPE:** High humus. Average moisture, good drainage, high fertility, 5.0–6.0 pH.

**PLANTING GUIDE:** Spring. Plant in full sun, 36″ (90 cm) apart.

**CARE TIPS:** Easy. Light moisture until established. Fertilize every 6 months. Prune or shear after bloom. Propagate by cuttings, seed.

**NOTES:** Thrives in borders, edgings, ground covers, massed plantings. Nice in arid, rock, wildlife gardens. Resists pests, diseases.

## *Euphorbia* spp. EUPHORBIACEAE

### Spurge

**SHAPE:** Numerous diverse, vigorous, mounded, bushlike, semi-evergreen shrubs and small trees, 4′–10′ (1.2–3 m) high and wide. Oval leaves, 1″–6″ (25–150 mm) long. See also *E. pulcherrima*, poinsettia.

**FLOWER:** Spring bloom. Clusters of varied, showy, flowers. Choose from cream, white, red, and yellow. Forms capsule-shaped fruit in summer.

**HARDINESS:** Many, zones 7–11.

**SOIL TYPE:** Sandy loam. High–average moisture, good drainage, medium–low fertility, 6.0–7.0 pH. Tolerates salt.

**PLANTING GUIDE:** Spring, as soil warms. Plant in full sun to partial shade, 12″–60″ (30–150 cm) apart.

**CARE TIPS:** Easy. Light moisture until established. Fertilize only in spring. Propagate by cuttings, division, seed.

**NOTES:** Thrives in borders, containers. Nice in formal, seaside, small-space gardens. Avoid planting near fishponds. Resists pests, diseases.

## *Euphorbia pulcherrima* EUPHORBIACEAE

### Poinsettia (Mexican Flameleaf)

**SHAPE:** Numerous erect, branched, semi-evergreen shrubs, 7′–10′ (2.2–3 m) high and to 6′ (1.8 m) wide. Smooth, textured, spoonlike or circular, veined leaves, 4″–7″ (10–18 cm) long.

**FLOWER:** Winter bloom. Terminal, inconspicuous flowers. Pink, red, white, yellow, variegated, and marbled rosettes of leaflike bracts to 10″ (25 cm) wide. Forms capsule-shaped fruit in spring.

**HARDINESS:** Zones 9–11. Protect from frost.

**SOIL TYPE:** Sandy loam. Average–low moisture, good drainage, medium–low fertility, 6.5–8.0 pH.

**PLANTING GUIDE:** Spring, as soil warms. Plant in full to filtered sun, 36″–60″ (90–150 cm) apart.

**CARE TIPS:** Average. Light moisture until established. Tolerates drought. Fertilize every 2 weeks as leaves turn color. Prune after bloom. Shelter from wind. Propagate by cuttings, seed.

**NOTES:** Thrives in accents, containers. Nice in small-space, tropical gardens. Resists pests, diseases.

## *Euryops pectinatus* ASTERACEAE (COMPOSITAE)

### Gray-Leaved Euryops

**SHAPE:** Few mounded, bushlike, evergreen shrubs, 36″–48″ (90–120 cm) high and wide. Alternate, velvety, featherlike, divided, cut leaves, 2″–3″ (50–75 mm) long with 8–10-paired leaflets.

**FLOWER:** Spring to autumn bloom. Numerous daisylike flowers, 1½″–2″ (38–50 mm) wide. Yellow. Forms dry, wingless seed.

**HARDINESS:** Zones 7–11. Protect from frost.

**SOIL TYPE:** Sandy loam. Average–low moisture, good drainage, medium–low fertility, 6.5–8.0 pH. Tolerates salt.

**PLANTING GUIDE:** Spring. Plant in full sun, 24″–36″ (60–90 cm) apart.

**CARE TIPS:** Easy. Light moisture until established. Tolerates drought, wind. Fertilize only in spring. Extend bloom by deadheading. Propagate by division, seed.

**NOTES:** Thrives in accents, beds, borders, containers, paths. Nice in cottage, seaside, small-space gardens. Resists diseases. Susceptible to aphids.

## Exochorda racemosa (E. grandiflora) ROSACEAE

### Common Pearlbush

**SHAPE:** Few vigorous, vertical, slender, deciduous shrubs, 10′–12′ (3–3.7 m) high and wide. Shiny, oval leaves, 2½″–3″ (63–75 mm) long.

**FLOWER:** Spring bloom, as leaves emerge. Pendulous clusters of spirea-like flowers, 1½″–2″ (38–50 mm) wide. Choose from cream and white. Forms dry, divided, capsule-shaped fruit in summer.

**HARDINESS:** Zones 4–9.

**SOIL TYPE:** High humus. High–average moisture, good drainage, medium fertility, 5.5–6.5 pH.

**PLANTING GUIDE:** Spring. Plant in full sun, 4′–6′ (1.2–1.8 m) apart.

**CARE TIPS:** Easy. Even moisture. Tolerates drought. Fertilize only in spring. Apply mulch in winter. Prune to maintain open form. Propagate by cuttings, layering, seed.

**NOTES:** Thrives in accents, borders, containers, screens. Nice in cottage, formal, meadow gardens. Resists pests, oak root fungus. Susceptible to powdery mildew.

## Forsythia × intermedia OLEACEAE

### Forsythia (Golden Bells)

**SHAPE:** Numerous vigorous, arched, open, deciduous shrubs to 10′ (3 m) high. Oval, simple, often 3-lobed leaves to 5″ (13 cm) long.

**FLOWER:** Spring bloom, before leaves emerge, on second-year wood. Showy clusters of 4-part, lobed flowers to 1″ (25 mm) long. Yellow. Forms winged seed in autumn.

**HARDINESS:** Zones 5–8.

**SOIL TYPE:** Loam. High moisture, average drainage, medium fertility, 6.5–8.0 pH.

**PLANTING GUIDE:** Spring. Plant in full sun, 8′–10′ (2.4–3 m) apart.

**CARE TIPS:** Easy. Even moisture. Fertilize every 10–12 weeks. Apply mulch, zones 5–6. Prune, thin oldest canes after bloom. Propagate by cuttings, layering, seed.

**NOTES:** Thrives in accents, backgrounds, borders, fence lines, hedges, mixed plantings. Nice in natural, woodland gardens. Cutting flower. Resists pests, diseases.

## Fothergilla gardenii HAMAMELIDACEAE

### Dwarf Fothergilla (Witch Alder)

**SHAPE:** Few slow-growing, bushlike, mounded, deciduous shrubs to 4′ (1.2 m) high. Oval to circular leaves, 1″–2″ (25–50 mm) long. Turns colors in autumn.

**FLOWER:** Spring bloom, before leaves emerge. Round, erect, bottle-brush–like clusters to 2″ (50 mm) long of tiny, thready flowers. White. Forms caplike fruit in summer.

**HARDINESS:** Zones 5–9.

**SOIL TYPE:** Loam. High moisture, good drainage, high-medium fertility, 5.5–6.5 pH.

**PLANTING GUIDE:** Spring. Plant in full sun to partial shade, 3″–48″ (90–120 cm) apart. Prefers full sun.

**CARE TIPS:** Easy. Even moisture until established. Fertilize only in spring. Mulch, zones 5–6. Prune after bloom. Propagate by cuttings, layering, seed.

**NOTES:** Thrives in accents, backgrounds, beds, borders. Nice in cottage, woodland gardens. Cutting flower. Resists pests, diseases.

## Fuchsia × hybrida ONAGRACEAE

### Fuchsia (Common Fuchsia, Lady's-Eardrops)

**SHAPE:** Numerous slow-growing, semi-evergreen or evergreen shrubs to 12′ (3.7 m) high. Shiny, lancelike, toothed leaves to 2″ (50 mm) long.

**FLOWER:** Summer bloom. Nodding, cup- to funnel-shaped, star-pointed flowers to 3″ (75 mm) long. Choose from blue, bronze, pink, purple, red, and violet with long, pink, red, white sepals. Forms purple, seedy berries in autumn.

**HARDINESS:** Zones 7–10. Protect from frost.

**SOIL TYPE:** High humus. High moisture, good drainage, high fertility, 6.0–7.0 pH.

**PLANTING GUIDE:** Spring, as soil warms. Plant in full to filtered sun, 36″–48″ (90–120 cm) apart.

**CARE TIPS:** Average. Even moisture. Fertilize every 4 weeks. Extend bloom by deadheading. Prune to main branches in autumn. Propagate by cuttings.

**NOTES:** Thrives in borders, containers, walls. Nice in cottage, formal, wildlife, woodland gardens. Good for espaliers, topiaries. Susceptible to aphids, spider mites, chlorosis.

## *Gardenia jasminoides* RUBIACEAE

### Common Gardenia (Cape Jasmine, Cape Jessamine)

**SHAPE:** Numerous slow-growing, bushlike, evergreen shrubs to 6′ (1.8 m) high. Shiny, thick, oval, veined leaves, 3″–4″ (75–100 mm) long.

**FLOWER:** Autumn to winter bloom. Double, fragrant flowers, 2″–3½″ (50–90 mm) wide. Choose from cream, white, and yellow.

**HARDINESS:** Zones 8–11. Protect from hot sun, frost.

**SOIL TYPE:** Loam; pond shorelines. High moisture, good drainage, medium fertility, 4.5–5.5 pH.

**PLANTING GUIDE:** Spring, as soil warms. Plant in partial shade, 24″–36″ (60–90 cm) apart.

**CARE TIPS:** Average. Even moisture; limit water in summer. Fertilize only in spring. Pinch tips for bushy plants. Extend bloom by deadheading. Prune after bloom. Propagate by cuttings.

**NOTES:** Thrives in containers, hedges, paths. Nice in rock gardens and ponds. Cutting flower. Susceptible to aphids, mealybugs, spider mites, scale.

## *Genista spp.* (*Cytisus* spp.) FABACEAE (LEGUMINOSAE)

### Broom

**SHAPE:** About 50 vigorous, sprawling, deciduous or semi-evergreen shrubs, 8″–180″ (20–460 cm) high. Usually alternate, divided, 1–3-leaflet or simple leaves, ½″–4″ (12–100 mm) long.

**FLOWER:** Late-spring bloom. Pairs or showy clusters of aromatic, pealike flowers to 1″ (25 mm) long. Choose from brown, red, white, and yellow. Forms beanlike pods in summer.

**HARDINESS:** Most, zones 4–9. Prefers dry climates. Protect roots from hot sun, frost.

**SOIL TYPE:** Sandy loam. Average–low moisture, good drainage, medium–low fertility, 6.5–8.0 pH.

**PLANTING GUIDE:** Spring. Plant in full sun, 12″–96″ (30–240 cm) apart. Avoid transplanting.

**CARE TIPS:** Easy. Light moisture until established. Fertilize every 6 months. Apply mulch. Prune after bloom. Propagate by cuttings, grafting, layering, seed.

**NOTES:** Thrives in beds, hedges. Nice in cottage, seaside gardens. Aggressive. Resists pests, diseases.

## *Hebe* **spp. and hybrids** SCROPHULARIACEAE

### Hebe

**SHAPE:** More than 70 vigorous, mounded, evergreen shrubs, 36″–72″ (90–180 cm) high and wide. Opposite, shiny, oval, often fine-toothed leaves to ½″–4″ (12–100 mm) long.

**FLOWER:** Summer bloom. Numerous tiny flowers in showy, spiking clusters to 3″ (75 mm) long. Choose from blue, pink, purple, and white. Forms flat, dry fruit with seed in autumn.

**HARDINESS:** Zones 8–9. Protect from frost.

**SOIL TYPE:** Sandy loam. Average–low moisture, good drainage, high–medium fertility, 6.5–7.5 pH.

**PLANTING GUIDE:** Autumn. Plant in full sun to partial shade, 24″–36″ (60–90 cm) apart.

**CARE TIPS:** Easy. Light moisture. Fertilize every 10–12 weeks. Prune after flowering. Propagate by cuttings, layering, seed.

**NOTES:** Thrives in beds, borders, containers, paths. Nice in cottage, seaside, small-space, woodland gardens. Resists pests. Susceptible to mildew.

## *Hibiscus rosa-sinensis* MALVACEAE

### Chinese Hibiscus (China Rose, Hawaiian Hibiscus)

**SHAPE:** Various vigorous, branched, upright or sprawling evergreen shrubs, 15′–30′ (4.5–9 m) high. Shiny, textured, oval leaves to 6″ (15 cm) long. See also *H. mutabilis*, Confederate rose.

**FLOWER:** Summer bloom. Single or double flowers, 4″–8″ (10–20 cm) wide, with ruffled petals. Choose from gold, orange, pink, red, and yellow. Forms hirsute, capsule-shaped fruit in autumn.

**HARDINESS:** Zones 9–11. Protect from frost.

**SOIL TYPE:** Loam. High moisture, good drainage, high fertility, 7.0–7.5 pH.

**PLANTING GUIDE:** Autumn. Plant in full sun to partial shade, 5′–10′ (1.5–3 m) apart.

**CARE TIPS:** Average. Even moisture. Fertilize every 4 weeks. Prune to shape. Shelter from wind. Propagate by cuttings, grafting, layering.

**NOTES:** Thrives in accents, beds, borders, containers, screens, walls. Nice in seaside, tropical, woodland gardens. Resists diseases. Susceptible to aphids, whiteflies.

## *Hydrangea* spp. HYDRANGEACEAE (SAXIFRAGACEAE)

### Hydrangea

**SHAPE:** More than 20 narrow or upright, bushlike, deciduous or evergreen shrubs, 4′–8′ (1.2–2.4 m) high. Opposite, shiny, broad, oval, lobate or deep-toothed leaves to 12″ (30 cm) long.

**FLOWER:** Summer to early-autumn bloom. Clusters to 18″ (45 cm) wide of star-shaped flowers. Choose from blue, lavender, pink, purple, and white. Forms seed in autumn.

**HARDINESS:** Most, zones 4–10.

**SOIL TYPE:** High humus. High moisture, good drainage, high fertility, 6.5–7.0 pH. For blue flowers, add aluminum sulfate; pink, garden lime.

**PLANTING GUIDE:** Spring. Plant in full sun to partial shade, 6′–10′ (1.8–3 m) apart.

**CARE TIPS:** Average. Even moisture. Fertilize every 6 weeks. Extend bloom by deadheading. Prune in autumn. Propagate by cuttings, division, seed.

**NOTES:** Thrives in borders, hedges, screens. Nice in cottage, woodland gardens. Cutting, drying flower. Susceptible to aphids, chlorosis, mildew.

## *Hydrangea anomala* subsp. *petiolaris* (H. petiolaris) HYDRANGEACEAE (SAXIFRAGACEAE)

### Climbing Hydrangea

**SHAPE:** Various sprawling or upright, woody deciduous vines to 20′ (6 m) high or more with rootlike holdfasts. Alternate, shiny, heart-shaped, toothed leaves to 4″ (10 cm) long.

**FLOWER:** Early-summer bloom. Flat clusters to 8″ (20 cm) wide of irregular, often sterile flowers to 1¼″ (32 mm) wide. White. Forms seed in autumn.

**HARDINESS:** Zones 4–9.

**SOIL TYPE:** High humus. High moisture, good drainage, high fertility, 6.0–7.0 pH.

**PLANTING GUIDE:** Spring. Plant in full sun to partial shade, 10′ (3 m) apart.

**CARE TIPS:** Average. Even moisture until established. Fertilize every 6–8 weeks. Prune after bloom. Renew by pruning to main stems. Propagate by cuttings, layering, seed.

**NOTES:** Thrives in arbors, trellises, screens. Nice in cottage, heritage, woodland gardens. Susceptible to aphids, chlorosis, mildew.

## *Hydrangea quercifolia* HYDRANGEACEAE (SAXIFRAGACEAE)

### Oak-Leaved Hydrangea

**SHAPE:** Various round, branched, stoloniferous, deciduous shrubs, 4′–6′ (1.2–1.8 m) high. Shiny, oaklike, broad, oval, 5-lobed leaves to 8″ (20 cm) long on woolly haired branches. Turns colors in autumn.

**FLOWER:** Late-summer to autumn bloom on second-year wood. Conelike clusters to 10″ (25 cm) long of simple flowers to ½″ (12 mm) wide. Choose from cream, rose, and white.

**HARDINESS:** Zones 5–9; zones 5–6, foliage plant.

**SOIL TYPE:** High humus. High–average moisture, good drainage, high fertility, 5.5–7.0 pH.

**PLANTING GUIDE:** Spring. Plant in full to filtered sun, 36″–48″ (90–120 cm) apart.

**CARE TIPS:** Average. Even moisture until established. Fertilize every 6–8 weeks. Extend bloom by deadheading. Prune after bloom. Propagate by cuttings, division, layering, seed.

**NOTES:** Thrives in edgings. Nice in woodland gardens. Susceptible to aphids, chlorosis, mildew.

## *Hypericum calycinum* HYPERICACEAE

### Aaron's Beard (Creeping St.-John's-Wort, Goldflower)

**SHAPE:** Several durable, vigorous, low, sprawling, stoloniferous, evergreen shrubs to 18″ (45 cm) high and 18″–24″ (45–60 cm) wide. Opposite, smooth, lancelike leaves to 4″ (10 cm) long.

**BLOOM:** Summer bloom. Simple, 5-petaled, open, round flowers to 2″ (50 mm) wide with feathery vertical centers. Choose from gold and yellow. Forms dry seed caps in autumn.

**HARDINESS:** Zones 5–10. Prefers mild-summer climates.

**SOIL TYPE:** Clayey soil. Average–low moisture, good drainage, medium–low fertility, 6.0–7.0 pH.

**PLANTING GUIDE:** Spring. Plant in full sun to partial shade, 9″–12″ (23–30 cm) apart.

**CARE TIPS:** Easy. Light moisture. Tolerates drought. Fertilize sparingly. Shear after bloom. Propagate by cuttings, division, seed, suckers.

**NOTES:** Thrives in banks, understory plantings. Nice in rock, woodland, Xeriscape gardens. Aggressive. Resists pests, diseases.

## *Indigofera* spp. FABACEAE (LEGUMINOSAE)

### Indigo Bush

**SHAPE:** About 750 vigorous, vertical, woody, deciduous shrubs, 18″–36″ (45–90 cm) high and wide. Alternate, smooth, oval, divided, circular leaves to 4″ (10 cm) long with 1–5-paired, oval leaflets to 1½″ (38 mm) long.

**FLOWER:** Summer bloom. Vertical, spiking clusters, 5″–8″ (13–20 cm) long, of pealike flowers to ¾″ (19 mm) long. Choose from pink, purple, rose, red, white, and yellow. Forms beanlike pods containing seed in autumn.

**HARDINESS:** Zones 5–10.

**SOIL TYPE:** Sandy loam. High moisture, good drainage, high-medium fertility, 6.0–7.0 pH.

**PLANTING GUIDE:** Spring. Plant in full sun, 10″–20″ (25–50 cm) apart.

**CARE TIPS:** Easy. Even moisture. Fertilize every 12 weeks. Prune severely in spring. Propagate by cuttings, division, seed.

**NOTES:** Thrives in borders, edgings. Nice in cottage, meadow gardens. Resists pests, diseases.

## *Isopogon formosus* PROTEACEAE

### Rose Coneflower

**SHAPE:** Various slow-growing, vertical, slender, evergreen shrubs, 4′–8′ (1.2–2.4 m) high and 36″–60″ (90–150 cm) wide. Shiny, featherlike, stiff, slender, deep-cut leaves to 3″ (75 mm) long with leaflets to 1″ (25 mm) long.

**FLOWER:** Late-winter or early-spring bloom. Short stalks from leaf axils bear circular flowers to 3″ (75 mm) wide. Choose from pink, purple, and rose. Forms hirsute, nutlike fruit in summer.

**HARDINESS:** Zones 8–11. Protect from frost, heat.

**SOIL TYPE:** Sandy soil. Average–low moisture, good drainage, medium fertility, 6.5–7.5 pH.

**PLANTING GUIDE:** Spring or autumn. Plant in full to filtered sun, 36″–48″ (90–120 cm) apart.

**CARE TIPS:** Average. Light moisture. Tolerates drought. Fertilize every 6–8 weeks. Pinch tips for bushy plants. Propagate by cuttings, seed.

**NOTES:** Thrives in accents, beds, borders, containers, screens, walls. Nice in arid, seaside gardens. Resists pests, diseases.

## *Jasminum* spp. OLEACEAE

### Jasmine (Jessamine)

**SHAPE:** About 200 upright, rambling, twining, deciduous or evergreen shrubs to 20′ (6 m) long. Alternate, divided leaves, with heart-shaped, fine-toothed, folded leaflets, to 3″ (75 mm) long.

**FLOWER:** Spring, summer, or autumn bloom. Diverse, often aromatic, pinwheel- or star-shaped flowers, ½″–2″ (12–50 mm) wide. Choose from pink, rose, white, and yellow. Forms black berries.

**HARDINESS:** Most, zones 8–11.

**SOIL TYPE:** Loam. Most moistures, good drainage, high-medium fertility, 6.5–8.0 pH.

**PLANTING GUIDE:** Spring. Plant in full to filtered sun, 6′–10′ (1.8–3 m) apart.

**CARE TIPS:** Average. Light moisture. Fertilize every 10–12 weeks. Support. Prune after bloom. Propagate by cuttings, layering, seed.

**NOTES:** Thrives in arbors, banks, trellises, walls. Nice in cottage, rock, tropical, wildlife, woodland gardens. Cutting flower. Resists pests, diseases.

## *Justicia brandegeana* (*Beloperone guttata*) ACANTHACEAE

### Shrimp Plant (False Hop, Shrimp Bush)

**SHAPE:** Various mounded, open, tropical evergreen shrubs to 36″ (90 cm) high. Soft, textured, hirsute, lancelike or oval leaves to 3″ (75 mm) long on weak leaf stalks.

**FLOWER:** Spring to autumn bloom. Prawnlike clusters to 6″ (15 cm) long of irregular, segmented, tubular, nodding flowers. Choose from purple, red, and white with contrasting bracts. Forms capsule-shaped fruit in autumn.

**HARDINESS:** Zones 9–11. Protect from frost.

**SOIL TYPE:** Loam. High–average moisture, good drainage, high–medium fertility, 6.5–7.5 pH.

**PLANTING GUIDE:** Spring, as soil warms. Plant in full to filtered sun, 36″–48″ (90–120 cm) apart.

**CARE TIPS:** Easy. Light moisture; limit water in winter. Fertilize every 4 weeks. Extend bloom by deadheading. Prune severely in spring. Propagate by stem cuttings, seed.

**NOTES:** Thrives in accents, containers. Nice in small-space, wildlife gardens. Resists pests, diseases.

## *Kalmia latifolia* ERICACEAE

### Mountain Laurel (Calico Bush)

**SHAPE:** Various slow-growing, thick-growing, mounded, evergreen shrubs to 10′ (3 m) high. Shiny, azalea-like, leathery, lancelike leaves to 5″ (13 cm) long. Turns colors in autumn.

**FLOWER:** Late-spring bloom on second-year wood. Mounded clusters to 8″ (20 cm) wide of cup-like, star-pointed flowers to 1½″ (38 mm) wide. Choose from brown, pink, red, rose, and white. Forms capsule-shaped seedpods in late summer.

**HARDINESS:** Zones 4–8. Protect from hot sun.

**SOIL TYPE:** High humus. High moisture, good drainage, high fertility, 5.5–6.5 pH.

**PLANTING GUIDE:** Spring. Plant in full sun to full shade, 6′–8′ (1.8–2.4 m) apart.

**CARE TIPS:** Easy. Even moisture. Fertilize every 10–12 weeks. Apply mulch. Prune lightly after bloom. Propagate by cuttings, layering, seed.

**NOTES:** Thrives in mixed plantings, screens. Nice in natural, woodland gardens. Susceptible to borers, lacebugs, fungal diseases, leaf spot.

## *Kerria japonica* ROSACEAE

### Japanese Rose (Kerria)

**SHAPE:** Various erect, bushlike, circular, deciduous shrubs, 4′–6′ (1.2–1.8 m) high and to 8′ (2.4 m) wide. Alternate, textured, oval, toothed, veined leaves to 2″ (50 mm) long.

**FLOWER:** Spring to early-summer bloom. Numerous single to very double flowers to 2″ (50 mm) wide. Choose from gold and yellow. Forms dry, clustered fruit in late summer.

**HARDINESS:** Zones 4–9.

**SOIL TYPE:** Sandy loam. High–average moisture, good drainage, medium fertility, 6.0–7.0 pH.

**PLANTING GUIDE:** Spring. Plant in full sun to partial shade, 36″–48″ (90–120 cm) apart.

**CARE TIPS:** Average. Light moisture. Fertilize every 10–12 weeks. Prune, thin after bloom. Propagate by cuttings, division, layering, seed.

**NOTES:** Thrives in accents, beds, borders. Nice in Asian, heritage, shade, woodland gardens. Cutting flower. Susceptible to Japanese beetles, blight, canker.

## *Kolkwitzia amabilis* CAPRIFOLIACEAE

### Beautybush

**SHAPE:** Lone vigorous, arched, deciduous, shrub to 15′ (4.5 m) high and wide with brown, flaking bark. Oval leaves to 3″ (75 mm) long. Turns colors in autumn.

**FLOWER:** Late-spring bloom, on second-year wood. Dense clusters of paired, 5-petaled flowers to ½″ (12 mm) long. Pink, with bristly, yellow centers. Forms bristly, brown fruit in summer.

**HARDINESS:** Zones 5–8. Protect from hot sun.

**SOIL TYPE:** Sandy loam. High moisture, good drainage, high–low fertility, 6.0–8.0 pH.

**PLANTING GUIDE:** Spring. Plant in full sun to partial shade, 12′ (3.7 m) apart.

**CARE TIPS:** Easy. Even moisture. Fertilize every 4 weeks. Apply mulch, zones 4–5. Prune after bloom. Propagate by cuttings.

**NOTES:** Thrives in accents, backgrounds, beds, borders, fence lines. Nice in natural, shade, small-space, wildlife, woodland gardens. Resists pests, diseases.

## *Lagerstroemia indica* LYTHRACEAE

### Crape Myrtle

**SHAPE:** Numerous slow-growing, sprawling, branched, dense, deciduous shrubby trees to 20′ (6 m) high and wide. Shiny, oval leaves to 3″ (75 mm) long. Turns colors in autumn.

**FLOWER:** Spring bloom. Cone-shaped clusters to 12″ (30 cm) long of aromatic, ruffled flowers to 1½″ (38 mm) wide. Choose from pink, purple, red, rose, and white. Forms brown, round fruit in autumn to winter.

**HARDINESS:** Zones 7–10.

**SOIL TYPE:** Sandy loam. Average moisture, good drainage, medium fertility, 6.5–7.5 pH.

**PLANTING GUIDE:** Spring or autumn. Plant in full sun, 5′–30′ (1.5–9 m) apart.

**CARE TIPS:** Easy. Light moisture until established. Fertilize sparingly. Prune in winter. Propagate by cuttings, seed.

**NOTES:** Thrives in accents, containers, paths. Nice in seaside, small-space gardens. Resists deer, insect pests. Susceptible to powdery mildew.

## *Lantana* spp. and hybrids VERBENACEAE

### Shrub Verbena (Lantana)

**SHAPE:** Many vigorous, often armed, evergreen, tropical shrubs to 6′ (1.8 m) high and wide. Shiny, oval, aromatic leaves to 5″ (13 cm) long.

**FLOWER:** Summer bloom, or year-round. Flat, mounded, or spiking clusters to 3″ (75 mm) wide, of tiny flowers. Choose from cream, gold, orange, pink, purple, red, yellow, and bicolored. Forms blackberry-like fruit in autumn.

**HARDINESS:** Zones 9–10. Protect from frost.

**SOIL TYPE:** Sandy soil. Average moisture, good drainage, high-medium fertility, 6.5–7.5 pH.

**PLANTING GUIDE:** Spring, as soil warms. Plant in full sun, 36″–48″ (90–120 cm) apart.

**CARE TIPS:** Easy. Light moisture. Fertilize only in spring. Prune to promote bushiness. Propagate by cuttings, seed.

**NOTES:** Thrives in accents, banks, borders, containers, edgings, ground covers. Nice in formal, meadow, wildlife gardens. Susceptible to aphids, mealybugs, whiteflies, orthezia.

## *Lantana montevidensis* and hybrids VERBENACEAE

### Trailing Lantana (Polecat Geranium, Weeping Lantana)

**SHAPE:** Several vigorous, sprawling woody, evergreen shrubs, 36″–60″ (90–150 cm) wide or long. Opposite or whorled, deeply textured, oval, toothed, aromatic leaves to 1″ (25 mm) long.

**FLOWER:** Spring to autumn bloom. Ball-shaped clusters to 2″ (50 mm) wide of tiny, 4-petaled, tubular flowers. Choose from lilac, pink, purple, and rose. Forms berrylike seed in autumn.

**HARDINESS:** Zones 8–11. Protect from frost.

**SOIL TYPE:** Sandy loam. Average moisture, good drainage, medium fertility, 6.5–7.0 pH.

**PLANTING GUIDE:** Spring, as soil warms. Plant in full sun, 18″ (45 cm) apart.

**CARE TIPS:** Easy. Light moisture. Tolerates drought. Fertilize every 10–12 weeks. Prune in spring, after bloom. Propagate by cuttings, seed.

**NOTES:** Thrives in banks, containers, foregrounds, hedges. Nice in cottage, meadow, natural, seaside, small-space gardens. Susceptible to aphids, mealybugs, whiteflies, orthezia, mildew.

## *Leonotis leonurus* LAMIACEAE (LABIATAE)

### Lion's-Ear (Lion's-Tail)

**SHAPE:** Various slow-growing, erect, branched evergreen shrubs, 5′–7′ (1.5–2.2 m) high and 4′–6′ (1.2–1.8 m) wide. Opposite, textured, soft, lancelike, toothed leaves, 2″–4″ (50–100 mm) long.

**FLOWER:** Summer to autumn bloom. Whorls to 6″ (15 cm) wide of lipped, tubular, hirsute flowers to 2½″ (63 mm) long. Choose from orange and red. Forms nutlike fruit bearing seed in autumn.

**HARDINESS:** Zones 8–11. Protect from frost.

**SOIL TYPE:** Sandy soil. Low moisture, good drainage, medium–low fertility, 6.0–7.0 pH.

**PLANTING GUIDE:** Spring, as soil warms. Plant in full sun, 24″–48″ (60–120 cm) apart.

**CARE TIPS:** Easy. Light moisture. Fertilize sparingly. Deadhead spent stalks. Shear in late autumn. Propagate by cuttings, seed.

**NOTES:** Thrives in accents, banks, fence lines, paths. Nice in cottage, formal, meadow, wildlife gardens. Cutting flower. Resists pests, diseases.

## *Leucothoe* spp. ERICACEAE

### Fetterbush (Doghobble, Sierra Laurel)

**SHAPE:** About 50 erect, arched, evergreen shrubs to 6′ (1.8 m) high and 4′–8′ (1.2–2.4 m) wide. Alternate, shiny, leathery, oval leaves to 7″ (18 cm) long. Turns colors in autumn.

**FLOWER:** Early-summer bloom. Nodding, clusters, 2″–4″ (50–100 mm) long, of tiny, bell-shaped flowers. Choose from cream, pink, and white. Forms capsule-shaped seedpods in autumn.

**HARDINESS:** Zones 5–9.

**SOIL TYPE:** Sandy loam. High–average moisture, good drainage, high fertility, 5.5–6.5 pH.

**PLANTING GUIDE:** Spring. Plant in full sun to partial shade, 36″–48″ (90–120 cm) apart.

**CARE TIPS:** Easy. Even moisture. Fertilize every 4 weeks during growth. Extend bloom by deadheading. Shelter from wind. Propagate by cuttings, division, runners, seed.

**NOTES:** Thrives in accents, beds, borders, containers, foregrounds. Nice in bog, woodland gardens. Cutting flower. Resists pests, diseases.

## *Lonicera* spp. CAPRIFOLIACEAE

### Honeysuckle

**SHAPE:** More than 150 erect or twining, deciduous or evergreen shrubs or vines, 3′–30′ (90–900 cm) high. Simple, shiny, leathery, oval leaves, 1″–6″ (25–150 mm) long. Turns colors in autumn.

**FLOWER:** Spring to autumn bloom. Numerous aromatic, tubular, lipped, flowers, ½″–2″ (12–50 mm) long. Forms black, purple, red berries in autumn. Choose from coral, pink, white, and yellow.

**HARDINESS:** Zones 4–9.

**SOIL TYPE:** Sandy loam. Average moisture, good drainage, high-medium fertility, 6.5–7.5 pH.

**PLANTING GUIDE:** Spring. Plant in full sun to partial shade. Space as recommended for cultivar.

**CARE TIPS:** Easy. Light moisture. Tolerates drought. Fertilize only in spring. Propagate by cuttings, layering, seed.

**NOTES:** Thrives in ground covers, hedges, trellises, walls. Nice in cottage, meadow, wildlife gardens. Aggressive. Resists diseases. Susceptible to aphids.

## *Loropetalum chinense* (*L. chinensis*) HAMAMELIDACEAE

### Loropetalum

**SHAPE:** An erect, arching, dense, woolly evergreen shrub to 12′ (3.7 m) high. Simple, oval, hirsute leaves, 1″–2″ (25–50 mm) long.

**FLOWER:** Early-spring bloom. Terminal clusters of irregular, open, wavy- and narrow-petaled, aromatic flowers to 2″ (50 mm) wide. Choose from green, pink, purple, and white. Forms capsule-shaped fruit in autumn.

**HARDINESS:** Zones 8–10. Protect from frost, hot sun, prolonged freezing of roots.

**SOIL TYPE:** High humus. High moisture, good drainage, high-medium fertility, 6.0–7.0 pH.

**PLANTING GUIDE:** Spring. Plant in partial to full shade, 8′–10′ (2.4–3 m) apart.

**CARE TIPS:** Easy. Even moisture. Fertilize every 6–8 weeks. Prune severely after bloom. Propagate by cuttings.

**NOTES:** Thrives in beds, borders, foregrounds, hedges. Nice in cottage, formal, woodland gardens. Resists pests, diseases.

## *Mahonia aquifolium* BERBERIDACEAE

### Oregon Grape (Mahonia)

**SHAPE:** Numerous slow-growing, sprawling, broad-leaved, evergreen shrubs to 12′ (3.7 m) high. Groups of 5 or 7, shiny, toothed, spiny leaves to 3″ (75 mm) long. Turns colors in autumn.

**FLOWER:** Spring bloom. Slender clusters of aromatic, bell-shaped flowers to ½″ (12 mm) wide. Yellow. Forms blueberry-like fruit in autumn.

**HARDINESS:** Most, zones 4–8.

**SOIL TYPE:** High humus. High moisture, good drainage, high fertility, 5.5–6.5 pH.

**PLANTING GUIDE:** Spring or autumn. Plant in partial to full shade, 5′–7′ (1.5–2.2 m) apart.

**CARE TIPS:** Easy to average. Even moisture. Tolerates drought. Fertilize every 10–12 weeks. Apply mulch, zones 7–8. Prune sparingly. Propagate by cuttings, layering, seed.

**NOTES:** Thrives in accents, backgrounds, barriers, fence lines, hedges. Nice in natural, woodland, Xeriscape gardens. Fruit attracts birds. Resists pests, diseases.

## *Mandevilla* × *amabilis* hybrids APOCYNACEAE

### Mandevilla

**SHAPE:** Numerous vigorous, vertical, twining, evergreen shrubs to 20′ (6 m) long. Opposite, shiny, oval, wavy-edged leaves, 4″–8″ (10–20 cm) long.

**FLOWER:** Late-spring to autumn bloom. Clusters of deep-throated, round, 5-petaled flowers, 3″–4″ (75–100 mm) wide. Choose from pink, red, white, bicolored. Forms hirsute fruit in autumn.

**HARDINESS:** Zones 8–11.

**SOIL TYPE:** Sandy loam. High moisture, good drainage, high fertility, 6.5–7.5 pH.

**PLANTING GUIDE:** Spring. Plant in full sun, 36″ (90 cm) apart.

**CARE TIPS:** Easy. Even moisture until established. Tolerates drought. Fertilize every 4 weeks. Stake to support. Pinch tips for bushy plants. Propagate by cuttings.

**NOTES:** Thrives in arbors, pillars, trellises, walls. Nice in arid, tropical, wildlife gardens. Cutting flower. Resists diseases. Susceptible to mealybugs, spider mites, whiteflies.

## *Musa spp.* MUSACEAE

### Ornamental Banana (Banana, Plantain)

**SHAPE:** About 25 vigorous, treelike, sprawling, tropical, rhizomatous, evergreen perennials to over 15' (4.5 m) high and 10' (3 m) wide. Smooth, shiny, often striped, broad-bladed fronds to 5' (1.5 m) long in a trunklike base.

**FLOWER:** Summer bloom. Pendulous, fleshy stem to 36" (90 cm) long with terminal flower bud to 5" (13 cm) long. Yellow, with purple, red bracts. Forms fruit in fingerlike clusters.

**HARDINESS:** Zones 9–11. Protect from frost.

**SOIL TYPE:** Sandy loam. High moisture, good drainage, high fertility, 6.0–7.0 pH.

**PLANTING GUIDE:** Spring, as soil warms. Plant in full to filtered sun, 4'–6' (1.2–1.8 m) apart.

**CARE TIPS:** Average to difficult. Even moisture. Fertilize every 4 weeks. Apply mulch; top dress annually. Propagate by division, offsets, seed.

**NOTES:** Thrives in backgrounds, fence lines. Nice in tropical gardens. Susceptible to aphids, mealybugs, spider mites, brown spot.

## *Nandina domestica* BERBERIDACEAE

### Heavenly Bamboo

**SHAPE:** A bushlike, open, evergreen shrub to 8' (2.4 m) high and 4' (1.2 m) wide. Bamboolike, delicate, oval leaves, 2" (50 mm) long. Turns colors in autumn. Dwarf cultivars available.

**FLOWER:** Late-spring to summer bloom. Lacy clusters to 12" (30 cm) long of tiny flowers. White. Forms red berries in autumn.

**HARDINESS:** Zones 7–10. Protect from frost.

**SOIL TYPE:** High humus. Most moistures, good drainage, high-medium fertility, 6.5–7.0 pH.

**PLANTING GUIDE:** Spring or autumn. Plant in full sun to partial shade, 24"–72" (60–180 cm) apart.

**CARE TIPS:** Easy. Even moisture until established. Tolerates drought. Fertilize every 6–8 weeks. Apply mulch, zones 6–7. Prune in early spring. Propagate by seed.

**NOTES:** Thrives in beds, borders, containers, fence lines, screens. Nice in tropical gardens. Resists deer, insect pests, oak root fungus. Susceptible to chlorosis.

## *Nerium oleander* APOCYNACEAE

### Common Oleander

**SHAPE:** Numerous vigorous, thick-growing, bushlike, arched evergreen shrubs to 20' (6 m) high and 12' (3.7 m) wide. Dull, leathery, slender leaves to 12" (30 cm) long.

**FLOWER:** Spring to autumn bloom. Clusters of aromatic, single to double flowers to 3" (75 mm) wide. Choose from pink, red, white, and yellow. Forms hirsute, tufted seed in autumn.

**HARDINESS:** Zones 6–11. Prefers hot, arid climates.

**SOIL TYPE:** Sandy loam. High moisture, good drainage, medium–low fertility, 6.5–7.0 pH.

**PLANTING GUIDE:** Autumn. Plant in full sun, 5'–10' (1.5–3 m) apart.

**CARE TIPS:** Easy. Even moisture until established. Tolerates drought. Fertilize only in spring. Apply mulch. Prune after bloom. Propagate by cuttings.

**NOTES:** Thrives in backgrounds, borders, containers, hedges, screens. Nice in arid, Xeriscape gardens. Resists deer, rodents. Susceptible to aphids, mealybugs, scale, leaf scorch.

## *Philadelphus coronarius* HYDRANGEACEAE (PHILADELPHACEAE, SAXIFRAGACEAE)

### Sweet Mock Orange

**SHAPE:** Numerous vigorous, thick-growing, sprawling, deciduous shrubs to 10' (3 m) high and wide. Dull to shiny, green, oval leaves, 1"–3" (25–75 mm) long.

**FLOWER:** Late-spring bloom. Radiating clusters of intensely fragrant, semi-double flowers to 1½" (38 mm) wide. Creamy white. Forms abundant seed in late summer.

**HARDINESS:** Zones 5–9.

**SOIL TYPE:** Compost or leaf mold. High moisture, good drainage, high-medium fertility, 6.5–7.5 pH.

**PLANTING GUIDE:** Spring. Plant in partial shade, 36" (90 cm) apart.

**CARE TIPS:** Easy. Even moisture until established. Tolerates drought. Fertilize every 6–8 weeks. Prune after bloom. Propagate by cuttings, layering, seed.

**NOTES:** Good for borders, edgings, hedges, paths. Nice in formal, small-space, woodland gardens. Resists pests, diseases.

## *Photinia* spp. and hybrids ROSACEAE

### Photinia

**SHAPE:** Numerous vigorous, vertical, circular, thick-growing, evergreen shrubs to 15' (4.5 m) high and wide. Alternate, shiny, oval to lancelike leaves, 2"–6" (50–150 mm) long.

**FLOWER:** Early-spring bloom. Clusters of aromatic, cup-shaped flowers to 3/8" (9 mm) wide with long stamens. Forms red, berrylike fruit in summer. Choose from cream, green, and white.

**HARDINESS:** Zones 6–9.

**SOIL TYPE:** Sandy loam. High–average moisture, good drainage, high–medium fertility, 6.0–7.5 pH.

**PLANTING GUIDE:** Spring. Plant in full sun, 4'–5' (1.2–1.5 m) apart.

**CARE TIPS:** Easy. Even moisture until established. Tolerates drought. Fertilize every 10–12 weeks. Apply mulch in winter. Prune or shear to shape. Propagate by cuttings, grafting, layering, seed.

**NOTES:** Thrives in backgrounds, hedges, screens. Nice in arid, wildlife, woodland gardens. Resists pests. Susceptible to chlorosis, fireblight, mildew.

## *Phygelius capensis* SCROPHULARIACEAE

### Cape Fuchsia

**SHAPE:** Few mounded, woody, deciduous subshrubs to 36" (90 cm) high and wide. Opposite, simple, oval to lancelike, lobate, fine-toothed leaves to 5" (13 cm) long.

**FLOWER:** Summer to autumn bloom. Spikes with nodding, tubular, flared flowers to 2" (50 mm) long. Choose from cream, rose, and yellow. Forms capsule-shaped fruit in autumn.

**HARDINESS:** Zones 8–10.

**SOIL TYPE:** Loam. High moisture, good drainage, high fertility, 6.0–7.0 pH.

**PLANTING GUIDE:** Spring, as soil warms. Plant in full to filtered sun, 36"–48" (90–120 cm) apart.

**CARE TIPS:** Easy. Even moisture. Fertilize every 4 weeks. Extend bloom by deadheading. Mulch in winter. Prune or shear in autumn. Propagate by cuttings, layering, seed.

**NOTES:** Thrives in accents, beds, containers, foregrounds. Nice in woodland gardens. Resists pests, diseases.

## *Pieris japonica* (*Andromeda japonica*) ERICACEAE

### Lily-of-the-Valley Bush (Japanese Andromeda)

**SHAPE:** Numerous slow-growing, circular, branched, evergreen shrubs, 10'–20' (3–6 m) high and wide. Shiny, rhododendron-like, oval to lancelike, fine-toothed leaves to 3" (75 mm) long.

**FLOWER:** Late-winter to spring bloom. Pendulous, lily-of-the-valley–like clusters to 6" (15 cm) long of bell-shaped flowers, 1/4"–3/8" (6–9 mm) wide. Choose from cream, pink, and white. Forms lobed, capsule-shaped fruit in summer.

**HARDINESS:** Zones 5–9.

**SOIL TYPE:** High humus. High moisture, good drainage, high–medium fertility, 5.0–6.5 pH.

**PLANTING GUIDE:** Spring, as soil warms. Plant in filtered sun to partial shade, 8' (2.4 m) apart.

**CARE TIPS:** Easy. Even moisture. Tolerates drought. Fertilize every 10–12 weeks. Prune after bloom to shape. Propagate by cuttings, layering, seed.

**NOTES:** Thrives in accents, backgrounds, fence lines, paths, screens. Nice in woodland gardens. Resists pests. Susceptible to fungal diseases.

## *Pittosporum tobira* PITTOSPORACEAE

### Japanese Pittosporum (Mock Orange)

**SHAPE:** Various slow-growing, mounded, evergreen shrubs or small trees to 18' (5.5 m) high. Shiny, leathery, oval leaves to 4" (10 cm) long. Dwarf cultivar, 'Wheeler's Dwarf', available.

**FLOWER:** Spring bloom. Showy, mounded clusters of aromatic, bell-shaped flowers to 1/2" (12 mm) wide. White. Forms orange, round berrylike fruit in autumn.

**HARDINESS:** Zones 9–10.

**SOIL TYPE:** Sandy loam. Average moisture, good drainage, medium fertility, 6.5–8.0 pH. Tolerates humidity, salt.

**PLANTING GUIDE:** Spring, as soil warms. Plant in full sun, 4'–6' (1.2–1.8 m) apart.

**CARE TIPS:** Easy. Light moisture until established. Tolerates drought. Apply mulch. Prune in spring. Propagate by cuttings, grafting, seed.

**NOTES:** Thrives in backgrounds, edgings, hedges, paths. Nice in arid, Asian, cottage, small-space gardens. Susceptible to aphids, scale, sooty mold.

## *Plumeria rubra* forms and cultivars APOCYNACEAE

### Plumeria (Frangipani, Nosegay, Temple Tree)

**SHAPE:** Various round, woody, tropical, deciduous shrubs, 20'–25' (6–7.5 m) high and to 18' (5.5 m) wide. Shiny, leathery, oval, veined leaves to 20" (50 cm) long with downy undersides.

**FLOWER:** Spring to early-winter bloom. Flat clusters of aromatic, 5-petaled, waxy, often reflexed flowers, 2"–5" (50–125 mm) wide. Choose from cream, gold, orange, pink, red, and white. Forms dry, winged seed in autumn.

**HARDINESS:** Zones 10–11.

**SOIL TYPE:** High humus; pond shorelines. Average –low moisture, good drainage, medium fertility, 6.0–7.0 pH.

**PLANTING GUIDE:** Spring, as soil warms. Plant in full to filtered sun, 7'–10' (2.2–3 m) apart.

**CARE TIPS:** Easy. Even moisture. Tolerates drought. Fertilize every 4 weeks. Propagate by cuttings.

**NOTES:** Thrives in accents, containers, hedges, screens. Nice in tropical, woodland gardens and ponds. Cutting flower. Resists pests, diseases.

## *Polygala* × *dalmaisiana* hybrids POLYGALACEAE

### Sweet-Pea Shrub

**SHAPE:** Various mounded to erect, circular, evergreen shrubs, 4'–8' (1.2–2.4 m) high and wide. Usually alternate, smooth, oval or lancelike leaves, ¾"–1" (19–25 mm) long.

**FLOWER:** Spring to autumn bloom. Pendulous clusters of pealike flowers to 1" (25 mm) long. Choose from pink, purple, and rose. Forms capsule-shaped pods with seed in autumn.

**HARDINESS:** Zones 9–11. Protect from frost. Prefers mild-winter, hot-summer climates.

**SOIL TYPE:** Sandy loam. High moisture, good drainage, high–medium fertility, 6.5–8.0 pH. Tolerates salt.

**PLANTING GUIDE:** Spring, as soil warms. Plant in full to filtered sun, 36"–48" (90–120 cm) apart.

**CARE TIPS:** Easy. Even moisture. Fertilize every 10–12 weeks. Shear in winter. Propagate by seed.

**NOTES:** Thrives in accents, backgrounds, fillers. Nice in arid, meadow, rock, seaside, tropical gardens. Resists pests, diseases.

## *Potentilla fruticosa* ROSACEAE

### Bush Cinquefoil (Shrubby Cinquefoil)

**SHAPE:** Numerous slow-growing, thick-growing, round, deciduous shrubs, 24"–48" (60–120 cm) high. Shiny, oval or lancelike, usually 5-lobed, divided leaves to ¾" (19 mm) long.

**FLOWER:** Late-spring to autumn bloom. Numerous open, single flowers to 1¼" (32 mm) wide. Choose from orange, pink, red, white, and yellow. Forms brown seed on female plants in autumn.

**HARDINESS:** Zones 3–9. Protect from hot sun.

**SOIL TYPE:** Sandy loam. High–average moisture, good drainage, high–low fertility, 6.0–8.0 pH.

**PLANTING GUIDE:** Spring. Plant in full sun to partial shade, 36"–48" (90–120 cm) apart.

**CARE TIPS:** Easy. Even moisture until established. Fertilize every 12 weeks. Apply mulch, zones 2–4. Prune after bloom. Propagate by division, seed.

**NOTES:** Thrives in backgrounds, beds, borders, edgings, hedges. Nice in cottage, formal, rock, small-space gardens. Resists diseases. Susceptible to spider mites.

## *Punica granatum* 'Nana' PUNICACEAE

### Dwarf Pomegranate

**SHAPE:** Various thick-growing, circular, spiny semi-evergreen trees to 36" (90 cm) high and 6' (1.8 mm) wide. Shiny, oval, fine-toothed leaves to ¾" (19 mm) long.

**FLOWER:** Summer to autumn bloom. Numerous open, tubular, fringed flowers to 1½" (38 mm) wide. Choose from orange and red. Forms red, leathery-skinned, edible fruit in autumn.

**HARDINESS:** Zones 8–11.

**SOIL TYPE:** Sandy loam. Average moisture, good drainage, high–low fertility, 6.0–8.0 pH.

**PLANTING GUIDE:** Spring. Plant in full sun, 5' (1.5 m) apart.

**CARE TIPS:** Easy. Even moisture until established. Tolerates drought. Fertilize every 10–12 weeks. Apply mulch. Prune in autumn. Propagate by cuttings, layering, seed.

**NOTES:** Thrives in foregrounds, containers, edgings, hedges. Nice in rock, small-space, wildlife gardens. Resists pests, diseases.

## *Pyracantha* spp. ROSACEAE

### Pyracantha (Fire Thorn)

**SHAPE:** Few erect or sprawling, thick-growing, spiny evergreen shrubs, 6'–20' (1.8–6 m) high. Shiny, leathery, lancelike leaves, ¾"–4" (19–100 mm) long.

**FLOWER:** Spring bloom. Dense, mounded clusters of small, single flowers. White. Forms bright red berries in autumn, lasting to winter.

**HARDINESS:** Zones 6–9. Prefers dry climates. Tolerates hot sun.

**SOIL TYPE:** Sandy loam. High moisture, good drainage, medium fertility, 6.0–8.0 pH.

**PLANTING GUIDE:** Spring, as soil warms. Plant in full sun, 6'–8' (1.8–2.4 m) apart. Best grown in garden soil.

**CARE TIPS:** Average. Even moisture until established. Fertilize only in spring. Prune after bloom. Propagate by cuttings, grafting, layering, seed.

**NOTES:** Thrives in accents, barriers, espaliers, fence lines, ground covers, hedges. Nice in arid, formal, small-space, wildlife gardens. Resists pests. Susceptible to fireblight, apple scab.

## *Rhododendron* spp. ERICACEAE

### Azalea

**SHAPE:** Various slow-growing, usually deciduous shrubs or small trees, 36"–120" (90–305 cm) high. Radiating clusters of waxy, oval leaves to 4" (10 cm) long. Turns colors in autumn.

**FLOWER:** Spring to summer bloom. Clusters of aromatic, trumpet-shaped flowers to 2" (50 mm) wide. Choose from orange, pink, red, white, and yellow. Forms capsule-shaped fruit in summer.

**HARDINESS:** Most, zones 7–9; some, zones 4–6.

**SOIL TYPE:** High humus. High moisture, good drainage, high fertility, 6.0–6.5 pH.

**PLANTING GUIDE:** Spring, as soil warms. Plant in filtered sun to full shade, 4' (1.2 m) apart.

**CARE TIPS:** Average. Even moisture until established; limit water thereafter. Fertilize every 4 weeks. Cultivate sparingly. Propagate by cuttings, layering.

**NOTES:** Thrives in accents, beds, containers, screens. Nice in meadow, small-space, woodland gardens. Susceptible to root weevils, powdery mildew.

## *Rhododendron* spp. ERICACEAE

### Rhododendron

**SHAPE:** Numerous diverse, slow-growing, sprawling, woody, usually evergreen shrubs or small trees to 25' (7.5 m) high and wide. Rosettes of waxy, oval to lancelike leaves to 12" (30 cm) long.

**FLOWER:** Spring to summer bloom. Round clusters, to 16" (40 cm) wide of aromatic, trumpet-shaped flowers to 8" (20 cm) long. Choose from cream, lavender, orange, pink, purple, red, white, and yellow. Forms capsulelike fruit in summer.

**HARDINESS:** Most, zones 6–10; some, zones 4–5.

**SOIL TYPE:** High humus. High moisture, good drainage, high fertility, 5.5–6.5 pH.

**PLANTING GUIDE:** Spring. Plant in filtered sun to partial shade, 6'–10' (1.8–3 m) apart.

**CARE TIPS:** Average. Even moisture until established. Fertilize every 4 weeks. Cultivate sparingly. Propagate by cuttings, layering.

**NOTES:** Thrives in accents, backgrounds, screens. Nice in meadow, woodland gardens. Resists diseases. Susceptible to root weevils.

## *Rosa banksiae* (*R. banksia*) ROSACEAE

### Lady Banks' Rose

**SHAPE:** Various vertical, arching, branched, thornless, semi-evergreen shrubs to 20' (6 m) long with alternate, shiny leaves, divided into 3–5-leaflet groups, 1"–2½" (25–63 mm) long.

**FLOWER:** Spring bloom; some remontant. Clusters of aromatic, very double flowers to 1" (25 mm) wide. Choose from white and yellow. Blooms on second-year wood.

**HARDINESS:** Zones 7–11.

**SOIL TYPE:** Sandy loam. Average moisture, good drainage, high fertility, 6.5–7.0 pH.

**PLANTING GUIDE:** Spring. Plant in full sun, 10' (3 m) apart.

**CARE TIPS:** Average. Even moisture. Drought tolerant. Fertilize every 4 weeks. Prune after bloom. Propagate by cuttings, layering.

**NOTES:** Thrives in arbors, fence lines, pillars, trellises. Nice in cottage, formal, small-space gardens. Resists diseases. Susceptible to aphids, spider mites, thrips.

## *Rosa* hybrids ROSACEAE

### Climbing Roses

**SHAPE:** Various vertical, climbing sports of bush-like, branched, deciduous shrubs to 12′ (3.7 m) tall with alternate, shiny leaves, divided into 3–5-leaflet groups, 1½″–3″ (38–75 mm) long.

**FLOWER:** Spring bloom; some remontant. Clusters of aromatic, single to very double flowers to 6″ (15 cm) wide. Choose from cream, orange, pink, red, white, yellow, and multicolored. Most bloom on second-year wood.

**HARDINESS:** Zones 4–10. Prefer dry climates.

**SOIL TYPE:** Sandy loam. High–average moisture, good drainage, high fertility, 6.5–7.0 pH.

**PLANTING GUIDE:** Spring. Plant in full sun, 6′ (1.8 m) apart.

**CARE TIPS:** Average. Light moisture. Fertilize every 4 weeks. Prune after bloom. Vegetative propagation usually restricted.

**NOTES:** Thrives in arbors, trellises. Nice in cottage, formal gardens. Susceptible to aphids, midges, spider mites, thrips, mildew, rust, black spot.

## *Rosa* hybrids ROSACEAE

### Floribunda Roses

**SHAPE:** Numerous erect, bushlike, deciduous shrubs and grafted standards, 36″–42″ (90–107 cm) high. Alternate, shiny leaves, divided into 3–5-leaflet groups, 1½″–2½″ (38–63 mm) long.

**FLOWER:** Spring to autumn bloom; remontant. Clusters of aromatic flowers to 5″ (13 cm) wide. Choose from orange, pink, purple, red, white, yellow, bicolored, blended, and striped.

**HARDINESS:** Most, zones 5–10; some, zones 2–4.

**SOIL TYPE:** Sandy loam. High–average moisture, good drainage, high fertility, 6.5–7.5 pH.

**PLANTING GUIDE:** Spring. Plant in full sun, 24″–30″ (60–75 cm) or more apart.

**CARE TIPS:** Average. Light moisture. Fertilize every 4 weeks. Pinch tips for bushy plants. Prune in late winter. Vegetative propagation usually restricted.

**NOTES:** Thrives in beds, borders, containers, fence lines. Nice in cottage, formal, small-space gardens. Cutting flower. Susceptible to aphids, midges, spider mites, thrips, mildew, rust, black spot.

## *Rosa* hybrids ROSACEAE

### Grandiflora Roses

**SHAPE:** Numerous upright, branched, deciduous shrubs and grafted standards, 6′–9′ (1.8–2.7 m) high and 4′–6′ (1.2–1.8 m) wide. Alternate, shiny leaves, divided into 3–5-leaflet groups, 1½″–3″ (38–75 mm) long.

**FLOWER:** Spring to autumn bloom; remontant. Clusters of double flowers to 8″ (20 cm) wide. Choose from cream, pink, red, and white.

**HARDINESS:** Most, zones 5–11; some, zone 3–4.

**SOIL TYPE:** Sandy loam. High–average moisture, good drainage, high fertility, 6.5–7.5 pH.

**PLANTING GUIDE:** Spring. Plant in full sun, 4′–5′ (1.2–1.5 m) apart.

**CARE TIPS:** Average. Light moisture. Fertilize every 4 weeks. Extend bloom by deadheading. Prune in spring. Vegetative propagation usually restricted.

**NOTES:** Thrives in accents, backgrounds, beds, paths, screens. Nice in cottage, formal gardens. Cutting flower. Susceptible to aphids, spider mites, thrips, mildew, rust, black spot.

## *Rosa* hybrids ROSACEAE

### Hybrid Tea Roses

**SHAPE:** Numerous upright, branched, deciduous shrubs and grafted standards, 4′–6′ (1.2–1.8 m) high and wide. Alternate, shiny leaves, divided into 3–5-leaflet groups to 3″ (75 mm) long.

**FLOWER:** Spring to autumn bloom; remontant. Single to double flowers to 8″ (20 cm) wide. Choose from cream, orange, pink, purple, red, white, yellow, bicolored, blended, and striped.

**HARDINESS:** Most, zones 5–11; some, zone 3–4.

**SOIL TYPE:** Sandy loam. High–average moisture, good drainage, high fertility, 6.5–7.5 pH.

**PLANTING GUIDE:** Spring. Plant in full sun, 36″–42″ (90–107 cm) apart.

**CARE TIPS:** Average. Light moisture. Fertilize every 4 weeks. Extend bloom by deadheading. Prune in spring. Vegetative propagation usually restricted.

**NOTES:** Thrives in borders, containers, paths. Nice in cottage, heritage, formal gardens. Cutting flower. Susceptible to aphids, midges, spider mites, thrips, mildew, rust, black spot.

## *Rosa* hybrids ROSACEAE

### Miniature Roses

**SHAPE:** Numerous mounded, bushlike, deciduous shrubs and grafted standards to 36″ (90 cm) high and wide. Alternate, shiny leaves, divided into 3–5-leaflet groups to 1½″ (38 mm) long.

**FLOWER:** Spring to autumn bloom; remontant. Clusters of double flowers to 2″ (50 mm) wide. Choose from cream, orange, pink, purple, red, white, yellow, bicolored, blended, and striped.

**HARDINESS:** Zones 3–10.

**SOIL TYPE:** Sandy loam. High–average moisture, good drainage, high fertility, 6.5–7.0 pH.

**PLANTING GUIDE:** Spring. Plant in full sun, 12″–18″ (30–45 cm) apart.

**CARE TIPS:** Average. Light moisture. Fertilize every 4 weeks. Pinch tips, flower buds. Prune in late winter. Vegetative propagation usually restricted.

**NOTES:** Thrives in beds, borders, containers, edgings. Nice in cottage, formal, small-space gardens. Cutting flower. Susceptible to aphids, midges, spider mites, thrips, mildew, rust, black spot.

## *Rosa* hybrids ROSACEAE

### Modern Shrub Roses

**SHAPE:** Numerous bushlike, deciduous shrubs and grafted standards, 4′–6′ (1.2–1.8 m) high and wide, with alternate, shiny leaves, divided into 3–5-leaflet groups, 1½″–3″ (38–75 mm) long.

**FLOWER:** Spring to autumn bloom; some remontant. Clusters of single to double flowers to 6″ (15 cm) wide. Choose from cream, orange, pink, red, white, yellow, bicolored, blended, and striped.

**HARDINESS:** Zones 3–10.

**SOIL TYPE:** Sandy loam. High–average moisture, good drainage, high fertility, 6.5–7.0 pH.

**PLANTING GUIDE:** Spring. Plant in full sun, 30″–36″ (75–90 cm) apart.

**CARE TIPS:** Average. Light moisture. Fertilize every 4 weeks. Pinch tips, flower buds. Prune in late winter. Vegetative propagation usually restricted.

**NOTES:** Thrives in beds, borders, containers, edgings. Nice in cottage, formal, small-space gardens. Cutting flower. Susceptible to aphids, midges, spider mites, thrips, mildew, rust, black spot.

## *Rosmarinus officinalis* 'Prostratus' LAMIACEAE (LABIATAE)

### Dwarf Rosemary

**SHAPE:** Numerous vigorous, short, sprawling or trailing, evergreen shrubs to 24″ (60 cm) high. Shiny, leathery, needlelike, very aromatic leaves, 1″–1½″ (25–38 mm) long.

**FLOWER:** Summer to autumn bloom. Upright, spiking clusters to 4″ (10 cm) long of tiny simple flowers. Choose from light blue and violet. Forms nutlets with seed in autumn.

**HARDINESS:** Zones 7–11.

**SOIL TYPE:** Sandy soil. Average–low moisture, good drainage, low fertility, 7.0–8.0 pH. Tolerates salt.

**PLANTING GUIDE:** Spring, as soil warms. Plant in full sun, 24″–36″ (60–90 cm) apart.

**CARE TIPS:** Easy. Light moisture. Fertilize sparingly. Prune, shear to shape form. Renew by dividing, removing centers. Propagate by cuttings, seed.

**NOTES:** Thrives in beds, borders, containers, edgings, ground covers, massed plantings, topiaries, walls. Nice in cottage, formal, kitchen, meadow gardens. Resists pests, diseases.

## *Solanum rantonnetii* (*Lycianthes rantonnetii*) SOLANACEAE

### Blue Potato Bush (Paraguay Nightshade)

**SHAPE:** Few vigorous, bushlike, twining or vertical, semi-evergreen or deciduous shrubs to 10′ (3 m) high and wide or 15′ (4.5 m) long. Alternate, smooth, oval leaves, 3″–4″ (75–100 mm) long.

**FLOWER:** Spring to autumn bloom. Clusters of round, 5-petaled, open-faced flowers to 1″ (25 mm) wide. Choose from blue, purple, violet, and white with yellow centers. Forms berrylike fruit in autumn.

**HARDINESS:** Zones 8–11. Protect from frost.

**SOIL TYPE:** Sandy soil. High–average moisture, good drainage, high–medium fertility, 5.5–7.0 pH.

**PLANTING GUIDE:** Spring, as soil warms. Plant in full sun to partial shade, 5′–7′ (1.5–2.2 m) apart.

**CARE TIPS:** Easy. Light moisture. Fertilize every 10–12 weeks. Support. Prune severely in winter. Propagate by cuttings.

**NOTES:** Thrives in accents, banks, fence lines, walls. Nice in informal, meadow, shade, woodland gardens. Resists pests, diseases.

## Spiraea spp. and hybrids ROSACEAE

### Spirea (Bridal-Wreath)

**SHAPE:** Numerous vigorous, arched or bushlike, deciduous shrubs to 6′ (1.8 m) high. Alternate, oval, lobate leaves to 3½″ (90 mm) long.

**FLOWER:** Spring to autumn bloom. Terminal or linear, ball-shaped clusters to 4″ (10 cm) wide of tiny, simple, aromatic flowers. Choose from pink, red, and white. Forms inconspicuous seed follicles in summer.

**HARDINESS:** Most, zones 5–10; some, zones 2–4.

**SOIL TYPE:** Sandy loam. High moisture, good drainage, medium fertility, 6.0–8.0 pH.

**PLANTING GUIDE:** Spring. Plant in full sun to partial shade, 6′–8′ (1.8–2.4 m) apart.

**CARE TIPS:** Easy. Even moisture. Fertilize every 6 months. Prune after bloom. Propagate by cuttings, layering, seed.

**NOTES:** Thrives in accents, backgrounds, fence lines, hedges, walls. Nice in cottage, small-space, woodland gardens. Susceptible to aphids, leafrollers, scale, fireblight, powdery mildew.

## Strelitzia reginae STRELITZIACEAE

### Bird-of-Paradise (Crane Flower)

**SHAPE:** Numerous vigorous, tropical, evergreen shrubs to 4′ (1.2 m) high and wide. Curved stems of shiny, frondlike, broadly lancelike, often cut leaves, 18″–36″ (45–90 cm) long.

**FLOWER:** Year-round bloom on mature plants, 4–6 years or older. Irregular, birdlike, crested, flowers to 12″ (30 cm) long. Multicolored. Forms capsule-shaped pods containing seed.

**HARDINESS:** Zones 9–11. Protect from frost.

**SOIL TYPE:** High humus. High–average moisture, good drainage, high fertility, 6.0–7.0 pH.

**PLANTING GUIDE:** Spring, as soil warms. Plant in full sun, 36″–48″ (90–120 cm) apart.

**CARE TIPS:** Difficult. Light moisture. Limit water in winter. Fertilize every 2 weeks. Extend bloom by deadheading. Propagate by division, seed.

**NOTES:** Thrives in accents, beds, containers, paths. Nice in formal, small-space, tropical gardens, ponds, and pools. Cutting flower. Resists pests, diseases.

## Syringa spp. OLEACEAE

### Lilac

**SHAPE:** More than 30 vigorous, sprawling, thick-growing, deciduous shrubs, 5′–20′ (1.5–6 m) high. Shiny, oval leaves to 5″ (13 cm) long.

**FLOWER:** Spring bloom on mature plants, 3–4 years or older. Showy clusters, 3½″–10″ (90–250 mm) wide, of tiny, aromatic flowers. Choose from blue, pink, purple, and white. Forms leathery seed-filled capsules in summer. Bloom requires 500 or more hours of chilling.

**HARDINESS:** Zones 3–9.

**SOIL TYPE:** Sandy loam. High moisture, good drainage, high fertility, 7.0–7.5 pH.

**PLANTING GUIDE:** Spring. Plant in full sun to partial shade, 5′–10′ (1.5–3 m) apart. Transplants readily.

**CARE TIPS:** Average. Even moisture. Fertilize every 12 weeks. Extend bloom by deadheading. Prune lightly after bloom. Propagate by cuttings, layering.

**NOTES:** Thrives in borders. Nice in cottage, woodland gardens. Cutting flower. Aggressive. Resists deer, insect pests. Susceptible to powdery mildew.

## Tibouchina urvilleana (T. semidecandra) MELASTOMATACEAE

### Glory Bush (Lasiandra, Pleroma, Princess Flower)

**SHAPE:** Various vigorous, open, branched, slender, evergreen shrubs, 10′–15′ (3–4.5 m) high and 5′–10′ (1.5–3 m) wide. Hirsute stalks of woolly or smooth, oval, veined leaves to 4″ (10 cm) long.

**FLOWER:** Spring to autumn bloom. Round, open, 5-petaled flowers, 1″–3″ (25–75 mm) wide. Choose from cobalt purple and violet. Forms capsule-shaped pods to ½″ (12 mm) wide containing seed in autumn.

**HARDINESS:** Zones 9–11. Protect from frost.

**SOIL TYPE:** High humus. High moisture, good drainage, high fertility, 6.0–7.0 pH.

**PLANTING GUIDE:** Spring, as soil warms. Plant in full sun to partial shade, 4′–5′ (1.2–1.5 m) apart.

**CARE TIPS:** Easy. Even moisture. Fertilize every 4 weeks. Pinch tips for bushy plants. Propagate by cuttings.

**NOTES:** Thrives in accents, containers, hedges. Nice in tropical, wildlife, woodland gardens. Resists diseases. Susceptible to budworms.

## *Viburnum opulus* CAPRIFOLIACEAE

### European Cranberry Bush (Whitten Tree)

**SHAPE:** Various elegant, open, deciduous shrubs to 12′ (3.7 m) high. Maplelike, 3–5-lobed, divided, veined leaves to 4″ (10 cm) long.

**FLOWER:** Late-spring bloom. Mounded clusters to 4″ (10 cm) wide of single, 4-petaled flowers to ¾″ (19 mm) wide. Choose from cream and white. Forms scarlet berries in autumn, lasting to winter.

**HARDINESS:** Zones 3–8. Protect from hot sun.

**SOIL TYPE:** Sandy loam; or, in ponds, margins. Most moistures, good drainage, high–medium fertility, 6.0–7.5 pH.

**PLANTING GUIDE:** Spring. Plant in full sun to partial shade, 6′–8′ (1.8–2.4 m) apart.

**CARE TIPS:** Easy. Even moisture. Fertilize every 10 weeks. Apply mulch. Prune after bloom. Propagate by cuttings, grafting, layering, seed.

**NOTES:** Thrives in accents, borders, screens. Nice in cottage, natural, rock, wildlife, woodland gardens and ponds. Resists diseases. Susceptible to aphids, spider mites.

## *Viburnum* spp. CAPRIFOLIACEAE

### Arrowwood

**SHAPE:** About 225 open, deciduous or evergreen shrubs, 5′–40′ (1.5–12 m) high. Textured, oval, toothed leaves, 3″–8″ (75–200 mm) long. Turns colors in autumn.

**FLOWER:** Late-spring bloom. Ball-like clusters of often fragrant, 5-petaled flowers, 3″–5″ (75–125 mm) wide. Choose from pink and white. Forms red or black berries in autumn.

**HARDINESS:** Most, zones 3–8.

**SOIL TYPE:** Sandy loam. High moisture, good drainage, high fertility, 6.0–7.5 pH.

**PLANTING GUIDE:** Spring. Plant in full sun to partial shade, 4′–10′ (1.2–3 m) apart.

**CARE TIPS:** Easy. Even moisture. Fertilize only in spring. Apply mulch, zones 6–8. Prune lightly after bloom. Propagate by cuttings, layering, seed.

**NOTES:** Thrives in accents, borders, paths. Nice in cottage, natural, wildlife, woodland gardens. Susceptible to aphids, spider mites, thrips, powdery mildew, leaf spot.

## *Weigela* spp. and hybrids CAPRIFOLIACEAE

### Weigela

**SHAPE:** Various vigorous, open, sprawling, deciduous shrubs to 10′ (3 m) high and 15′ (4.5 m) or more wide. Opposite, shiny, oval leaves to 4″ (10 cm) long.

**FLOWER:** Late-spring bloom, on second-year wood. Dense clusters of cone-shaped flowers to 1½″ (38 mm) long. Choose from pink, purple, red, white, and yellow. Forms woody seedpods in summer.

**HARDINESS:** Zones 4–9.

**SOIL TYPE:** Sandy loam. High–average moisture, good drainage, medium fertility, 6.5–7.0 pH.

**PLANTING GUIDE:** Spring. Plant in full sun to partial shade, 8′ (2.4 m) apart.

**CARE TIPS:** Easy. Even moisture. Fertilize every 6–8 weeks. Apply mulch. Prune after bloom. Propagate by cuttings.

**NOTES:** Thrives in accents, borders, hedges. Nice in cottage, woodland gardens. Cutting flower. Resists pests, diseases.

## *Wisteria* spp. FABACEAE (LEGUMINOSAE)

### Wistaria (Wisteria)

**SHAPE:** About 10 vigorous, upright, twining, woody deciduous tropical lianas or vines to 100′ (30 m) or longer. Alternate, soft, plumelike, divided leaves, with 9–19 leaflets to 3″ (75 mm) long. Turns colors in autumn.

**FLOWER:** Summer bloom. Pendulous clusters, 6″–48″ (15–120 cm) long, of aromatic, pealike flowers to ¾″ (19 mm) long. Choose from blue, lilac, and white. Forms dry seedpods in autumn.

**HARDINESS:** Zones 4–10.

**SOIL TYPE:** Loam. Average moisture, good drainage, medium–low fertility, 6.0–7.0 pH.

**PLANTING GUIDE:** Spring, as soil warms. Plant in full sun, 8′–10′ (2.4–3 m) apart.

**CARE TIPS:** Easy. Light moisture. Fertilize sparingly. Support. Pinch tips for bushy plants. Propagate by cuttings, division, grafting, seed.

**NOTES:** Thrives in accents, arbors, trellises, walls. Nice in cottage, formal, heritage gardens. Aggressive. Resists pests, diseases.

# Flowering Succulents and Cacti

Match care to each plant's needs and grow these intriguing and beautiful desert and tropical plants.

Proper light and watering are the secrets to growing healthy cacti. Provide them with bright, indirect light and even moisture until they are established. When mature, most cacti and succulents require a full-sun location; in hot climates, however, they may need some shade during the hot summer months. In the wild some species grow in the shelter of rocks or under bushy plants. Place them in an eastern exposure where they will receive sun in the morning and some shade during the hot afternoon. Tropical cacti, such as epiphyllums and Christmas cactus, require bright shade similar to that found beneath trees in the rain forest and jungle.

A sunny, dry courtyard with afternoon shade is an ideal spot for pots full of blooming cacti.

**Watering.** Proper watering is also important to growing healthy cacti and succulents. The most common cause of failure in these plants after light exposure is overwatering, which leads to root rot. Use a moisture meter to determine when your cacti or succulents require water. Hold off watering until the gauge shows almost dry for cacti and slightly dry for succulents—they will need more frequent watering than cacti. For potted plants, lightweight containers provide good clues to the dryness of their soil. Place containers on pot feet to raise them for good drainage. Avoid using trays or catch pots that trap moisture around the plants' roots.

**Cactus and Succulent Containers.** In general, containers are the right choice for planting cacti and succulents. Both categories of plants require only shallow containers for their shallow roots. Make certain that the pot you use has plenty of drainage holes. For plants fewer than six inches (15 cm) high, choose pots that are one inch (25 mm) wider than the plants. Pot larger plants in containers that are two to four inches (50 to 100 mm) wider than the plants.

When repotting a cactus, wear gloves to protect yourself from the spines or wrap the plant with a thick paper collar and use it to maneuver the cactus as you plant. Remember that large specimens are heavy as well as hazardous to the unwary.

**Soil and Planting.** Cacti and succulents can and do survive in a variety of soil types, including heavy clay. They will be much healthier, however, if you use a potting mix that has an open, fast-draining texture yet retains moisture. Choose one with equal parts of soil, vermiculite, and sand for best results.

In frost-free areas, plant cacti and succulents in the outdoors. The soil should be fast draining and near neutral in pH, or slightly acidic. Plant cacti in raised beds or on a slope so that they don't become too wet at the root zone for long periods in regions where there is frequent rainfall. As an alternative, plant them under the shelter of an overhang to prevent them from becoming waterlogged. Use a soil mixture with ample sand to assure quick drainage. In cold-winter climates, plant both plant types in buried containers you can dig and move indoors in winter or choose species that are hardy in your zone.

**Fertilizing.** Cacti and succulents are heavy feeders during the growing season leading up to their bloom. Feed them a complete fertilizer with minor and trace minerals at half strength during active growth. A good NPK analysis for cacti fertilizer is 15–15–30; many tomato fertilizers work well. Add granular or dry fertilizer to the soil when you plant or repot a cactus and use a liquid organic fertilizer the rest of the time. Fertilize quarterly during the slow-growth or semi-dormant periods unless the recommendation for the specific cultivar is to withhold all fertilizer at such times.

**General Recommendations.** Other than these care recommendations, cacti and succulents are in many ways ideal garden plants. They thrive on neglect that would be fatal to other flowering plants. They are a staple of most Xeriscape gardens, and planting succulent ground covers instead of turfgrass lawns can save large volumes of water. Only in true arid-garden conditions do most of them need shelter and

shade; in most other gardens, they will slowly grow to fill the bed and burst forth with a showy display of flowers in winter, spring, or summer, depending on the species and cultivar. Cacti and succulents are also ideal for plantings in landscape rock gardens. Make them a focal point in these settings by choosing several of the vertical and ball-shaped cacti, arranging them in a group, and filling the soil around them with a sprawling or mounding succulent ground cover. Allow the boulders and large rocks to protrude through the planting. The texture of the rocks, the spines of the cactus, their colorful flowers, and the foliage of the succulents will combine to make the Xeriscape or rock garden memorable.

Plant carefree ground-cover succulents in rock gardens for a blend of interesting textures and flowers.

**CAUTION!**
The spines of cacti and succulent plants are hazardous; avoid placing these plants near paths or in gardens frequented by pets and children.

## *Agave* spp. AGAVACEAE

### Agave (Aloe, Century Plant)

**SHAPE:** Various mounded, fleshy evergreen shrubs, 18"–60" (45–150 cm) high and 24"–96" (60–240 cm) wide. Succulent, arched, lancelike, toothed, often hirsute leaves, 6"–60" (15–150 cm) long, with terminal spines.

**FLOWER:** Summer bloom. Stalks, 4'–18' (1.2–5.5 m) tall, with upright, branching clusters of fragrant, tubular flowers to 3" (75 mm) long. Choose from cream, red, greenish white, and yellow.

**HARDINESS:** Zones 8–10.

**SOIL TYPE:** Sandy loam. Average–low moisture, good drainage, medium–low fertility, 6.5–7.5 pH.

**PLANTING GUIDE:** Spring. Plant in full to filtered sun. Space as recommended for cultivar.

**CARE TIPS:** Easy. Light moisture. Limit fertilizing, pruning. Propagate by offsets, seed.

**NOTES:** Thrives in accents, containers, hedges, screens. Nice in arid, desert, seaside, wildlife gardens. Susceptible to borers, mealybugs, scale, fungal diseases.

## *Aloe* spp. LILIACEAE

### Aloe

**SHAPE:** Numerous diverse, evergreen perennials, shrubs, and trees, from 6" (15 cm) to 20' (6 m) high. Succulent, thick, lancelike, toothed leaves, 2"–24" (50–610 mm) long, with terminal spines, often in basal rosettes.

**FLOWER:** Winter to summer bloom; some, year-round. Spiking stalks, 3" (75 mm) to 20' (6 m) tall, with upright, branching clusters of tubular flowers to 5" (13 cm) long. Choose from cream, green, orange, red, rose, white, and yellow.

**HARDINESS:** Most, zones 9–10.

**SOIL TYPE:** Sandy loam. Average–low moisture, good drainage, medium fertility, 6.5–8.0 pH.

**PLANTING GUIDE:** Spring. Plant in full to filtered sun. Space as recommended for cultivar.

**CARE TIPS:** Easy. Light moisture. Limit fertilizing, pruning. Propagate by cuttings, seed, suckers.

**NOTES:** Thrives in accents, containers, edges. Nice in arid, desert, seaside, wildlife gardens. Resists pests and diseases.

## *Aptenia cordifolia* (*Mesembryanthemum cordifolium*) AIZOACEAE

### Candy Apple (Hearts and Flowers, Baby Sun Rose)

**SHAPE:** Various short-lived, sprawling, evergreen succulent perennial shrubs to 16" (40 cm) high and 36" (90 cm) wide. Opposite, succulent, flat, oval, wavy leaves to 1" (25 mm) long.

**FLOWER:** Spring to summer bloom. Double, slim-petaled, open flowers to 1" (25 mm) wide. Choose from purple, red, and rose.

**HARDINESS:** Zones 8–11. Tolerates drought. Protect from hot sun.

**SOIL TYPE:** Sandy soil. Average–low moisture, good drainage, medium fertility, 6.5–7.5 pH.

**PLANTING GUIDE:** Spring, after soil warms. Plant in full to filtered sun, 24" (60 cm) apart.

**CARE TIPS:** Easy. Light moisture; water when soil dries 4"–6" (10–15 cm) deep. Propagate by cuttings, seed.

**NOTES:** Thrives in banks, containers, slopes. Nice in arid, seaside, small-space, Xeriscape gardens. Resists insect pests and diseases. Susceptible to slugs, snails.

## *Astrophytum ornatum* CACTACEAE

### Star Cactus

**SHAPE:** Various low, round, ribbed, waxy, leafless cacti to 15" (38 cm) high, with brown, orange, awl-like spines in radiating clusters.

**FLOWER:** Summer bloom. Ringlike clusters at the top of the plant of frilly, very double flowers, 2"–3½" (50–90 mm) wide. Pale yellow. Forms round fruit in autumn.

**HARDINESS:** Zones 7–11. Prefers arid, mild-winter climates.

**SOIL TYPE:** Sandy soil. Average–low moisture, good drainage, medium fertility, 7.0–8.5 pH. Salt tolerant.

**PLANTING GUIDE:** Spring. Plant in partial shade, 6"–9" (15–23 cm) apart.

**CARE TIPS:** Easy. Water and fertilize only in spring to summer; limit water in winter. Propagate by offsets, seed.

**NOTES:** Thrives in accents, containers edges. Nice in arid, natural, small-space gardens. Good as houseplant. Resists pests, diseases.

## *Cephalocereus senilis* CACTACEAE

### Old-Man Cactus

**SHAPE:** Various long-lived, upright and columnar, ribbed cacti, 15′ (4.5 m) or more high, with yellow spines to 2″ (50 mm) long, clothed in woolly bristles to 12″ (30 cm) long.

**FLOWER:** Spring bloom on mature plants. Tubular, flared flowers to 2″ (50 mm) long. Rose pink. Open at night. Forms pearlike fruit in summer.

**HARDINESS:** Zones 9–11. Protect from frost. Prefers arid climates.

**SOIL TYPE:** Sandy soil. Average–low moisture, good drainage, medium–low fertility, 6.5–8.0 pH. Tolerates salt.

**PLANTING GUIDE:** Spring. Plant in full to filtered sun, 4′–5′ (1.2–1.5 m) apart.

**CARE TIPS:** Easy. Withhold water until ribs are prominent; water deeply thereafter. Tolerates drought. Fertilize only in autumn. Propagate by offsets, seed.

**NOTES:** Thrives in accents, borders, containers. Nice in arid gardens. Resists pests, diseases.

## *Delosperma cooperi* AIZOACEAE

### Purple Ice Plant

**SHAPE:** Several long-lived, sprawling, evergreen succulent perennial shrubs, 4″–8″ (10–20 cm) high and 18″ (45 cm) wide. Opposite, bristly, tubular, succulent, flat leaves to 2½″ (63 mm) long with rows of tiny bumps.

**FLOWER:** Summer bloom. Single, many-petaled, open flowers to 2″ (50 mm) wide. Choose from bright to deep purple and rose, with gold centers.

**HARDINESS:** Most, zones 8–11; some, zones 6–7. Tolerates drought, hot sun.

**SOIL TYPE:** Sandy soil. Average–low moisture, good drainage, medium–low fertility, 7.0–8.0 pH.

**PLANTING GUIDE:** Spring, after soil warms. Plant in full to filtered sun, 10″–12″ (25–30 cm) apart.

**CARE TIPS:** Easy. Light moisture; water when soil dries 4″–6″ (10–15 cm) deep. Propagate by cuttings, seed.

**NOTES:** Thrives in banks, containers. Nice in seaside, small-space, Xeriscape gardens. Resists insect pests and diseases. Susceptible to slugs, snails.

## *Dudleya* spp. CRASSULACEAE

### Dudleya

**SHAPE:** Numerous erect to sprawling, powdery, evergreen succulent perennials to 24″ (30 cm) high and 18″ (45 cm) wide. Rosettes of angular, succulent, narrow, thick leaves, 2–8″ (50–200 mm) long.

**FLOWER:** Spring bloom. Erect clusters of starlike, tiny flowers. Choose from pink, red, and yellow.

**HARDINESS:** Most, zones 10–11; some, zones 8–9. Protect from frost.

**SOIL TYPE:** Sandy soil. Average moisture, good drainage, low fertility, 7.0–8.0 pH. Tolerates salt.

**PLANTING GUIDE:** Spring, after soil warms. Plant in full to filtered sun, 10″ (25 cm) apart.

**CARE TIPS:** Easy. Water when soil dries 4″–6″ (10–15 cm) deep. Avoid wetting foliage. Shelter from rain. Propagate by cuttings, seed.

**NOTES:** Thrives in banks, containers. Nice in arid, rock, seaside, small-space, Xeriscape gardens. Resists insect pests. Susceptible to slugs, snails, fungal diseases.

## *Echinocactus grusonii* CACTACEAE

### Barrel Cactus (Golden Ball Cactus)

**SHAPE:** Various round, ribbed cacti to 4′ (1.2 m) wide with brown, white, golden yellow, needle-like spines in flat, radiating clusters and vertical, central spines. Offsets form groups.

**FLOWER:** Summer bloom. Ringlike clusters at the top of the plant, of open, very double flowers, 1½″–2″ (38–50 mm) wide. Choose from green and yellow.

**HARDINESS:** Zones 9–11. Prefers arid, mild-winter climates.

**SOIL TYPE:** Sandy soil. Average–low moisture, good drainage, medium fertility, 7.0–8.5 pH. Tolerates salt.

**PLANTING GUIDE:** Spring. Plant in full sun to partial shade, 12″–24″ (30–60 cm) apart.

**CARE TIPS:** Easy. Water, fertilize spring to summer; limit in winter. Propagate by offsets, seed.

**NOTES:** Thrives in accents, borders, containers. Nice in arid, natural, small-space gardens. Good as houseplant. Resists pests, diseases.

### *Echinocereus* spp. CACTACEAE

#### Hedgehog Cactus (Hedgehog Cereus, Pitaya)

**SHAPE:** About 35 vertical to low, round and columnar, ribbed cacti, 12″–36″ (30–90 cm) high, usually with brown, white bristles or needlelike spines in vertical, radiating clusters.

**FLOWER:** Spring bloom. Lone, open or tubular, double flowers, 2″–4″ (50–100 mm) wide. Choose from purple, red, yellow, and white with yellow centers. Open at night.

**HARDINESS:** Zones 4–10. Prefers arid, cold-winter climates.

**SOIL TYPE:** Sandy soil. Average–low moisture, good drainage, medium fertility, 6.0–7.5 pH.

**PLANTING GUIDE:** Spring. Plant in full sun, 24″–36″ (60–90 cm) apart.

**CARE TIPS:** Easy. Water, fertilize only in spring to autumn. Propagate by layering, offsets, seed.

**NOTES:** Thrives in accents, barriers, borders, containers. Nice in arid, mountain, natural, small-space gardens. Resists pests. Susceptible to fungal diseases.

### *Ferocactus* spp. CACTACEAE

#### Barrel Cactus (Fishhook Cactus, Strawberry Cactus, Visnaga)

**SHAPE:** About 25 vertical, stout, round to columnar, ribbed cacti to 10′ (3 m) high, with flat, hooked spines and woolly, bristly hairs.

**FLOWER:** Spring to early-summer bloom. Bell- or cup-shaped, double flowers to 3″ (75 mm) wide. Choose from orange, red, yellow, and multicolored. Forms fleshy, round fruit to ½″ (12 mm) wide in late summer to winter.

**HARDINESS:** Zones 10–11. Prefers arid, mild-winter climates.

**SOIL TYPE:** Sandy loam. Average–low moisture, good drainage, medium fertility, 6.5–8.0 pH.

**PLANTING GUIDE:** Spring. Plant in full sun, 24″–36″ (60–90 cm) apart.

**CARE TIPS:** Easy. Water when soil dries 6″–8″ (15–20 cm) deep. Tolerates drought. Fertilize only in summer. Propagate by offsets, seed.

**NOTES:** Thrives in accents, containers, edges. Nice in arid, natural, small-space gardens. Good as houseplant. Resists pests, diseases.

### *Gymnocalycium saglione* *(Echinocactus saglionis)* CACTACEAE

#### Chin Cactus

**SHAPE:** Few erect or low, columnar to round, deeply ribbed cacti, 18″–36″ (45–90 cm) high, with black, brown, needlelike spines in flat, radiating clusters, and a few vertical, central spines to 2″ (50 mm) long.

**FLOWER:** Summer bloom. Open, double flowers to 1½″ (38 mm) wide. Choose from pink and white. Forms fleshy, oval fruit in autumn.

**HARDINESS:** Zones 9–11. Prefers arid, mild-winter climates.

**SOIL TYPE:** Sandy soil. Average–low moisture, good drainage, medium fertility, 6.0–7.5 pH.

**PLANTING GUIDE:** Spring. Plant in full sun, 24″–36″ (60–90 cm) apart.

**CARE TIPS:** Easy. Water and fertilize in spring to autumn; limit water in winter. Tolerates drought. Propagate by layering, offsets, seed.

**NOTES:** Thrives in accents, containers, barriers. Nice in arid, natural gardens. Good as houseplant. Resists pests, diseases.

### *Kalanchoe* spp. CRASSULACEAE

#### Kalanchoe (Airplant)

**SHAPE:** About 125 short-lived, erect or sprawling, evergreen succulent perennials and shrubs, 18″–60″ (45–150 cm) high. Usually opposite, fleshy, flat, oval, lobed basal leaves, 2″–8″ (50–200 mm) long.

**FLOWER:** Winter to spring bloom. Branched clusters of single, open or tubular flowers, ⅛″–1″ (3–25 mm) wide. Choose from purple, red, white, and yellow.

**HARDINESS:** Zones 8–11. Protect from frost, hot sun.

**SOIL TYPE:** High humus. High–average moisture, good drainage, high fertility, 6.0–7.0 pH.

**PLANTING GUIDE:** Autumn. Plant in filtered sun to partial shade, 36″ (90 cm) apart.

**CARE TIPS:** Easy. Even moisture; water when soil dries 2″–4″ (10–15 cm) deep. Propagate by cuttings, leaf plantlets, seed.

**NOTES:** Thrives in accents, containers. Nice in tropical gardens. Resists insect pests and diseases. Susceptible to slugs, snails.

## *Lampranthus* spp. AIZOACEAE

### Ice Plant

**SHAPE:** About 160 low, sprawling, evergreen succulent perennials, 3″–24″ (75–610 mm) high and 12″–36″ (30–90 cm) wide. Opposite, smooth or shiny, succulent, tubular, often 3-sided, curved leaves, ¾″–1½″ (19–38 mm) long.

**FLOWER:** Year-round bloom. Single to double flowers, ½″–2½″ (12–63 mm) wide. Choose from orange, pink, purple, red, rose, white, and yellow.

**HARDINESS:** Zones 9–11. Tolerates hot sun.

**SOIL TYPE:** Sandy soil. Average–low moisture, good drainage, medium–low fertility, 7.0–8.0 pH.

**PLANTING GUIDE:** Spring, after soil warms. Plant in full sun, 18″–24″ (45–60 cm) apart.

**CARE TIPS:** Easy. Light moisture. Fertilize only in spring. Deadhead spent seed caps. Propagate by cuttings, seed.

**NOTES:** Thrives in hanging baskets, containers, massed plantings, slopes. Nice in meadow, seaside gardens. Resists insect pests, diseases. Susceptible to slugs, snails.

## *Mammillaria bocasana* CACTACEAE

### Snowball Cactus (Powder-Puff Cactus, Puff Cactus)

**SHAPE:** Numerous round to columnar, ribbed cacti to 3″ (75 mm) high, with cream, white, yellow, needlelike spines in flat clusters, vertical, central spines; and bristly hairs to 1″ (25 mm) long.

**FLOWER:** Winter bloom. Ringlike cluster of open, often threadlike flowers to ¾″ (19 mm) wide at the top of the plant. Choose from pink, purple, red, and white. Forms woolly fruit in autumn.

**HARDINESS:** Zones 9–10. Prefers arid, mild-winter climates.

**SOIL TYPE:** Sandy soil. Average–low moisture, good drainage, medium fertility, 7.0–8.0 pH.

**PLANTING GUIDE:** Spring, plant in full sun to partial shade, 4″–6″ (10–15 cm) apart.

**CARE TIPS:** Easy. Water and fertilize only in spring to autumn; limit in winter. Propagate by offsets, seed.

**NOTES:** Thrives in accents, containers, edgings. Nice in arid, natural gardens. Good as houseplant. Resists pests, diseases.

## *Opuntia* spp. CACTACEAE

### Prickly Pear (Cholla)

**SHAPE:** Nearly 300 diverse, branched cacti, 4″–180″ (10–455 cm) high, with either jointed, padlike "tuna" or tubular stems, and usually with white, yellow, needlelike, barbed, vertical, often brittle bristles and spines, ¼″–1″ (6–25 mm) long.

**FLOWER:** Winter to spring bloom. Double flowers, ½″–4″ (12–100 mm) wide. Choose from green, pink, purple, red, rose, white, yellow, and multicolored. Forms oval, edible fruit in summer.

**HARDINESS:** Most, zones 8–10; some, zones 4–7.

**SOIL TYPE:** Sandy soil. Average–low moisture, good drainage, medium–low fertility, 6.5–7.0 pH.

**PLANTING GUIDE:** Spring. Plant in full sun. Space as recommended for cultivar.

**CARE TIPS:** Easy. Light moisture. Fertilize only in summer. Propagate by cuttings, layering, seed.

**NOTES:** Thrives in accents, barriers. Nice in arid gardens. Fruit and pads of most cultivars are edible. Resists pests, diseases.

## *Schlumbergera bridgesii* (*S. × buckleyi*) CACTACEAE

### Christmas Cactus

**SHAPE:** Few semi-epiphytic, arched, sprawling, cacti to 24″ (60 cm) high. Wavy-edged, succulent, jointed stems, with silver, white bristles.

**FLOWER:** Winter bloom. Tubular, terminal flowers to 3″ (75 mm) long. Choose from cherry and red.

**HARDINESS:** Zones 8–11. Protect from frost.

**SOIL TYPE:** Sandy loam; pond shorelines. Average–low moisture, good drainage, high–medium fertility, 5.5–6.5 pH.

**PLANTING GUIDE:** Autumn. Plant in open to full shade, 18″–24″ (45–60 cm) apart.

**CARE TIPS:** Average to difficult. Light moisture in late spring to autumn; limit water in autumn until bloom, then water until blooms fade. Fertilize every 4 weeks. Propagate by cuttings, layering, seed.

**NOTES:** Thrives in hanging baskets, containers. Nice in tropical and subtropical, woodland gardens and ponds. Good for holiday decorations, houseplant. Resists pests, diseases.

## *Sedum* spp. CRASSULACEAE

### Stonecrop (Orpine)

**SHAPE:** About 600 low, evergreen succulent perennials, 3″–12″ (75–305 mm) high. Mounded rosettes of alternate, smooth, succulent, over-lapping, round leaves to 3″ (75 mm) long.

**FLOWER:** Spring to autumn bloom. Round clusters to 2″ (50 mm) wide of tiny, starlike flowers. Choose from pink, purple, white, red, and yellow.

**HARDINESS:** Most, zones 4–10; some, zones 2–3.

**SOIL TYPE:** Sandy soil. Average–low moisture, good drainage, medium–low fertility, 6.0–7.5 pH.

**PLANTING GUIDE:** Spring, after soil warms. Plant in full sun to partial shade, 12″–24″ (30–60 cm) apart.

**CARE TIPS:** Easy. Light moisture; water when soil dries 4″–6″ (10–15 cm) deep. Limit fertilizing. Propagate by cuttings, division, seed.

**NOTES:** Thrives in accents, borders, containers, edgings, massed plantings. Nice in arid, natural, seaside, small-space, wildlife gardens. Resists pests, diseases.

## *Sempervivum tectorum* CRASSULACEAE

### Hen-and-Chickens

**SHAPE:** Many short, mounded, hirsute, evergreen succulent perennials to 12″ (30 cm) high and 24″ (60 cm) wide. Succulent, smooth, curving leaves, 2″–4″ (50–100 mm) long, with sharp-tipped spines in a basal rosette.

**FLOWER:** Summer bloom. Wiry, fibrous stems to 24″ (60 cm) tall with branching clusters of star-like flowers, 1″–1½″ (25–38 mm) wide. Choose from purple, red, and yellow.

**HARDINESS:** Zones 4–10.

**SOIL TYPE:** Sandy soil. High moisture good drain-age, low fertility, 6.5–7.5 pH.

**PLANTING GUIDE:** Spring or autumn. Plant in full sun, 6″–9″ (15–23 cm) apart.

**CARE TIPS:** Easy. Light moisture; water when soil dries 2″–4″ deep. Tolerates drought. Limit fertilizing. Propagate by cuttings, seed.

**NOTES:** Thrives in borders, containers, ground covers. Nice in rock, seaside, Xeriscape gardens. Resists pests. Susceptible to fungal diseases.

## *Stenocereus thurberi* (*Lemaireocereus thurberi*) CACTACEAE

### Organ-Pipe Cactus

**SHAPE:** Various vertical, branched, columnar, ribbed cacti, 12′–15′ (3.7–4.5 m) high, with brown, black, needlelike spines to 2″ (50 mm) long. Offsets form groups.

**FLOWER:** Spring bloom. Tubular to cuplike flowers to 3″ (75 mm) long. Choose from cream, pink, purple, and white. Open at night. Forms fleshy, round fruit to 3″ (75 mm) wide in summer.

**HARDINESS:** Zones 7–11. Prefers arid, mild-winter climates.

**SOIL TYPE:** Sandy soil. Average–low moisture, good drainage, medium–low fertility, 6.5–8.0 pH.

**PLANTING GUIDE:** Spring. Plant in full sun, 6′–10′ (1.8–3 m) apart.

**CARE TIPS:** Easy. Water and fertilize only in spring to autumn; limit water in winter. Tolerates drought. Propagate by offsets, seed.

**NOTES:** Thrives in accents, containers, fence lines. Nice in arid, natural gardens. Resists pests. Susceptible to fungal diseases.

## *Yucca filamentosa* (*Y. smalliana*) AGAVACEAE

### Adam's-Needle (Yucca)

**SHAPE:** Various mounded, evergreen shrubs, 24″–36″ (60–90 cm) high and to 5′ (1.5 m) wide. Shiny, stiff, swordlike leaves to 30″ (75 cm) long with threadlike edges and terminal, thorny spines, in a basal rosette.

**FLOWER:** Late-spring to summer bloom. Spiking woody stems to 8′ (2.4 m) tall with clusters of fragrant, saucer-shaped flowers to 2″ (50 mm) long. Choose from cream and white.

**HARDINESS:** Zones 4–10.

**SOIL TYPE:** Sandy loam. Average–low moisture, good drainage, medium fertility, 6.0–7.5 pH.

**PLANTING GUIDE:** Spring. Plant in full sun, 36″–120″ (90–305 cm) apart.

**CARE TIPS:** Easy. Water when soil dries 6″–8″ (15–20 cm) deep. Tolerates drought. Fertilize every 10–12 weeks. Propagate by cuttings, seed.

**NOTES:** Thrives in accents, containers. Nice in arid, meadow, Xeriscape gardens. Good for cutting, drying. Susceptible to aphids and leaf spot.

# Aquatic Flowering Plants

Fill garden ponds and container fountains with flowering aquatic plants and open the door to a completely new way of gardening.

There are four categories of aquatic plants, each with its own particular growth habits and cultural requirements.

**Bog Plants.** Bog plants love moisture but grow with their roots sitting in saturated soil. You can plant them just outside a pond in a marshy area. This category includes golden-ray (*Ligularia* spp.) and marsh marigold (*Caltha palustris*). In addition, many shade garden plants do well as bog plants, including cannas, forget-me-nots, plantain lilies, and irises. Most aquatic plants require at least five hours of sun per day.

**Margin Plants.** Margin plants thrive around a pond's edges. Plant them so that their crowns are three to four inches (75 to 100 mm) below the water surface and their stems, leaves, and flowers are above it. Arrowhead (*Sagittaria latifolia*), cattail (*Typha* spp.), and pickerel weed (*Pontederia cordata*) are examples of margin plants.

**Floating Plants.** Anchored floating plants include the best-known water plants such as lotuses and water lilies, which grow with their leaves floating on the surface and their roots in soil shallowly or deeply underwater. A few free-floating plants that need little or no soil for their roots also are found in this group, including water hawthorn (*Aponogeton distachyus*) and water hyacinth (*Eichhornia crassipes*).

**Oxygenating Plants.** Unlike floaters, oxygenating plants grow below the water's surface. They play a critical role in limiting algae by taking up carbon dioxide from the water and releasing oxygen used by other plants and fish. One particularly effective flowering oxygenator is Washington grass (*Cabomba caroliniana*).

Some aquatic plants spread slowly; a few are invasive and their cultivation is prohibited in some regions. Check with your local agricultural commissioner's office to determine the status of a plant. Introduced plants can crowd out native species if they find their way into natural waterways, ponds, and rivers.

Water lilies have many-petalled, showy flowers that stand on erect stalks high above the water. For best growth, plant them with their roots deeply submerged.

## Planting Aquatics

Different techniques are used to plant each category of aquatic plant. Follow the directions given for each category for best results.

### Bog Plants

Plant non-aggressive species as you would terrestrial plants. Turn the soil in the bed to at least 18 inches (45 cm) deep, loosening it and adding amendments as needed. With a shovel or trowel, open a planting hole. Set the plant in the hole so it is at the same depth in the soil as it grew in the nursery container.

Plant creeping species in a plastic basket lined with porous, nonwoven landscape fabric to block the spread of rhizomes and stolons. Fill the basket with the soil mixture recommended for the cultivar. Use a trowel to open a planting hole in the prepared basket's soil mix. Baskets can hold more than one plant, provided you follow the recommended spacing for the species. Bury the basket in the garden soil, leaving its top edge exposed at least one inch (25 mm) above the surrounding soil.

Fertilize the soil mixture when planting aquatics. Special slow-release aquatic fertilizers are available. Replace them as required by the cultivar or when the plants' foliage shows signs of nutrient deficiency.

### Margin Plants

Plant non-aggressive species in the same manner you would use for terrestrial plants. Plant aggressive species in lined plastic baskets, as for bog plants.

### Floaters

Gently place floating plants in still water with their roots trailing beneath them. Remember that most floaters grow vigorously; try a few and allow them to grow to mature size before adding more. Some floaters drop air sacs and dead leaves. Remove them from the pond to prevent the clogging of filters, pumps, and fountains. If floaters drift into a pump intake or skimmer box opening, tether them with monofilament nylon line attached to a fishing sinker.

### Anchored Floaters

Floaters with deeply submerged roots are planted in plastic baskets, as for bog plants. Weight the bottom of the basket with gravel to keep it from floating. After planting is complete, set the basket into a basin of water, and submerge it until it stops releasing bubbles. Transfer the basket to the pond's bottom, setting it at the recommended depth for the cultivar.

### Oxygenators

Plant rooted oxygenators in the same manner you would use for anchored floaters. It's important to let them float around the surface while still in their transport containers until the water temperature inside the container matches that of the water in the surrounding pond. Once the temperatures have equalized, pour them directly into the pond.

Garden centers and nurseries devoted to water gardening and aquatic plants have low tanks filled with plants rather than racks and rows of nursery containers.

## *Aponogeton distachyus* APONOGETONACEAE

### Cape Pondweed (Water Hawthorn)

**SHAPE:** A tropical tuberous, aquatic perennial to 12″ (30 cm) wide. Floating, spreading rosettes of stiff, slender, lancelike, leathery leaves to 6″ (15 cm) long. Semi-dormant in summer.

**FLOWER:** Spring, autumn bloom. Short stalks with branched, clustered pairs to 1½″ (38 mm) long of irregular, vanilla-scented, aromatic flowers to ½″ (12 mm) wide. White, speckled with black.

**HARDINESS:** Zones 8–11. May self-seed. Water 40°–90° F (4°–32° C).

**SOIL TYPE:** Clay loam–humus mix; pond margins. High to saturated moisture, average drainage, high fertility, 6.0–8.0 pH.

**PLANTING GUIDE:** Spring to summer. Plant in baskets in full sun to partial shade, 12″–24″ (30–60 cm) apart, 8″–24″ (20–60 cm) deep.

**CARE TIPS:** Easy. Fertilize every 4 weeks. Lift in winter. Propagate by division, offsets, seed.

**NOTES:** Thrives in still water. Nice in ponds as alternative to water lilies. Resists pests, diseases.

## *Bacopa caroliniana* (*B. amplexicaulis*) SCROPHULARIACEAE

### Lemon Hyssop (Blue Water Hyssop)

**SHAPE:** Stoloniferous, erect, creeping, semi-aquatic, evergreen perennials to 24″ (60 cm) tall. Opposite, oval, succulent, citrus-scented, aromatic leaves to 1″ (25 mm) long.

**FLOWER:** Summer to autumn bloom. Short, hirsute stalks with single, cup-shaped, 5-petaled flowers to ⅜″ (9 mm) wide. Blue. Water hyssop, *B. monneiri*, is available in blue, white.

**HARDINESS:** Zones 8–11. Water 34°–90° F (1°–32° C).

**SOIL TYPE:** Loam–peat moss mix; pond shallow margins, shorelines. Saturated moisture, medium fertility, 6.0–7.0 pH.

**PLANTING GUIDE:** Spring. Plant in full sun, 24″–36″ (30–60 cm) apart, 6″ (15 cm) deep.

**CARE TIPS:** Easy. Even moisture. Fertilize every 6–8 weeks. Propagate from cuttings.

**NOTES:** Thrives in banks, amid rocks. Nice in ponds, fountains, and tropical, woodland gardens. North American native plant. Resists pests, diseases.

## *Caltha palustris* RANUNCULACEAE

### Marsh Marigold (Kingcup)

**SHAPE:** Vigorous, low, succulent perennials, 8″–36″ (20–90 cm) tall. Glossy, textured, heart-shaped, leathery, toothed leaves to 7″ (18 cm) wide. Dormant in summer.

**FLOWER:** Early-spring bloom. Erect stems with pairs of single or double, starlike, waxy flowers, 2″ (50 mm) wide. Yellow.

**HARDINESS:** Zones 3–10. May self-seed. Water 34°–70° F (1°–21° C).

**SOIL TYPE:** Humus-loam mix; pond shallow margins, shorelines. High to saturated moisture, average drainage, high fertility, 6.0–8.0 pH.

**PLANTING GUIDE:** Spring. Plant in full sun to full shade, 6″ (15 cm) apart in clusters 24″–36″ (60–90 cm) apart, 6″ (15 cm) deep.

**CARE TIPS:** Easy. Even moisture. Fertilize only in spring. Apply mulch. Propagate by division, seed.

**NOTES:** Thrives in borders, edgings. Nice in bog, woodland gardens and ponds. North American native plant. Resists pests, diseases.

## *Eichhornia crassipes* PONTEDERIACEAE

### Water Hyacinth

**SHAPE:** Vigorous, tropical, rhizomatous, evergreen, aquatic perennials to 12″ (30 cm) tall and wide with trailing roots. Rosettes of shiny, round leaves, 2″–5″ (50–125 mm) wide, with air pockets, form floating mats.

**FLOWER:** Summer bloom. Spikes with circular clusters of open, 6-petaled flowers to 2″ (50 mm) wide. Choose from blue, lilac, pink, and yellow with single yellow spot.

**HARDINESS:** Zones 9–11. Water 60°–90° F (16°–32° C). Protect from frost.

**SOIL TYPE:** Water; surface floater. High fertility, 5.5–9.0 pH.

**PLANTING GUIDE:** Spring, as water warms. Plant in full sun.

**CARE TIPS:** Easy. Fertilize every 4–6 weeks. Lift, store at 60°–70°F (16–21° C). Propagate by division.

**NOTES:** Thrives in warm water. Nice in fish ponds. Protect from turtles. Very invasive; culture may be prohibited in some regions.

## *Ligularia* spp. and hybrids ASTERACEAE (COMPOSITAE)

### Golden-Ray

**SHAPE:** Nearly 150 mounded, round, deciduous perennials, 24″–60″ (60–150 cm) tall. Textured, circular to heart-shaped, veined leaves, 12″–18″ (30–45 cm) long and wide.

**FLOWER:** Summer bloom. Tall spikes with loose clusters of daisylike, many-rayed, reflexed flowers, 1″–4″ (25–100 mm) wide with buttonlike centers. Choose from orange, white, and yellow.

**HARDINESS:** Zones 3–9.

**SOIL TYPE:** Sandy loam; pond shallow margins, shorelines. High to saturated moisture, good drainage, high fertility, 5.5–7.0 pH.

**PLANTING GUIDE:** Early spring. Plant in partial to full shade, 36″–48″ (90–120 cm) apart.

**CARE TIPS:** Easy. Even moisture. Fertilize every 4 weeks. Deadhead spent stalks. Propagate by division, seed.

**NOTES:** Thrives in edgings. Nice in bog, natural gardens and ponds. Cutting flower. Resists insect pests, diseases. Susceptible to slugs, snails.

## *Lobelia cardinalis* CAMPANULACEAE (LOBELIACEAE)

### Cardinal Flower (Indian Pink)

**SHAPE:** Erect, clumping, creeping perennial, 24″–48″ (60–120 cm) tall and 12″ (30 cm) wide. Alternate, lancelike, toothed leaves to 4″ (10 cm) long.

**FLOWER:** Summer to autumn bloom. Stalks with branched clusters of irregular, tubular, lipped flowers, 1″–2″ (25–50 mm) long, over narrow bracts. Choose from purple, red, and white.

**HARDINESS:** Zones 3–11. Water 33°–70° F (1°–21° C).

**SOIL TYPE:** Loam; pond margins and shorelines. High to saturated moisture, good drainage, high fertility, 6.0–8.0 pH.

**PLANTING GUIDE:** Spring. Plant in full sun to partial shade, 12″ (30 cm) apart, up to 6″ (15 cm) deep.

**CARE TIPS:** Easy. Even moisture. Lift in winter, zones 3–6. Mulch. Propagate by division, seed.

**NOTES:** Thrives in edgings. Nice in bog gardens and ponds. North American native plant. Resists insect pests, diseases. Susceptible to slugs, snails.

## *Menyanthes trifoliata* GENTIANACEAE

### Marsh Trefoil (Bogbean, Buckbean)

**SHAPE:** Slow-growing, low, rhizomatous, creeping, perennial, 9″–12″ (23–30 cm) tall. Sheathed stalks with alternate, oval, 3-lobed, often bristly leaves to 4″ (10 cm) long.

**FLOWER:** Late-spring bloom. Spikes with branched clusters of bearded, fringed flowers to ½″ (12 mm) wide. Choose from white and purple.

**HARDINESS:** Zones 3–11. Water 40°–80° F (4°–27° C). Prefers cold-winter climates.

**SOIL TYPE:** Loam–peat moss mix; pond margins and shorelines. High to saturated moisture, good drainage, medium fertility, 5.0–6.0 pH.

**PLANTING GUIDE:** Spring. Plant in full sun to partial shade, 16″ (40 cm) apart, up to 12″ (30 cm) deep.

**CARE TIPS:** Easy. Fertilize every 8–10 weeks. Divide when crowded. Propagate by division, layering, root cuttings, or seed.

**NOTES:** Thrives in accents, edgings. Nice in bog, natural, woodland gardens and ponds. Aggressive. Resists pests, diseases.

## *Nelumbo lutea* (*Nelumbium luteum*) NYMPHAEACEAE

### American Lotus (Water Chinquapin)

**SHAPE:** Vigorous, rhizomatous, creeping perennial, 30″–84″ (75–215 cm) tall. Stalks above the water surface with circular leaves, 12″–24″ (30–60 cm) wide.

**FLOWER:** Summer to autumn bloom. Erect stems of single to double, cup-shaped flowers, 7″–11″ (18–28 cm) wide. Choose from cream, white, and yellow. Forms woody seedpods in autumn.

**HARDINESS:** Zones 3–11. Water 33°–70° F (1°–21° C).

**SOIL TYPE:** Clay-loam–peat moss mix; pond deeply submerged. Saturated moisture, good drainage, high fertility, 6.0–8.0 pH.

**PLANTING GUIDE:** Spring. Plant in full sun to partial shade, 5′ (1.5 m) apart, up to 18″ (45 cm) deep.

**CARE TIPS:** Easy. Fertilize every 4 weeks. Lift in winter, zones 3–5. Propagate by division, seed.

**NOTES:** Thrives in accents, deep water. Nice in still ponds. North American native plant. Edible seeds and tubers. Resists pests, diseases.

## *Nymphaea* spp. NYMPHAEACEAE

### Water Lily

**SHAPE:** Numerous topical and hardy, tuberous or rhizomatous, deciduous perennials to 8″ (20 cm) high and 4′ (1.2 m) wide. Shiny, circular leaves, 9″–10″ (23–25 cm) wide.

**FLOWER:** Summer bloom. Stalks with usually double, slim-petaled flowers, 2″–10″ (50–250 mm) wide. Choose from pink, red, white, and yellow.

**HARDINESS:** Hardy cultivars, zones 4–10; tropicals, zones 9–11. Water 70°–90° F (21°–32° C). Prefers mild climates. Protect from hot sun.

**SOIL TYPE:** Clay-humus mix; in ponds, deeply submerged. Saturated moisture, average drainage, high fertility, 6.0–8.0 pH.

**PLANTING GUIDE:** Spring, when water warms. Plant in baskets in full sun, 4′ (1.2 m) apart, up to 18″ (45 cm) deep.

**CARE TIPS:** Easy. Fertilize every 4 weeks. Lift tropicals in winter. Propagate by division, seed.

**NOTES:** Thrives in deep water. Nice in still ponds. Cutting flower. Susceptible to aphids, beetles.

## *Nymphoides* spp. GENTIANACEAE

### Floating-Heart (Water Snowflake, Banana Lily)

**SHAPE:** About 20 creeping, deciduous perennials to 8″ (20 cm) high and 6′ (1.8 m) wide. Opposite, shiny, simple, round or heart-shaped leaves, 3″–12″ (75–305 mm) wide.

**FLOWER:** Summer bloom. Open, single, fringed flowers to ¾″ (19 mm) wide. Choose from white, yellow, and orange.

**HARDINESS:** Most, zones 5–11. Water 40°–80° F (4°–27° C).

**SOIL TYPE:** Clay-loam mix; pond margins.

Saturated moisture, average drainage, medium fertility, 6.0–8.0 pH.

**PLANTING GUIDE:** Spring. Plant in baskets in full sun to partial shade, 36″ (90 cm) apart, 6″–24″ (15–60 cm) deep.

**CARE TIPS:** Average. Fertilize every 4 weeks. Lift tropicals in winter. Propagate by cuttings, division, seed. Avoid algae control agents.

**NOTES:** Thrives in accents. Nice in fountains, small ponds. Aggressive. Resists pests and diseases.

## *Pontederia cordata* PONTEDERIACEAE

### Pickerel Weed (Blue Pickerel Rush)

**SHAPE:** Clumping aquatic, perennial. Grows 24″–48″ (60–120 cm) tall. Erect, translucent, arrow- or heart-shaped, veined leaves, 6″–8″ (15–20 cm) long. Dormant in winter.

**FLOWER:** Summer to autumn bloom. Spiking clusters of tubular, 6-petaled flowers, 6″ (15 cm) wide. Blue with a yellow dot on the upper petal. Long blooming.

**HARDINESS:** Zones 3–11. Water 33°–70° F (1°–21° C).

**SOIL TYPE:** Sand-clay-loam mix; in ponds, shallow or deep margins. Saturated moisture, average drainage, medium fertility, 6.0–8.0 pH.

**PLANTING GUIDE:** Spring. Plant in full sun to partial shade, 4′ (1.2 m) apart, up to 12″ (30 cm) deep.

**CARE TIPS:** Easy. Fertilize every 10–12 weeks. Extend bloom by deadheading. Propagate by division.

**NOTES:** Thrives in accents. Nice in bog, natural gardens and ponds. Aggressive. North American native plant. Resists pests, diseases.

## *Typha* spp. TYPHACEAE

### Cattail (Bulrush)

**SHAPE:** About 15 creeping, rhizomatous or stoloniferous, deciduous perennials, 12″–96″ (30–240 cm) tall. Slender, straplike leaves to 6′ (180 cm) long. Dwarf cultivars available.

**FLOWER:** Summer to autumn bloom. Stiff, woody stems to 8′ (2.4 m) high of sausage-shaped flower heads or catkins, 4″–10″ (10–25 cm) long.

**HARDINESS:** Zones 3–10. Water 33°–70° F (1°–21° C).

**SOIL TYPE:** Sandy loam; in ponds, deeply submerged. Saturated moisture, average drainage, high fertility, 6.0–8.0 pH.

**PLANTING GUIDE:** Spring. Plant in baskets in full sun to partial shade, 24″ (60 cm) apart, up to 12″ (30 cm) deep.

**CARE TIPS:** Easy. Fertilize every 6–8 weeks. Remove catkins in autumn. Propagate by division or seed.

**NOTES:** Thrives in accents, screens. Nice in bog, natural gardens and ponds. Cutting flower. Aggressive. Resists pests, diseases.

# Ornamental Grasses

Add movement and the unusual form of grasses to those sites
in your garden where flowers struggle due to exposure, soil, or moisture.

Mix tall ornamental grasses with shorter species to make a layered screen to divide areas of your yard or block views of a neighbor's home.

Ornamental grasses need very little maintenance once they're established. The majority prefer sunny sites and will adapt to wide ranges of soil, temperature, and moisture conditions. Some are ideal bog plants. Others are drought-tolerant, making them well-suited for Xeriscape gardens. A few combine tolerance for both wet and dry conditions.

There are two categories of ornamental grasses. Warm-season grasses grow from spring through summer, bloom in autumn, and then go dormant, leaving their dry, brown foliage and flower plumes standing into winter. Plant warm-season grasses any time the soil is at least 65°F (18°C), from midspring to early autumn. This category includes fountain grass, eulalia grass, tall purple moor grass, and switch-grass. Many arid-climate turfgrasses also are included among warm-season grasses.

Cool-season grasses are generally evergreen in nature, although in cold climates some will die back completely, becoming dormant until temperatures begin to warm again. Cool-season grasses begin their new root growth in autumn and continue it through winter. They flower in spring and summer. Plant them in early spring or any time in autumn. This group includes autumn moor grass (*Sesleria autumnalis*), blue fescue, blue oat grass, feather reed grass (*Calamagrostis* × *acutiflora*), and tufted hair grass.

Some ornamental grasses spread by rhizomes or underground stolons, others create a larger clump, still others creep, and many reseed themselves. Some species and cultivars of ornamental grasses such as pampas grass grow very large and can be aggressive in a home landscape; always check the mature growth pattern of grasses before adding them to your landscape. Some grasses are prohibited because they crowd out native plants or clog natural waterways.

Ornamental grasses and grasslike perennials are popular plants in mixed plantings. Their popularity stems from these advantageous features:

- Need little maintenance or care
- Are free of pests and diseases
- Have vigorous, often single-season growth
- Turn color in autumn, with stalks and seed heads that often persist into winter
- Tolerate dry, low-nutrient soils
- Tolerate boggy, acidic, and alkaline soils

Plant ornamental grasses in average soil, working in some additional sand and compost. Most species grow best in a full-sun location, although a number of cultivars have been developed to grow in filtered sun, partial shade, or even deep shade. Give them sufficient room to grow. In general, plant grasses as far apart as they will be tall. Place narrow, upright growers close together, mounding grasses farther apart. Use mulch to keep weeds down, but keep it clear of the plant's crown. Plant those cultivars with creeping rootstocks and aggressive tendencies in baskets or containers lined with porous, non-woven landscape fabric, then bury them in the garden soil. This measure will contain their roots; shear self-seeding cultivars after they bloom to keep them from broadcasting their seed.

Water young ornamental grasses often until they become established. They vary in their water needs. Some can go very dry, while others need more frequent watering. Avoid overfertilizing, as some grasses will die when the soil is too rich.

Like perennials, ornamental grasses benefit from an annual cleanup, which will rejuvenate them for the following season. Cut the dried tops of warm-season grasses back to about eight inches (20 cm) before they resume growth in spring. Cut cool-season grasses back in the autumn after they've bloomed or wait until early spring if you enjoy their dried plumes throughout the winter months.

Divide ornamental grasses every few years, whenever the center of the clump dies back. Divide warm-season types in spring before growth is ten inches (25 cm) tall. Cool-season grasses can be divided in autumn or early spring. To divide, use a spade or

other sharp instrument to cut the roots into sections, then pry them apart with a garden fork. Replant the sections in other areas. Sections on the outside of the clump are younger and tend to be the most vigorous.

Many ornamental grasses make good cutting and drying plants. Harvest their stems and seed heads soon after they emerge, dry them in bunches hung upside down, and spray them with floral fixative to help them retain their seeds. Use grasses by themselves or to add visual interest to floral arrangements.

The feathery seed plumes and wiry leaf-stalks of many ornamental grasses make them ideal foreground plants to grow in the front of flower beds.

## Grasses and Grassy Plants

Perennial plants with grasslike leaves are frequently used in plantings as substitutes for true ornamental grasses. Below, you will find a list of species that look like grasses, but actually are broadleaved plants or rushes.

*Acorus gramineus*—Japanese sweet flag (pg. 271)
*Armeria maritima*—sea pink (pg. 164)
*Baumea rubingosa*—Variegated rush (pg. 271)
*Campanula poscharskyana*—Serbian bellflower (pg. 169)
*Catananche caerulea*—Cupid's-dart (pg. 169)
*Colchicum autumnale*—Meadow saffron (pg. 218)

*Ipheion uniflorum*—Spring starflower (pg. 224)
*Juncus patens*—California gray rush (pg. 275)
*Luzula sylvatica*—Greater woodrush (pg. 275)
*Ophiopogon japonicus*—Mondo grass (pg. 276)
*Sisyrinchium* spp.—Blue-eyed grass (pg. 277)
*Zephyranthes* spp.—Zephyr lily (pg. 231)

# Selecting Grasses

| Grasses | USDA Plant Hardiness | Season of Interest | Exposure | Soil Moisture |
|---|---|---|---|---|
| *Acorus gramineus*—Japanese sweet flag | Zones 6–10 | Year-round | Full to filtered sun | High |
| *Andropogon gerardii*—Big bluestem | Zones 3–10 | Late spring to summer | Full to filtered sun | Average–low |
| *Arundo donax*—Giant reed | Zones 6–11 | Summer | Full sun to partial shade | High–saturated |
| *Baumea rubingosa*—Variegated rush | Zones 8–11 | Summer | Full sun | High |
| *Bouteloua gracilis*—Blue grama | Zones 4–10 | Summer to autumn | Full sun | Average–low |
| *Briza media*—Quaking grass | Zones 4–10 | Spring to summer | Full sun | Low |
| *Calamagrostis* × *acutiflora*—Feather reed grass | Zones 4–9 | Spring to autumn | Full sun to partial shade | High |
| *Calamagrostis nutkaensis*—Pacific reed grass | Zones 7–10 | Autumn | Full sun to partial shade | Average |
| *Carex* spp.—Sedge | Zones 3–9 | Summer | Full sun to full shade | High–saturated |
| *Chasmanthium latifolium*—Northern sea oats | Zones 4–10 | Summer to autumn | Full sun to partial shade | Average |
| *Cortaderia selloana*—Pampas grass | Zones 6–11 | Summer | Full sun | High–low |
| *Deschampsia caespitosa*—Tufted hair grass | Zones 4–9 | Late spring to summer | Full sun to full shade | High |
| *Festuca glauca*—Blue fescue | Zones 4–9 | Spring to summer | Full sun | High–average |
| *Helictotrichon sempervirens*—Blue oat grass | Zones 4–9 | Spring | Full sun | High |
| *Imperata cylindrica* 'Rubra'—Japanese blood grass | Zones 4–10 | Late summer | Full sun to partial shade | High |
| *Juncus effusus*—Soft rush | Zones 4–11 | Summer | Full sun to partial shade | High |
| *Juncus patens*—California gray rush | Zones 7–10 | Summer | Full sun | Average–saturated |
| *Leymus arenarius*—Blue European dune grass | Zones 4–10 | Summer | Full sun to partial shade | High |
| *Luzula sylvatica*—Greater woodrush | Zones 4–10 | Summer | Full sun to full shade | Low–average |
| *Miscanthus oligostachyus*—Flame grass | Zones 4–10 | Late summer | Full to filtered sun | High–average |
| *Miscanthus sinensis*—Eulalia grass | Zones 4–10 | Late summer to autumn | Full sun to partial shade | High–average |
| *Molinia caerulea*—Purple moor grass | Zones 4–10 | Late summer to autumn | Full sun to partial shade | High–average |
| *Ophiopogon japonicus*—Mondo grass | Zones 7–11 | Summer | Partial to full shade | High |
| *Panicum virgatum*—Switch-grass | Zones 4–9 | Summer to autumn | Full to filtered sun | High–average |
| *Pennisetum alopecuroides*—Fountain grass | Zones 5–11 | Summer to autumn | Full sun to partial shade | High–average |
| *Phalaris arundinacea*—Ribbon grass | Zones 4–10 | Summer to autumn | Full sun | High |
| *Schizachyrium scoparium*—Little bluestem grass | Zones 3–10 | Late summer to autumn | Full sun | High–low |
| *Scirpus cyperinus*—Woolgrass bulrush | Zones 3–11 | Summer | Full sun to partial shade | High–saturated |
| *Sesleria autumnalis*—Autumn moor grass | Zones 4–10 | Spring | Full sun to partial shade | Average |
| *Sisyrinchium* spp.—Blue-eyed grass | Zones 4–8 | Spring | Full sun to partial shade | High |
| *Sorghastrum avenaceum*—Wood grass | Zones 4–9 | Late summer | Full sun | High |
| *Stipa gigantea*—Giant feather grass | Zones 6–10 | Summer | Full sun | Average–low |

## *Acorus gramineus* ARACEAE

### Japanese Sweet Flag (Dwarf Sweet Flag, Grassy-Leaved Sweet Flag)

**SHAPE:** Numerous mounded, rhizomatous, semi-evergreen, herbaceous perennials to 18″ (45 cm) high and wide. Low, fan-shaped, tufts of shiny, often variegated, slender, straplike, fragrant leaves to 12″ (30 cm) long.

**FLOWER:** Insignificant flowers; grow for foliage.

**HARDINESS:** Zones 6–10.

**SOIL TYPE:** High humus; pond shallow margins or shorelines. High moisture, good drainage, high fertility, 6.0–8.0 pH.

**PLANTING GUIDE:** Spring. Plant in full to filtered sun, 12″–24″ (30–60 cm) apart, up to 10″ (25 cm) deep.

**CARE TIPS:** Easy. Even moisture during growth. Fertilize only in spring. Divide when crowded. Propagate by division, seed.

**NOTES:** Thrives in accents, borders, containers, edgings, ground covers, massed plantings. Nice in bog, meadow, prairie, shade gardens, and ponds. Resists pests, diseases.

## *Andropogon gerardii* POACEAE (GRAMINEAE)

### Big Bluestem (Beard Grass, Turkeyfoot)

**SHAPE:** Various erect, bunched perennial grasses, 36″–84″ (90–215 cm) high and 24″–36″ (60–90 cm) wide. Soft, hirsute stalks of flat, slender leaf sheaths to ⅜″ (9 mm) wide. Turns colors in autumn.

**SEED HEAD:** Late-spring to summer bloom. Grasslike stems with branched clusters to 4″ (10 cm) long of whorled florets to ⅛″ (3 mm) long. Choose from red and purple.

**HARDINESS:** Zones 3–10.

**SOIL TYPE:** Loam. Average–low moisture, good drainage, high–medium fertility, 6.0–7.5 pH.

**PLANTING GUIDE:** Spring. Plant in full to filtered sun, 18″–24″ (45–60 cm) apart.

**CARE TIPS:** Easy. Even moisture during growth. Fertilize only in spring. Shear in spring before new growth begins. Propagate by division, seed.

**NOTES:** Thrives in accents, massed plantings, screens. Nice in meadow, prairie, seashore, wildlife gardens. Resists pests, diseases.

## *Arundo donax* and hybrids POACEAE (GRAMINEAE)

### Giant Reed (Carrizo, Variegated Mediterranean Rush)

**SHAPE:** Various erect, bunched, rhizomatous, deciduous perennial grasses, 6′–30′ (1.8–9 m) high and 36″–48″ (90–120 cm) wide. Canelike, reedy stalks of striped, flat, broadly spear-shaped leaf sheaths to 24″ (60 cm) long.

**SEED HEAD:** Summer bloom. Plumelike, terminal, seed heads to 24″ (60 cm) long. Choose from green, and purple.

**HARDINESS:** Zones 6–11.

**SOIL TYPE:** High humus; pond shorelines.

High–saturated moisture, good drainage, high fertility, 6.0–8.0 pH.

**PLANTING GUIDE:** Spring. Plant in full sun to partial shade, 9′ (2.7 m) apart.

**CARE TIPS:** Easy. Even moisture. Fertilize every 10–12 weeks. Shear in autumn. Propagate by division, seed.

**NOTES:** Thrives in containers, screens, windbreaks. Nice in meadow, prairie gardens and ponds. Drying plant. Aggressive. Resists pests, diseases.

## *Baumea rubingosa* 'Variegata' (CYPERACEAE)

### Variegated Rush

**SHAPE:** Erect, bunching, rhizomatous, evergreen herbaceous perennials, 12″–24″ (30–60 cm) high and 12″ (30 cm) wide. Basal stalks with shiny, often striped, round to flat, swordlike leaf sheaths to 24″ (60 cm) long.

**SEED HEAD:** Summer bloom. Inconspicuous, tiny, tightly clustered seed. Brown.

**HARDINESS:** Zones 8–11.

**SOIL TYPE:** Sandy loam; pond deep margins or shorelines. High moisture, good drainage,

medium fertility, 6.0–8.0 pH.

**PLANTING GUIDE:** Spring. Plant in a basket, in full sun, 12″ (30 cm) apart, 1″–4″ (25–100 mm) deep.

**CARE TIPS:** Easy. Even moisture during growth. Fertilize only in spring. Shear in late autumn. Propagate by division.

**NOTES:** Thrives in accents, containers, edgings. Nice in bog, small-space, woodland gardens and ponds. Good for mixed plantings with ferns. Resists pests, diseases.

## *Bouteloua gracilis* POACEAE (GRAMINEAE)

### Blue Grama (Mosquito Grass)

**SHAPE:** Various fine, upright, bunched perennial grasses, 16″–20″ (40–50 cm) high and 4″ (10 cm) wide. Basal stalks of flat, slender leaf sheaths to ⅛″ (3 mm) wide. Turns colors in autumn.

**SEED HEAD:** Summer to autumn bloom. Grasslike stems with curved, pointed, brushlike clusters to 2″ (50 mm) long. Tan.

**HARDINESS:** Zones 4–10.

**SOIL TYPE:** Sandy loam. Average–low moisture, good drainage, medium fertility, 6.0–7.5 pH.

**PLANTING GUIDE:** Spring. Plant in full sun, 18″–24″ (45–60 cm) apart.

**CARE TIPS:** Easy. Even moisture during growth. Fertilize only in spring. Shear in spring before new growth begins. Propagate by division, seed.

**NOTES:** Thrives in accents, edgings, massed plantings. Nice in meadow, prairie, seaside, wildlife, woodland gardens. Cutting and drying plant. Resists pests, diseases.

## *Briza media* POACEAE (GRAMINEAE)

### Quaking Grass (Rattlesnake Grass)

**SHAPE:** Various fine, upright, bunched perennial grasses, 12″–24″ (30–60 cm) high and 12″ (30 cm) wide. Basal stalks of slender leaf sheaths to 6″ (15 cm) long and ¼″ (6 mm) wide. Turns colors in autumn.

**SEED HEAD:** Spring to summer bloom. Grasslike stems with plumelike, drooping, segmented seed clusters to ¼″ (6 mm) long. Yellow turning white.

**HARDINESS:** Zones 4–10.

**SOIL TYPE:** Sandy loam. Low moisture, good drainage, medium fertility, 6.0–7.5 pH.

**PLANTING GUIDE:** Spring. Plant in full sun, 12″ (30 cm) apart.

**CARE TIPS:** Easy. Limit moisture. Fertilize only in spring. Shear in spring before growth begins. Propagate by division, seed.

**NOTES:** Thrives in accents, edgings, massed plantings. Nice in cutting, meadow, prairie, wildlife, woodland gardens. Cutting and drying plant. Resists pests, diseases.

## *Calamagrostis* × *acutiflora* POACEAE (GRAMINEAE)

### Feather Reed Grass

**SHAPE:** Various vigorous, vertical, bunched, herbaceous perennial grasses, 4′–7′ (1.2–2.2 m) high and 6″–12″ (15–30 cm) wide. Round, stiff stalks with textured, arched, slender, lancelike, veined leaf sheaths to 36″ (90 cm) long.

**SEED HEAD:** Spring to autumn bloom. Slim, stiff stems to 6′ (1.8 m) long with plumelike clusters to 12″ (30 cm) long of feathery bracts and seed. Green turning gold.

**HARDINESS:** Zones 4–9.

**SOIL TYPE:** Sandy loam. High moisture, good drainage, medium fertility, 6.5–7.5 pH.

**PLANTING GUIDE:** Spring. Plant in full sun to partial shade, 12″–24″ (30–60 cm) apart.

**CARE TIPS:** Easy. Water when soil dries to 4″ (10 cm) deep. Fertilize only in spring. Shear in spring before growth begins. Propagate by seed.

**NOTES:** Thrives in accents, borders, containers, walls, windbreaks. Nice in cottage, meadow gardens. Good for drying. Resists pests, diseases.

## *Calamagrostis nutkaensis* POACEAE (GRAMINEAE)

### Pacific Reed Grass

**SHAPE:** Various vigorous, vertical, bunched, herbaceous perennial grasses, 6′–7′ (1.8–2.2 m) high and 12″–24″ (30–60 cm) wide. Basal stalks, with arched, slender, lancelike leaf sheaths to 4′ (1.2 m) long.

**SEED HEAD:** Autumn bloom. Slim, stiff stems to 6′ (1.8 m) long with branched clusters to 8″ (20 cm) long of bracts and seed. Yellow.

**HARDINESS:** Zones 7–10.

**SOIL TYPE:** Sandy loam. Average moisture, good drainage, medium fertility, 6.0–7.5 pH. Tolerates salt.

**PLANTING GUIDE:** Spring. Plant in full sun to partial shade, 12″–24″ (30–60 cm) apart.

**CARE TIPS:** Easy. Water when soil dries to 4″ (10 cm) deep. Fertilize only in spring. Shear in spring before growth begins. Propagate by seed.

**NOTES:** Thrives in accents, borders, containers, screens. Nice in meadow, prairie, woodland gardens. Good for drying. Resists pests, diseases.

## Carex spp. CYPERACEAE

### Sedge

**SHAPE:** About 2,000 diverse, vigorous, bunching or matting, rhizomatous perennial sedges, 12″–60″ (30–150 cm) high. Shiny, often variegated, slender leaves, 6″–60″ (15–150 cm) long.

**SEED HEAD:** Summer bloom. Wiry spikes, 12″–60″ (30–150 cm) high, of inconspicuous flowers. Choose from green, purple, white, and yellow.

**HARDINESS:** Zones 3–9. Prefers cool-summer, humid climates.

**SOIL TYPE:** Sandy loam; pond shallow margins. High–saturated moisture, good drainage, medium fertility, 6.0–7.5 pH.

**PLANTING GUIDE:** Spring. Plant in full sun to full shade, as recommended for cultivar.

**CARE TIPS:** Easy. Even moisture. Fertilize only in spring. Propagate by division, seed.

**NOTES:** Thrives in banks, containers, ground covers. Nice in bog, cutting, natural, wildlife, woodland gardens and ponds. Drying plant. Aggressive. Resists pests, diseases.

## Chasmanthium latifolium (Uniola latifolia) POACEAE (GRAMINEAE)

### Northern Sea Oats

**SHAPE:** Few arching, clumping, creeping perennial grasses, 24″–60″ (60–120 cm) high. Basal stalks of flat, broad, lance- or bamboolike leaf sheaths to 2″ (50 mm) wide.

**SEED HEAD:** Summer to autumn bloom. Arched stems with nodding, flat, segmented seed clusters to 2″ (50 mm) long. Choose from silver and tan turning copper in autumn.

**HARDINESS:** Zones 4–10.

**SOIL TYPE:** Sandy loam. Average moisture, good drainage, medium fertility, 6.0–8.0 pH.

**PLANTING GUIDE:** Spring. Plant in full sun to partial shade, 24″ (60 cm) apart.

**CARE TIPS:** Easy. Even moisture during growth. Fertilize only in spring. Shear in spring. Support with stakes. Propagate by division.

**NOTES:** Thrives in accents, containers, edgings. Nice in bog, meadow, prairie, small-space, wildlife, woodland gardens. Cutting and drying plant. Resists pests, diseases.

## Cortaderia selloana POACEAE (GRAMINEAE)

### Pampas Grass

**SHAPE:** Various erect, bunched, evergreen perennial grasses, 6′–20′ (1.8–6 m) high and 4′–10′ (1.2–3.0 m) wide. Flat, narrow, spearlike, saw-tooth-edged leaf sheaths to 6′ (1.8 m) long. Dwarf, sterile cultivars available.

**SEED HEAD:** Summer bloom. Woody round stalks with plumelike, terminal, seed heads to 4′ (1.2 m) long. Choose from green, purple, white.

**HARDINESS:** Zones 6–11. May self-seed.

**SOIL TYPE:** Sandy loam. High–low moisture, good drainage, average fertility, 6.5–8.0 pH.

**PLANTING GUIDE:** Spring. Plant in full sun, 10′ (3 m) apart.

**CARE TIPS:** Easy. Even moisture until established. Fertilize only in spring. Shear in spring before growth begins. Propagate by division, seed.

**NOTES:** Thrives in containers, screens, windbreaks. Nice in cutting, meadow, prairie gardens. Drying plant. Invasive; culture may be prohibited in some areas. Resists pests, diseases.

## Deschampsia caespitosa POACEAE (GRAMINEAE)

### Tufted Hair Grass

**SHAPE:** Numerous vigorous, vertical, bunching, herbaceous perennial grasses to 4′ (1.2 m) high and 24″ (60 cm) wide. Stalks, 6″–10″ (15–25 cm) long, with smooth, slender, spearlike leaf sheaths.

**SEED HEAD:** Late-spring to summer bloom. Slim, stiff stems to 48″ (1.2 m) long with tufted clusters to 6″ (15 cm) long of florets, feathery bracts, and seed. Choose from bronze, gold, and green turning yellow, white.

**HARDINESS:** Zones 4–9. May self-seed. Prefers cool-summer climates.

**SOIL TYPE:** Sandy loam. High moisture, good drainage, high fertility, 6.5–7.0 pH.

**PLANTING GUIDE:** Spring. Plant in full sun to full shade, 24″–36″ (60–90 cm) apart.

**CARE TIPS:** Easy. Even moisture. Fertilize every 4 weeks. Shear in spring. Propagate by seed.

**NOTES:** Thrives in accents, borders, massed plantings. Nice in bog, cottage, meadow, woodland gardens. Aggressive. Resists pests, diseases.

## Festuca glauca *(F. ovina* var. *glauca)* POACEAE (GRAMINEAE)

### Blue Fescue (Sheep Fescue)

**SHAPE:** Numerous vigorous, mounded, bunching, herbaceous perennial grasses, 4″–24″ (10–60 cm) high, 6″–18″ (15–45 cm) wide. Shiny, wiry, very slender, needle-shaped leaf sheaths to 12″ (30 cm) long. Dwarf cultivars available.

**SEED HEAD:** Spring to summer bloom. Tiny, flowers in nodding clusters. Grow for foliage. Silver turning tan.

**HARDINESS:** Zones 4–9.

**SOIL TYPE:** Sandy loam. High–average moisture, good drainage, medium–low fertility, 6.5–7.5 pH.

**PLANTING GUIDE:** Spring. Plant in full sun, 6″–15″ (15–38 cm) apart.

**CARE TIPS:** Easy. Water when soil dries 2″–4″ (50–100 mm) deep. Limit fertilizing. Shear after flowering, winter. Propagate by division, seed.

**NOTES:** Thrives in banks, beds, borders, edgings, ground covers, massed plantings. Nice in meadow, natural, seaside, Xeriscape gardens. Resists pests, diseases.

## Imperata cylindrica POACEAE (GRAMINEAE)

### Japanese Blood Grass

**SHAPE:** Various vigorous, vertical, bunching, herbaceous perennial grasses, 12″–24″ (30–60 cm) high and wide. Short, branched leafstalks to 6″ (15 cm) long with shiny, slender, spearlike leaf sheaths to 24″ (60 cm) long. Turns colors when mature.

**SEED HEAD:** Late-summer bloom. Stems with white clusters of florets, feathery bracts, and seed.

**HARDINESS:** Zones 4–10.

**SOIL TYPE:** Sandy loam; pond shorelines. High moisture, good drainage, high–medium fertility, 6.5–7.5 pH.

**PLANTING GUIDE:** Spring. Plant in full sun to partial shade, 12″–24″ (30–60 cm) apart.

**CARE TIPS:** Easy. Even moisture. Water when soil dries to 4″ (10 cm) deep. Fertilize every 10–12 weeks. Shear in spring. Propagate by division.

**NOTES:** Thrives in accents, edgings, massed plantings. Nice in meadow, natural, rock, small-space gardens and ponds. Resists pests, diseases.

## Helictotrichon sempervirens *(Avena sempervirens)* POACEAE (GRAMINEAE)

### Blue Oat Grass

**SHAPE:** Various vigorous, vertical, tufted, herbaceous, semi-evergreen perennial grasses to 5′ (1.5 m) high and 24″–36″ (60–90 cm) wide. Smooth, slender, spear-shaped, arched leaf sheaths to 24″ (60 cm) long.

**SEED HEAD:** Spring bloom. Slim, stiff stems to 5′ (1.5 m) long with tufted clusters to 6″ (15 cm) long of florets, feathery bracts, and seed.

**HARDINESS:** Zones 4–9.

**SOIL TYPE:** Sandy soil. High moisture, good drainage, high–medium fertility, 7.0–8.0 pH.

**PLANTING GUIDE:** Spring. Plant in full sun, 18″–24″ (45–60 cm) apart.

**CARE TIPS:** Easy. Even moisture. Fertilize every 6–8 weeks. Remove spent seed heads, stalks. Shear in autumn. Propagate by division, seed.

**NOTES:** Thrives in accents, borders, fillers, massed plantings. Nice in meadow, natural, rock, seaside, woodland, Xeriscape gardens. Resists pests, diseases.

## Juncus effusus JUNCACEAE

### Soft Rush

**SHAPE:** Numerous erect, clumping, grasslike, semi-evergreen herbaceous perennials to 32″ (80 cm) high and wide. Round, slender, tubular, sometimes variegated leaves to 32″ (80 cm) long and ¼″ (6 mm) wide. Turns brown in autumn. Lesser corkscrew rush, *J. effusus* 'Spiralis', grows leaves in spiraling patterns.

**FLOWER:** Summer bloom. Insignificant flowers; grow for foliage.

**HARDINESS:** Zones 4–11.

**SOIL TYPE:** High humus; pond shallow margins or shorelines. High–saturated moisture, good drainage, high fertility, 5.5–7.5 pH.

**PLANTING GUIDE:** Spring. Plant in full sun to partial shade, 18″ (45 cm) apart, up to 4″ (10 cm) deep.

**CARE TIPS:** Easy. Even moisture. Fertilize every 4–6 weeks. Propagate by division, seed.

**NOTES:** Thrives in accents, borders, containers, ground covers. Nice in bog, shade, small-space gardens and ponds. Resists pests, diseases.

## *Juncus patens* JUNCACEAE

### California Gray Rush

**SHAPE:** Few erect, clumping, grasslike, semi-ever-green herbaceous perennials to 24″ (60 cm) high and wide. Basal sheaths with round, slender, tubular leaves to 24″ (60 cm) long and ¼″ (6 mm) wide.

**FLOWER:** Summer bloom. Insignificant flowers; grow for foliage. Choose from blue, gray, and green foliage.

**HARDINESS:** Zones 7–10.

**SOIL TYPE:** High humus; pond shallow margins or shorelines. Average–saturated moisture, good drainage, high fertility, 5.5–8.0 pH.

**PLANTING GUIDE:** Spring. Plant in full sun, 12″ (30 cm) apart, up to 6″ (15 cm) deep.

**CARE TIPS:** Easy. Even moisture until established; tolerates drought thereafter. Fertilize every 4–6 weeks. Propagate by division.

**NOTES:** Thrives in accents, borders, containers, ground covers. Nice in bog, small-space, wood-land gardens and ponds. Resists pests, diseases.

## *Leymus arenarius* (*Elymus arenarius, Agropyron magellanicus*) POACEAE (GRAMINEAE)

### Blue European Dune Grass (Lyme Grass, Wild Rye)

**SHAPE:** Various vigorous, mounding, bunched, rhizomatous, evergreen perennial grasses to 4′ (1.2 m) high and wide. Basal stalks, with arched, slender, lancelike leaf sheaths to 4′ (1.2 m) long and ¼″ (6 mm) wide.

**SEED HEAD:** Summer bloom. Slim, stiff stems to 10″ (25 cm) long with linear sprays of tiny bracts and seed. Grow for blue or silver foliage.

**HARDINESS:** Zones 4–10.

**SOIL TYPE:** Sandy loam. Average–low moisture, good drainage, medium fertility, 6.0–8.0 pH. Tolerates salt.

**PLANTING GUIDE:** Spring. Plant in full sun to partial shade, 12″–24″ (30–60 cm) apart.

**CARE TIPS:** Easy. Water when soil dries to 4″ (10 cm) deep. Tolerates drought. Fertilize in spring. Shear in autumn. Propagate by division.

**NOTES:** Thrives in accents, containers, ground covers. Nice in meadow, prairie, seaside gardens. Aggressive. Resists pests, diseases.

## *Luzula sylvatica* 'Marginata' JUNCACEAE

### Greater Woodrush

**SHAPE:** Few erect, clumping, grasslike, semi-evergreen stoloniferous perennials to 36″ (90 cm) high and wide. Basal sheaths with flat, slender, lancelike, often variegated, hirsute leaves, 4″–12″ (10–30 cm) long, ⅝″ (16 mm) wide.

**FLOWER:** Summer bloom. Tufted tiny flowers; grow for foliage. Choose from blue, gray, and green foliage.

**HARDINESS:** Zones 4–10.

**SOIL TYPE:** High humus. Low–average moisture, good drainage, high fertility, 5.5–8.0 pH.

**PLANTING GUIDE:** Spring. Plant in full sun to full shade, 12″ (30 cm) apart, up to 6″ (15 cm) deep.

**CARE TIPS:** Easy. Even moisture until established. Tolerates drought. Fertilize in spring. Propagate by division.

**NOTES:** Thrives in accents, borders, ground covers. Nice in bog, shade, small-space, woodland, Xeriscape gardens. Resists pests, diseases.

## *Miscanthus oligostachyus* POACEAE (GRAMINEAE)

### Flame Grass

**SHAPE:** Various vigorous, upright, bunching, herbaceous perennial grasses, 36″–48″ (90–120 cm) high and wide. Short, branched leafstalks to 6″ (15 cm) long with shiny, slender, spearlike leaf sheaths to 24″ (60 cm) long. Turns colors in autumn.

**SEED HEAD:** Late-summer bloom. Stems with white clusters of florets, feathery bracts, and seed.

**HARDINESS:** Zones 4–10.

**SOIL TYPE:** Sandy loam; pond shorelines. High–average moisture, good drainage, high–medium fertility, 6.0–7.5 pH.

**PLANTING GUIDE:** Spring. Plant in full to filtered sun, 12″–24″ (30–60 cm) apart.

**CARE TIPS:** Easy. Even moisture. Water when soil dries to 4″ (10 cm) deep. Fertilize every 10–12 weeks. Shear in spring. Propagate by division.

**NOTES:** Thrives in accents, massed plantings, screens. Nice in meadow, natural gardens and ponds. Resists pests, diseases.

## *Miscanthus sinensis* POACEAE (GRAMINEAE)

### Eulalia Grass (Japanese Silver Grass)

**SHAPE:** Various vigorous, erect, bunching, herbaceous perennial grasses, 4'–6' (1.2–1.8 m) high and 36"–48" (90–120 cm) wide. Short, branched leafstalks with shiny, slender, spearlike leaf sheaths, 24"–36" (60–90 cm) long. Turns colors in autumn.

**SEED HEAD:** Late-summer to autumn bloom. Slender, stiff stems to 7' (2.2 m) high with plumelike seed clusters to 12" (30 cm) long. Choose from bronze, copper, and pink.

**HARDINESS:** Zones 4–10.

**SOIL TYPE:** Sandy loam. High–average moisture, good drainage, medium fertility, 6.5–7.5 pH.

**PLANTING GUIDE:** Spring. Plant in full sun to partial shade, 5'–6' (1.5–1.8 m) apart.

**CARE TIPS:** Easy. Even moisture. Fertilize every 6–8 weeks. Shear in spring. Propagate by division, seed.

**NOTES:** Thrives in accents, backgrounds, screens, windbreaks. Nice in meadow, natural, rock gardens. Resists pests, diseases.

## *Molinia caerulea* POACEAE (GRAMINEAE)

### Purple Moor Grass

**SHAPE:** Various vigorous, vertical, bunching, herbaceous perennial grasses, 12"–36" (30–90 cm) high and wide. Short, branched leafstalks with shiny, slender, spearlike, often variegated leaf sheaths to 32" (80 cm) long.

**SEED HEAD:** Summer to autumn bloom. Slender, stiff stems to 36" (90 cm) high with plumelike seed clusters to 10" (25 cm) long. Choose from purple and white turning yellow.

**HARDINESS:** Zones 4–10.

**SOIL TYPE:** Sandy loam. High–average moisture, good drainage, medium fertility, 6.0–7.0 pH.

**PLANTING GUIDE:** Spring. Plant in full sun to partial shade, 24' (60 cm) apart.

**CARE TIPS:** Easy. Even moisture. Fertilize every 6–8 weeks. Shear in spring. Propagate by division, seed.

**NOTES:** Thrives in accents, backgrounds, borders, containers, edgings, massed plantings. Nice in meadow, natural, rock, Xeriscape gardens. Resists pests, diseases.

## *Ophiopogon japonicus* LILIACEAE

### Mondo Grass (Dwarf Lilyturf)

**SHAPE:** Various durable, bunching, grasslike, stoloniferous, tuberous, evergreen, herbaceous perennials to 6" (15 cm) high and wide. Shiny, slender, spear-shaped leaves to 6" (15 cm) long.

**SEED HEAD:** Summer bloom. Stiff, wiry stems with spiking clusters of nodding, bell-shaped flowers to ¼" (6 mm) wide. Choose from pink, violet, and white. Forms berrylike fruit in autumn.

**HARDINESS:** Zones 7–11.

**SOIL TYPE:** Sandy loam; pond shorelines. High moisture, good drainage, high–medium fertility, 6.5–7.0 pH.

**PLANTING GUIDE:** Spring. Plant in partial to full shade, 6"–12" (15–30 cm) apart.

**CARE TIPS:** Easy. Even moisture. Fertilize every 6–8 weeks. Propagate by division, seed, stolons.

**NOTES:** Thrives in banks, edgings, ground covers, paths. Nice in natural, shade, woodland gardens. Aggressive. Resists insect pests, diseases. Susceptible to slugs, snails.

## *Panicum virgatum* POACEAE (GRAMINEAE)

### Switch-Grass (Panic Grass)

**SHAPE:** Various vigorous, bunching, rhizomatous perennial grasses, usually to 7' (2.2 m) high. Vertical, shiny, leafstalks with smooth, vertical, spearlike leaf sheaths to 48" (1.2 m) long. Turns brown, red, yellow in autumn.

**SEED HEAD:** Summer to autumn bloom. Branched sprays to 20" (50 cm) long of erect seed clusters. Choose from bronze and pink turning brown, cream, and white.

**HARDINESS:** Zones 4–9.

**SOIL TYPE:** Sandy loam. High–average moisture, good drainage, medium fertility, 6.5–7.5 pH.

**PLANTING GUIDE:** Late winter to early spring. Plant in full to filtered sun, 24"–36" (60–90 cm) apart.

**CARE TIPS:** Easy. Even moisture until established. Tolerates drought. Fertilize every 10–12 weeks. Shear in spring. Propagate by division, seed.

**NOTES:** Thrives in accents, backgrounds, screens, windbreaks. Nice in meadow, natural, seaside gardens. Drying plant. Resists pests, diseases.

## *Pennisetum alopecuroides* POACEAE (GRAMINEAE)

### Fountain Grass (Chinese Pennisetum)

**SHAPE:** Various vigorous, bunching, mounded, herbaceous perennial grasses to 48″ (1.2 m) high and wide. Shiny leafstalks to 16″ (40 cm) long, with arched, slender, spearlike leaf sheaths to 5′ (1.5 m) long. Turns colors in autumn.

**SEED HEAD:** Summer to autumn bloom. Erect, bristly, plumelike clusters, 4″–6″ (10–15 cm) long. Pink turning cream and yellow.

**HARDINESS:** Zones 5–11. May self-seed. Best in hot-summer climates.

**SOIL TYPE:** Sandy loam. High–average moisture, good drainage, medium fertility, 6.0–7.0 pH.

**PLANTING GUIDE:** Early spring. Plant in full sun to partial shade, 12″–36″ (30–90 cm) apart.

**CARE TIPS:** Easy. Even moisture until established. Tolerates drought. Fertilize only in spring. Shear in spring. Propagate by division, seed.

**NOTES:** Thrives in accents, beds, containers, fence lines, screens. Nice in cottage, meadow, natural gardens. Drying plant. Resists pests, diseases.

## *Phalaris arundinacea* POACEAE (GRAMINEAE)

### Ribbon Grass (Gardener's-Garters, Reed Canary Grass)

**SHAPE:** Various durable, upright, rhizomatous perennial grasses to 5′ (1.5 m) high and 24″ (60 cm) wide. Leafstalks with opposite, ribbon-like, striped leaf sheaths to 7″ (18 cm) long.

**SEED HEAD:** Summer to autumn bloom. Clusters to 6″ (15 cm) long of inconspicuous, feathery florets, bracts, and seed to ⅛″ (3 mm) wide. Choose from purple and white turning tan.

**HARDINESS:** Zones 4–10.

**SOIL TYPE:** High humus; pond shorelines. High moisture, good drainage, medium fertility, 6.0–8.0 pH.

**PLANTING GUIDE:** Spring. Plant in containers in full sun, 24″ (60 cm) apart.

**CARE TIPS:** Easy. Water as soil dries 4″–6″ (10–15 cm) deep. Tolerates drought. Limit fertilizing. Shear in spring. Propagate by division, seed.

**NOTES:** Thrives in accents, containers, ground covers. Nice in meadow, rock, Xeriscape gardens and ponds. Aggressive. Resists pests, diseases.

## *Schizachyrium scoparium* POACEAE (GRAMINEAE)

### Little Bluestem Grass (Broom Beard Grass, Wire Grass)

**SHAPE:** Numerous erect, bunching, tufted, herbaceous perennial grasses to 5′ (1.5 m) high and 36″ (90 cm) wide. Jointed leafstalks to 24″ (60 cm) long with smooth, slender, spearlike, leaf sheaths to 5′ (1.5 m) high.

**SEED HEAD:** Late-summer to autumn bloom. Open clusters to 6″ (15 cm) long of florets, feathery bracts, and seed. Choose from blue green, green, and purple. Turns colors in autumn to winter.

**HARDINESS:** Zones 3–10.

**SOIL TYPE:** Sandy loam. High–low moisture, good drainage, medium fertility, 6.5–7.5 pH.

**PLANTING GUIDE:** Spring. Plant in full sun, 12″ (30 cm) apart.

**CARE TIPS:** Easy. Even moisture until established. Drought tolerant. Fertilize only in spring. Shear in spring. Propagate by seed.

**NOTES:** Thrives in borders, containers, massed plantings. Nice in meadow, natural, prairie, wildlife gardens. Resists pests, diseases.

## *Scirpus cyperinus* (*Isolepsis cyperinus*) CYPERACEAE

### Woolgrass Bulrush

**SHAPE:** Various upright, bunching, stoloniferous, perennial sedges to 5′ (1.5 m) high and 24″ (60 cm) wide. Smooth, closed, triangular leaf sheaths to 5′ (1.5 m) long.

**SEED HEAD:** Summer bloom. Woolly, spike- or tassel-like clusters of arched, branched bracts, 12″–36″ (30–90 cm) long, with tiny, sterile or fertile flowers. Choose from green or variegated.

**HARDINESS:** Zones 3–11.

**SOIL TYPE:** Sandy loam; pond shorelines or margins. High–saturated moisture, good drainage, low fertility, 6.0–8.0 pH.

**PLANTING GUIDE:** Spring. Plant in containers in full sun to partial shade, 24″ (60 cm) apart, up to 4″ (10 cm) deep.

**CARE TIPS:** Easy. Even moisture. Limit fertilizing. Shear in spring. Propagate by division, seed.

**NOTES:** Thrives in accents, borders, edgings. Nice in bog, wildlife gardens and ponds. Aggressive. Resists pests, diseases.

## *Sesleria autumnalis* POACEAE (GRAMINEAE)

### Autumn Moor Grass

**SHAPE:** Various vigorous, erect, tufted, evergreen, herbaceous perennial grasses, 12″–18″ (30–45 cm) high and wide. Short, branched leafstalks with shiny, flat, spearlike leaf sheaths to 12″ (30 cm) long.

**SEED HEAD:** Spring bloom. Slender, stiff stems to 24″ (60 cm) high with plumelike seed clusters to 10″ (25 cm) long. Purple turning white.

**HARDINESS:** Zones 4–10.

**SOIL TYPE:** Sandy loam. Average moisture, good drainage, medium fertility, 6.5–8.0 pH.

**PLANTING GUIDE:** Spring. Plant in full sun to partial shade, 12″ (30 cm) apart.

**CARE TIPS:** Easy. Even moisture until established. Tolerates drought. Fertilize every 6–8 weeks. Shear in spring. Propagate by division, seed.

**NOTES:** Thrives in accents, borders, containers, ground covers, massed plantings. Nice in meadow, natural, rock, seaside, Xeriscape gardens. Resists pests, diseases.

## *Sisyrinchium* spp. IRIDACEAE

### Blue-Eyed Grass

**SHAPE:** About 75 vertical, bunching, grasslike, deciduous herbaceous perennials to 36″ (90 cm) high and wide. Shiny, arched, slender, grasslike leaves to 12″ (30 cm) long.

**FLOWER:** Spring bloom. Stiff stalks with erect, branched, open clusters to 6″ (15 cm) long of star-shaped, round, 6-petaled flowers to ½″ (12 mm) long. Choose from blue, purple, white, and yellow. Forms capsulelike fruit.

**HARDINESS:** Zones 4–8. May self-seed.

**SOIL TYPE:** Loam; pond shorelines. High moisture, good drainage, medium fertility, 6.0–8.0 pH.

**PLANTING GUIDE:** Spring or autumn. Plant in full sun to partial shade, 16″–36″ (45–90 cm) apart.

**CARE TIPS:** Easy. Even moisture. Fertilize in spring. Shear in winter. Propagate by division, seed.

**NOTES:** Thrives in accents, banks, beds, borders, ground covers. Nice in bog, meadow, natural, seaside, woodland gardens and ponds. Resists pests and diseases.

## *Sorghastrum avenaceum* (*S. nutans*) POACEAE (GRAMINEAE)

### Wood Grass (Indian Grass)

**SHAPE:** Various vigorous, upright, bunching, rhizomatous perennial grasses to 5′ (1.5 m) high and 36″ (90 cm) wide. Erect leafstalks with shiny, slender, spearlike leaf sheaths, 24″–36″ (60–90 cm) long. Turns colors in autumn.

**SEED HEAD:** Late-summer bloom. Stiff, slender stems to 48″ (1.2 m) high with branched, spikelike clusters to 12″ (30 cm) long of florets, chafflike bracts, and seed. Choose from white and yellow turning red brown.

**HARDINESS:** Zones 4–9. May self-seed.

**SOIL TYPE:** Loam. High moisture, good drainage, medium fertility, 6.5–7.5 pH.

**PLANTING GUIDE:** Spring. Plant in full sun, 12″ (30 cm) apart.

**CARE TIPS:** Easy. Even moisture. Drought tolerant. Shear in spring. Propagate by division, seed.

**NOTES:** Thrives in accents, backgrounds, massed plantings. Nice in arid, meadow, natural, wildlife gardens. Aggressive. Resists pests and diseases.

## *Stipa gigantea* POACEAE (GRAMINEAE)

### Giant Feather Grass (Needlegrass)

**SHAPE:** Various vigorous, sprawling, tufted perennial grasses to 36″ (90 cm) high and 42″ (107 cm) wide. Erect leafstalks with shiny, slender, spearlike leaf sheaths, 24″–36″ (60–90 cm) long.

**SEED HEAD:** Summer bloom. Hollow, slender stems to 7′ (2.2 m) high with branched, spikelike clusters to 20″ (50 cm) long of florets, chafflike bracts, and seed. Yellow turning white.

**HARDINESS:** Zones 6–10.

**SOIL TYPE:** Loam. Average–low moisture, good drainage, medium fertility, 6.5–8.0 pH.

**PLANTING GUIDE:** Spring. Plant in full sun, 36″ (90 cm) apart.

**CARE TIPS:** Easy. Even moisture until established. Drought tolerant. Shear in spring. Propagate by division, seed.

**NOTES:** Thrives in accents, backgrounds, edgings, massed plantings. Nice in arid, meadow, natural, seaside, wildlife gardens. Aggressive. Resists pests and diseases.

# Plant Index

# Subject Matter Index

# Credits

All Photographs by John M. Rickard, except as noted below.

**All-American Rose Selections, Inc.:**
pg. 252 (2nd)

**Gerald A. Bates:** pgs. 73 (G, O, P, Q), 79 (C bot.), 81 (C2, & F), 111 (bot.), 145, 147 (2nd & 3rd), 148 (1st & 3rd), 150 (2nd & 4th), 153 (1st, 3rd & 4th), 155 (2nd), 156 (2nd), 157 (1st & 3rd), 160 (3rd), 163 (2nd), 169 (2nd), 171 (3rd), 174 (2nd), 175 (2nd, 3rd & 4th), 176 (1st & 3rd), 178 (3rd), 179 (2nd), 182 (4th), 183 (1st), 189 (2nd), 193 (3rd), 194 (1st), 195 (3rd), 196 (3rd & 4th), 197 (2nd), 200 (1st), 205 (3rd), 207 (3rd), 211 (3rd), 216 (3rd), 218 (1st), 218 (3rd), 219 (2nd), 226 (1st), 227 (1st & 2nd), 230 (3rd), 231 (1st), 235 (2nd), 236 (3rd), 237 (2nd), 240 (3rd), 243 (1st), 244 (4th), 247 (2nd & 4th), 248 (1st & 3rd), 253 (1st & 3rd), 254 (2nd), 260 (4th), 261 (4th), 262 (2nd), 268, 271 (4th), 272 (1st & 4th), 273 (2nd), 275 (1st & 2nd), 276 (1st), 277 (3rd)

**Bipfloral.com:** pg. 170 (4th)

**Doug Dealey:** pg. 53 (top)

**Robert J. Dolezal:** pgs. 2, 16, 22 (top), 25 (top), 26 (top), 28 (mid. left), 36 (bot.), 37 (top), 40 (all), 41 (top), 42 (bot. left), 48, 49 (bot.), 51 (all), 52 (mid.), 54 (mid. & bot.), 55 (mid.), 59 (top right), 63 (top), 66 (top), 69 (top), 74 (all), 75 (E1), 78 (all), 79 (A, B, C mid.), 80 (mid.), 81 (A, B1, B2, C1, D1, E, H, I), 82 (top),104 (top), 106 (bot.), 107 (top), 110, 111 (top),

112 (top), 117 (bot. right), 118 (bot.), 120 (top), 136 (bot. left, bot. mid., bot. right), 138 (bot.), 146 (3rd), 149, (1st & 3rd), 151 (2nd), 152 (2nd), 157 (2nd), 160 (2nd), 161 (4th), 162 (1st), 164 (4th), 167 (1st), 168 (1st & 3rd), 175 (1st), 176 (4th), 179 (1st), 180 (2nd), 183 (3rd & 4th), 185 (2nd), 186 (1st), 187 (1st), 189 (4th), 191 (1st), 195 (1st), 201 (1st), 204 (4th), 205 (2nd), 206 (4th), 211 (4th), 213, 221 (4th), 223 (2nd & 4th), 224 (1st & 3rd), 228 (3rd), 232, 237 (1st), 238 (3rd), 240 (4th), 241 (1st), 248 (4th), 251 (4th), 254 (1st & 3rd), 256, 258 (2nd), 259 (1st, 3rd & 4th), 262 (3rd & 4th), 277 (1st)

**Hortiphoto.com:** pg. 217 (2nd)

**International Flower Bulb Centre:**
pgs. 20 (top right & mid. right), 30 (bot. left)

**Intl. Flower Bulb Centre © IBC/ Doronfoy:**
pg. 20 (top left)

**Ikeda Shoji:** pg. 112 (bot.)

**Donna Krischan:** pgs. 53 (bot.), 163 (1st & 3rd), 165 (1st), 166 (2nd & 4th), 170 (2nd),176 (2nd), 184 (2nd), 187 (2nd), 188 (4th), 190 (1st), 198 (2nd), 199 (1st & 3rd), 200 (1st), 201 (2nd), 206 (3rd & 4th), 207 (4th), 208 (2nd & 3rd), 209 (1st), 215 (1st), 217 (1st), 220 (2nd), 222 (1st), 224 (2nd), 227 (3rd), 243 (3rd), 265 (3rd), 266 (1st & 3rd)

**Sandi Mehler:** pgs. 7 (4th), 13 (bot.), 27 (top), 29 (bot.), 37 (mid.), 38 (bot.), 59 (top left), 68 (top), 99, 154 (4th), 160 (1st), 188 (2nd), 235 (1st), 240 (2nd)

**Netherland Flower Bulb Information Center:** 214 (1st), 216 (1st), 222 (2nd), 228 (1st), 229 (1st), 230 (1st)

**Jerry Pavia:** pgs: 150 (3rd), 152 (3rd), 154 (2nd), 155 (1st), 160 (4th), 161 (1st), 162 (4th), 167 (3rd), 169 (1st), 170 (1st), 171 (1st), 172 (3rd & 4th), 173 (1st), 174 (3rd), 177 (4th), 186 (4th), 187 (3rd), 188 (3rd), 190 (2nd, 3rd & 4th), 191 (2nd, 3rd & 4th), 192 (2nd), 193 (1st), 194 (3rd), 196 (2nd), 200 (2nd), 201 (4th), 202 (1st), 203 (2nd, 3rd & 4th), 205 (1st), 206 (1st & 2nd), 209 (2nd), 215 (2nd), 217 (3rd), 218 (2nd), 221 (1st), 221 (3rd), 222 (4th), 223 (1st), 225 (1st), 226 (2nd), 228 (2nd & 4th), 229 (3rd & 4th), 235 (3rd & 4th), 236 (1st), 237 (3rd & 4th), 238 (4th), 241 (3rd), 243 (2nd), 244 (1st & 2nd), 245 (1st), 246 (4th), 249 (1st & 2nd), 258 (3rd), 271 (2nd & 3rd), 278 (3rd)

**Jacqueline Ramseyer:** pg. 59 (bot.)

**Charles Slay:** pg. 8

**USDA/Agricultural Research Station (Scott Bauer):** pg. 219 (3rd)

**Yvonne Williams:** pg. 233 (top)

# Acknowledgments

The editors acknowledge with grateful appreciation the contribution to this book of Jamie Coleman of Petals Florists, Mt. Shasta, California; Dan Durant and David Newton of Country Willows Bed & Breakfast Inn, Ashland, Oregon; and Beverly Shannon.